FABRIC OF VISION

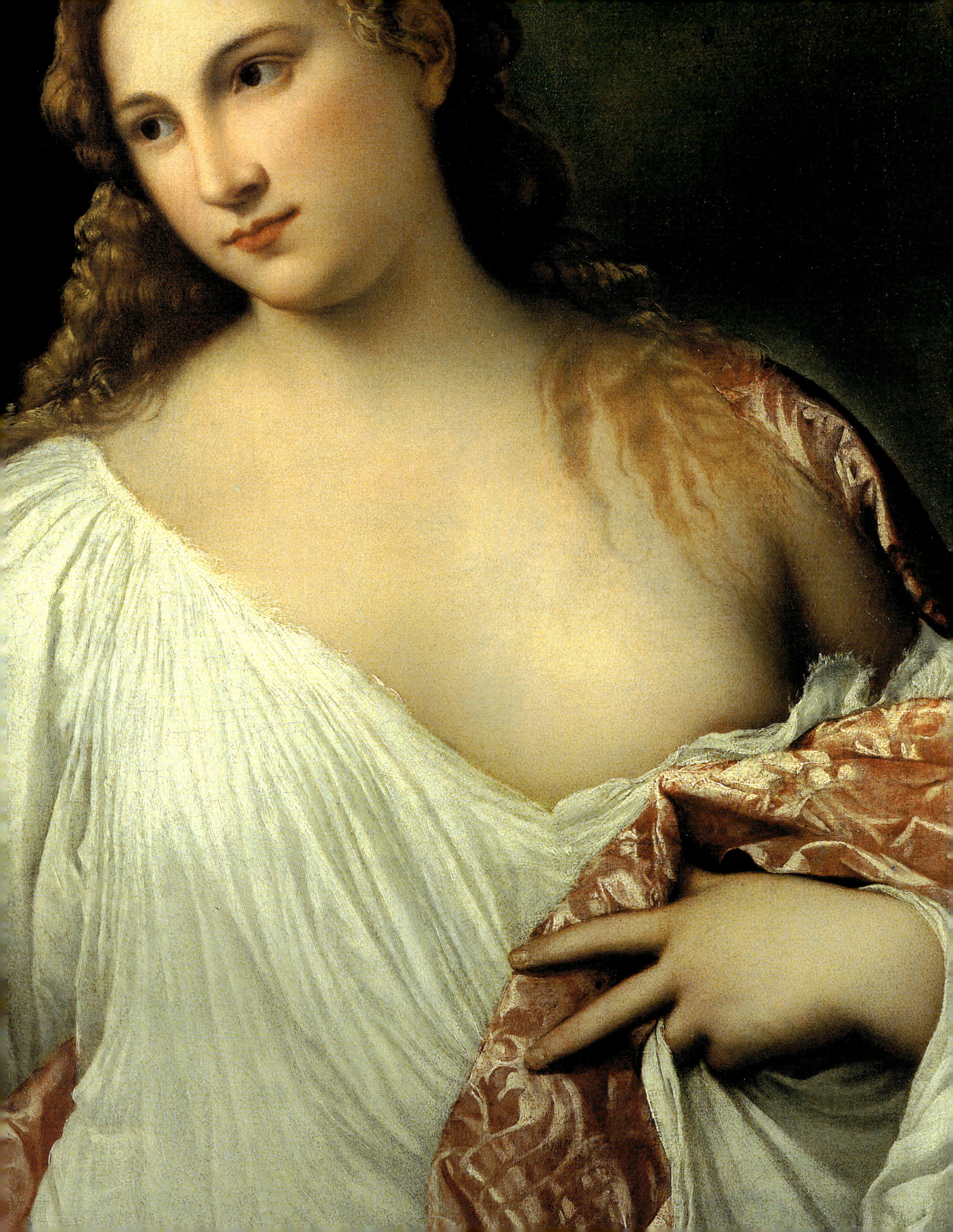

Fabric of Vision

DRESS AND DRAPERY IN PAINTING

ANNE HOLLANDER

National Gallery Company, London

DISTRIBUTED BY YALE UNIVERSITY PRESS

This book was published to accompany an exhibition at the National Gallery, London 19 June 2002–8 September 2002

Supported by the Corporate Members of the National Gallery

First published in Great Britain in 2002 by
National Gallery Company Limited
St Vincent House, 30 Orange Street,
London WC2H 7HH
www.nationalgallery.co.uk

ISBN 1 85709 907 9
525083

British Library Cataloguing-in-Publication Data
A catalogue record is available from the British Library
Library of Congress Catalog Card Number 2001095558

PUBLISHER Kate Bell
EDITOR Paul Holberton
EDITORIAL ASSISTANCE Tom Windross
DESIGNER Philip Lewis
PICTURE RESEARCHERS Xenia Corcoran and Catharina Tesdorpf
PRODUCTION Jane Hyne and Penny Gibbons

Printed and bound in Italy by Conti Tipocolor srl

Cover: Gottlieb Schick, *Frau Wilhelmine von Cotta*, 1802, Staatsgalerie Stuttgart (detail of fig. 80)
Frontispiece: Titian, *Flora*, about 1516–18, Galleria degli Uffizi, Florence (detail of fig. 41)
Contents page: Ernst Ludwig Kirchner, *The Red Cocotte*, 1914, Staatsgalerie Stuttgart (detail of fig. 110)

Contents

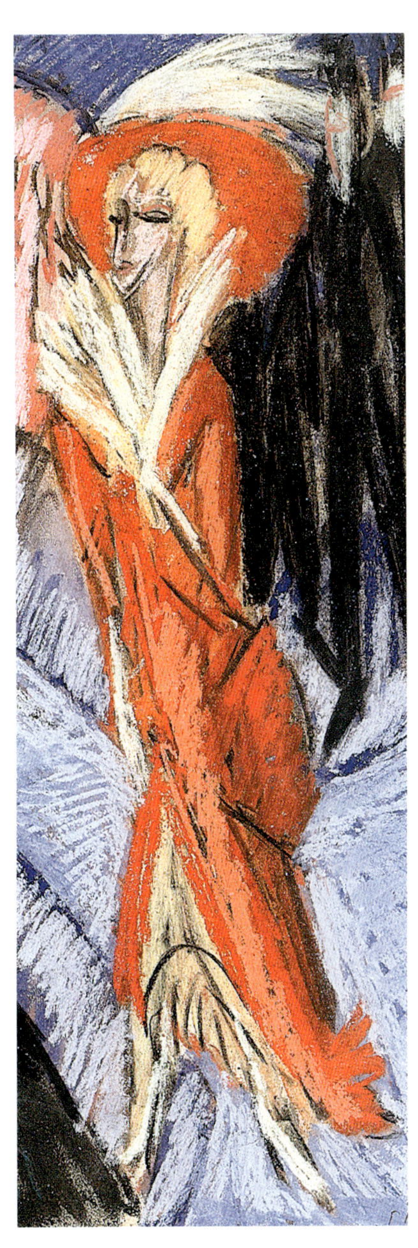

Author's Acknowledgements

THE IDEA FOR THIS EXHIBITION and its accompanying book is due to Patricia Williams, who was then Publishing Director of the National Gallery Company. Having heard me talk often and at length about the image of cloth and clothing in painting, it was Patricia who conceived it as the subject for a possible exhibition at the National Gallery. She told me how to transform this conception into a proposal, and then brought it to the attention of the Gallery, with gratifying results. Patricia also helped to shape the character of this book during its formative stage, when it began assuming an identity separate from that of the actual show. I am doubly indebted to her, for thinking up and helping to realise this undertaking.

I had no museum experience when I began to work on it, except as a constant visitor to many galleries. I want especially to thank Michael Wilson, Head of Exhibitions and Display, for taking such amiable charge of my unforgettable, if somewhat exhausting, education in precisely how an exhibition comes into being.

I wish to thank Neil MacGregor, at the time Director of the National Gallery, for agreeing to make this one possible. I am also grateful for the pointed questions he asked and the apt suggestions he made, once the effort was underway.

But I thank him mainly as representing the National Gallery itself, which was such an inspiring revelation to me when I first entered it long ago, as an American student of art history, across the Atlantic for the first time. I went to the Gallery again and again with my sketch pad, to copy the drapery in the Mantegna, in the El Greco and in the Rogier van der Weyden, all three now in this exhibition, which were among the first to set my thoughts in motion about the folds and the clothes in pictures.

ANNE HOLLANDER
New York, June 2002

Foreword

AN EXHIBITION ON DRESS AND DRAPERY at the National Gallery might strike some as incongruous. In Britain in particular, where high-mindedness and puritanism go hand in hand and personal display is viewed with suspicion, an interest in clothing and fashion may seem frivolous. But as Anne Hollander points out, clothing is an important feature of all figurative art. Although it might appear self-effacing, directing attention away from itself to faces and hands or bodies in movement, it is present, doing its job, contributing to the meaning and expressive force of the artist's work.

The fashions in which painters like Titian, Van Dyck and Delacroix depict their subjects serve to dignify and beautify them. The authority of their images has provided men and women with a standard of how to appear in life, a poetic ideal which carries with it the aspirations of an era. Just as a painter like Constable provided a way of responding to the English countryside and its hitherto unappreciated beauties, so great artists have shown each age how it wants to appear, how to dress, and even the desirable shape to be when undressed. It is through painting – and through photography – that clothes are elevated to become an embodiment of a society's highest ideals about itself. In his essay *The Painter of Modern Life*, Charles Baudelaire expounded a new theory of beauty recognising the importance of fashion, which he defined as 'a symptom of the taste for the ideal' and 'a sublime deformation of nature'. Artists of all ages acknowledge this, creating beautiful images from the current modes of dress that surround them.

Anyone who has had the experience of hearing a great lecturer speaking on art knows how a perceptive and original mind can reawaken one's own aesthetic responses, and how easy it is, in the first place, for those responses to become habitual and jaded. It is difficult to maintain a high level of receptivity and sensibility in front of works of art, and this is where interpreters and writers can help. In her book – and in the exhibition it accompanies – Anne Hollander brings to bear a lifetime's meditation on the relationship between dress and art, and her formidable talents as a writer, to open our eyes to the power and meaning of dress and drapery in painting. In so doing she enables us to see familiar and unfamiliar paintings in a new way, drawing our attention to the poetry of fabric and the skills of the painter.

Fabric of Vision is not a conventional art-historical exhibition, focusing on a single artist or a recognised style or period of painting. We therefore owe special thanks to those museums and collectors who have so generously supported the project with the loan of their paintings, and made the exhibition possible. And we are particularly grateful to Anne Hollander for opening our eyes to the beauties of dress and drapery in paintings.

MICHAEL WILSON
Head of Exhibitions and Display
National Gallery, London

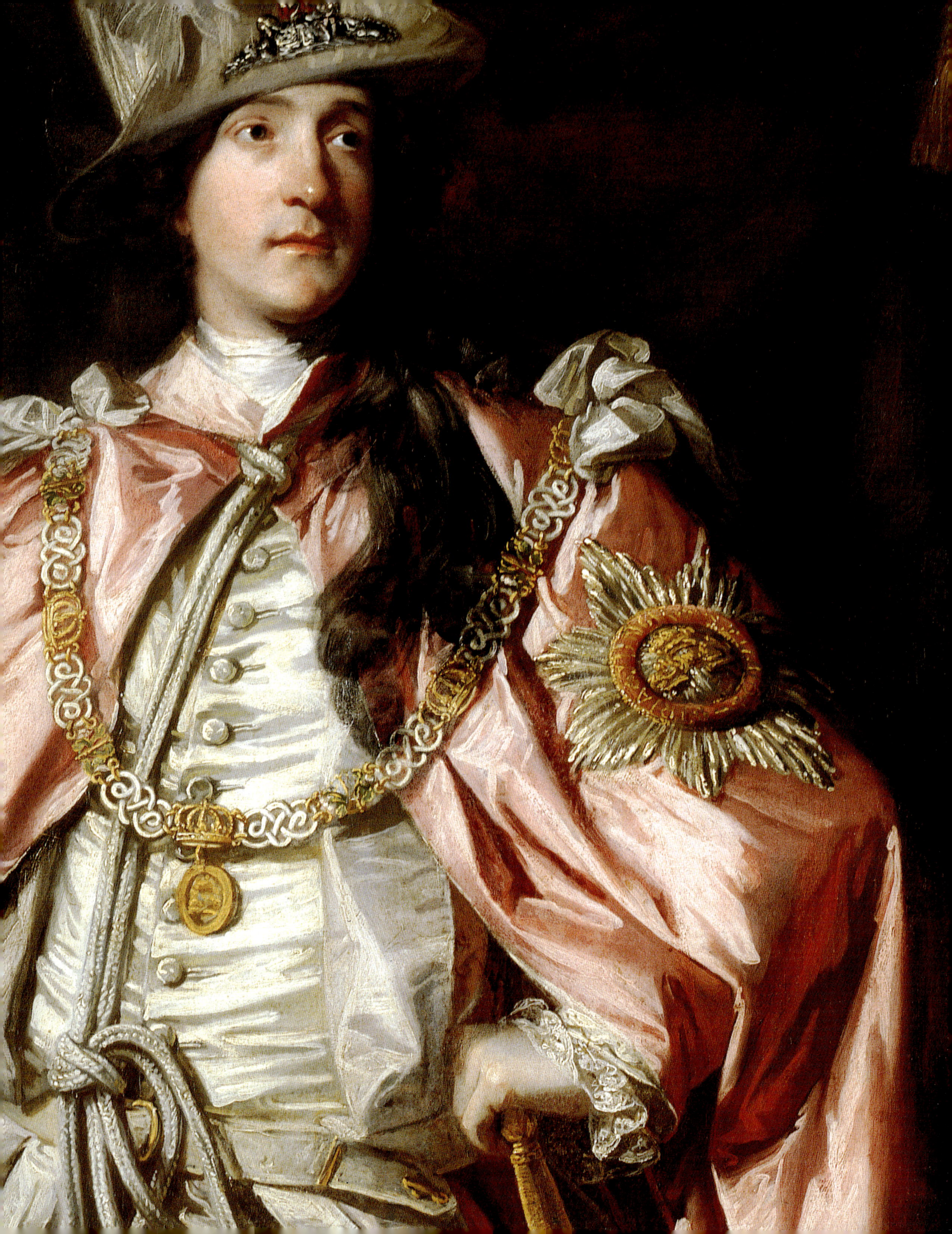

Introduction

CLOTHING APPEARS IN all traditions of figurative painting, often filling two thirds of the frame without seeming to be there. Even when monopolising the space, dress seems to make no separate claim, assimilating itself to the person wearing it, so that clothes serve chiefly for quick identification, to show who's king or angel, slave or soldier, man or woman, just as in the theatre. In dramatic scenes, the artist's rendering of the figures' clothing may go unnoticed unless he calls attention to it, and even then the faces and gestures that tell the story tend to seize the eye at the expense of the folds.

Any figurative artist is in fact equally interested in every part of the pictorial space. Whatever he does with the clothes is an expressive device and represents a formal decision with as much importance as those he makes about the faces and the setting. The amount of suggestive freight that clothing can carry in a picture is therefore all the greater if the painter knows how to integrate it with the faces and gestures, so it will do its work – direct the eye, adjust the emotional temperature, make subtle allusions whether noticeably or unnoticeably. The force of the *Mona Lisa*, for example, lies to a not inconsiderable degree in the thin veil darkly silhouetted alongside her falling hair, the one-sided wrap of her mantle, the many regular and subdued folds descending from the narrow band at her neckline. Different decisions about the details of the veil, dress and scarf would have produced different effects in the smile.

In the same way, although the clothing always matters a great deal in Ingres's portrait drawings, it has been so subtly rendered that it enhances the power of the face without seeming to. Using only a pencil, Ingres records every detail of the garments, but a few degrees less precisely than the details of the skin and features of the face; and he makes them gradually more sketchy and cursive, though no less accurate, the further they are from the exquisitely fine finish of the eyes, nose and mouth. The effect is to rivet attention on the face, but without cheating at all on the elegant details of the costume.

This book traces one uneven path through one part of the huge realm of painted folds and clothes. These chapters are concerned with pointing out some of the ways Western artists used garments and draperies as expressive ingredients in paintings, from

Detail of fig. 73

the middle of the fifteenth century to the middle of the twentieth. The theme is articulated in three different epochs of major change in Western painting – in the Renaissance, at the Neoclassic end of the eighteenth century and at the beginning of the Modern twentieth.

We will see how far, during the long period between the sixteenth century and the late eighteenth, comprising the aesthetic shifts called Mannerist, Baroque and Rococo, painters developed the Renaissance conceptions of pictured drapery, and in what directions, to free it from the restraints of fact and make it an entirely pictorial substance, with a dynamic relation to both legendary and contemporary dress in art. During the short nineteenth-century period, we can see how drapery for its own sake became marginalised in figurative painting, largely confined to the realm of historical or classical fantasy (although it did appear in still life), while painters' attention focused more on the emotional and erotic qualities of modern men and women's clothing.

In the first half of the nineteenth century, painters' handling of the different dress of the two sexes shows a strong Romantic cast. In the second half, we can see added to that a much greater interest in the way formal differences in male and female clothing could be manipulated to determine the atmosphere of paintings, and artists began to display the psychological character of dress directly through formal strategies. The path of this essay ends with the painters of the first half of the twentieth century who were again emphasising the formal considerations important to medieval painters, who had worked in the flat, stylised mode the early Renaissance painters strove to transcend. Modern artists once more applied them to dress and drapery, but this time for individual expressive aims, sustained by a century of Romantic and Realist belief in individual artistic freedom.

Because of the creative force and compelling vision of artists, dress in pictures has a great deal of power over the perception of dress in life. In art, it's possible to see how clothes are really supposed to look – that is, how an imaginative, sympathetic and understanding visual artist has made them look, emphasising their form in a desirable way, adjusting their style with masterly skill. The eye, trained by art, often sees these effects in the real world, even if the actuality fails, slightly or substantially, to meet the standard of art. But the sense of a standard is there – the belief in a right way of looking that exists in pictures and is always being lived up to in life, consciously or unconsciously. We invented the mirror, the empty picture we constantly re-create, to show us how we are measuring up.

The images we measure ourselves against are now usually the various works of camera art, created with kinds of emphasis and stylisation as potent as those once employed by the fresco and easel painters of the pre-camera past. We can imagine fashionable people in Renaissance Venice feeling that they were living up to Titian's visions of perfect clothed elegance, or those in Baroque England watching themselves living up to Van Dyck's. We can also imagine citizens of Siena in 1340 looking at the *Good and Bad Government* frescoes by Ambrogio Lorenzetti in the Town Hall and seeing themselves rightly portrayed, looking just as they knew they really looked. Centuries later, we believe that they did look exactly like that, despite the unbelievably smooth stockings everybody has on, which undoubtedly wrinkled in actual wear. The knitting machines and synthetic fibres had not yet been invented that truly put an end to wrinkled stockings; but Lorenzetti indicates that nobody wished to notice wrinkles in the stockings of 1340; and so their true look was always smooth, as the pictures show.

The earliest painters discussed in this essay, those from the fourteenth and fifteenth centuries in Europe, were very much aware of the artists of classical antiquity, whose works of sculpture had survived to set a standard for the convincing representation of draped clothed appearance. The Renaissance painters, inspired and instructed by the classical standard, went on to develop their own authoritative ways to render the modified draped garments of their own day. Their brilliant legacy of realistic folds compelled generations of later painters, in whose lives draped clothing had no everyday use, to find the rendering of drapery a constant artistic challenge and resource. Painters might use drapery to infuse their canvases with extra vitality and raw beauty, whether to suggest human power or true divinity, to enhance the tailored clothing they were scrupulously recording, or to improve the look of fruit on a plate.

Draped or not, it's obvious that clothes in themselves have mattered enormously to artists, since they are potent visual phenomena in the human world, as strong as faces. It's also obvious that viewers of paintings have learned from artists how to lead richer visual lives, how to see more fully and imaginatively. Therefore, just as painted landscape has shown us ways to look at scenery, so painted clothing has shown us how clothes contribute to the way human life looks. These chapters are concerned with pointing out how painters have made dress and drapery come alive in pictures, sharpening our eyes so that we can forever perceive them with insight, comprehension and feeling, in art and in life.

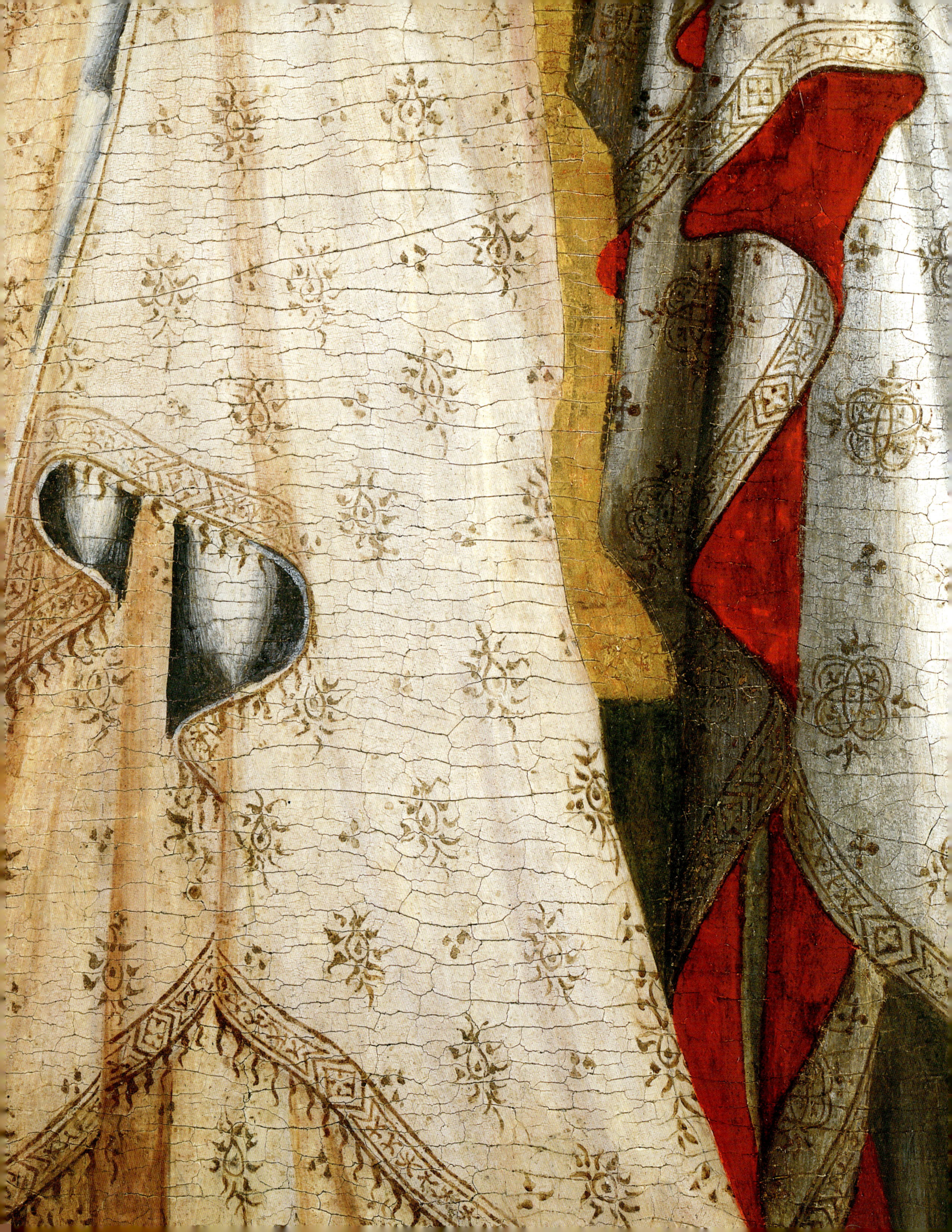

I Cloth of Honour

In classical Greece, clothes were very simple. Most civil garments were lengths of stuff woven to size and worn as they came off the loom, hung and wrapped or tied and pinned around the body. A suit of clothes consisted of one garment on the body and a wrap over that; both these differed in size and length, and in styles of draping and fastening, according to the wearer's sex, occupation and region, along with the garment's function. Tailoring, the cutting out and piecing together of shaped cloth segments to make a three-dimensional garment, was unknown. The beauty of clothing dwelt in the distinction of its woven fabric and in the elegance or aptness with which it was draped around the individual body. Any ugliness or awkwardness in clothing would arise from the lack of such aptness and distinction, or from noticeable disrepair of the stuff. Beyond that, the aesthetic quality of clothing might be enhanced or diminished or made absurd according to the way its folds behaved when the wearer moved, or how they were acted on by wind or other circumstance.

The drapery in classical Greek art was always a version of real clothes. Artists varied their methods of enhancing the visual qualities of such clothing in use, so as to make the stone folds create the motion or the repose in any given group, to make it dignify the procession on one carved relief and agitate the battle-scene on another (fig. 1). Broken surfaces of carved cloth, placed to one side or falling down behind, might set off the smooth nudity of undressed free-standing figures; the overall caress of marble ripples might emphasise the underlying nudity of dressed ones (fig. 2).

Artistic licence was needed to render the behaviour of loose, mutable textiles in a dense, static medium. To read convincingly as thin or heavy, sober or active, folds had to be shaped with carefully evocative stylisation at all epochs. Before the Classical period, Greek sculptors depended on schematic patterns to convey the look of cloth, but during and after the fifth century BC the effort to reproduce the appearance of free-falling and free-flying drapery appears clearly, both in Greek originals and in Roman copies and approximations. All of it is artistically modified as always, but now into an extraordinary credibility, with extraordinary variety. The result is that, from the time of the Parthenon

Detail of fig. 10

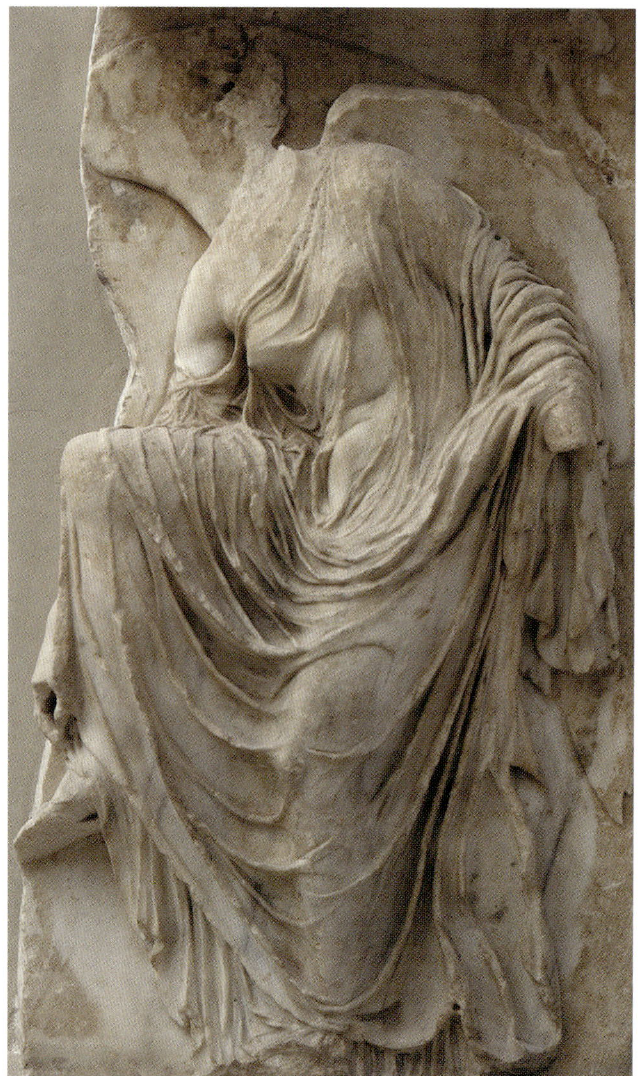

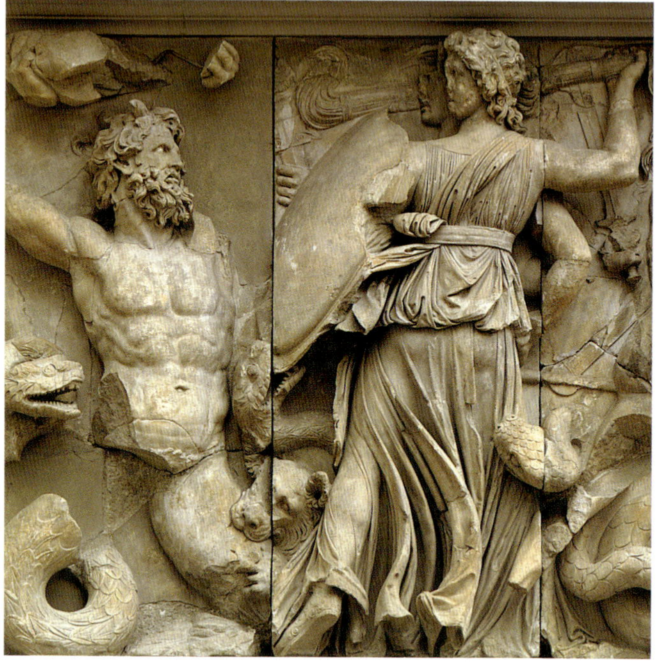

LEFT **1**
Athenian, about 410 BC
A Nike adjusting her Sandal,
from the Temple of Athena
Nike on the Acropolis
Pentelic marble, height 107 cm
Acropolis Museum, Athens

ABOVE **2**
Pergamene, about 164–156 BC
Hecate fighting a Monster,
from the east frieze of
the Pergamum Altar
Marble, height 230 cm
Staatliche Museen zu Berlin,
Antikensammlung

sculptures onwards, the lifelikeness in carved Greek clothes and bodies has often given viewers the idea that the sculptor has produced perfection – a stylisation of natural appearances so subtle as to seem absent.

Because real clothes were always the basic reference in ancient Greek works, authenticity inhabits the whole range of drapery tropes adopted by Greek sculptors, a truth that evoked the respect they have received ever since they were made. Even when the sculptured folds are shown to fly or cling in extreme ways, or to fall in a hyper-regular rhythm not found in direct experience, the viewer gives credit to a basic fidelity in the representation. The draped cloth, however rhetorical its folds, is never conjured out of nowhere as a notional addition to scenes or figures, extra amounts of it are not inserted where they could not go, or used for purposes in a work of art that they could never serve in reality. All parts of it reflect a constant fact of life understood by contemporary viewers, just as the skilfully applied visual rhetoric reflects a constant fact of art.

Many generations later, in the European Renaissance, dress and drapery were no longer synonymous in real life, but multiple folds of cloth were still common in everyday experience. Looking at paintings from the fifteenth century, we can see that both Italian and Netherlandish painters, in their different ways of rendering drapery's behaviour, were seeking to develop pictorial stylisations analogous to the antique ones for sculpture, that would produce that same look of perfection. To support that effect, the fifteenth-century painters sought the look of basic accountability in the cloth, whatever painted editing the folds might need for the sake of the picture.

In the early Middle Ages, the ancient way of rendering truthful-looking draped bodies had gradually become abstracted and ritualised for use in the Christian art of figuring the divine. Painted representations of folds had come to vary not so much in their adaptation from the direct observation of cloth in use, but in the arrangement of pictorial formulae for representing clothes. If we compare a thirteenth-century Tuscan Madonna (fig. 3) with the female figure on a Classical Greek stele (fig. 4), we can see how the memory of antique three-dimensionality and lifelike mobility in art, with its look of plastic artlessness for drapery, had become preserved in painting in the form of decorative linear pattern and vivid arrangement of flat colour.

BELOW LEFT **3**
Tuscan, 13th century
The Virgin and Child with Two Angels
Tempera on wood, 36.5 × 26.7 cm
National Gallery, London
NG 4741

BELOW RIGHT **4**
Greek, mid 4th century BC
Fragment of a grave relief:
Seated Woman
Marble, height 122 cm
The Metropolitan Museum of Art, New York, Harris Brisbane Dick Fund, 1948 (inv. 48.11.4)

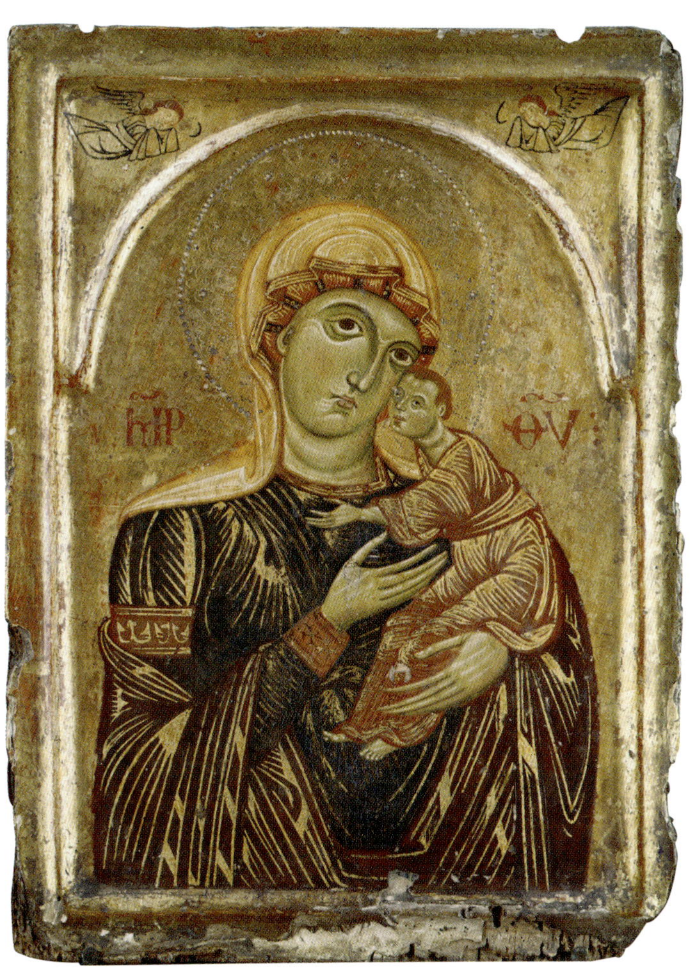

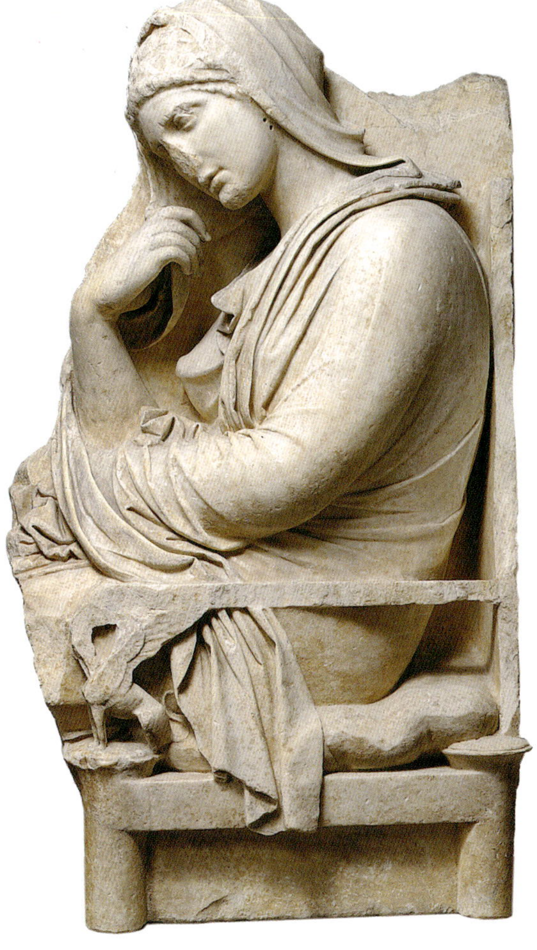

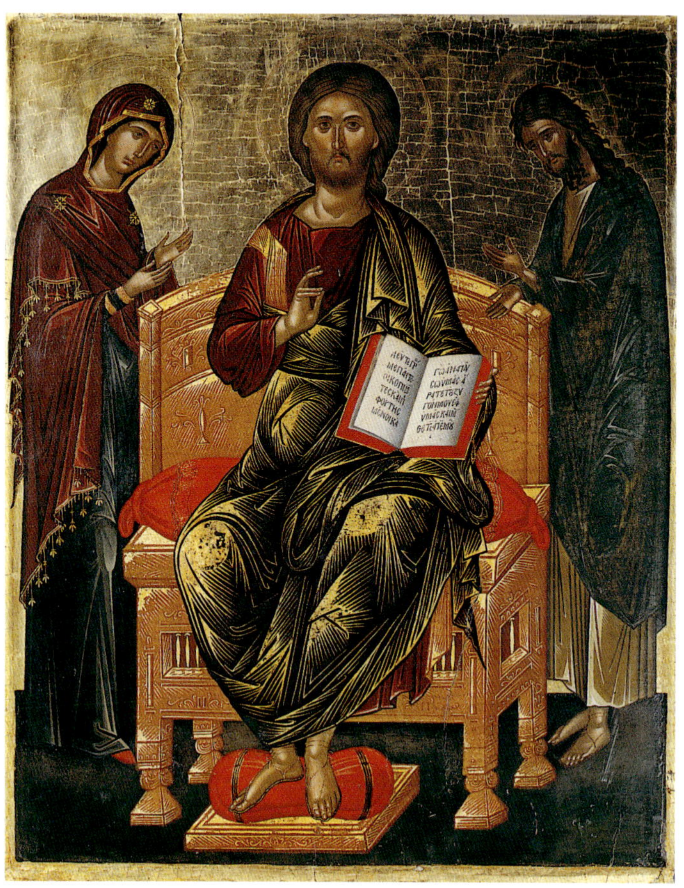

5
Cretan, about 1425–50
The Deesis (Christ with the Virgin and Saint John the Baptist)
Tempera and gold on wood, 68 × 48 cm
Private collection

A Cretan icon (fig. 5) that preserves the Byzantine tradition into the fifteenth century still shows a predominantly linear rendering of folds, as well as for the form of full-length bodies. The garments are part of pictorial legend, not life.

From about 1300 the Florentine artist Giotto began representing drapery with what appears to be a freshly direct eye on how it really behaved. In the *Decameron*, Boccaccio referred to Giotto as an extraordinary genius who 'brought back to light an art which had been buried for centuries', also saying that he followed nature and made things look actual, not painted; Boccaccio never says that he followed ancient examples. The folds on Giotto's painted draped figures nevertheless show a strong affinity with some of the ones in ancient Greek sculpture, even though European medieval clothing had become more complex and had long since included tailored components.

In Giotto's Arena Chapel scene of *Joachim and the Shepherds*, for example (fig. 6), the draped garments seem to surround the figures as they stand in real space, and the folds seem to swing down or tuck up in unaffected obedience to the law of gravity and the rules of real cloth. We can see a quite similar effect in an Imperial Roman statue, copying Classical Greek style, of a boy in a cape (fig. 7). Giotto's shepherds wear cut and sewn sleeved tunics, not uncut fabric, but one of them has a rectangular cape just like the Roman boy's, and the painted folds fall with notably sculptural effect. Joachim wears

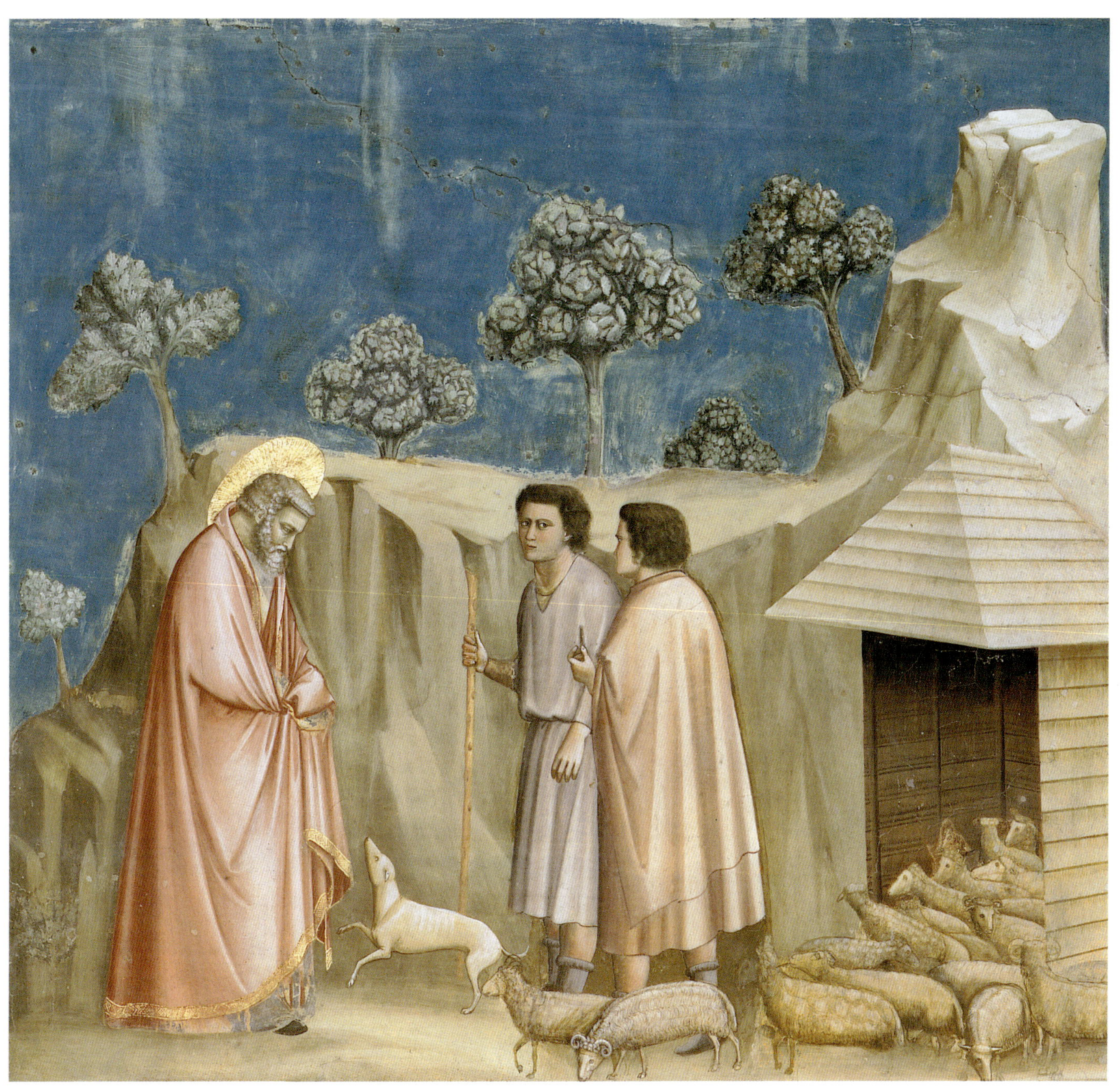

6
Giotto di Bondone
(about 1266/7; died 1337)
Joachim and the Shepherds,
from *The Life of the Virgin*,
about 1305–13
Fresco
Cappella degli Scrovegni, Padua

RIGHT **7**
Greco-Roman, 1st century AD
The Tralles *Boy*
Marble, height with plinth 147.5 cm
Archaeological Museum, Istanbul

FAR RIGHT **8**
Roman copy after a Greek original, about 440–430 BC
Sophocles
Marble, height 204 cm
Musei Vaticani, Rome

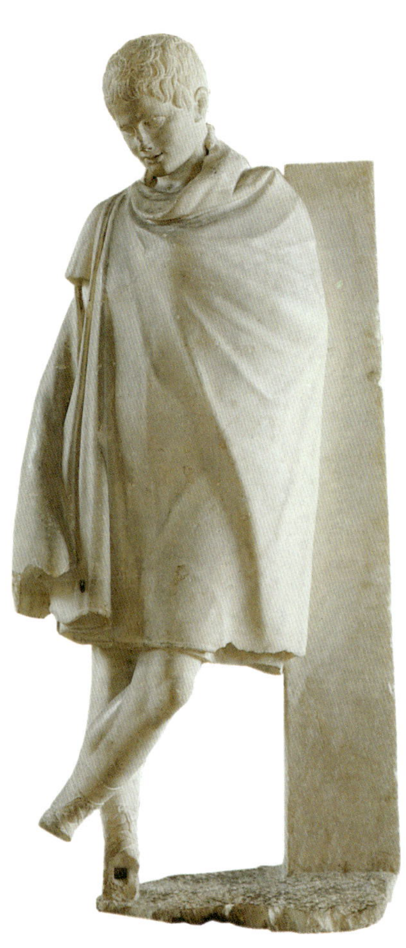

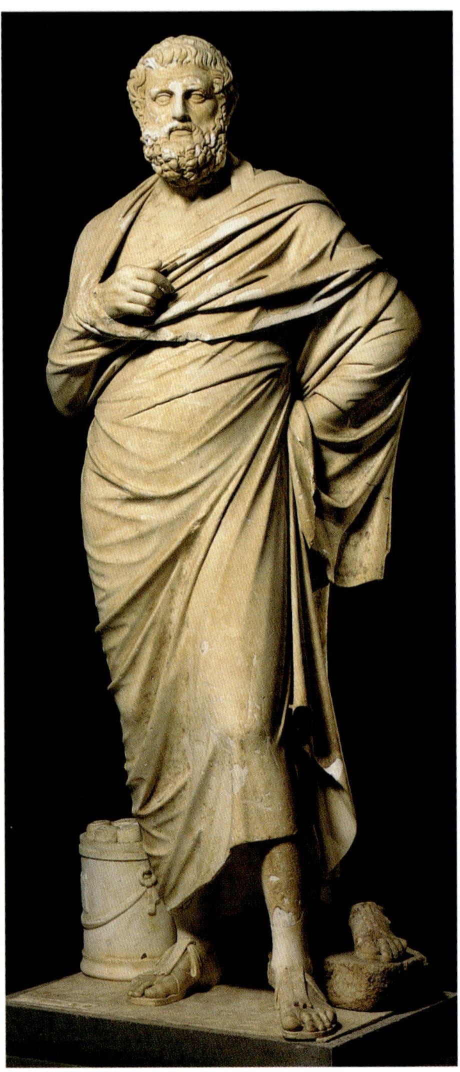

a longer version that seems to drape in painterly harmony with what carved Sophocles was wearing in the fifth century BC (fig. 8).

Most painters in the two generations following Giotto were less radically original than he; but we can see in Bernardo Daddi's *Marriage of the Virgin* of the 1330s how progress was being made in escaping old rituals for painting the drapery in religious art (fig. 9). The painter has combined rather formulaic hair and hands with a new effort, supported by a new programme for shading and foreshortening, to represent the way long loose garments actually sweep, fall and drag. Still later, about 1350, the noble figures of Saint Catherine and Saint Bartholomew, in a panel attributed to Allegretto Nuzi (fig. 10), show the new technique for modelling folds. Bartholomew in particular seems to stand out from his background as his draped mantle recedes around him, the folds catching strips of light on their narrowing ridges and showing larger lighted areas in the foreground. His beard, too, gives the illusion of hair. Saint Catherine's coiffure,

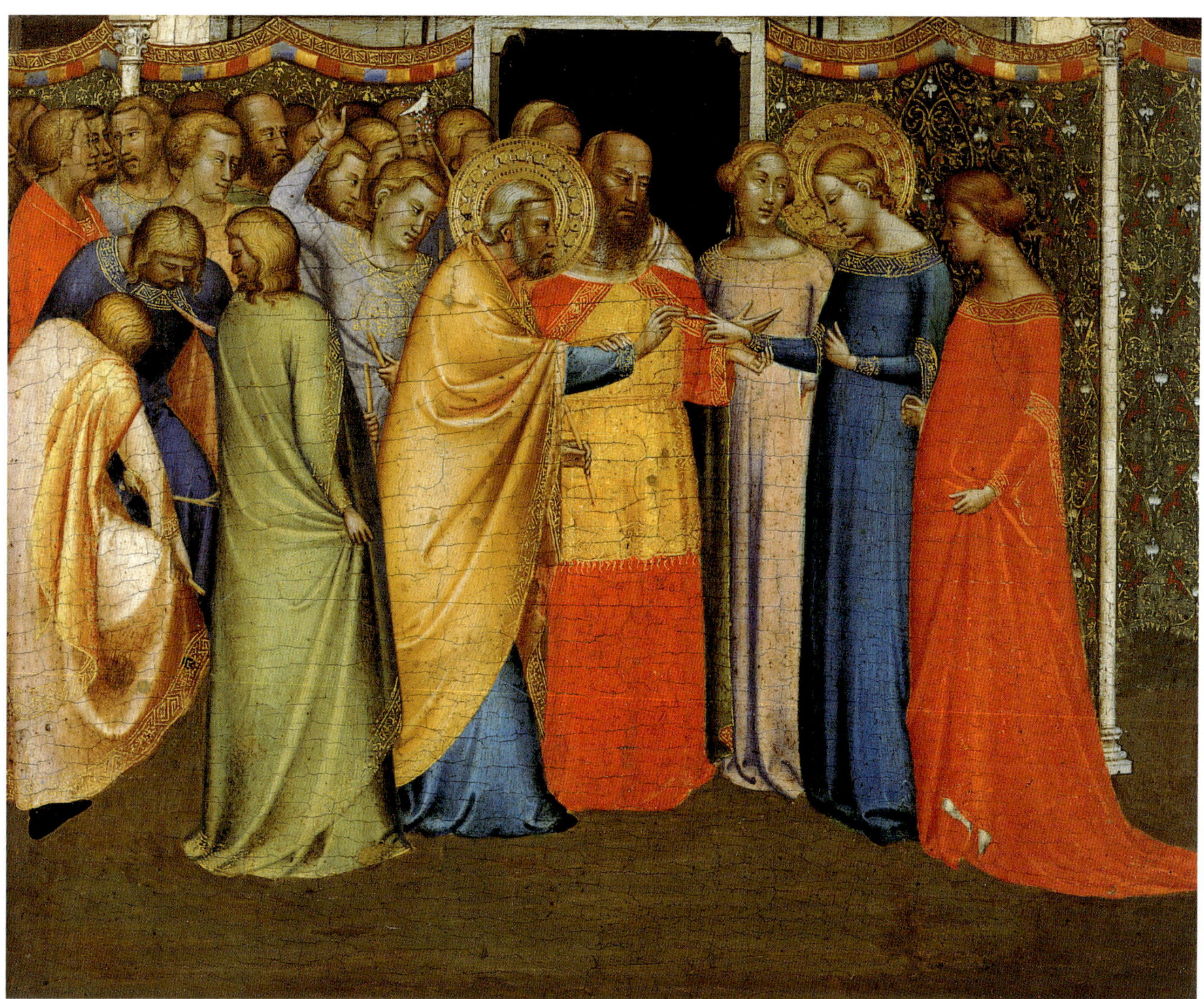

however, does not; and both saints are wearing robes with applied overall patterns, the edges rippling down in arabesques enhanced by contrasting linings. Despite the new modelling, these decorative effects tend to distance this painting from Giotto's sculpture-like innovations, and make these figures harmonise better with the more decorative style that prevailed in Florence during the rest of the century.

In our examples, Giotto's painted clothes and those on the classical carvings are alike in showing a unified texture for the fabric. The garments Giotto painted for both holy Joachim and the humble shepherds seem to be made from the same flexible, opaque and closely woven stuff, which resembles the stuff forming the drapery worn by Sophocles and the Roman boy, the woman on the stele and many figures on the Parthenon reliefs. Giotto seems to apply the different colours for the characters to a sort of universal perfect wool, with a matt finish suitable for the fresco medium, and quite apt for suggesting sculpture. He gives extra richness to Joachim's cape with a discreet gold border and not

9
Bernardo Daddi
(about 1300–1348)
The Marriage of the Virgin, about 1330–40
Tempera on wood, 25.5 × 30.7 cm
The Royal Collection
The Queen's Gallery, Buckingham Palace, London

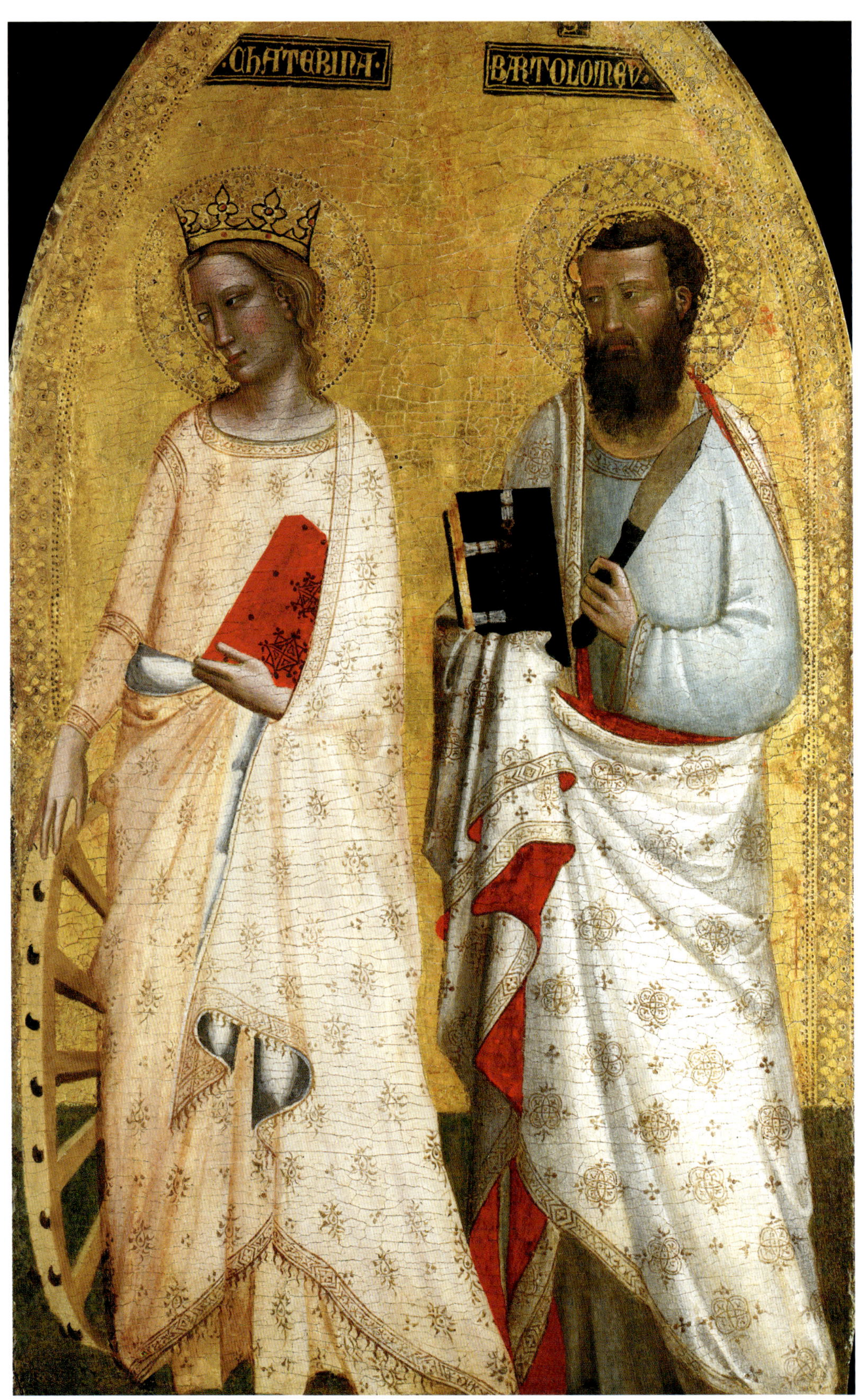

10
Attr. to **Allegretto Nuzi**
(1316/20–1373/4)
Saint Catherine and Saint Bartholomew, about 1350
Tempera on wood, 83 × 51 cm
National Gallery, London
NG 5930

with a patterned textile, as if to keep the viewer's attention on the natural look of all the folds in the picture, and avoid distracting the eye with any interesting surface or glimpses of contrasting colour.

A century later, in the 1420s, Masaccio again followed Giotto's sculptural rule for painted cloth. He dressed all figures in the same neutral stuff so as to display most clearly the simple, solidly modelled and well-lit accuracy of its folds, dyeing it in different colours for different figures as the theme and composition required. He, too, would usually add only gold bands or borders to indicate richness. Tailoring to fit the body, however, was now a more important element in real clothing, and a greater aesthetic consciousness of bodily form than Giotto shows began to appear in artists' rendering of clothes, in conjunction with developments in the knowledge of anatomy and in actual fashion.

Masaccio's fresco in the Brancacci Chapel called *The Tribute Money* (fig. 11) shows the rear view of a modern tax-collector engaging with a biblical Jesus and Saint Peter, who face the viewer. The man, perhaps an anxious underling and not the official himself, wears a short and full belted doublet, pieced at the centre back to fit his shoulders, its long sleeves tapered to the wrist, the right one unfastened, a thin line of shirt showing above the neckline. At the same time his clothed body offers a graceful classical pose, supported by antique bare feet and legs below the folds of his short skirt. In the curves of the two girdles and the style of the folds, Masaccio closely integrates the clothing of this modern figure with that of Christ and the Apostles in biblical costume, the tight grouping of all these fully realised figures going beyond Giotto's more stage-like encounter between the biblical Joachim and his modern shepherds. By biblical costume, I mean the clothes worn in works of art for roughly sixteen centuries by Jesus and many male saints, consisting of a full-length, long-sleeved robe belted or unbelted, with a large mantle wrapped over it, which often goes over one shoulder and under the other arm, and sometimes over both shoulders as a cape, like Joachim's. Varieties of these two garments were the common basis of European male dress beginning in about the fourth century and continuing in the Byzantine empire – the costume appears in late antique sculpture and is repeated in Byzantine icons over centuries (see fig. 5).

Long, loose gowns for men were of Eastern origin, and they were at first looked down on as effeminate by the leg-baring male Romans of antiquity, whose descendants nevertheless adopted them; and they were indeed eventually abandoned in Europe, frozen into elements of monastic dress and church vestments. From about the seventh century ordinary male dress came to consist of narrow, short tunics worn with under-pants, hose and footgear, all emphasising the separately clad look of male legs and feet. These below-the-waist elements were of Gaulish and Frankish and Danish origin, initially seen by the Romans as barbaric and very virile indeed. Eventually they would be refined into tight hose with a codpiece, varieties of breeches and the whole boot wardrobe. Short male doublets came to include carefully pleated folds by the twelfth century, by which time new styles of long gown, with sophisticated fit above and controlled folds below, had come back as elegant dress for noblemen, who no doubt wished to recover the dignity of long robes with no loss of masculine chic. These modes continued through the fifteenth century, and variously wrapped capes and mantles never went out of use in all classes.

In Masaccio's day, therefore, gathered and draped fabric on the male body was visible in contemporary dress; of which the chief modern effect was nevertheless the separate articulation of male legs – something which could now, as the *Tribute Money* suggests, be turned into a classical allusion with the help of some bare skin. Jesus and his disciples continued to wear long, loose fourth-century-style gowns in works of art, in Masaccio as in Giotto and their successors, and in everybody's imagination ever since, along with all the saints and martyrs of the early Christian centuries and many hosts of angels.

Female biblical garb in art has some of the same character as the masculine version, and it, too, follows the costume of fourth-century late antiquity, meaning a similar long dress with long sleeves and a wrap over it, part of which may drape the female head. But while living men in the ancient world were baring their legs and often appearing nude with only a wrap, and while later medieval men began showing off their legs and letting their clothes show off their figure, women kept the appearance of modesty that had required long, flowing dresses in classical antiquity and went on requiring them until the twentieth century of the Christian era.

It was only in the later fourteenth century that European women began to tighten their long dresses alluringly around the torso, and to lower their necklines seductively, at the same time widening or trailing their skirts and inventing new shapes for their sleeves. This means that the shoe-length, long-sleeved, high-necked shapeless robe (dress, kirtle, *cotte*) stayed in the European female wardrobe without much change for more than a thousand years. In actual use, it was worn belted or unbelted over a shift (smock, chemise, *camicia*) in daily life and under an equally shapeless overdress with wider sleeves (gown, *cote-hardie*, surcoat) for festive appearances. Over everything might go a big mantle; on the head would be a veil in some form, sometimes arranged to cover neck and chin; under that, or combined with it, the hair would be arranged in coiled plaits or otherwise bound up. Only young unmarried girls might wear loose and uncovered hair.

In religious art up to the middle of the fourteenth century, the Virgin and the female saints could wear this costume as both up-to-date and biblical at the same time. You can see in the Daddi (see fig. 9) that the long, straight dress the Virgin wears on the right is very similar to those worn by her disappointed suitors grouped together at the left, behind triumphant Joseph. These suitors' gowns, however, may be read as old-days dress, not modern clothing, since elegant young men in 1340 were wearing short form-fitting doublets with long tight hose, while Mary's dress is as right for that year as it is for ancient times. Anyone looking at this painting at that date could see the Virgin and her attendant as somehow generic, their costume as properly eternal as womanhood itself, while the men appear in the correct ancient gear for a specifically ancient event.

This basic style of female dress – Mary here wears both kirtle and gown, her inner sleeves emerging from outer ones – can be seen clothing the Virgin and saints in hundreds of works by European painters working after 1350. We can watch them varying the fit, the sleeves, the neckline and the waistline so as to harmonise with fashion, which had begun to change more quickly. Daddi's bridal Virgin wears no mantle, but later painters usually draped one over her single or double dress, often letting part of it serve as a veil, as the custom was in classical and late antiquity, or adding a separate veil, as the later custom was in real life – or both.

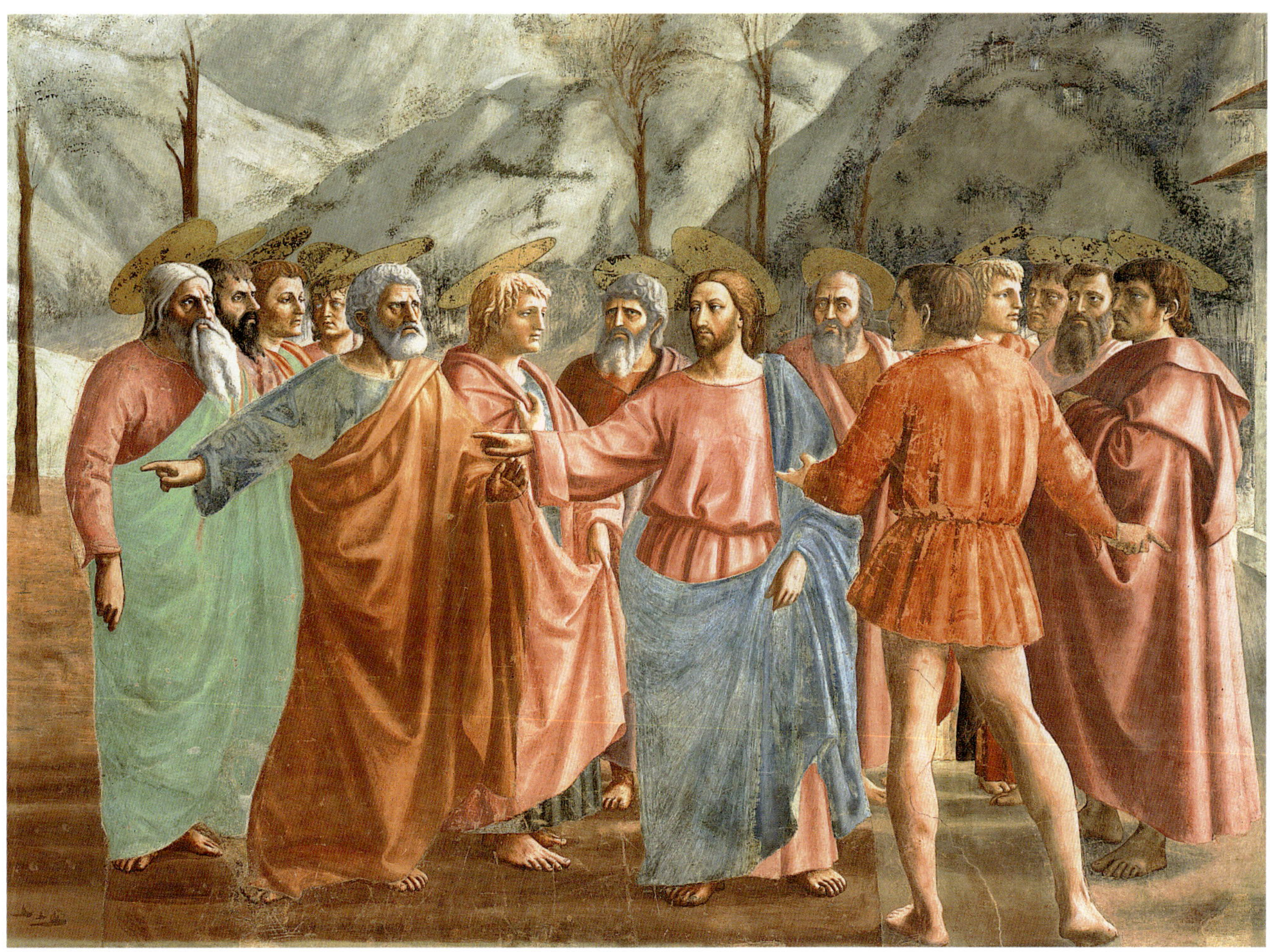

11
Masaccio (1401–1428)
The Tribute Money (detail), from *The Life of Saint Peter*, about 1423–8
Fresco
Brancacci Chapel, Santa Maria del Carmine, Florence

During the later fifteenth century, after Masaccio, dress in Italian painting shows more developments in what I have called biblical, old-days or legendary costume. 'Legendary' may in fact be the better term for garb worn in paintings by characters not only in Old and New Testament events, but in stories from the Apocrypha and the Lives of the Saints and early chronicles, in episodes from Greek and Roman history and mythology, or from the medieval romances – anything that is part of legend, sacred or secular, true or not. The design of the clothes for such personages shows considerable variety, combining references to fashions of earlier centuries and to dress in famous ancient works of art (or to other painters' works that refer to those) with references to current fashions in dress and its representation, and to the costumes currently in use for pageants and other performances. Those, too, showed a similar mixture.

Such pictorial clothing was sometimes used to indicate legendary associations for real portrait subjects – in which case we have to wonder if the sitter owned and wore such a garment, if it was made specially to be worn in the painting, or if it was wholly invented by the painter. The design of legendary dress in art has to be distinguished from the style of its rendering – in the Masaccio, for example, Jesus is in legendary clothes and the tax-collector is not; but the character of their drapery is the same.

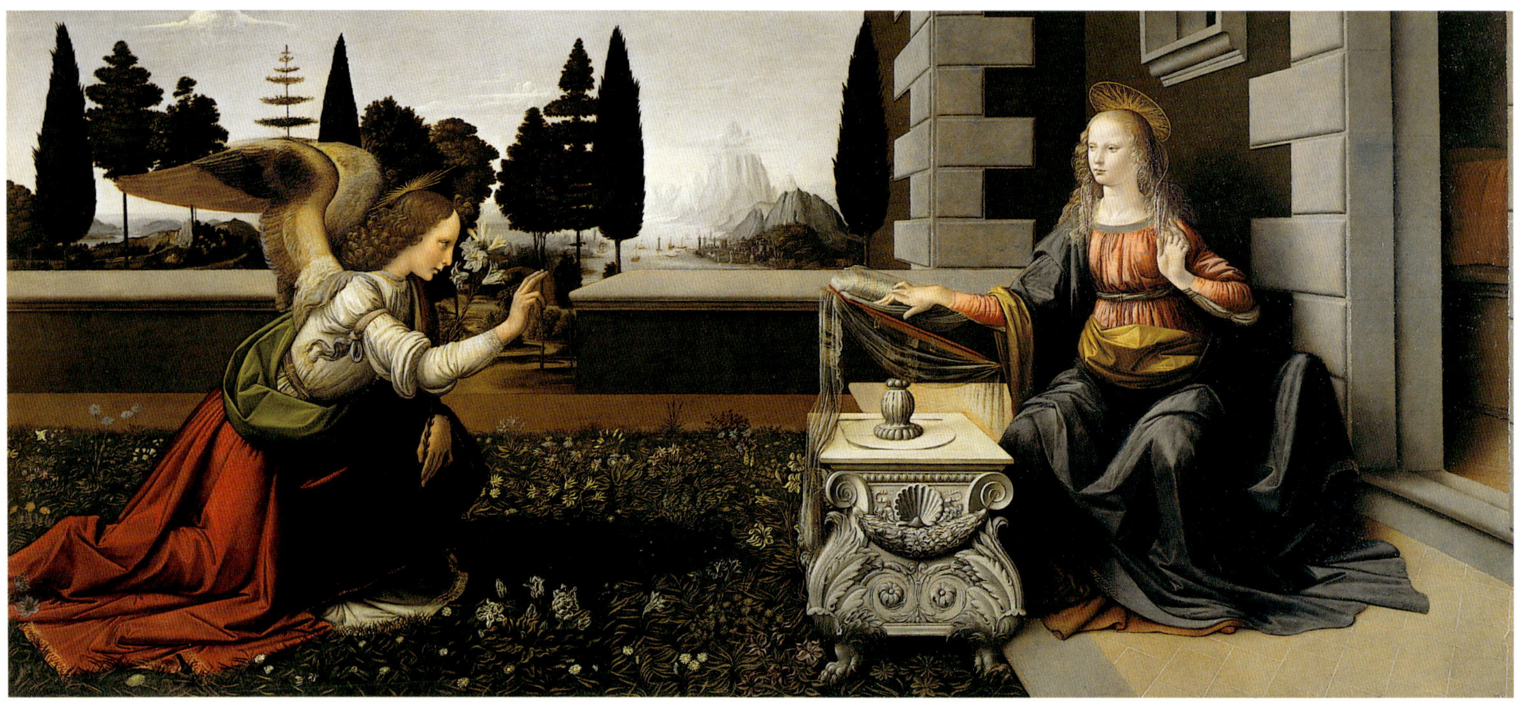

12
Leonardo da Vinci (1452–1519)
The Annunciation, about 1472–5
Tempera on wood, 98 × 217 cm
Galleria degli Uffizi, Florence

In Leonardo da Vinci's early 1470s *Annunciation* (fig. 12), Mary's dress is a new version of the legendary fourth-to-fourteenth-century kirtle and mantle. These styles were now a hundred years out of date, and their legendary appearance displays modern editing by the painter. The ornamental gold neckband is traditional for the Virgin in Florentine art – we saw it in the Daddi – but the rich folds gathered on to it are modern in their fresh rendering. The entire vestimentary effect now transcends Giotto and Masaccio, and contrasting linings and silken texture only add more power to the magnificent effect of weight, movement and the display of underlying form in the folds of the two mantles. The soft drapery above the Virgin's waist that suggests the bosom underneath now has overtones of classical Greek dress (see fig. 2).

Entirely contemporary and fashionable, however, are the tight sleeves attached along the forearm across the white chemise sleeves underneath. Though the announcing angel wears a legendary wrapped mantle and long robe, too, the robe has a fashionably modern high neck and tied-around sleeves. We can see the single sweep of his graceful body and leg through the differing draperies of the two garments, and his hair is that of a modern young man. The Virgin's veiled hair, however, is traditional, not modern, and we may note that Leonardo's *Mona Lisa* is wearing very similar hair and clothing in her portrait from around thirty years later (begun 1503). Mona Lisa wears a dress gathered on a band, a thick scarf over one shoulder and a shadowy veil over her loose dark hair, as if Leonardo wished to clothe her smile with both ancient suggestions and an ambiguously virginal ambience.

In direct contrast to this kind of legendary clothing for the Virgin, however, is Piero della Francesca's earlier *Madonna del Parto* of about 1450 (fig. 13), who wears a completely up-to-date veil, its neat bands interacting with her hair, and a neatly tailored, strictly falling modern dress with padded and pleated upper sleeves and tight lower ones, its

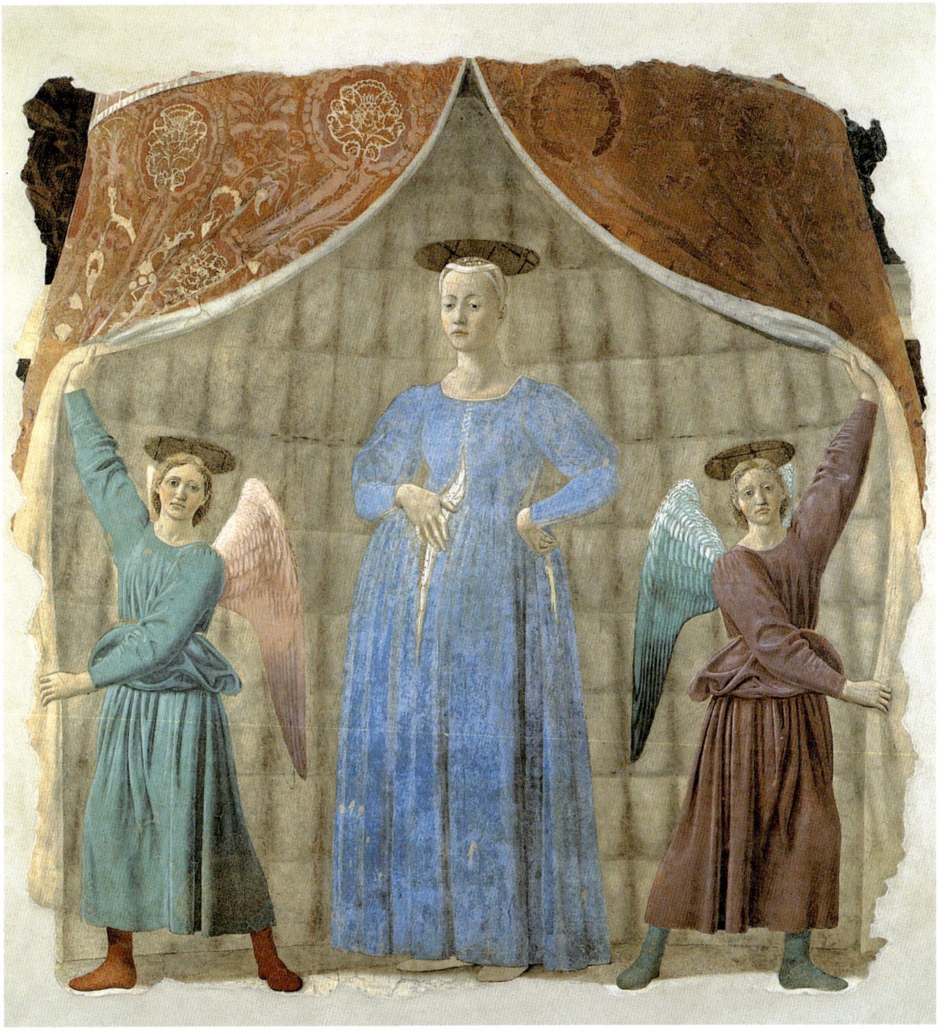

RIGHT **13**
Piero della Francesca
(about 1415/20–1492)
The Virgin pregnant with the Child (*Madonna del Parto*), about 1450
Detached fresco, 206 × 203 cm
Santa Maria a Nomentana, Monterchi

BELOW **14**
Alesso Baldovinetti
(about 1426–1499)
Portrait of a Lady in Yellow, about 1465
Tempera and oil on wood, 62.9 × 40.6 cm
National Gallery, London
NG 758

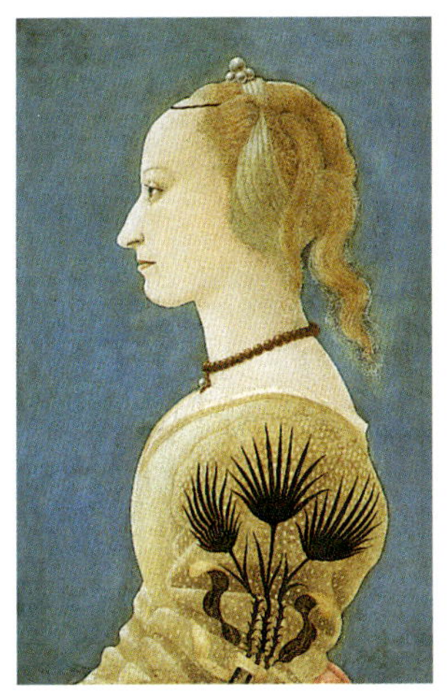

modern front and side lacings undone to show her pregnancy, her shirt visible through the slits. Draped legendary effects appear on the angels instead, who wear Gothic versions of fourth-century gowns, such as angels might wear in pageants.

This Virgin's simple dress corresponds to current trends in elegance, of which we can see a later example in Alesso Baldovinetti's coin-like profile portrait of about 1465 (fig. 14). Here the padding of the sitter's sleeves is carefully managed so that the large *palmetto* leaves embroidered on them can form the most vivid motif both in her costume and in the painting. Her headdress is a complicated arrangement of hair, veiling and ornament, with limited freedom for three wavy locks falling right, left and centre rear. There is no freely draped fabric contributing to the charm of this costume; the regular folds around her two arms balance the beginning of skirt we can see at the back of her waist.

Andrea Mantegna worked in Padua and Mantua, visiting Rome between 1488 and 1490, and he made a serious study of surviving antique sculpture. He has made three elegant approximations of draped classical statuary in his 1490s painting of the Virgin

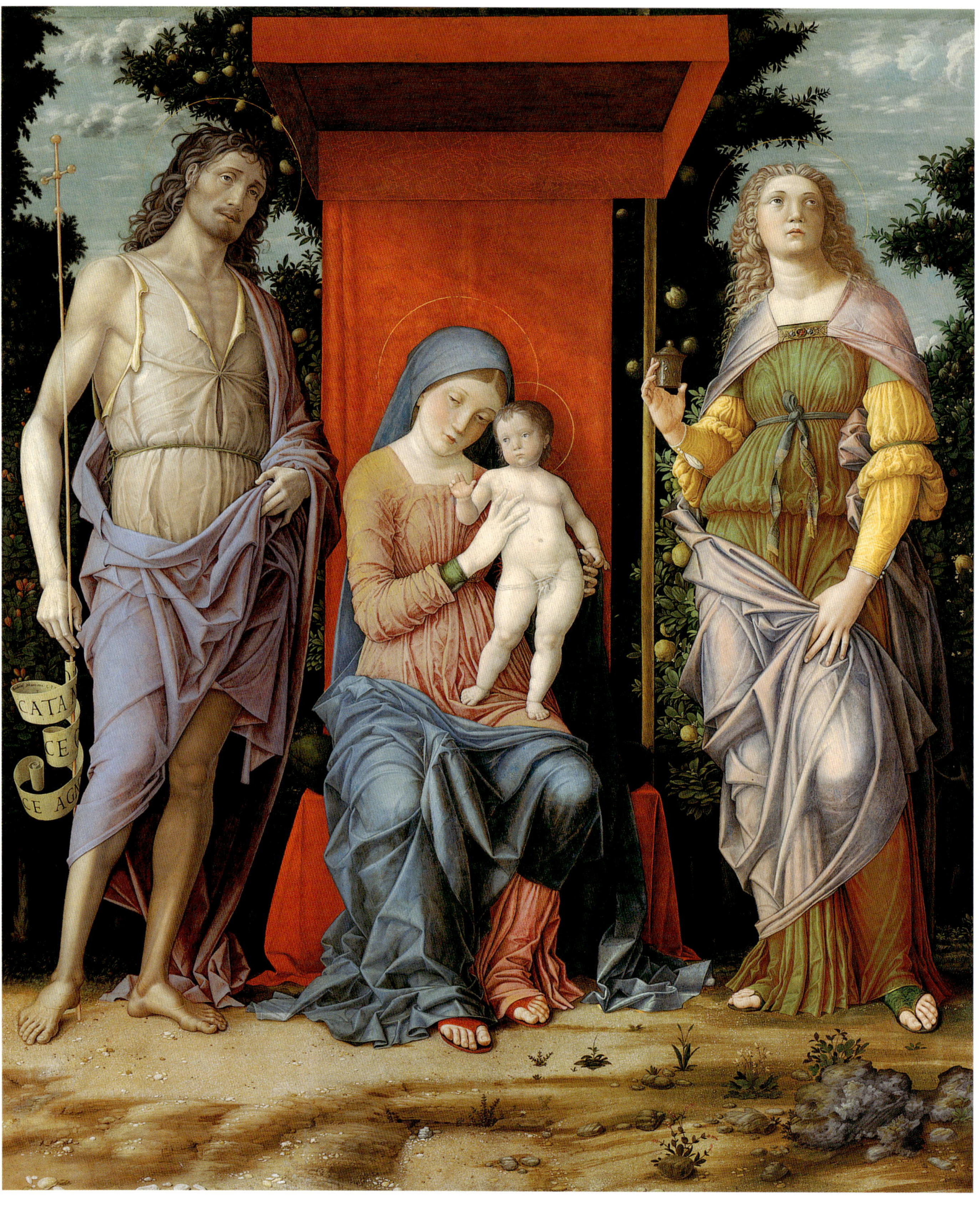

OPPOSITE **15**
Andrea Mantegna
(1430/1–1506)
The Virgin and Child with the Magdalen and Saint John the Baptist, about 1490–1500
Tempera on canvas,
139.1 × 116.8 cm
National Gallery, London
NG 274

flanked by two saints, including the signature *contrapposto* pose for both standing figures (fig. 15). The clothing they wear is a mixture of ancient Greco-Roman dress and the proper legendary gear for the biblical characters as they appear in art; and Mantegna has effectively classicised the way the garments behave. A classical marble figure of *Tyche* (Luck or Fortune; fig. 16) wears draped clothing carved into folds quite like those he painted for his Christian altarpiece.

This Virgin's fourth-century gown drapes very closely to her body, and, although a kirtle-sleeve appears above her wrist, her two dresses and implied chemise produce no bulk. Her mantle, covering her round head with a Byzantine effect (see fig. 3), drapes elaborately over her knees in folds to which the painter has applied his own unique stylisation. Saint John the Baptist wears his Scriptural camel-skin (Matthew 3:40), although the painter makes it look as delicate as the garment Ulysses compares to onion-skin (*Odyssey* 19:230–5). Over it, his classically worn wrap is again unmistakably folded by Mantegna.

Mary Magdalen has had the most varied wardrobe of all the female saints in art, and her clothes – here including a classical dress with modern sleeves under an eleventh-century mantle – identify her less certainly than does her ointment jar, here gracefully held up for us to notice, and her long, loose hair (Luke 7:38). Most notable on each of these three adult figures is the carefully wrought co-ordination between the multi-coloured draped garments and each articulated body; and this harmony is pointed up by the marmoreal Greek anatomy of the nude infant in the centre, who nearly copies the Baptist's classical posture.

Here again the painter doesn't use patterned stuff, but dwells intently on the shapes of the folds as they connect with the torsos and limbs. The draped figures are isolated to seem like statues, each with its individual scheme of coloured folds. For the mantles, Mantegna's idiosyncratic folds are singularly weightless, seeming to clutch at the knees and thighs of each figure so we can be sure to see their size and placement. He doesn't mind suggesting that the stuff is not woven but carved and then painted, and none of it shows a contrasting lining.

Quite different is the effect achieved in *The Virgin and Child with Two Angels* by Andrea Previtali, a follower of Giovanni Bellini working in Venice and Bergamo, the picture dated to the 1510s (fig. 17). There is no emphatic classical idea shaping these figures, or the folds of the brilliant garments sweeping broadly around them as they kneel or sit on the ground; and these mantles turn back their edges more than once to show the equal brilliance of their linings. Knees and thighs are barely evident, the Virgin's torso seems padded by her thick chemise, and the angels display their elegant sleeves and shining hair, not their figures. The rear angel even hides himself under a conventionally angelic mantle, which echoes the Virgin's traditional garb. This nude infant is not displaying his divine shape but concentrating on the red cherries he holds, even barring our view of his bare body with his other arm.

Previtali clearly stays away from using detailed human anatomy as an armature for showing off draped garments, on the classical model. The richly dyed smooth textiles are instead painted as if they enveloped the characters with their own authority; and we can see that the appeal of this picture is essentially chromatic, in the famous Venetian Renaissance manner. It's a simple group of solid figures in a landscape, brought to life by

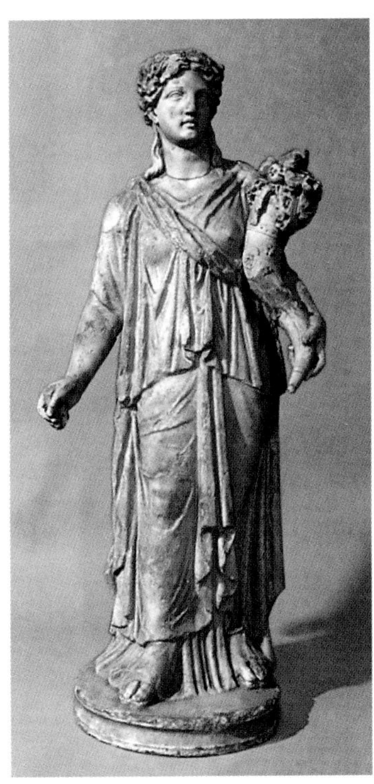

16
Greco-Roman, probably 2nd century
Tyche with Cornucopia
Marble, height 98 cm
The British Museum, London

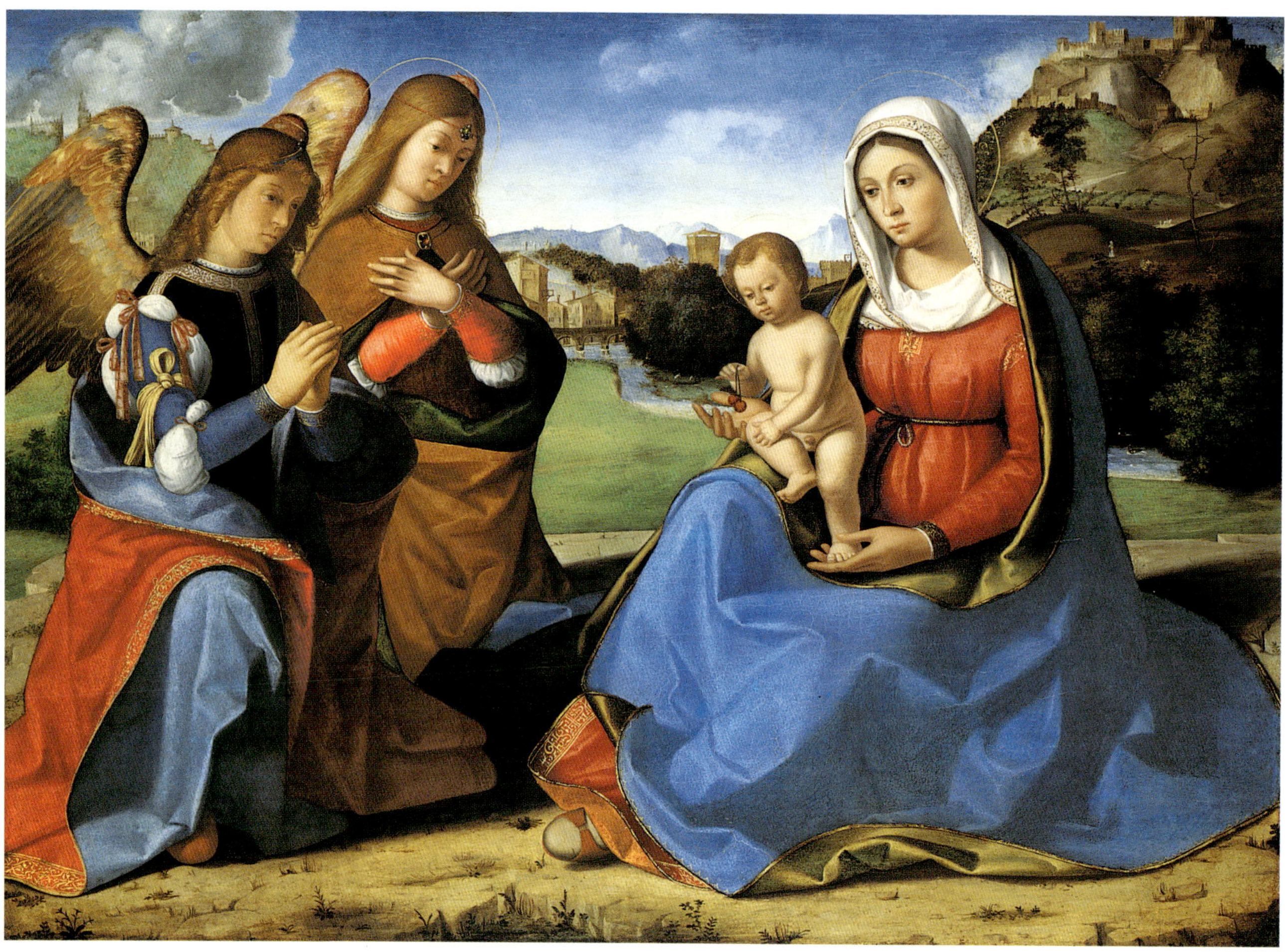

17
Attr. to **Andrea Previtali**
(active 1502; died 1528)
The Virgin and Child with Two Angels, about 1510–20
Oil on canvas, transferred from wood, 63.7 × 92.7 cm
National Gallery, London
NG 3111

an integrated ensemble of a few glowing and expertly modulated colours, most of them conveyed in the arrangement of beautiful silk folds.

The painter deploys smaller specimens of this concordant drapery to integrate the angels' complex modern sleeves with the Virgin's legendary veil and bodice, adding white linen accents to all the radiant silks; but he invests most of the drapery in the trio of heavy, two-sided silken cloaks. To them he adds the gold-faced silken skirt-hem, using all the draperies to bind the figures together into a warm fabric symphony of red and blue, green and gold, a touch of black and a little white. We must infer the anatomy of the bodies supporting it all; they could be straw dummies.

The folds on Previtali's holy personages were modelled primarily to emphasise the colour, weight and sheen of actual fabric. They are a reminder that in all Renaissance Europe woven textiles were themselves treasures, just as they had been in Mediterranean antiquity, where the naturalistic vision of drapery in art had begun. The exquisite silk fabrics and magnificent wool carpets arriving in Europe from the East were matched by the beautiful wool, silk and linen fabrics woven in the British Isles and in Europe itself. Remarkable ways to process different fibres produced satin and gold-brocaded satin, velvet and cut velvet and crushed velvet, changeable silk of two colours at once, shimmering silk shot with metallic thread, stiff linen damask and floating linen gauze, thick wool felt, supple wool serge, silken veiling like mist and woollen veiling like a spider's web.

Huge sums might be spent on dress and decoration made from such wonders, rivalling those spent on glazed and golden marvels studded with gems, or indeed on exquisitely wrought paintings and statues. It's no wonder that Renaissance painters and sculptors clothed the citizens of Paradise and Parnassus in gloriously draped garments. Fine stuffs themselves seemed to have celestial claims, equal to the Scriptural pearl, jasper and emerald. Their renowned high value demanded expressions of painterly reverence in the form of truthful representation, however different the painters' styles of truth.

We have so far been looking at some fourteenth- and fifteenth-century Italian painters' responses, both direct and indirect, to the carved folds of Greek and Roman sculpture, noting that these artists working in Tuscany, Lombardy and the Veneto had different ways of painting fabric draped on figures, even though each may have seen himself as following the heritage of classical sculpture, in which an interaction of bodies and draperies had been so important. That heritage had been based on the classical ideal of rendering visual reality in a subtly perfected form, to let art create a stable beauty for fleeting natural appearances.

In fifteenth-century northern Europe, the same drive to rival or outdo sculpture, but with a Gothic rather than a classical model, resulted in the rise of a different style of pictorial naturalism for cloth in the work of Jan van Eyck, Rogier van der Weyden and their successors. In their version, rendering the atmospheric effects of light, as it revealed the colours and the qualities of textile surfaces, was more important than striving for the formal and spatial harmony and conviction achieved in the ancient Greco-Roman drapery, as well as in the bodies wearing it.

Such a different stylisation for making fabric look real was based on a different sense of perceived reality. In northern European painting, the look of fleeting actualities was valued for itself, and the idealising aim of art was to intensify it. The aim was to make a painting look revelatory, rather than rendered, as if the scene in it were in progress and nothing had been set in position by the painter. Creating perfection might lie simply in showing how the shifting daylight reveals the sleek surface hairs and underlying downiness of a squirrel-fur cuff. We see one of these around the Virgin's right sleeve in the centre of an altarpiece from the workshop of Dirk Bouts (fig. 18), where it is her one notable ornament. The painter seems to put it there to honour her hand, as it touches the sacred book held by Saint Peter. More discreet is the small bit we see lining the hem of her dress as it turns up a little in front.

In the idealising art of these lands with wet cold weather, rare sunshine and no direct classical heritage, the details of clothing were painted as if dress were far more naturally beautiful than the shape of human bodies, since undress was so non-natural and non-ideal a condition. Northern painters promoted an opposing beauty in their precise rendering of the various ways that differently woven fabrics looked, as light fell over their motions and positions while in use. For the dress of the Virgin and the saints, it was most often the wayward behaviour of abundant wool that was celebrated, its folds never regulated, tidied or stilled, always shown as a part of a constantly shifting sea.

Bouts's 1460s version of the enthroned Madonna with her baby and two attendant saints shows such woollen drapery cascading and breaking over inarticulate bodies, replacing them with its superior textile anatomy and action. In contrast to Mantegna's image, this woollen fabric looks much more essential to these three saintly figures than any human anatomy could. These ample clothes put even greater emphasis on the well-defined nakedness of the baby, as if sharply reminding us that Christ is naked in his later moments of sacrifice and death; and we see Saint Paul in the act of handing him a carnation, symbol of the Passion. Mary wears her traditional costume and loose hair, her mantle again veiling her head; her entire ensemble seems made of many more metres of material than appear on Mantegna's Virgin, as if to take up the space a solid body would occupy. Peter and Paul have tailored shoulders and collars above the downward-falling

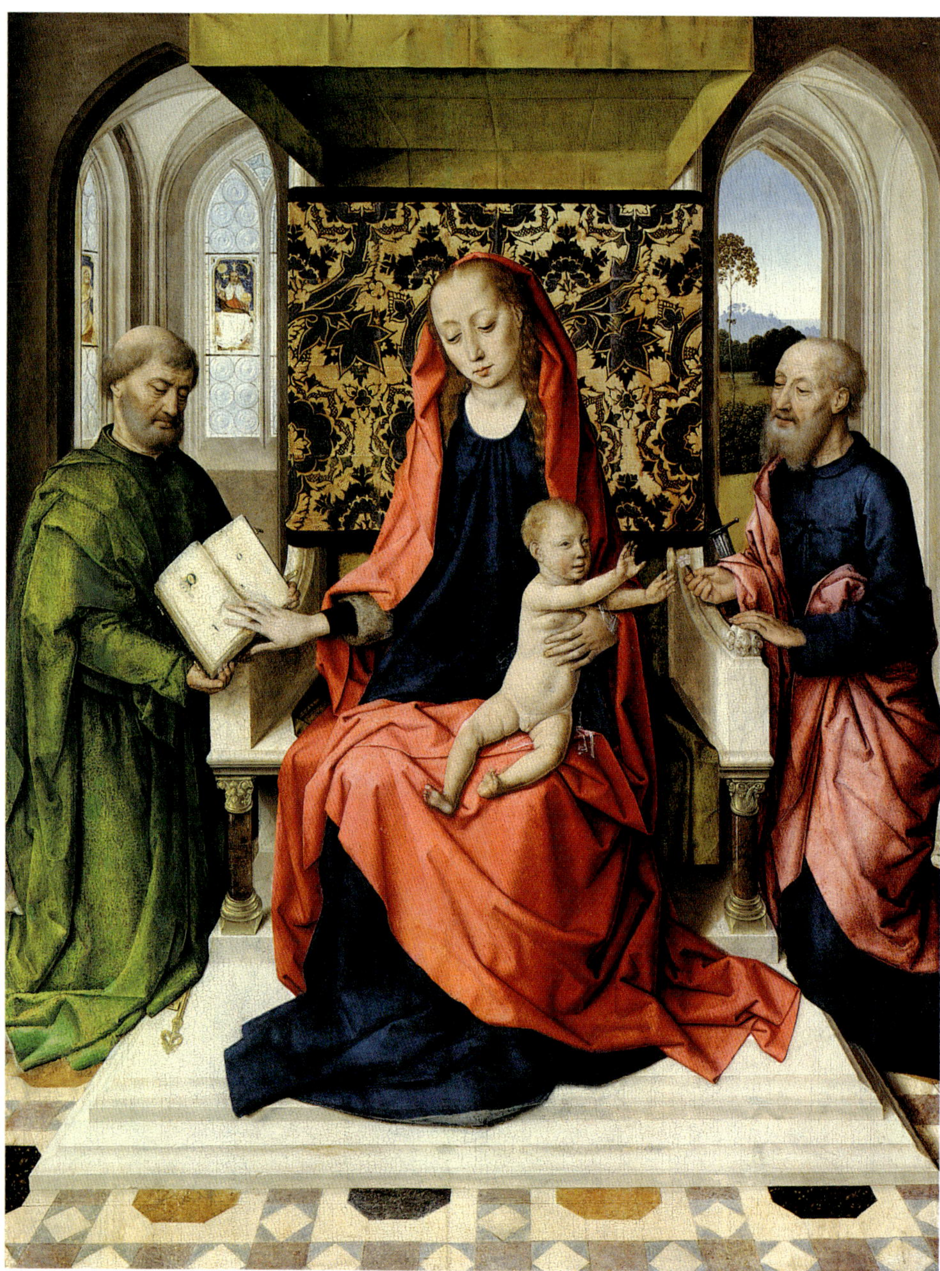

18
Workshop of Dirk Bouts
(about 1400?–1475)
The Virgin and Child with Saints Peter and Paul, probably 1460s
Oil on oak, 68.8 × 51.6 cm
National Gallery, London
NG 774

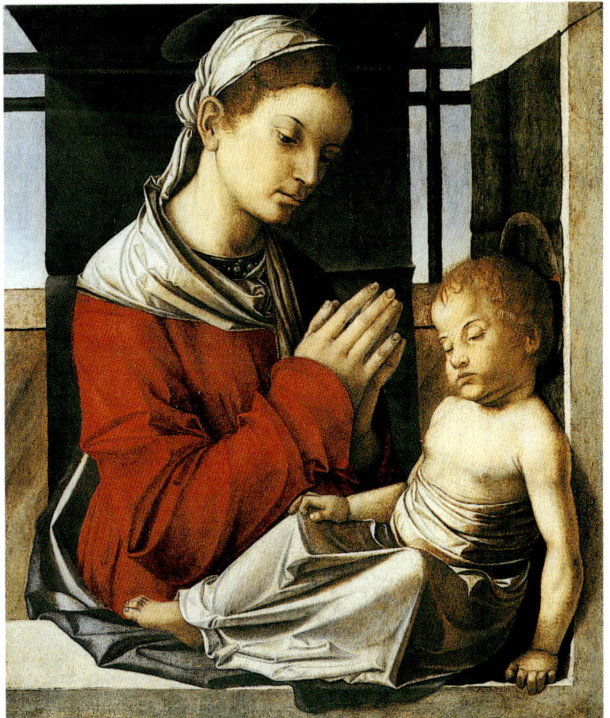

19
Bartolomeo Montagna
(about 1450–1523)
The Virgin and Child,
about 1504–6
Oil on canvas, transferred from wood, 59 × 51 cm
National Gallery, London
NG 1098

drapery of their gowns and mantles, which seems to be compelling them to sink to their knees on the top step. The light on the wool binds these separately draped masses into a more contemplative unit than the luscious one Previtali created with silk.

In both Italian and Flemish painting, a ceremonial hanging is often spread flat behind the figure of the seated Madonna, in imitation of the cloth of honour hung behind rulers when they sat to hold audience; and for the Virgin in paintings, it's often extended forwards at a right angle to form a canopy over her head. Bouts sets up his Virgin's throne on a dais inside a Gothic church, with floors of inlayed marble and two stained glass windows balancing one archway to the garden. The pale cloth of honour and canopy behind it are made regal by the great rectangle of black and gold brocade stretched just behind her, a sumptuous tribute to this Queen of Heaven who wears no crown or other jewel, no golden bands and borders on her plain woollen clothes.

Mantegna's vivid tomato-red version is placed among fruit trees under the sky, to make a garden pavilion for the Madonna and Child, and its flat red folds make a sharp contrast to the rhythmic play of the saints' and Virgin's cool draperies (see fig. 15). In an even more dramatic use of this motif, Bartolomeo Montagna's Virgin of about 1505 (fig. 19) adores her son as if oblivious to the stiff, dark fabric hung behind and above her, of which the creases still show where it was folded in storage. Her sleeping infant has his own draped garment to emphasise his graceful legs, and his own small, unfolded cloth of honour hung on a cord against the stuccoed stone embrasure where he leans.

With these dark shapes hung at right angles, joined with a few upright and horizontal beams, the painter creates the exact perspective of the setting and gives it an abstract character, enhanced by the empty blue sky behind it. Against them the matt white, red and blue-grey draperies crisply swathing the rounded forms of the two figures make a measured, brilliant display. These two honorific cloths and the other, richer ones we've looked at show how attentively painters were considering the character of fabric at this period, not just for pictured garments but for itself, as if to represent faithfully the honour it received in life.

The fifteenth-century Flemish painter's delight in the multiform crumple of layered garments shows intensely in part of an altarpiece painted in about 1435 by Rogier van der Weyden, showing Mary Magdalen sitting on the floor reading (fig. 20) with her ointment jar beside her. She has an expressive face, a delicate neck and finely articulated hands; the rest of her is made entirely of closely observed folds that give her a vibrant presence. For this Magdalen Rogier has followed the convention of showing the saint in fashionable dress, so we can see how the different folds of her real-life garments behave – very rigidly in the bodice above her tight and high black belt, very freely in the two skirts and wide sleeves.

We may also note that for her headdress she has abandoned fashion for legendary effects. Female portraits show us that hair in this period was tightly arranged and often hidden, while head-veils (however band-like) were symmetrically wrapped, or pleated or folded, and always held firmly in place. In art, casually draped veils and loose hair were correct headwear only for legendary costume, reserved for the Virgin and the saints or for the citizens of ancient, mythical and biblical places. Where most painters would leave the Magdalen's loose hair uncovered as Mantegna does, Rogier has added a seriously draped veil (with just a little ruching) suited to her present contemplative act and humble pose. Her loose hair flows unnoticeably out from under it over her shoulders.

Her veil can be compared to the neatly pinned and folded real-life headdress of Rogier's portrait subject (fig. 21), who wears a similar dress. The Magdalen's spread skirts show variably tumbled stuffs – her green wool overskirt has been raised in front to show its grey fur lining and the gold brocade underskirt, just as she would hold it while walking – but below her belt the emerging folds remain closely and regularly pleated. We can imagine the lady in the portrait similarly clad below the waist, perhaps in a less luxurious kirtle, lifting up and carrying the long fur-lined overskirt in front to make fine folds with it, and to expose the kirtle underneath. By contrast, Mantegna's Magdalen wears a clinging pictorial ensemble of classical, modern and traditional components, all organised into a poetic arrangement very different from anything normally worn by living ladies such as Baldovinetti's sitter.

By the fifteenth century, casually bunched or draped fabric had become only one element in normal European dress. Fashion, having gradually emerged in Europe by the later thirteenth century after ages of simple tunics, robes and mantles in many versions, now required much more discipline for draped folds, to blend with advances in the discipline of cut and fit. Random drapery now occurred in episodes – the strict folds of a man's cape freely draped up on to one shoulder, a woman's symmetrically pleated skirt bursting into free folds for its train. For both sexes, garments were now made closely fitted to the arms and upper body and tight in the waist, every little wrinkle smoothed by clever padding or avoided by adroit cutting. The ideal torso looked upholstered – sometimes with strictly controlled folds, such as those on Rogier's sitter, where they make a fine counterpoint to her randomly crushed sleeves. Folds in gentlemen's doublets, too, were made perfectly regular by hidden tapes and interlining on skirt, body and

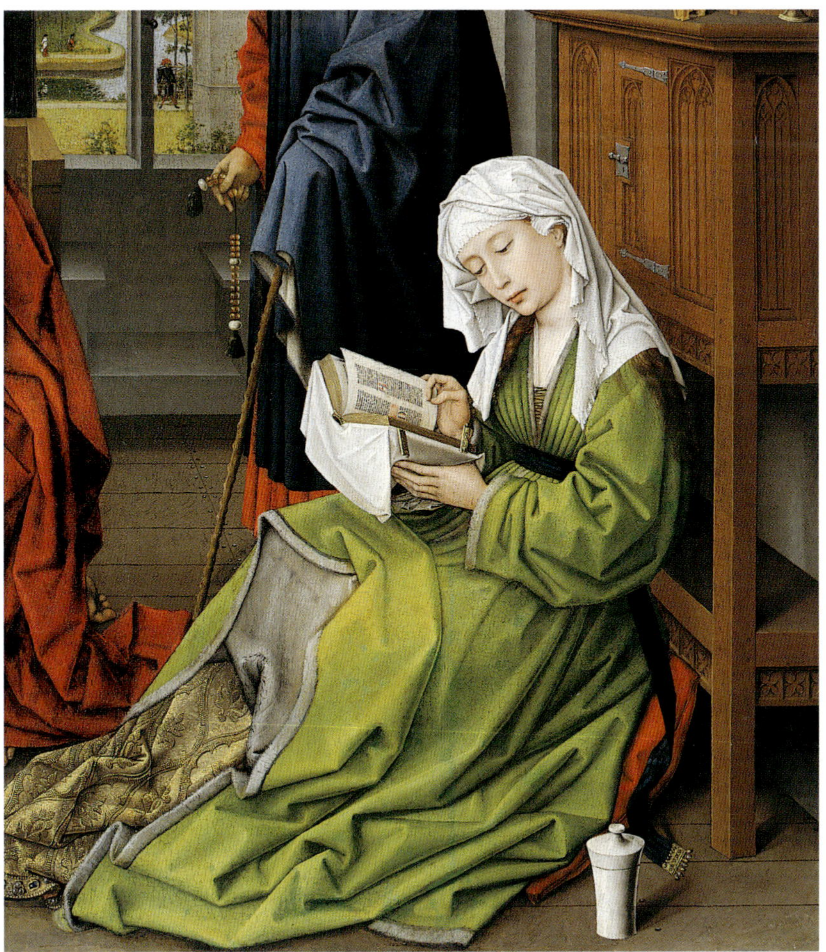

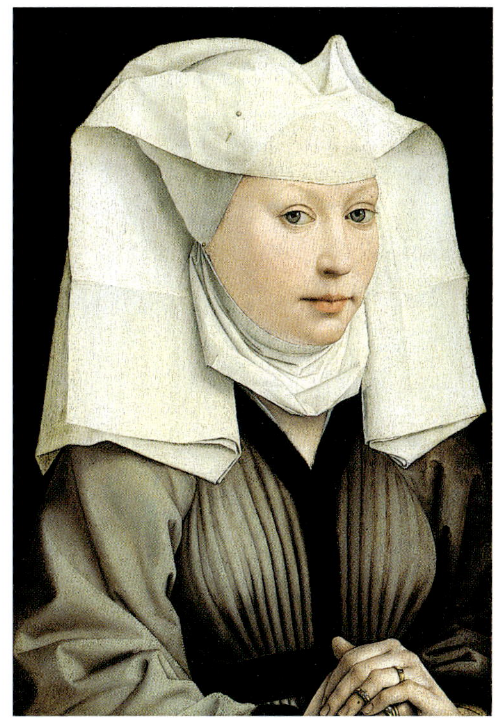

sleeves, to keep the outline orderly. So were the upper folds of ladies' skirts, to control the perfect fall we can see on the kirtle skirt of Piero's pregnant Virgin (see fig. 13).

Piero was one of the many fifteenth-century painters who used fashionable dress quite straightforwardly as legendary clothing, without creating a fanciful or antique look with more free folds than fashion permitted. In the second of two panels by Dirk Bouts illustrating the Justice of Otto, a thirteenth-century legend about the late tenth-century Holy Roman emperor Otto III, the scene is a trial by fire (fig. 22). A noblewoman is demanding justice for her falsely accused and beheaded husband, and proving his innocence by holding a red-hot bar that does not burn her. Everyone is in the most elegant Burgundian court modes for 1473, when the picture was delivered.

We can see the tight fit of the lady's bodice, and by this decade her sleeves are tight too, and her veil drapes from a magnificent high hood; but she still holds up her extra-long fur-lined skirt in front, now to cradle her husband's severed head. Most striking are the two long-legged gentlemen's very short, very rich tailored gowns with padded shoulders, their tight waists accentuated by narrowing folds, worn over even shorter, tighter doublets and long, tight hose ending in extravagantly pointed shoes. This fashionable group makes a strong contrast to Bouts's altarpiece of a few years earlier,

ABOVE LEFT **20**
Rogier van der Weyden
(about 1399–1464)
Fragment of an altarpiece:
The Magdalen reading,
probably about 1435
Oil on mahogany, transferred from another panel,
61.6 × 54.6 cm
National Gallery, London
NG 654

ABOVE RIGHT **21**
Rogier van der Weyden
(about 1399–1464)
Portrait of a Lady, about 1435
Oil on oak, 47 × 32 cm
Staatliche Museen zu Berlin, Gemäldegalerie

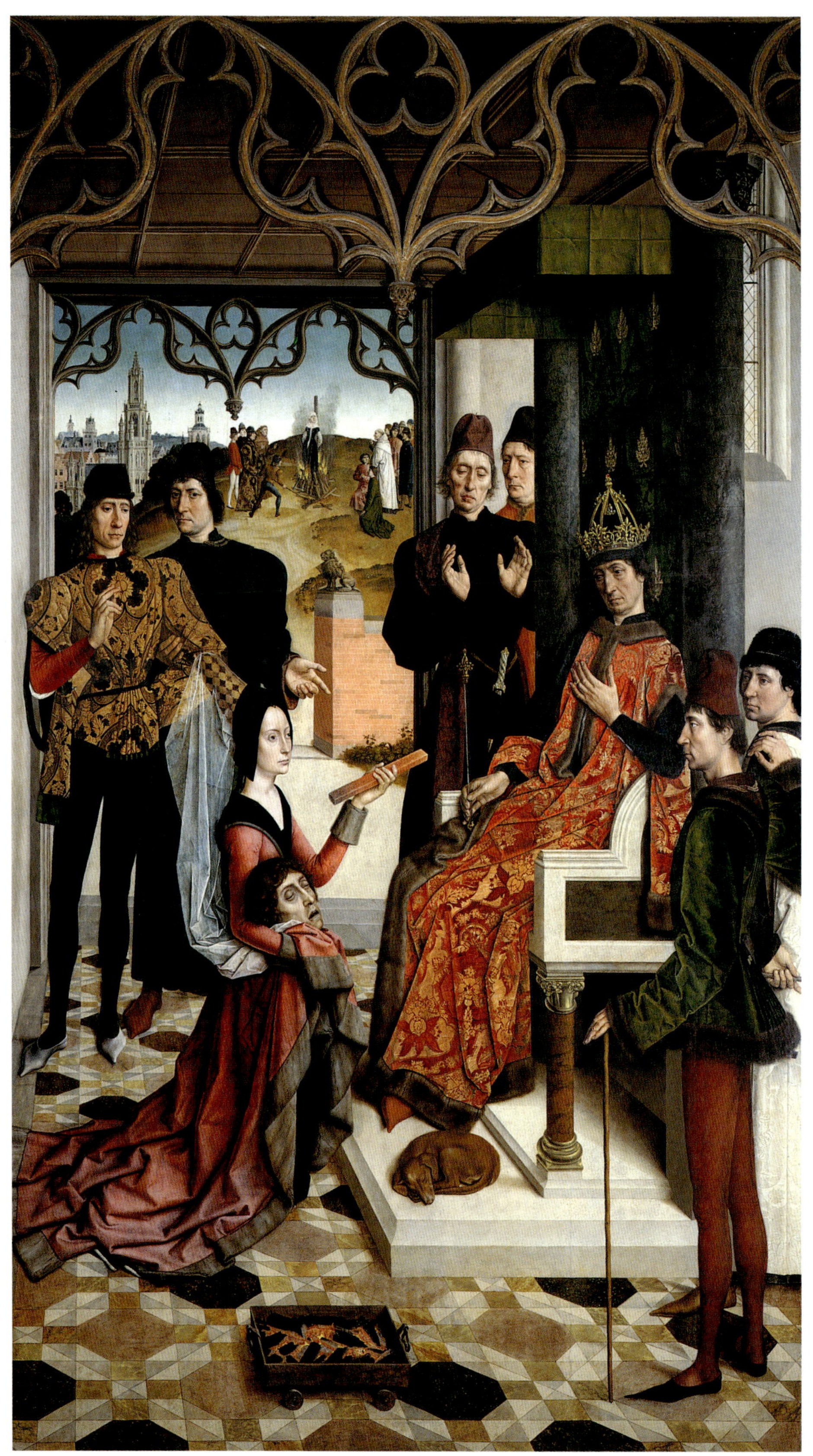

22
Dirk Bouts (about 1400?–1475)
The Trial of the Countess, from
The Justice of Otto, about 1471–3
Oil on oak panel, 344 × 201.5 cm
Musées royaux des Beaux-Arts
de Belgique, Brussels

where the saints' bodies are expressed only in miles of legendary wool, and the gold brocade is confined to the stiff cloth of honour.

On a less exalted social level at about the same date, Hans Memling's youth (fig. 23) wears a velvet doublet so black that no folds appear, and the focus here is on the two sequences of delicate black cord that attach the red jerkin under it. These mark the whiteness of the shirt under that, which also emerges delicately bunched around each arm-hole between the tight doublet and its pinned-on sleeves. His costume itself makes a vivid pattern out of his upper body with no use of drapery, an effect we also saw in the Baldovinetti; but his hands, face and hair, the columns and the book are all material phenomena with delicate surface details. This young man is praying, and his bare head is a sign of humility. A full and fluffy coiffure, however, was a proud male privilege at the time, an ornament usually on view in public below neat hats like those worn by the Bouts gentlemen. Angels in Italian art, as we have seen, often sport such hair, too.

Neither our three examples nor other fifteenth-century portraits show loose fabric draping freely behind the subject, decoratively swagged to fill the flat surface behind the painted person. Woven stuffs did sometimes appear in the background, but stretched flat with a minimal fold or two in the cloth-of-honour manner. Apparently lacking in both Italian and Flemish portrait painters of this time was the impulse to use unaccountable fabric to give extra expression to a sitter's image.

In every kind of European image at this period, it's evident that all painters were offering cloth in its true character, even in legendary costumes. No textile is shown used in any way that's vain or purely rhetorical. Curtains hang from visible supports in believable ways; it's clear that the draped clothing shown on figures would still clothe them even if the standing characters turned around and walked away, or the moving ones stopped moving and sat down. Every floating scarf or sash has a beginning and an end. Every sleeve has a visible parent garment, and it matches the size and shape of its fellow. No draped cloak in whatever style drapes illogically, or has more stuff than it needs to behave as it does; no skirt would have an uneven hemline if the seated wearer stood up. The integrity of draped fabric, honoured by contemporary society and by ancient history, was clearly seen as expressing the integrity of the artist and his art.

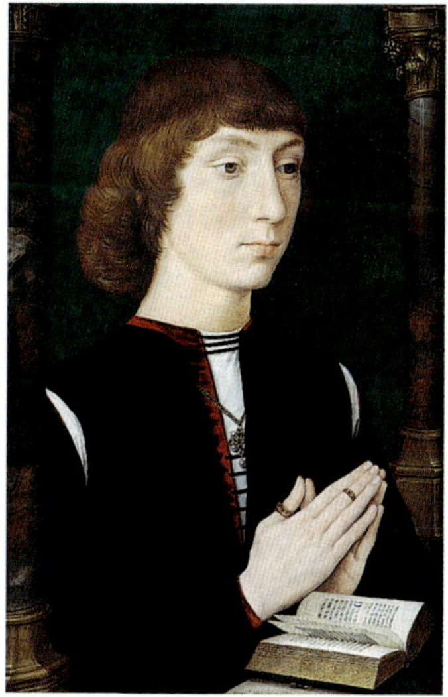

23
Hans Memling (active 1465; died 1494)
A Young Man at Prayer, probably about 1475
Oil on oak, 39 × 25.4 cm
National Gallery, London
NG 2594

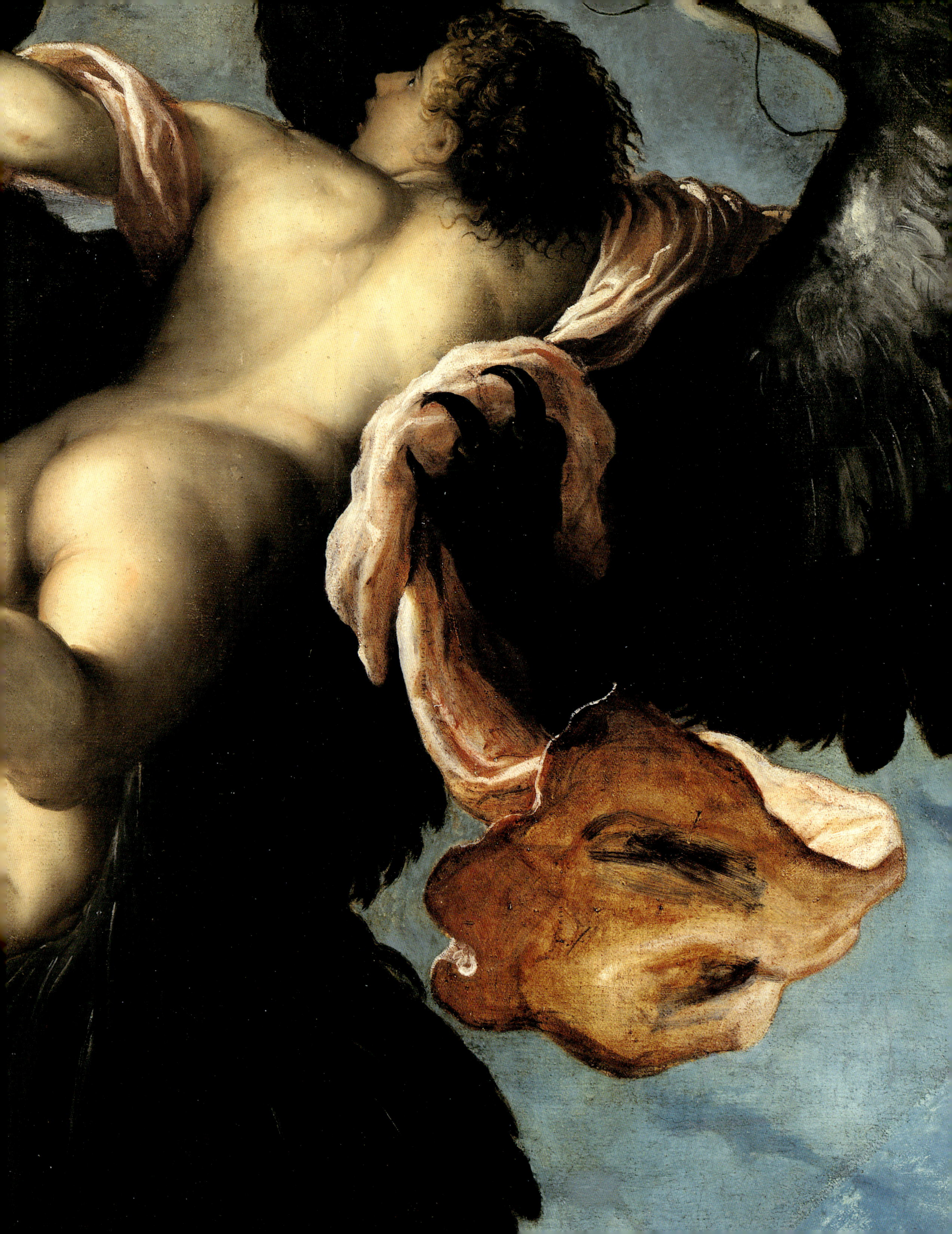

II Liberated Draperies

We have seen how fifteenth-century painters, like antique sculptors, showed their deep respect for the properties of cloth itself, whether draped and tailored as clothing, or hung and stretched as decoration. We saw this respect extended to the artistic use of fabric for legendary clothing, including traditional garb for Christian saints, as well as to the rendering of modern tailored garments; and that the real and legendary garments combined in pictures were all responsibly constructed and made of equally sane stuff. During the next century, however, painters found other ways to build on the prestige of the draped cloth in earlier works of art, both in antiquity and in the recent past. Sixteenth-century painters began to emphasise the purely artistic life of draped fabric, turning it into a painterly component with much wider scope, enabling the cloth represented in pictures to enjoy a new freedom from the practical rules constraining a man-made substance with specific technical qualities and uses.

They seemed to suggest that draped fabric might renew its role as man's natural, elemental accompaniment in works of art – the role drapery had originally enjoyed in antique art before fashion existed, when it was rendered as a constant element in everyone's experience. In sixteenth-century art, after the advances in realism of the previous century, the representation of draped fabric could again claim universal status for itself, now in reference not only to antiquity, but to art's own draped Christian past, which was indeed founded in that same classical art that everyone acknowledged as the ultimate source.

Painting itself had come to seem founded on draperies, fully as much as on bodies; and as fashion had more noticeably and more variously taken over living bodies, so draped fabric could become a separate painterly element, whether to form the clothing for visionary bodies in art, or to appear visionary in itself. Just as outdoor scenery might show storm clouds in the sky or a spring gushing from a rock, so indoor scenes might have swatches of drapery gushing between columns or swagging under cornices. Painters came to feel they could bring drapery into the picture as needed to meet expressive demands, never forgetting the pictorial rule that it must look like drapery, to make the necessary connection with the revered art of the past.

Detail of fig. 35

Fashion during the sixteenth century was in fact growing ever more distant from its medieval draped past. From about 1520, at the start of what is called the Mannerist epoch, the trend in elegant clothing was increasingly towards more width and mass, more padding and more surface complexity in the ways cloth was used. Elegance was no longer expressed in straight-falling regular folds and a long, dragging sweep for sleeves, gowns, cloaks and skirts. Fabric was now made to bunch up and puff out in smaller-scale, more random ways and to stand out stiffly, especially to amplify the look of the upper body with the addition of padded shoulders and big complex sleeves. The overall smooth fit and orderly fall of cloth, emphasising the slimness and length admired in the fifteenth century, gave way to a busy, mobile bulk emphasising fleshiness and substance.

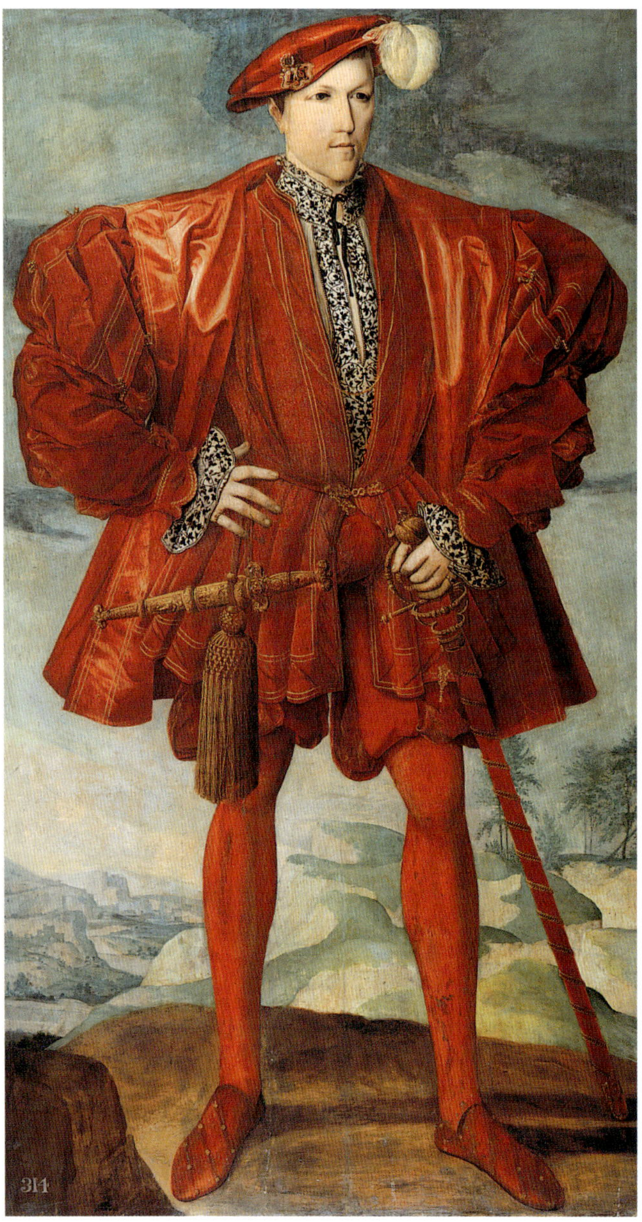

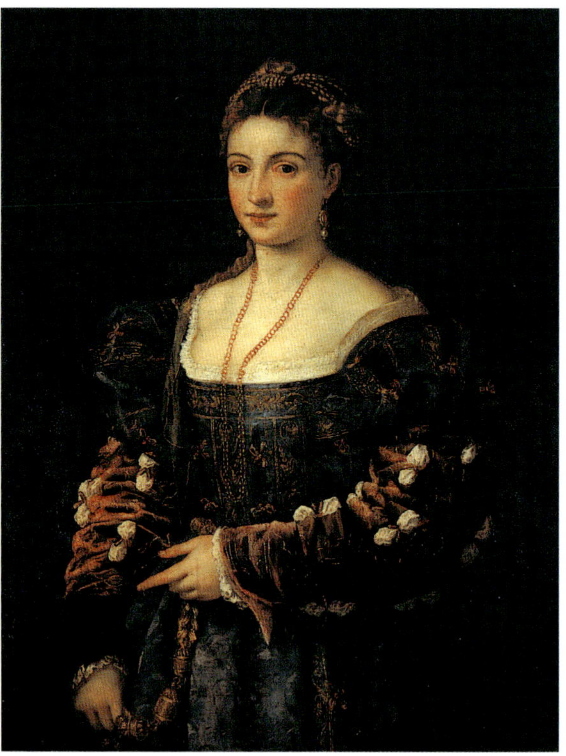

LEFT **24**
Flemish, about 1540
Portrait of a Young Man in Red
Oil on canvas, 190.2 × 105.7 cm
The Royal Collection,
Hampton Court

ABOVE **25**
Titian (about 1485/90–1576)
'La Bella', 1536
Oil on canvas, 89 × 75.5 cm
Galleria Palatina, Palazzo Pitti,
Florence

For women, the most important development in fashion was the new use of straight stays built into the bodice, not to contract the waist and ribcage but to stiffen and thicken them in accordance with the bulk now desired for the total effect. The most notable development for men was that of elaborate breeches for the pelvic area and thighs, along with the stiffened and padded codpiece and the general use of short gowns, now worn unbelted for greater fullness. Eventually stays were also used in masculine doublets.

The standing portrait dated to 1540 of an unknown Englishman by an unknown painter (fig. 24) gives the ideal full-length masculine look for the first half of the century, with the head very small in proportion to the huge shoulders, the torso clad in bunched and broken stuffs with the focus on the codpiece, and the long legs now shortened by the breeches. Titian's magnificent image of ideal female beauty from 1536 (fig. 25) shows the new stiff, thick and highly ornamented bodice with its thick puffed and padded sleeves and thick folds of skirt at the hips. All these turn the dress itself into a brilliant living organism, which fills much of the space and makes the beauty's head, neck and white bosom seem proportionately small and all the more fair. We can see that these styles for men and women suggest that the ideal body under them is massive and muscular.

Paradoxically, delight in the natural flow and lengthy fall of drapery had less expression in fashion itself at the time when new interest in its aesthetic capacities appeared in art; artists also began to delight less in using precise fashionable details as components for the costumes in legendary scenes. In the sixteenth century, as opposed to all previous ones, many painters began to put realistic-looking but not very specifically or believably deployed cloth into the design of legendary clothing, or add it to the scenery – primarily for emotional impact and psychological effect, to maintain the idea of draped fabric as a basic element in pictures, a test of the painter's originality and skill, whether as a classical allusion or a reference to traditional Christian art. In the course of the century, we can see to what degree the flavour and the power of a picture might depend on what such painterly draperies were made to do.

In the very early 1500s, Michelangelo was already showing, in his unfinished *Entombment of Christ* (fig. 26), how draped clothing in pictures could shake off all the rules of real garments and become a freely malleable element. The standing woman who supports Christ's body on the right wears two dresses, a long-sleeved pink one under a sleeveless dark-grey one; but the pink one behaves very strangely. The right sleeve is much fuller and larger than the left one, and only half the skirt seems to exist. Meanwhile the skirt of the overdress is draped up to the left by no visible means, while its vertical folds above the waist seem too numerous to allow the garment to stay on the shoulders as it does, even with the band across it, and too full to be part of the same garment as the skirt. The painter has added and subtracted and manipulated folds in this costume as he likes, using them to increase the unearthly and unstable look of the figure by hiding her rear leg and by denying these garments the look of real ones.

The standing man on Christ's other side wears a clinging red dress lined in grey, of which the front neckline is sharply cut down and peeled back on one side. Michelangelo has blatantly violated this dress entirely for the sake of this picture, so as to expose the man's shoulder and link its anatomical beauty with the beautiful bare forearm below. No fifteenth-century painter would ever have done this to a garment, nor would any

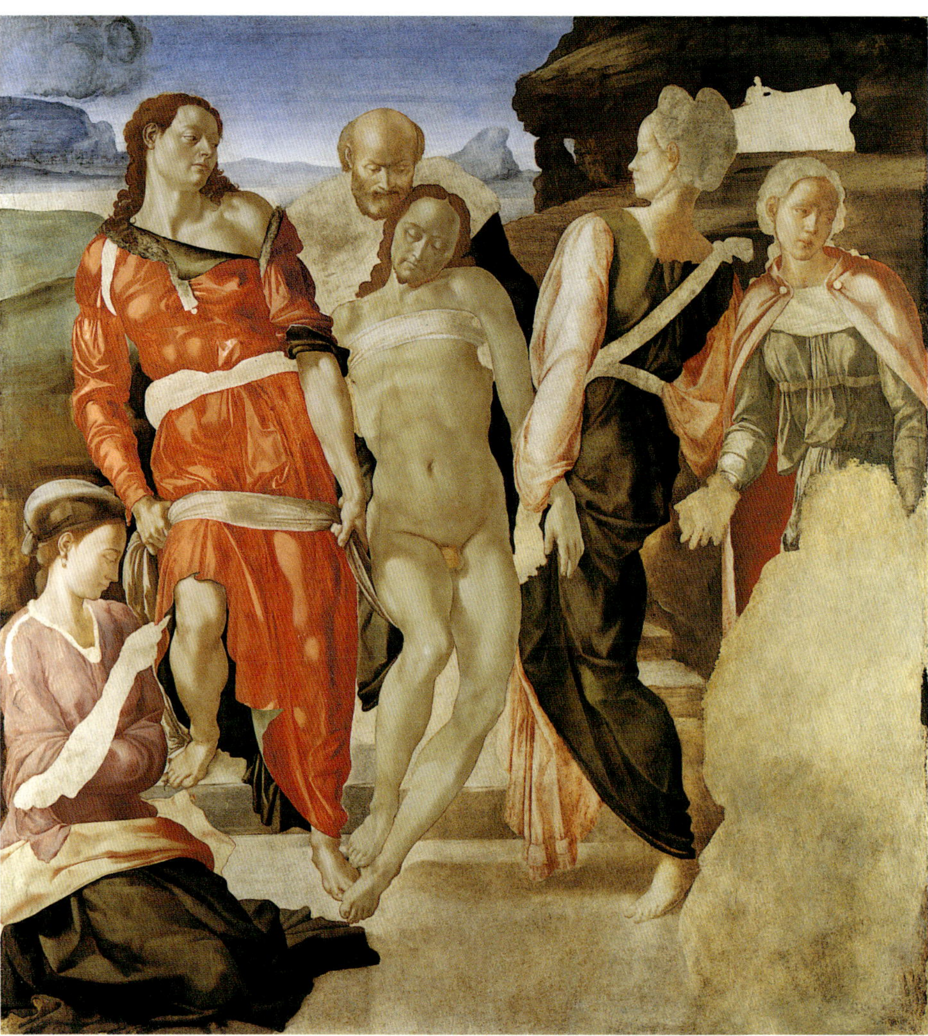

26
Michelangelo (1475–1564)
The Entombment of Christ, about 1500–1
Oil on wood, 161.7 × 149.9 cm
National Gallery, London
NG 790

antique artist; and Michelangelo is not suggesting that any dress was ever so treated before, in life, legend or art – he is doing it only now, and only here. Meanwhile, above this same painted forearm, the rolled up sleeve looks quite reasonable for what this body-bearing arm is doing.

At the bottom, the rear hemline of the skirt seems to exist in two separate parts, reflecting two separate schemes of draped folds designed for the separate legs, one bent and bare to match the nude forearm, one straight and covered to match the opposite sleeved arm. This dress thus has two different lengths of skirt for its right and left sides, a disparity again not permitted in fifteenth-century pictorial dress, and unheard of in life, but visually perfect for the painted costume of this male figure.

Each separate fold in both costumes is authoritatively represented, so that they give the visual impression of being made of real cloth; but the realism of the folds only strengthens the disturbing effect of the irregular clothing, which acts subtly on the viewer's eye to keep this scene from resembling anything that might happen in real life. The blend of lifelike folds with unlikely clothes increases the surreal and elegiac mood of the picture, while the rhyming leftward rise of their two strangely draped skirts unites these opposing figures as they share the weight of Christ's nude body. Michelangelo's very personal and emotive use of the painted fabric in this picture is an early example of the new freedom artists were beginning to give it.

Jacopo da Pontormo, born a generation later than Michelangelo, is a key figure in the advance of Florentine painting of the Mannerist period. One of his masterpieces is *The Deposition of Christ* in the Capponi Chapel in Santa Felicita in Florence (fig. 27), painted between 1526 and 1528, where eleven interlaced figures and their draperies seem to form a floating cloud – and there is an actual cloud floating in the picture, as if to allow the association. None of these eleven wears intelligible garments except the dead Christ,

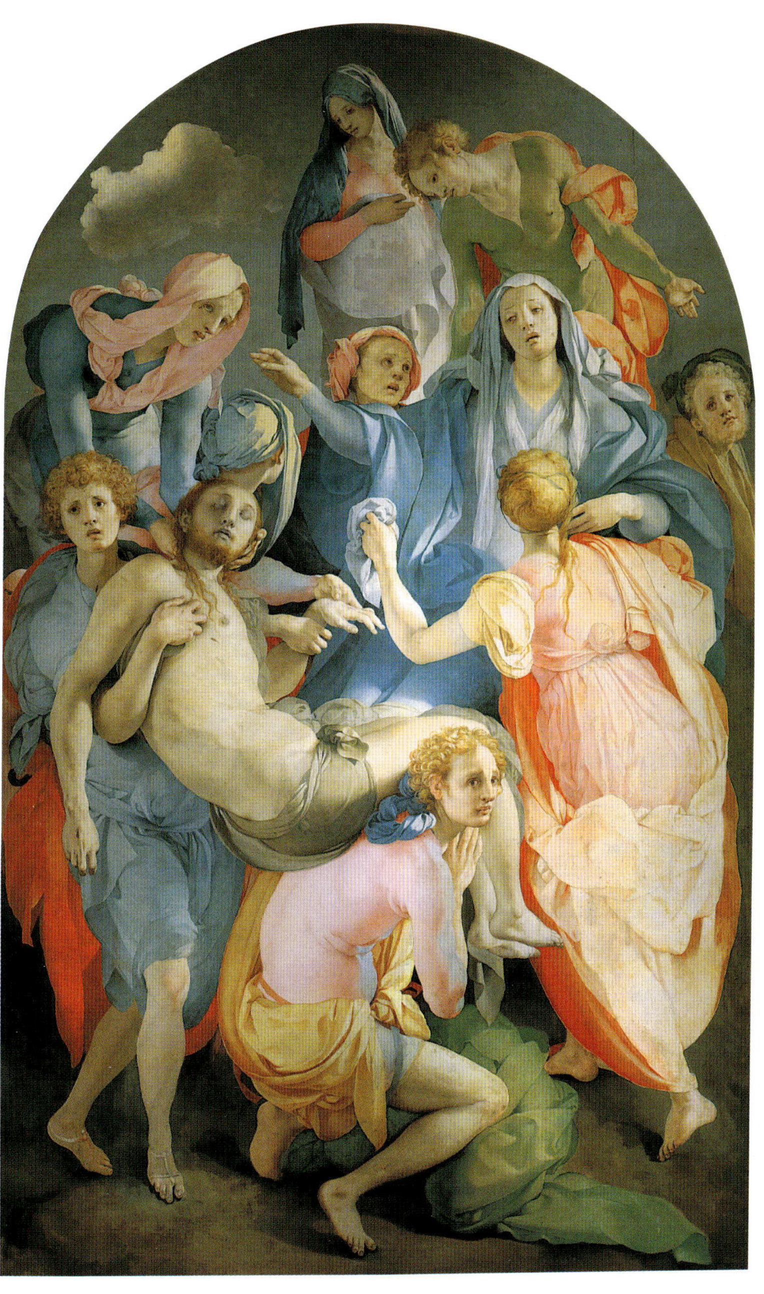

27
Jacopo da Pontormo (1494–1557)
The Deposition of Christ, 1526–8
Oil on canvas, 313 × 192 cm
Santa Felicita, Florence

whose earthly loincloth is painted a pale dun colour not found elsewhere among the repeating rainbow of shades in which all the other draperies appear. The irrationality of the others' garments – the quasi veils, almost mantles, perhaps sashes and not-really gowns – is wonderfully consistent. None of the drapery can be clearly understood as occurring in a real length of woven fabric or in a garment of known shape, nor could most of it actually stay where it is placed – something true of most of the figures. But consistent, too, is the truthful clarity of the individual folds that form the draperies, like that of all the figures' perfect anatomy; and the texture of the cloth is its most consistent, and most Florentine element. Just as in Giotto and Masaccio so many years before, all the draperies are made of the same stuff in different colours.

The painter has further increased the unearthly beauty of this composition by coating the skin of at least six of the figures with partial painted-on garments under the drapery, most notably the pink one on the crouching youth in the centre foreground who bears Christ's lower body on his shoulder, and the green one on the bending youth at the top. A tinted anatomy is thus shown to be part of this pictorial wardrobe – even the Virgin has blue arms and bosom under her blue draperies. Another unearthly effect appears on the foreground woman seen from the back, whose dramatically wrapped mantle-like drape has been painted in one colour for the front half and another for the rear half, the two colours turning into each other along her leg and sides – not, as might happen in life, in one colour lined with another colour, nor two changeable colours throughout one garment. The painter has brought all these miraculous clothes into existence expressly for this swirling sacred event, which we see could only take place where the earth blends effortlessly into the sky, and gravity has ceased to prevail.

At almost the same moment, about 1525, Titian painted drapery with quite another effect for his *Entombment* (fig. 28), an example of the Venetian master's different sort of expressive miracle. This sombre drama for six persons has also been beautifully composed and costumed; but these legendary draped garments, of which stylised versions can be found in thirteenth-century art, are here offered with a gripping modern truthfulness, evident in one glance, of structure, texture and behaviour. Right away we accept the white linen folds in the foreground that focus and intensify the light falling on Christ's beautiful dead legs. We watch the sheet stretch tight under his weight, and unfold crisply under the hands of the man holding the legs, we see them and the linen gleaming against his dark garment. The lower half of this dead, linen-held body dominates the picture and forces the event on us.

The two men holding Christ's shadowed upper body both wear classical sandals, as if they were in a Mantegna; and each wears a differently dignified silk gown, of which the elegant sleeves have been differently tucked up, so they can undertake this unprecedented task – on the left, straight sleeves rolled up; on the right, hanging sleeves tied behind the back, leaving long tight ones showing. These men bend towards each other with dance-like grace, while the disarrangement of each visible sleeve is concentrated and highlighted – small folds in white linen at left, large knotted swags in red and brown damask at right.

Completing the tight male group at the centre is John the Evangelist in plain red with long hair, open-mouthed with woe as he lifts one pale wrist in his ruddy hand; and at far

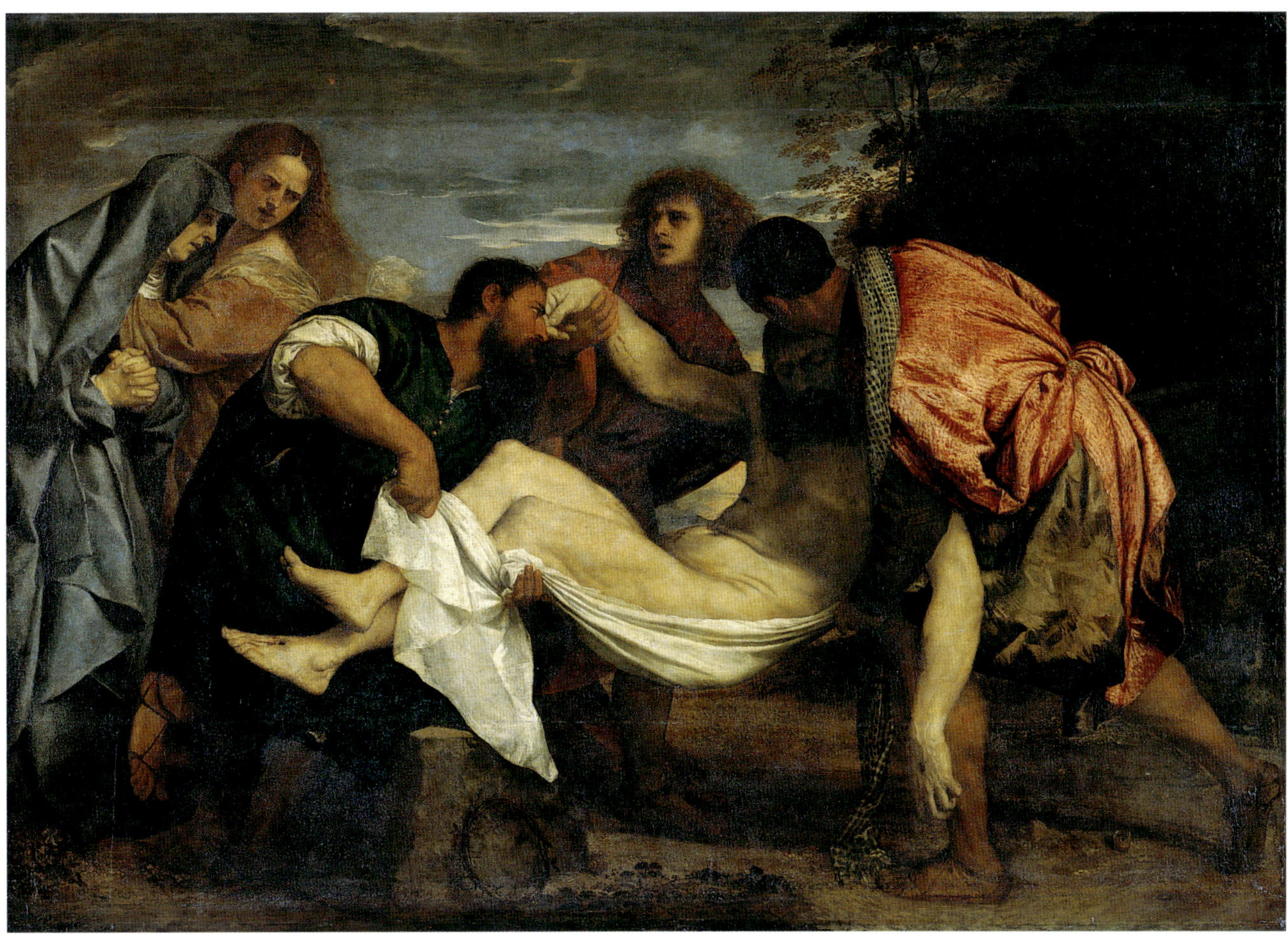

left the loose-haired Magdalen, her red sleeve moving to embrace the bent Virgin under her blue mantle, looks back to frown at the corpse. These three attendant saints are clad in minimal indications of their traditional dress – one or two real-looking square metres each, the Virgin's full-length blue folds having the most scope, as in many fifteenth-century works. The Magdalen adds a trace of modern Venetian scarf across her shoulder; and a legendary scarf – that is, an unwound biblical turban – is falling over those of the man on the right.

The uniform candour of these variable silk and linen folds and Titian's great tact in rendering these old-days clothes have served to charge this canvas with immediate tragedy. The care he has taken with the classical simplicity of their composition and the subtlety of their lighting has become invisible. The draperies look as unaffected as the grief on the faces and the action of the bodies, and they add their own intensely moving look of perfect spontaneity.

Not everyone was a great genius. We can contrast the masterpieces of Michelangelo, Pontormo and Titian with a work of about 1540 by the Milanese artist Gaudenzio Ferrari, whom we see using deliberately expressive drapery in a version of *Christ rising from the Tomb* (fig. 29). This Christ wears a neat pair of underpants, of which you can see part of

28
Titian (about 1485/90–1576)
The Entombment of Christ, about 1525
Oil on canvas, 148 × 212 cm
Musée du Louvre, Paris

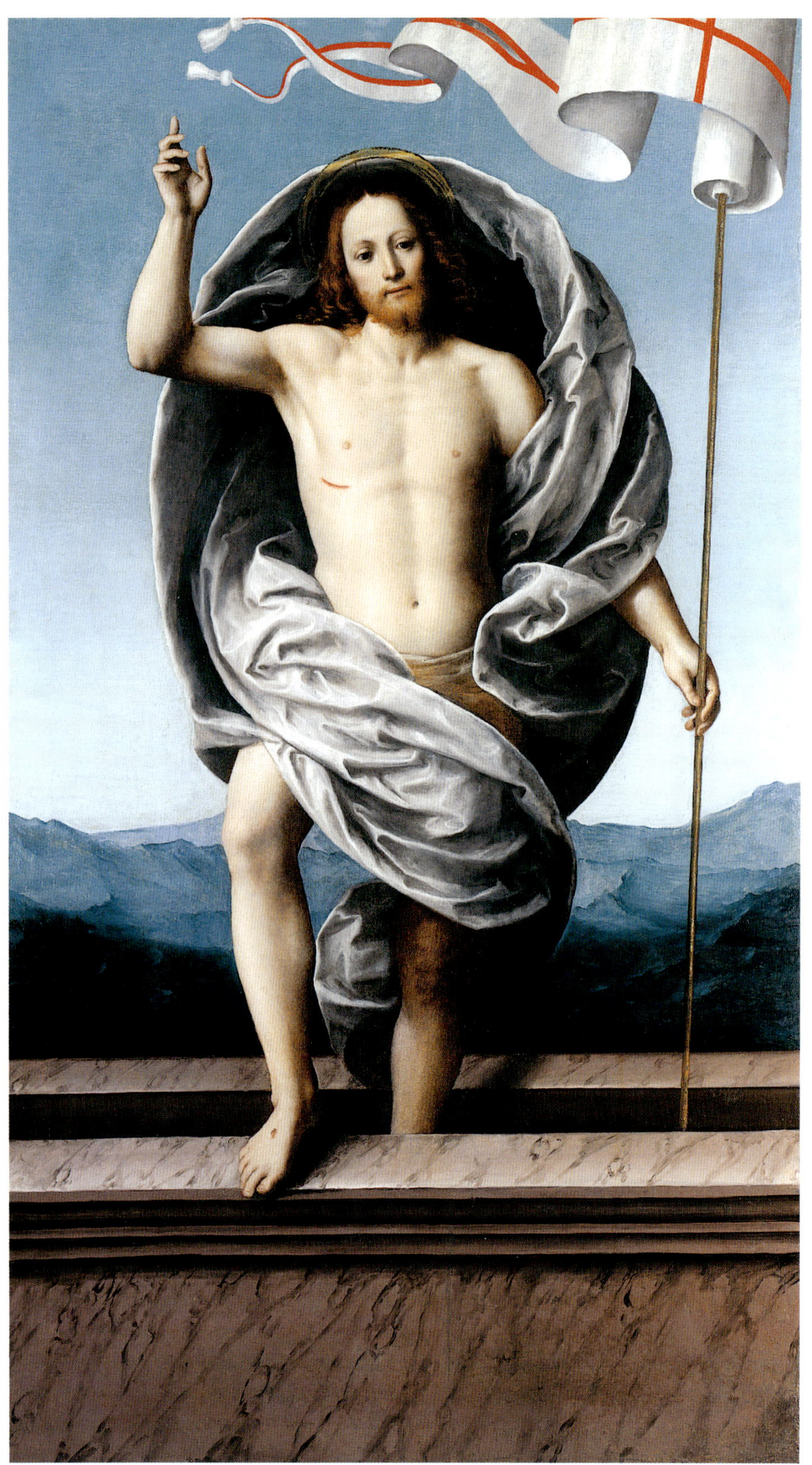

29
Gaudenzio Ferrari
(1475/80–1546)
Christ rising from the Tomb, about 1540
Oil on poplar, 152.4 × 84.5 cm
National Gallery, London
NG 1465

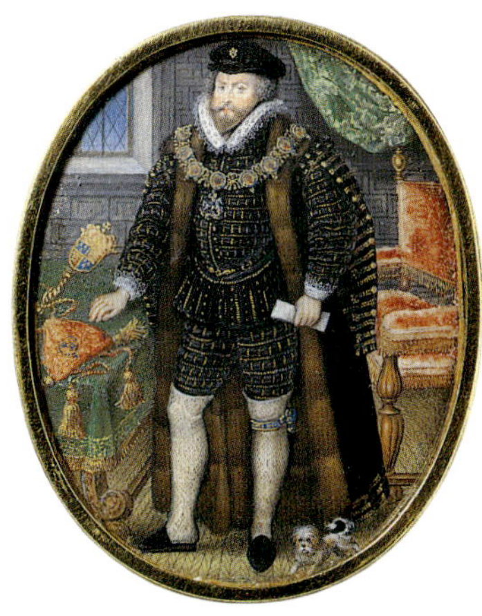

30
Nicholas Hilliard (about 1547–1619)
Sir Christopher Hatton, about 1588–91
Watercolour on vellum, 5.6 × 4.3 cm
The Victoria and Albert Museum, London

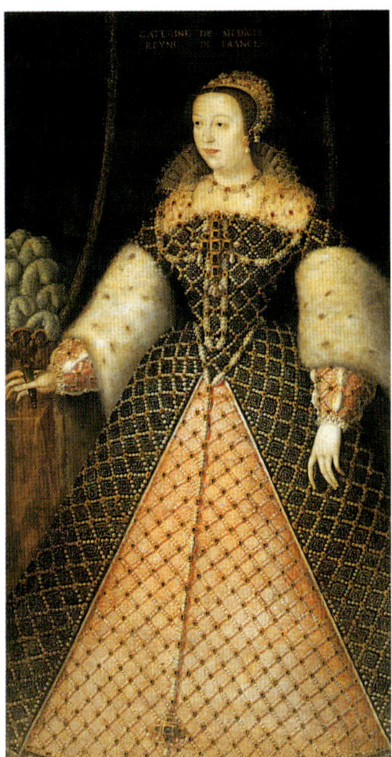

31
French School, about 1550
Catherine de' Médici
Oil on canvas, 146 × 105 cm
Museo Mediceo, Palazzo Medici-Riccardi, Florence

a seam, a detail quite in keeping with the respectable if uninteresting draped clothing this artist was painting in the first decade of the century. Around Christ's whole figure, however, now swirls a large cloud of unspecific cloth, a sort of notional cloak with no definite edges and corners, no width or length, no inside or outside, no visible means of support, and considerable rigidity of shape. The heavy unreality of this object now strikes the eye, as nothing about the painter's conventional gowns and mantles from thirty years before does. He seems to be trying out something new to him.

A soft wind is blowing the banner Christ holds; but that same wind could make no difference to this formidable drape. It has the look of being held in place by the force of artistic convention, which insists that its strict oval outline look mandorla-like, that its carved marmoreal folds suggest antique draperies to match Christ's classical nudity, and also that it stand figuratively for the grave-clothes from which he has escaped. We can, moreover, see that Christ is actually wearing none of this stuff, not wrapping it around him to dress in after he climbs out, not letting it fall away from him as he rises up. It's congealed around his body to fix him forever in this iconic pose, as if to prevent him from rising further, or even from moving at all. As in Michelangelo's *Entombment* and Pontormo's *Deposition*, each fold looks quite real; but this painter, perhaps born before Michelangelo and certainly dead before Pontormo, hadn't yet found the daring or the flair, the instinct for mould-breaking, the painterly imagination to create an unreal arrangement for real drapery that would break free, lift off and hold good. This effort to try it shows him held back by the inherited authority of an earlier way.

Ornament for elegant dress was changing its character as sixteenth-century fashion became more sophisticated in its second half. We can see why the term Mannerism, which can mean excessive attention to stylish detail at the expense of basic form, has been applied to European fashion as well as to painting in the middle decades of the sixteenth century. Instead of sweeping or controlled folds giving a costume its chief beauty, elaborate workmanship came to be applied to the surface of all parts of an elegant ensemble, no longer just to the embroidering of borders, the scalloping of edges or the weave of the stuff. Tailors excelled at inventive pinking and slashing for sleeves, hats, doublets and bodices, wrought lace became an important public element of rich dress, precious metals and gems were sewn right on to garments, and the fashionably thickened arms and torsos, along with the increasingly stiffened skirts and breeches, offered a larger ground for surface treatment. Elegant portraiture of these decades makes a fine display of such fashionable details, recording every pearl and pickadil with care (fig. 31; see fig. 25).

Drapery was losing its chic in fashion, but the prestige of painted draped fabric was higher than ever, as painters began to play with its pictorial role in sacred and secular legend. As its elemental character was being demonstrated by great and less great painters, freely draped fabric also began to appear in portraits, even if the subject was not wearing any of it. In portraiture throughout the rest of the sixteenth century, beginning in the 1520s, we find floating, falling or looped-up fabric, with no visible source or use, near or behind the formidably padded, stiffened and decorated bodies of ladies and gentlemen (fig. 30; see fig. 31).

This drapery could be said to have a painterly precedent in the cloth of honour we saw stretched flat behind draped Virgins in the fifteenth century, when it was sometimes stretched flat behind portrait subjects, too. It might also be said to have a rational excuse, since curtains had long since been used for closing off openings in rooms leading to alcoves or balconies or other rooms. But in most sixteenth-century portraits where it appears, the attendant drapery looks irrational and emotional, sensual and allusive, sometimes ridiculous, and not at all practical. The idea had clearly taken root that draped fabric in a picture has a virtue and power of its own. If drapery is in the picture with Jesus or with Venus, it can add to their force and importance; and by extension, if it's there with a portrait subject, it can add to his or hers.

In his 1533 portrait of a gentleman (fig. 32), Jörg Breu of Augsburg has recorded the sitter's pinked brown gloves, well-tailored and feathered red hat, fully paned (that is, made of adjacently set strips) white doublet and paned sleeves, frilled shirt-collar and sleeveless black gown with shoulder-tabs – all suggesting that no big, raw folds of stuff should have any prominence in his apparel. The drapery instead hangs above his shoulder from no visible rod, looped up for no visible purpose other than to show its own green beauty, which makes a foil for the green landscape outside the window and for the sitter's many strips, slits, straps, frills and tabs.

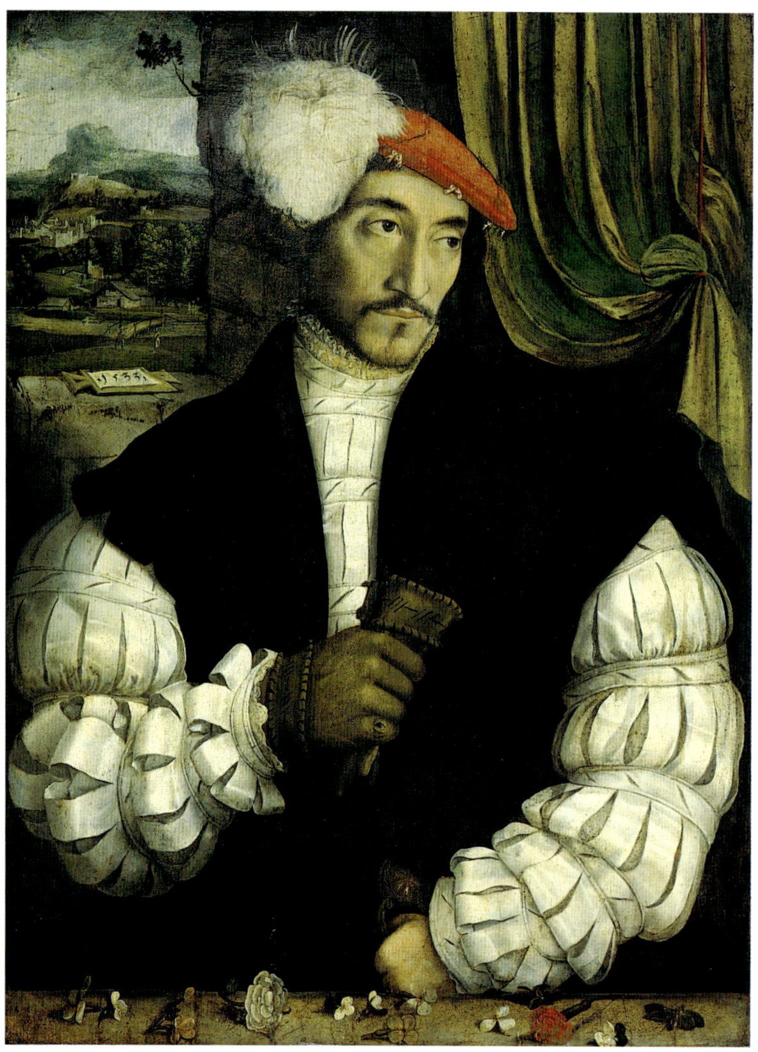

32
Jörg Breu the Elder
(about 1475/6–1537)
Portrait of a Man, 1533
Oil on panel, 67.8 × 49.2 cm
Courtauld Institute Gallery, London

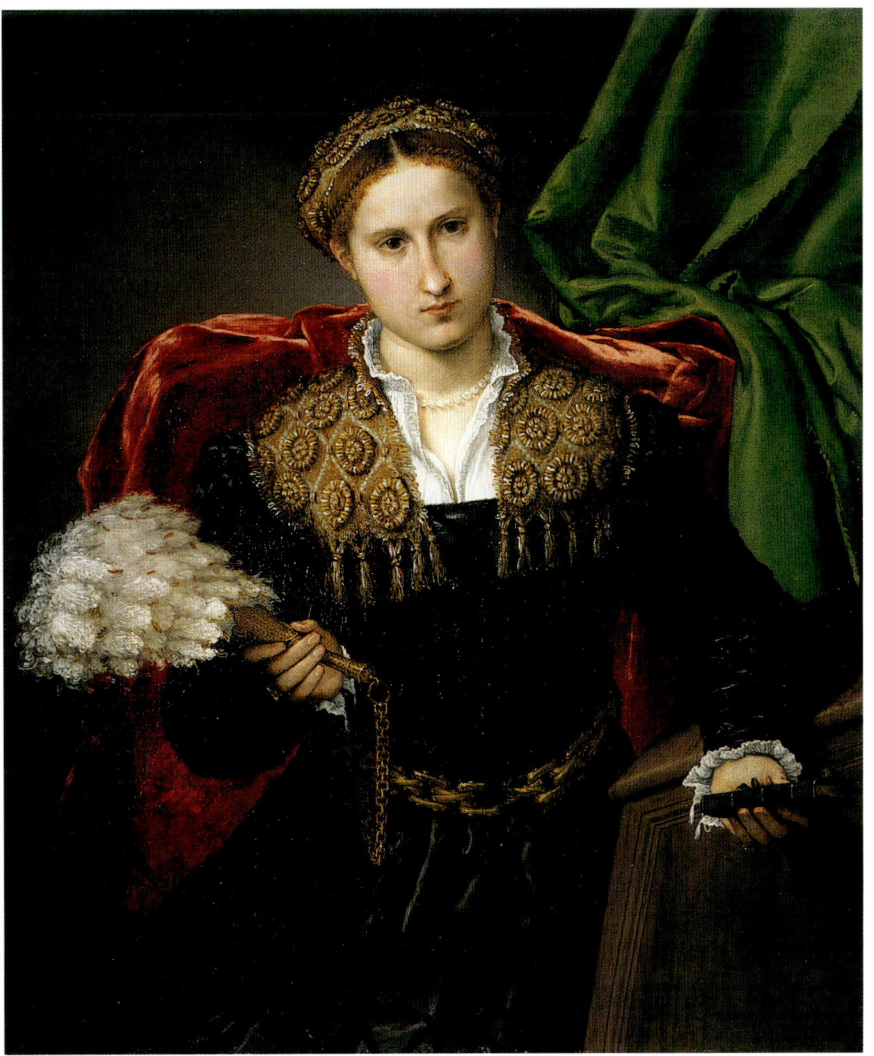

33
Lorenzo Lotto (about 1480–after 1556)
Laura da Pola, 1543
Oil on canvas, 91 × 76 cm
Pinacoteca di Brera, Milan

As the century went on, attendant drapery showed more lush and free behaviour and a consistent lack of clear source or function in the setting, while the subject's dress showed more fragmented, decorative uses of cloth, along with further adornments and accessories. Lorenzo Lotto's 1543 portrait of Laura da Pola (fig. 33) shows heavy draperies encroaching on the back of the sitter's chair and looking ready to swamp her in folds, as she sits laden with weighty gold embroideries on her head, chest and shoulders. A huge gold chain confines the waist of her long-sleeved black cut-velvet dress, to which another big gold chain attaches the many-feathered, gold-handled fan she lifts in one hand – the little book in her other hand is weightless by comparison.

The spotlight, however, is focused on the undone frilly collar of the sitter's white chemise, which reveals her incandescent throat in its gentle pearl rope. We see a tender creature chained in a black and gold prison, soon to drown in an uncontrollable torrent of red and green silk. The heavy black and gold dress with touches of white defines the woman, and so do her accessories; the red and green fabric appears as a separate agency, an influence, an ambience.

Agnolo Bronzino's portrait of Lodovico Capponi from about 1550 (fig. 34) shows the sitter encased in an armour-like doublet of black silk puckered by vertical bands of black velvet, his white trunk-hose paned, his codpiece slashed and padded, his white sleeves pinked and further puckered with vertical white braid. The few folds of black cape over his rear shoulder are subdued, the better to emphasise the action of the brilliant green drapery behind him, and to show that the green folds are emphatically not part of his costume. This stuff comes from nowhere expressly to fill the whole space behind the man, to bunch and ripple in happy textile play while the youthful sitter's image remains grave, elegant and commanding.

It's as if this background fabric were there to suggest things about the subject that his face and clothing may not convey, a sense of what he would rather be doing than posing. This is an example of painterly drapery used for its own expressiveness, looking quite unlike anything used in life for clothes or curtains, bearing instead the look of Pontormo's unearthly swatches in the *Deposition*, with each fold perfect, but the whole unlikely. We can see that fabric in paintings has come to refer to itself, to display its painted nature in the image and its elemental character in art.

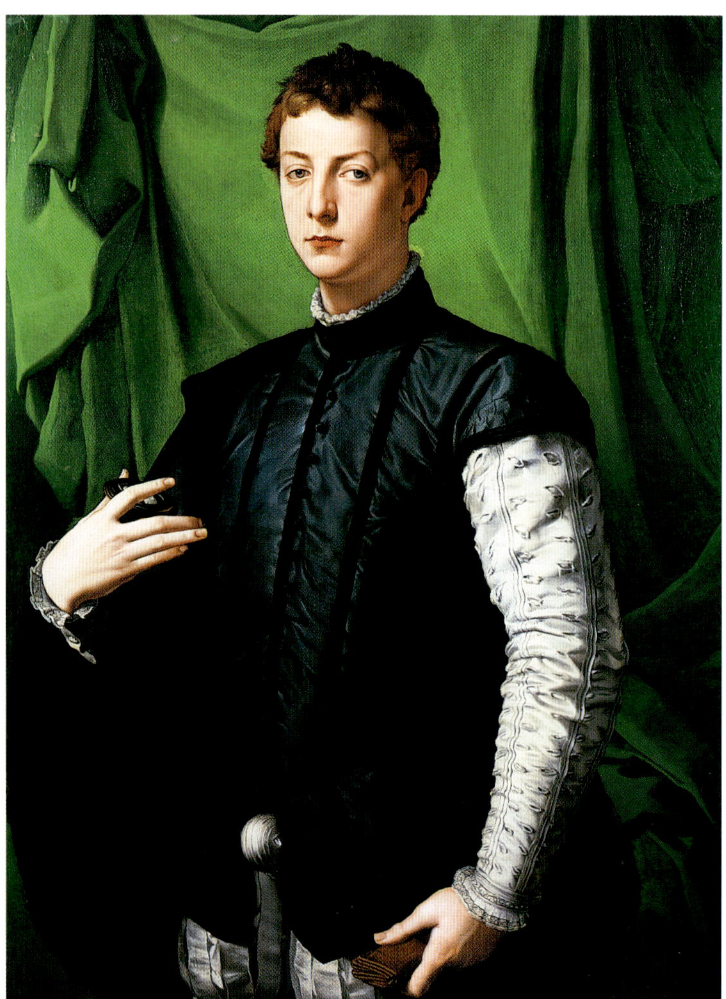

34
Agnolo Bronzino (1503–1572)
Lodovico Capponi, about 1550–5
Oil on poplar, 116.5 × 85.7 cm
The Frick Collection, New York

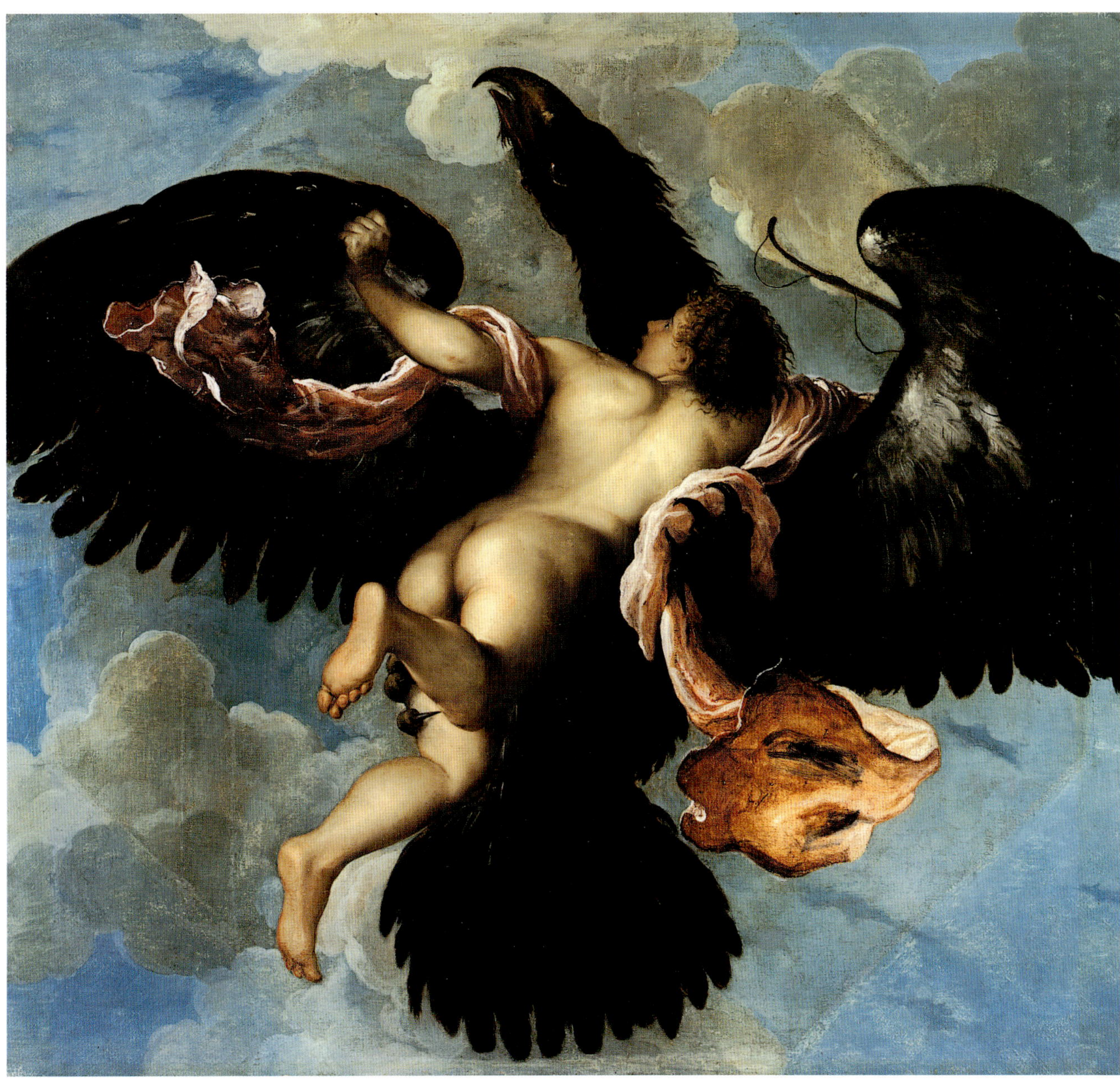

35
Damiano Mazza
(active about 1570–90)
The Rape of Ganymede,
probably about 1570–90
Oil on canvas, 177.2 × 188.6 cm
National Gallery, London
NG 32

In the second half of the century, painters had come to feel quite at ease inventing pictorial drapery gestures for their own expressive value, without conveying any idea of use but also without distorting the way cloth is. Such gestures, especially in connection with nude figures, could suggest the draperies of antiquity without imitating any particular ones. Damiano Mazza was a Paduan pupil and imitator of Titian, active between 1570 and 1590. Like Gaudenzio's *Christ rising*, his *Rape of Ganymede* (fig. 35) offers a nude male figure accompanied by a length of stuff that fails to clothe it, but this time with much more aptitude. The subject of Jupiter's rape of Ganymede requires showing an eagle – that is, Jupiter in one of his seducer's disguises – carrying a nude boy through the air; but Mazza's version of the scene is exceptionally violent. The painter has highlighted the plump boy's twisted back and kicking legs against the huge feathery spread of the black bird that surrounds him on all sides, digging its claw into one tender thigh, flapping its vast wings to gain altitude, and stretching its neck to thrust its beak upwards. But between the dark feathers and the pale flesh flows a stream of coral-coloured silk, like a metaphor of heated blood, a whip of desire. It wraps around each arm of the youth and flies out sideways, giving him his own pair of fluttering wings, one even clutched in the other black claw as the boy's pale hand grabs at the eagle's black wing. This piece of stuff – never a garment, but a classical allusion like Gaudenzio's marbly one for Jesus, here providing a whiff of antique Eros, a silken caress in this nightmare of rape – has edges, corners and clear dimensions, along with believable texture and agitation. It's real, just like what it's there to convey, the amorous nature of this airborne embrace.

Jacopo Tintoretto was a past master at visionary tailoring, as he also was at visionary landscape, blending realistic fiction and unreal fantasy with deft genius. Like Pontormo and other Florentine painters of the Mannerist period, he also used what look like painted body-suits on some of his unearthly characters, also in connection with swirling draperies. The distressed princess kneeling in the foreground of his *Saint George and the Dragon* (fig. 36) is costumed as if for the role of a character in a pageant, wearing a clinging blue dress with a belt and a brooch instead of modern stays and padded sleeves. She has a fairy-tale crown and hair ornaments, but modern pearl earrings; and like many North Italian ladies of her time, she has added a small transparent scarf to soften the neckline of her bodice, just as Titian's beauty does (see fig. 25), even though her dress is of a loose, exotic cut. It looks like a real costume, because it's much more intelligibly designed and made than similar ones worn by some of Tintoretto's allegorical characters in the Scuola di San Rocco, for example, whose dresses have vague sleeves and hems. The dress here has neat sleeves and a clearly defined hem, even a neckline with turned over points as well as her scarf; we can see she is a personage, not an allegory.

To this believable figure the artist has added a strong mythic dimension by surrounding it with an immense, shapeless but multiform swatch of unbelievable carmine drapery. The wind that lifts it is not the offshore breeze that causes Saint George's cape to flutter behind him as he attacks the dragon in the background. The largest portion of this stuff leaps out from behind the princess towards the sea, backing up her distracted gaze and gesture as if to fill her immediate space with a painterly version of her leaping hope and terror.

More of it is draped around her hips, insufficiently knotted there to support its backward and downward swing. We can see that it will keep her forever kneeling in despair, since if she stood up it would undo and fall. One more bit wraps thickly around her rearward upper arm, so as to unite the hip-drape with the whipping stuff behind her, and thus to make one vibrant non-garment out of all three busy, rosy elements. Tintoretto has sold us this uneasy piece of painterly goods with mesmerising skill. It's as though he had enveloped his princess in a lengthy and compelling phrase of music, suitable to her plight and state of mind. This feast of textile beauty entrances our eager gaze, making us feel and believe in her feeling, just as such music would do.

El Greco applied his distinctive mode of expression to all the fabric in his pictures, giving cloth not only new scope for pictorial action but new ways of resembling phenomena

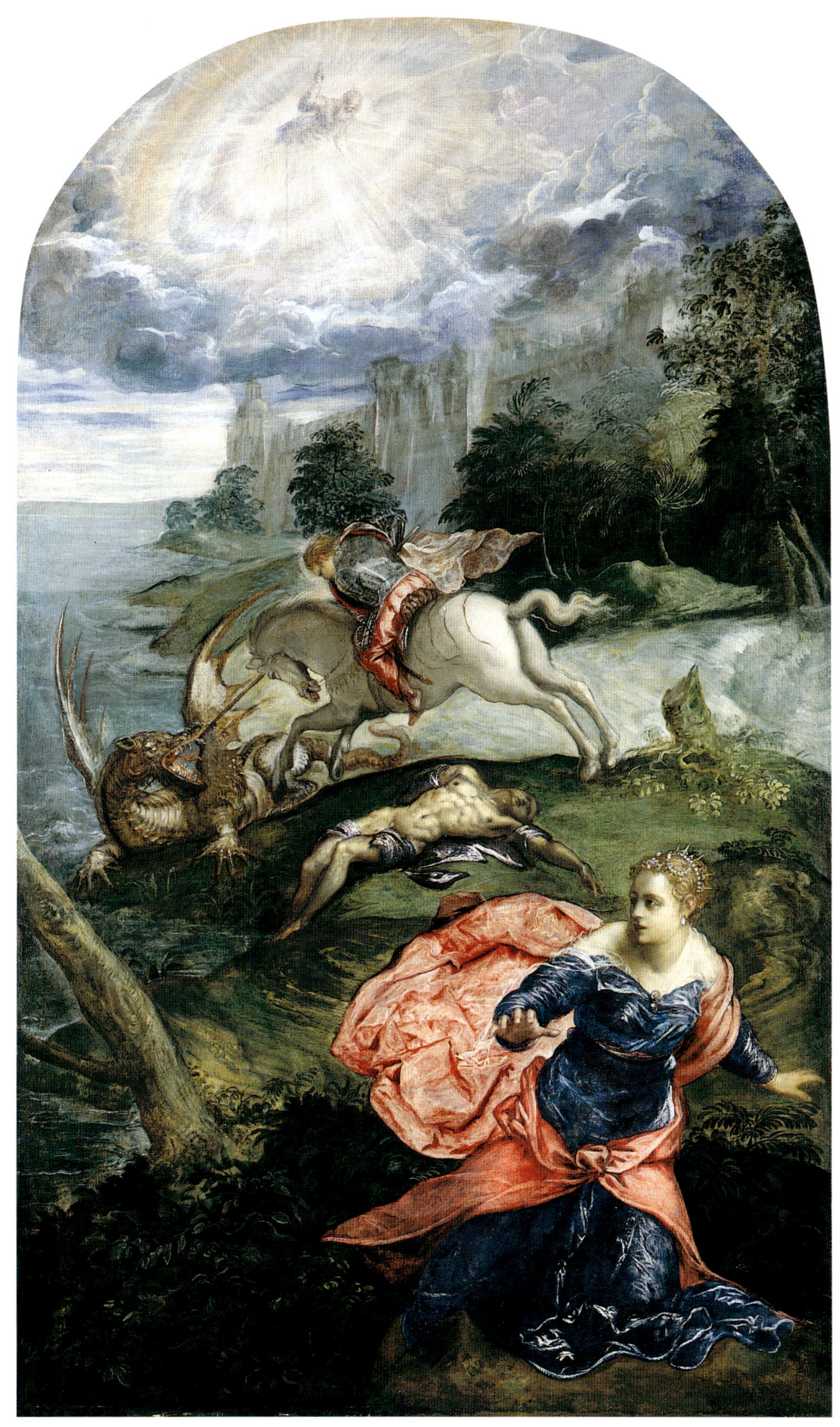

36
Jacopo Tintoretto (1518–1594)
Saint George and the Dragon, about 1560
Oil on canvas, 158.3 × 100.5 cm
National Gallery, London
NG 16

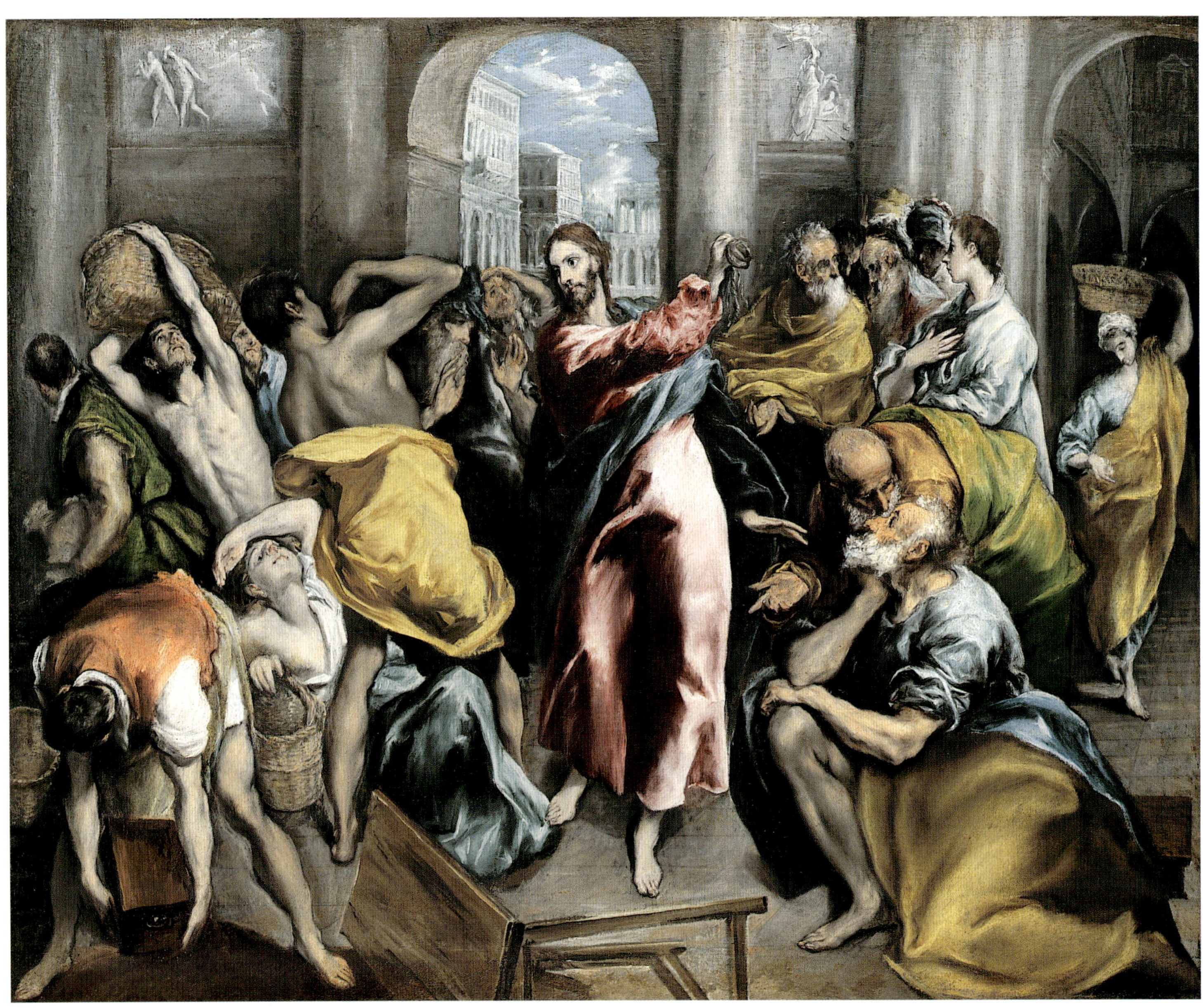

37
El Greco (about 1541–1614)
Christ driving the Traders from the Temple, about 1600
Oil on canvas, 106.3 × 129.7 cm
National Gallery, London
NG 1457

other than cloth – something not done by the other sixteenth-century painters whose works we've looked at. This version of his *Christ driving the Traders from the Temple* (fig. 37), dated to about 1600, shows how El Greco has abandoned all need to account for the structure of garments, for the shapes taken by woven textiles, or for their effective attachment to human trunks and limbs. The yellow drape covering the middle of the figure about to receive a blow from Christ's lash is held up by painterly magic, a flange of it uncannily standing away from his ribs and another curling up away from his thighs. This wrap is thick but has no weight and no corners; it could be a crushed circle of stiff paper, while the yellow skirt on the lower half of the right foreground disciple seems made of dented rubber, quite unlike his shirt of watery blue ripples.

Although Tintoretto covered hosts of figures in similarly invented draperies, he made the painted folds expound the painted bodies in a way El Greco did not, and Tintoretto's, with all their brushy freedom, never suggest any substance other than cloth or paint. In El Greco's scene the colours of Christ's robe and mantle derive from Tintoretto, but the mantle's shape from clouds and streams, and the robe's surface from sheet metal or the faces of cliffs. This robe nevertheless has a sharp and even hem – the only one in the picture – so that Christ's feet, always significant, may come into due prominence below it.

These are legendary costumes, but real clothes do appear on the scene's periphery. At far left among the wicked, a man holding a jug wears a green doublet with ivory sleeves and small white ruff above a high collar, and on the right a beardless young disciple wears an open-collared white shirt with a visible arm-hole seam. These garments, and the ones on the two figures limiting the space – the woman at far right rear and the man at near left foreground – are blurry and turbulent, the painter visibly reminding us that they are made wholly of brushstrokes, not cloth. But they are certainly clothes, which throw into relief the strange shapes and textures covering the bodies of the central characters, with their lifted arms on the left and nervous fingers on the right. Everybody's stiff or rippling or rubbery or metallic folds are made to bunch or collide with each other, to mix up or separate these figures, to create common or opposing channels for the zeal, fright and indifference this picture brings together. They create an opposite effect to that of Pontormo's *Deposition*, where all the folds and faces agree to a single anxiety, except those of the dead.

So much mastery of textile expression on the part of great sixteenth-century painters permitted similar flights of fabric in much later painting. Among other artists in the middle of the nineteenth century, Honoré Daumier, who is most famous for a realism extending to caricature in his accounts of modern dress, occasionally ventured into Arcadian fantasy. We can see in his *Nymphs pursued by Satyrs* (fig. 38), painted in 1850, that he has absorbed the lessons of both Titian and Tintoretto. These fleeing women are loosely wrapped in bright fluttering draperies of no specific shape or fabric, which have been carefully disposed to leave their feet, legs, shoulders and breasts bare. Just as in Titian's *poesie* on classical themes, where the painter gave the women white drapery under coloured drapery, to suggest a *camicia* under a dress, Daumier gives these girls upper draperies in white to suggest modern blouses and chemises, and lower draperies in strong colours to suggest modern skirts and petticoats.

The invention of these draperies to create selective exposure and general excitement is a sensual tease for the viewer. They show, in an echo of Tintoretto's methods, that if the girls stopped running all this cloth would instantly fall off. Daumier used this stuff to suggest that the girls are to be imagined as already naked, the draperies simply standing for the titillation of that fact, and of course for the encompassing fact that these are Arcadian circumstances, in which satyrs pursue nymphs, and that they inhabit draped classical antiquity, where Titian spent so much painterly time.

Pictorial drapery, once free from any constraints to look functional or even possible, was obviously perfect for creating a range of felicitous effects in any later school of portraiture. Portraits ever since the sixteenth century have been likely to contain some, and often a great deal, beginning with Van Dyck's noble images, where cascades of stuff

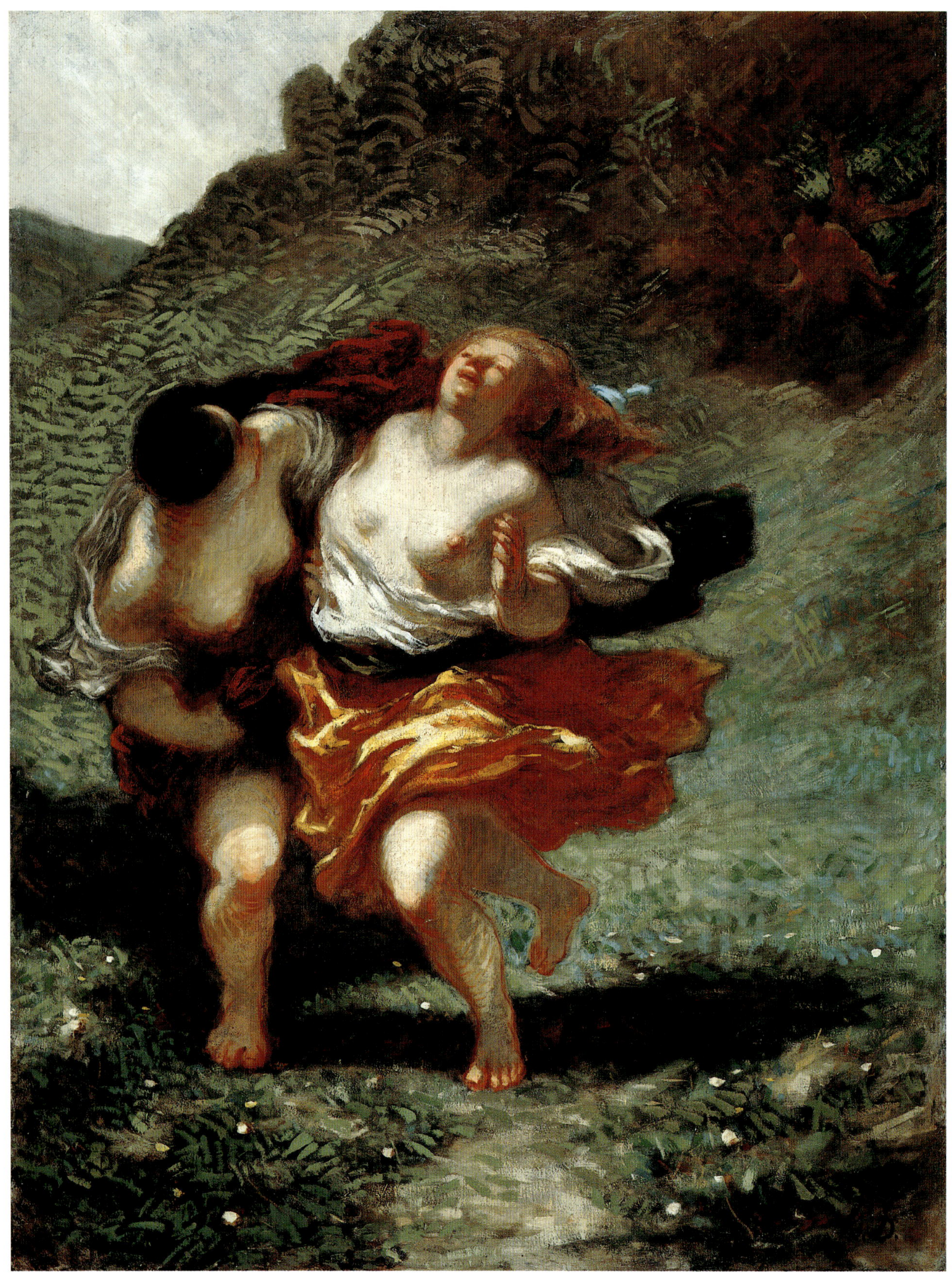

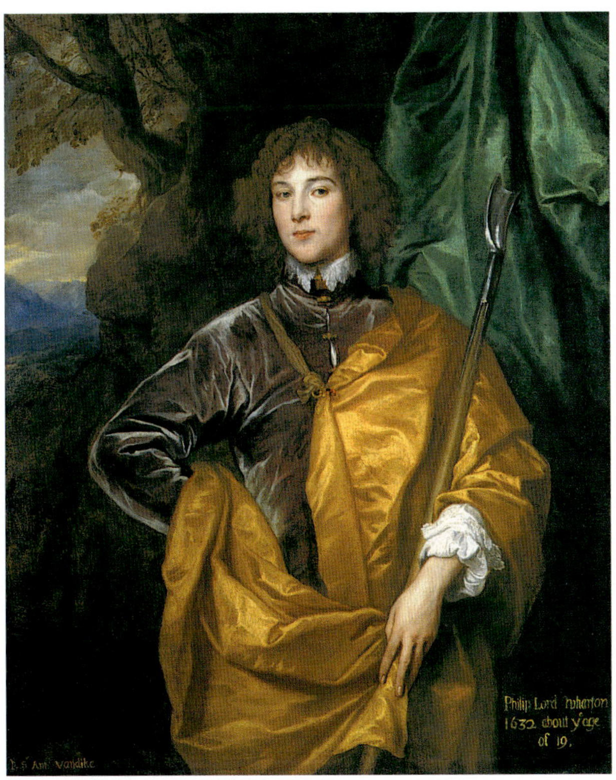

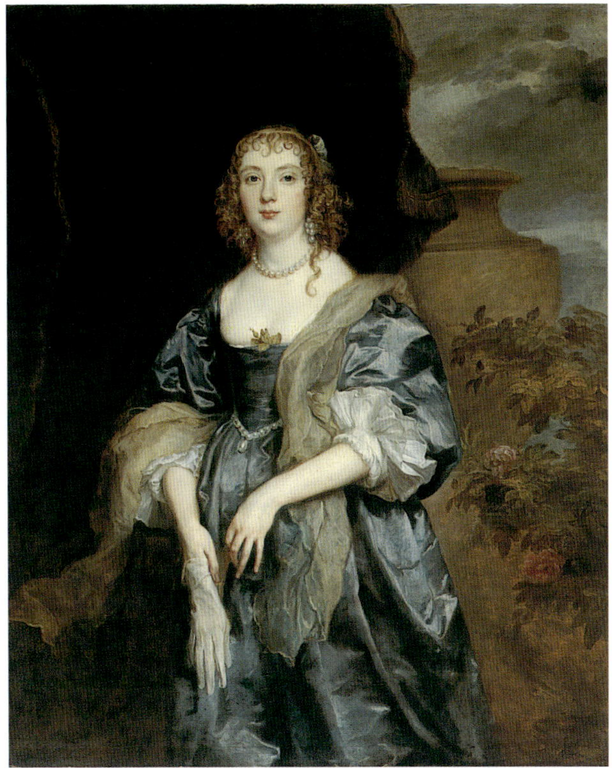

ABOVE LEFT **39**
Anthony van Dyck (1599–1641)
Philip, Lord Wharton, 1632
Oil on canvas, 133.4 × 106.4 cm
National Gallery of Art, Washington, Andrew W. Mellon Collection

ABOVE RIGHT **40**
Anthony van Dyck (1599–1641)
Lady Anne Carr, Countess of Bedford, about 1638
Oil on canvas, 136.2 × 109.9 cm
Private collection

OPPOSITE **38**
Honoré-Victorin Daumier (1808–1879)
Nymphs pursued by Satyrs, 1850 (with later additions)
Oil on canvas, 131.8 × 97.8 cm
The Montreal Museum of Fine Arts, Adaline Van Horne Bequest

are likely to be adorning not just interiors but rocks, trees and the outsides of buildings (fig. 39). During the seventeenth century, fashion itself was again making use of flowing fabrics, so that the torrents of attendant drapery in elegant portraits might appear in dark colours and stay in the shadows, to let the light focus more on the sitters' skirts, sleeves and cloaks (fig. 40). But the idea persisted that its painted presence was essential – always existing in some separate dimension from the clothing of the sitter, even if the folds in it were similar. The drapery in a portrait would be there for the picture's sake, not to record something customarily found behind the sitter in real life. You could say it was there for art's sake, to show that drapery by itself had come to stand for art.

When draped fabric had become normal clothing only in sacred and legendary pictures, individual artists used such painted drapery as a personal expressive vessel, often selectively departing from reality – folds were dressing the picture, not just the people. Painters of portraits also came to place sitters in their real clothes among expressive pictorial folds, so that painted drapery became the clothing of portraits, not of sitters. It was perceived to obey the rules of painters, whatever they were, and not those of the draped textiles in real life, whatever they had become; and so it could remain forever in use. Cloth placed near the sitter in a portrait could evoke pictorial drapery's whole past – the cloth of honour of the Virgin and royalty, the seductively draped undress of Venus and her votaries, the robes of saints and Apostles, the capes of antique heroes.

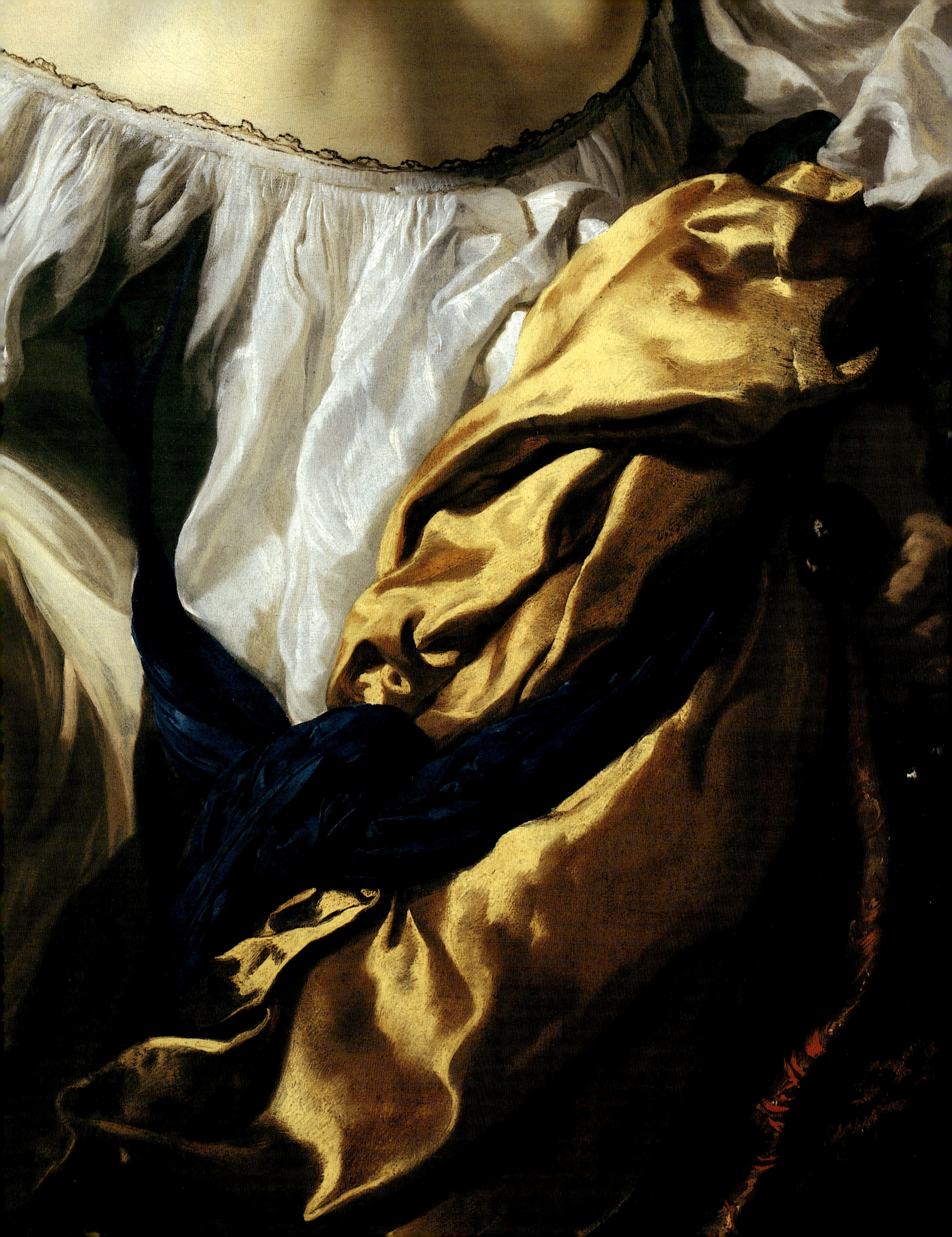

III Sensuality, Sanctity, Zeal

In the last chapter we saw some examples of the way sixteenth-century portrait painters set off static formal clothing with fluid scenic drapery. But another potent tradition had already arisen, notably in Renaissance Venice, of painting half-length, semi-erotic quasi-portraits, perhaps with a classical or biblical title, perhaps with none, which required putting seductive drapery on the sitter and leaving the rest of the setting bare of folds. Girls might be the Roman goddess Flora or the Christian Mary Magdalen; boys might be Orpheus or John the Baptist. Male models might wear a drape or skins across a bare chest; female models wore semi-adorned, semi-loose hair with a pictorial costume that often included the folds of a real chemise, opened enough to show most of one breast.

Titian provides a peerless example in his *Flora* of about 1516–18 (fig. 41). He offers this half-dressed, dyed-blonde, loose-haired model as a perfect classical beauty with great delicacy of feeling, much of both conveyed in the draperies. While its white folds are exposing one of Flora's shoulders and half her bosom, in a sequence of textile curves that slide in a manner proper to the ancient world, this garment has at the same time been rendered with scrupulous accuracy and absolutely no fudging as a modern chemise. This is real clothing transformed with almost unnoticeable discretion into pictorial costume.

You can locate the seam where the sleeve meets the body of the shirt; you can see the narrow fringed band gathering the folds, and if you look along the neckline you can see where it ends, at the two spread corners where the wide front opening begins – one above the covered breast, one below the deep shadow where the nude breast meets the nude arm; and you can see the front seam that begins at the bottom of the opening. But these details register slowly; what evokes response is how gracefully Titian has draped the folds over arms, bosom and flanks to show the slight torsion in the figure, how well the crushed crescents of pink damask contribute to the sensual effect, one curving around this hip, an opposing one curving over that shoulder, the largest and busiest held in a curve just below the nude breast. You can see only a fraction of Flora's nipple, as the expanse of her chest very gradually modulates into the subtle forms of two breasts, one

Detail of fig. 53

41
Titian (about 1485/90–1576)
Flora, about 1516–18
Oil on canvas, 79.7 × 63.5 cm
Galleria degli Uffizi, Florence

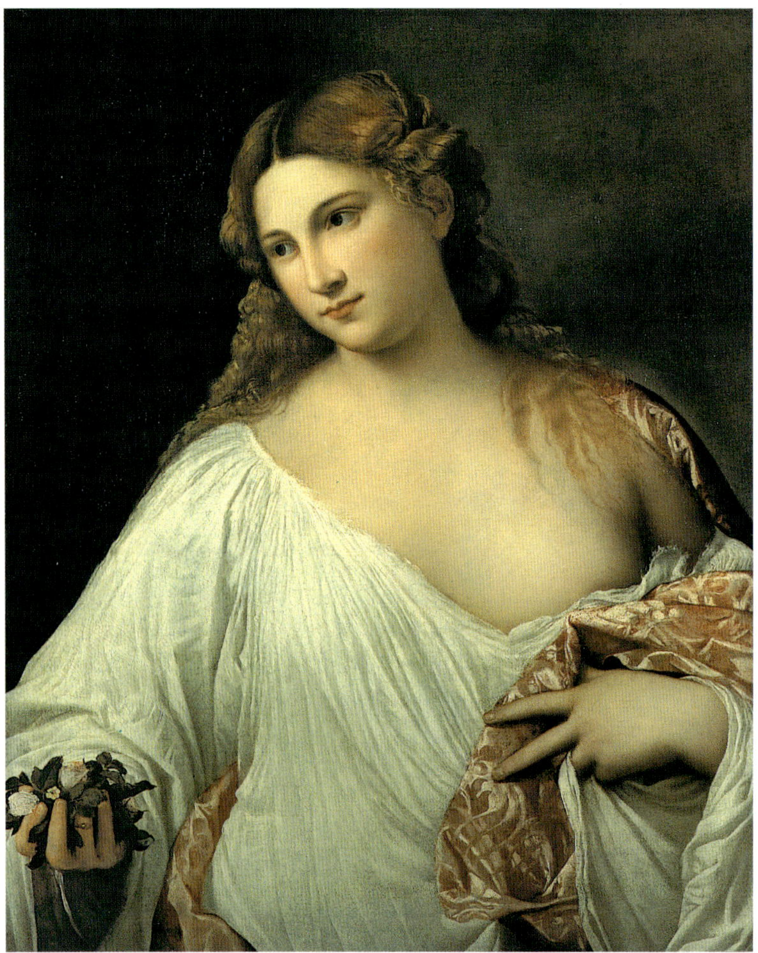

barely indicated under the shirt. Her left hand, its fingers managing the two kinds of folds, seems to be unconsciously keeping the damask stole and open shirt from slipping further down, as if the exposure already on view were also unconscious: Flora's full attention is naturally on the invisible person soon to receive the leaves and flowers from her right hand.

In Tintoretto's striking essay in the erotic half-length figure from around 1570 (fig. 42), we can feel that a degree of Mannerist turbulence has affected its sensuality, as the model deliberately exposes both breasts. Ample folds of thin silk have been draped over her two nude shoulders, leaving visible the frill of chemise cupping one breast, to suggest that the feel of thin tissue moving over sensitive skin underlies the idea of antique drapery the scarf is adding to this picture. The model's action is almost ceremonious, she looks solemnly away from our gaze, her disciplined hair and the symmetrical folds lend a touch of antique dignity to her image. But it has been carefully unsettled by her double pearls and modern frill, and most of all by the way she bunches up the gauzy stuff between her naked breasts, to insist on their fullness and separation as Titian's model notably did not. The painter also shows each of her hands touching skin and silk together, so we feel a multiple sensory thrill.

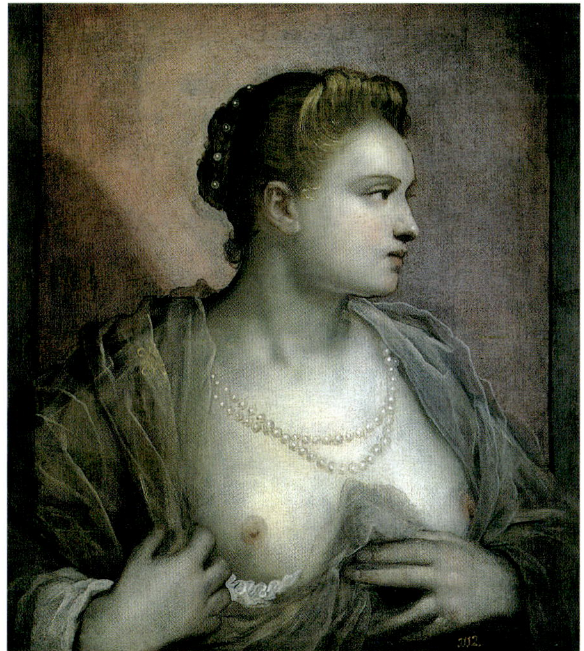

42
Jacopo Tintoretto
(1518–1594)
Woman uncovering her Breasts, about 1570
Oil on canvas, 61 × 55 cm
Museo Nacional del Prado, Madrid

43
After Titian
(about 1485/90–1576)
The Toilet of Venus, after about 1555
Oil on canvas, 94.3 × 73.8 cm
Courtauld Institute Gallery, London

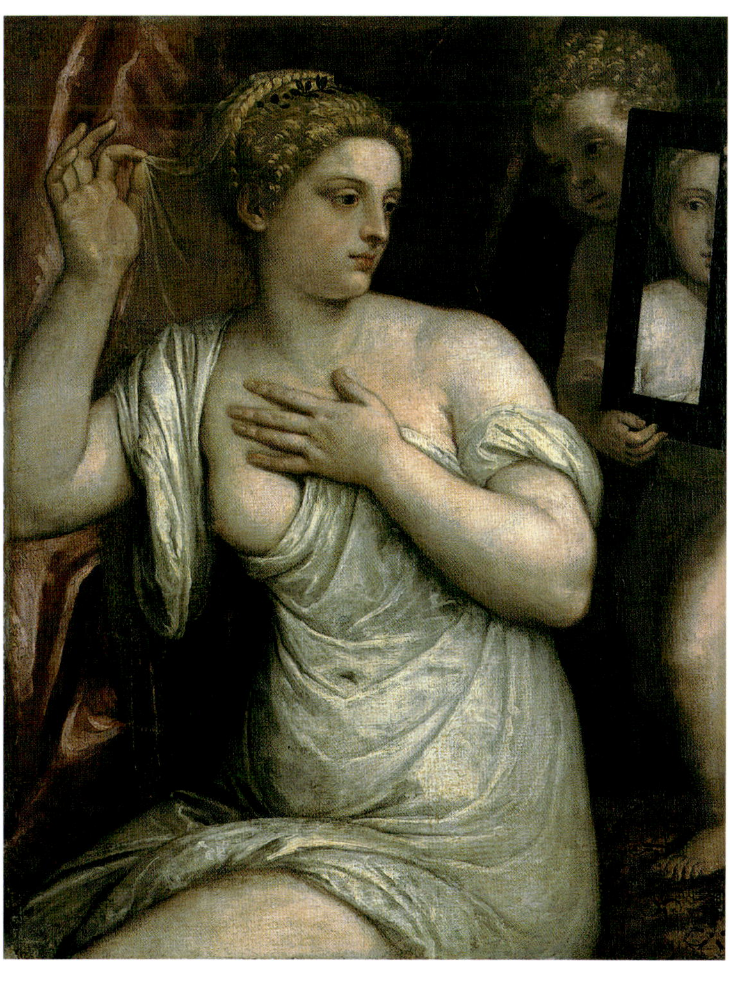

Cupid holds the mirror for a Venus who eyes us from it, in an unattributed variation based on a *Venus* by Titian, this one wearing wholly pictorial draperies remote from the chemise idea (fig. 43). Like the other two, however, this painter concentrates on showing how the model's hands relate her drapery to her body, so here we can plainly see the stuff giving a caress, not just concealment. The hand sliding over her breasts also strokes them with the thin folds, while the other hand prepares the fringed veil to stroke her neck. The painter has now created a divine unreality for the rest of immortal Venus's draperies, which improbably indent her navel – a rhetorical motif that appears both in Mannerist painting and in Hellenistic sculpture – and otherwise have no clear shape or aim as they softly come and go around parts of her.

Under the evolving Baroque dispensation, one new role for drapery in painting was to intensify the sensual quality of such figures. Given the established associations of pictorial drapery with painted classical nudity, it was clear that sensuality could quickly be heightened by causing specific modern garments to assume the folds of unspecific, classical-looking draperies, which could then behave in unaccountable ways. Part of a modern tailored coat or shirt might resemble the easy agent of exposure that a loose Greek tunic once had been. Delicious arms and shoulders or backs and breasts could be revealed by slippery drapery that was really just modern clothing momentarily undone, as if by its own lust for the model.

This pictorial fashion could make a strong appeal to the viewer's senses, since, by the seventeenth century, painters were certainly as skilled in evoking the caress of fabric as they were in making it whip or hang. It is subtly thrilling that the suave draperies surrounding a peasant boy's white shoulder really belong to a ragged shirt and outsize coat, and that he, smiling at something we can't see, is feeling them slide over his skin as we watch him (fig. 44). Comparing this bare-shouldered image painted in about 1680 with the bare shoulder on the *Venus* of about 1555, we can see that this naked Baroque shoulder is now emphatically shrugged up out of the cloth, so that the drapery makes it fix our attention, whereas *Venus*, like *Flora* before her, allowed her draperies to blend her bare shoulder with the rest of her nude beauties.

The author of all such new emphasis on the hunched erotic shoulder in painting was undoubtedly Michelangelo Merisi da Caravaggio (perhaps inspired by Michelangelo

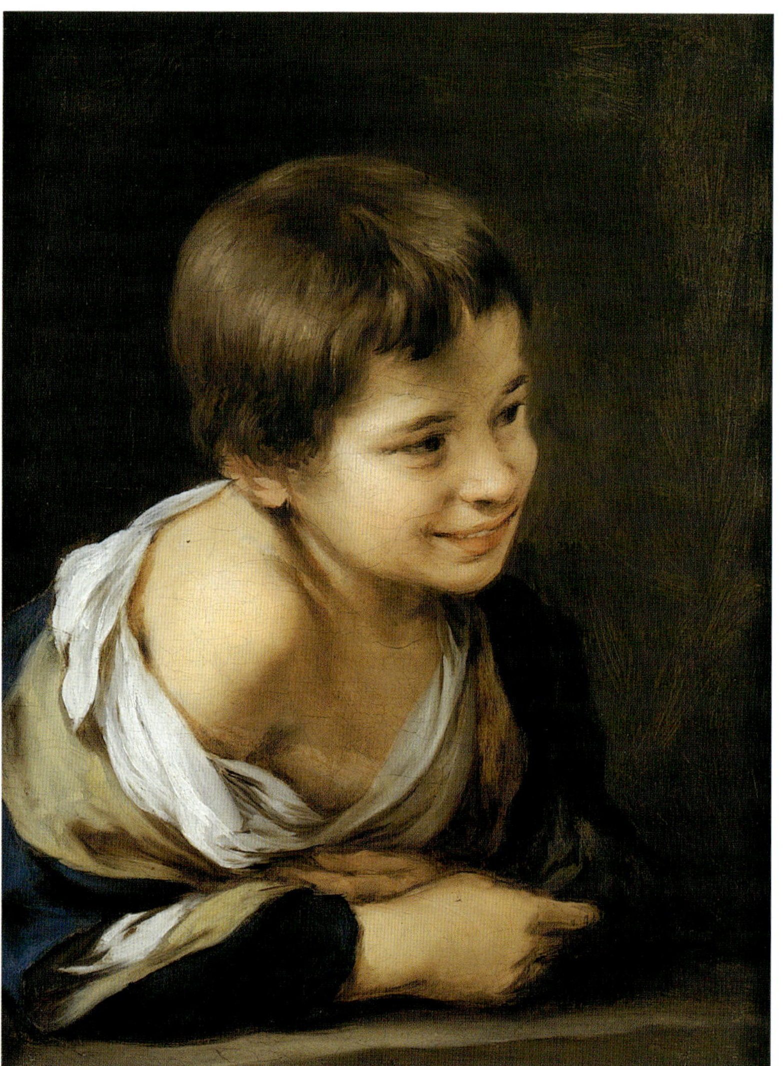

44
Bartolomé Esteban Murillo
(1617–1682)
A Peasant Boy leaning on a Sill, about 1670–80
Oil on canvas, 52 × 38.5 cm
National Gallery, London
NG 74

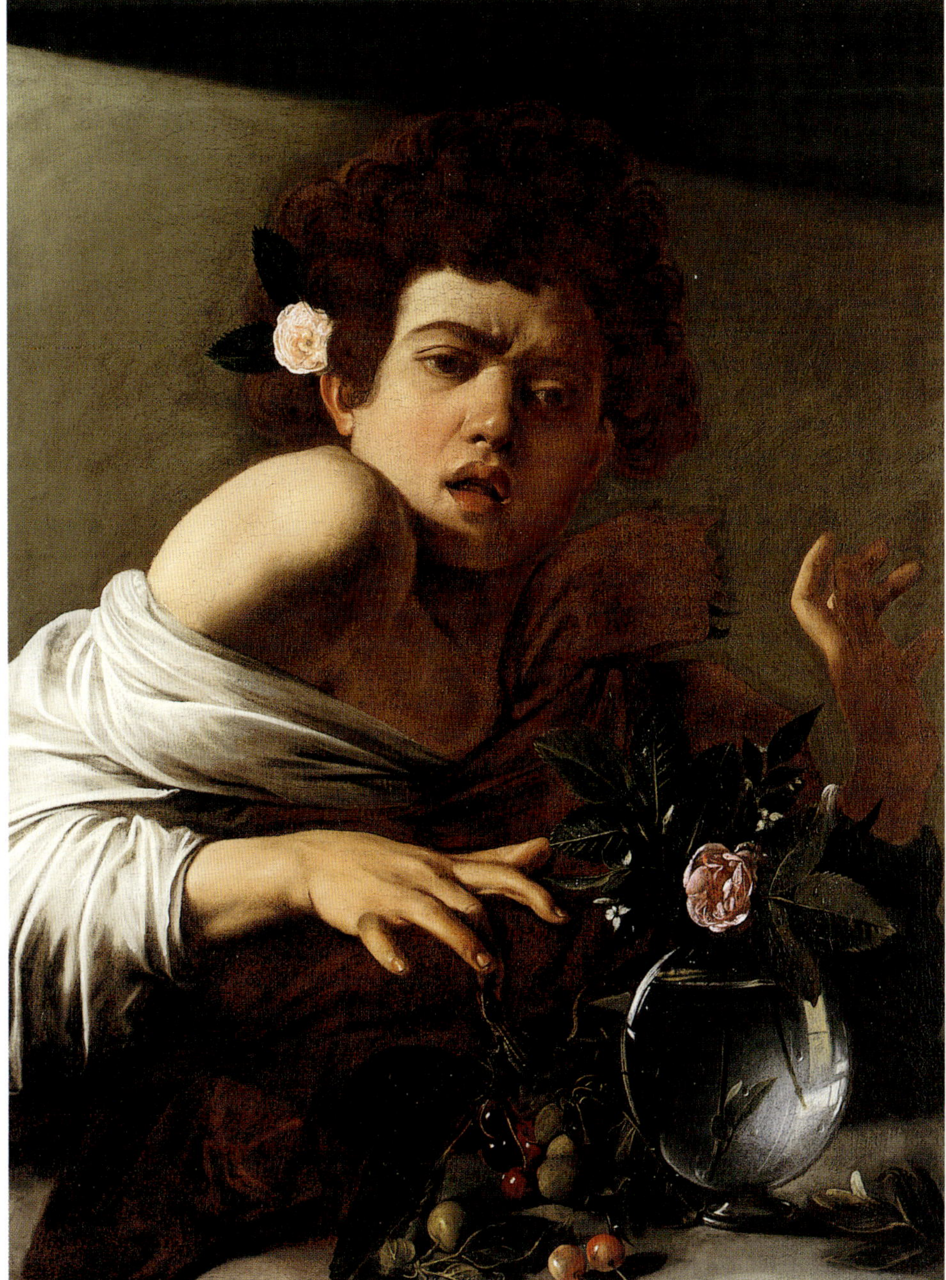

45
Michelangelo Merisi da Caravaggio (1571–1610)
Boy bitten by a Lizard, about 1595–1600
Oil on canvas, 66 × 49.5 cm
National Gallery, London
NG 6504

Buonarroti, see fig. 26), who had been developing the theme well before 1600. The ancients, used to the public sight of bare shoulders, had never thought of isolating them with drapery to increase their erotic charge, and Renaissance artists had exposed shoulders without making much of them, preferring to harmonise them with nude chests and backs. Caravaggio seems to have been the first painter to show a naked shoulder thrusting itself up into the light, as if eager to be bitten like an apple. At a time when European male dress was concealing and wadding the upper body, his paintings of *Bacchus* and other half-length figures of the 1590s (fig. 45) were pointedly showing off young boys' bare

46
Michelangelo Merisi da Caravaggio (1571–1610)
The Magdalen weeping, 1606
Oil on canvas, 106.5 × 91 cm
Private collection

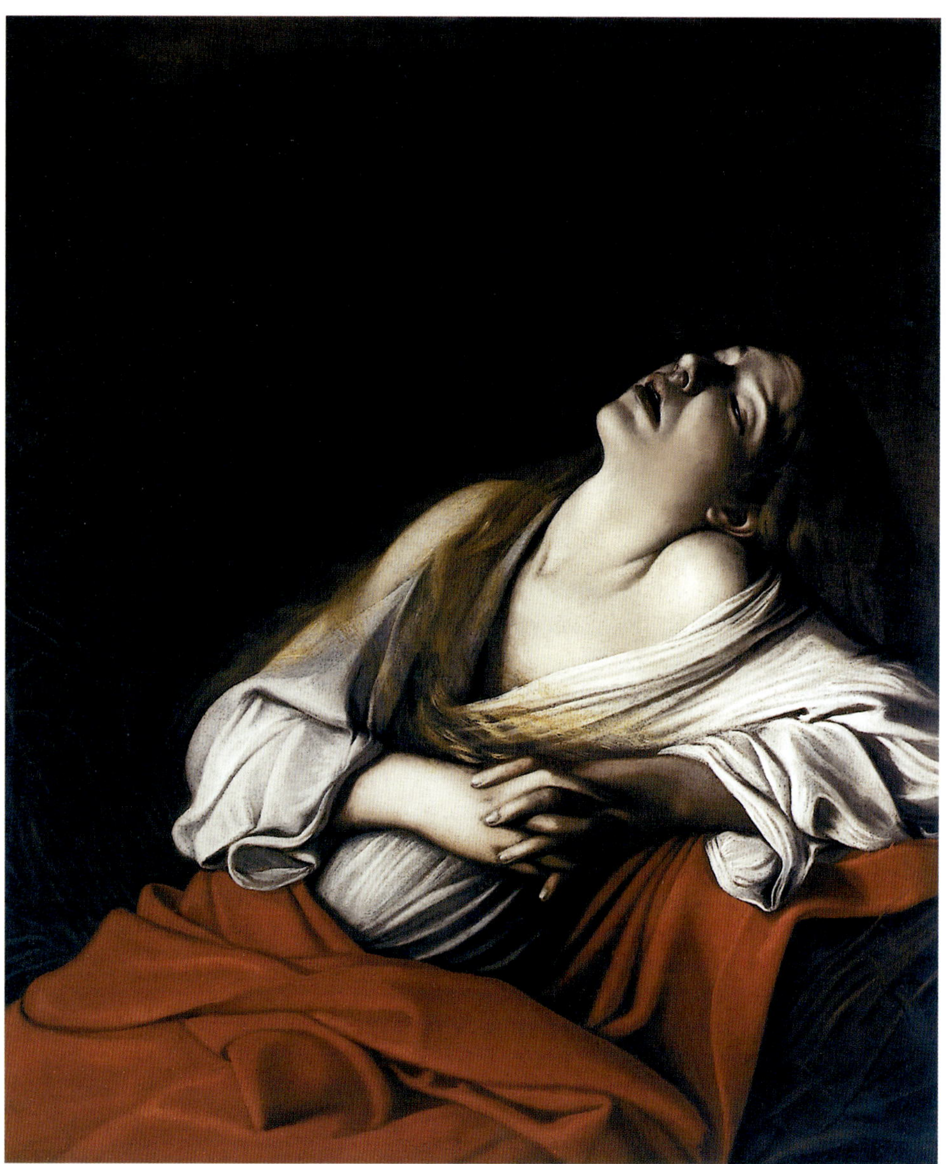

shoulders. Caravaggio was applying his vigorous new brand of awkward realism to figures in the Venetian erotic-half-length convention, which had held to a calm antique look for shoulders. Building dramatically on Titian's serene early examples, he intensified the way a normal white shirt could be transmuted into fictional draperies, on purpose to sharpen the allure of a real-looking shoulder as it pushed upwards out of its unreal wraps and grazed the sitter's own cheek.

Caravaggio painted several female models again and again, portraying them fully dressed in contemporary and sometimes elegant clothes, self-possessed in the role of the Virgin, a heroine or a saint. It was usually on male models, most of them representing angels and biblical characters, that this painter explored the uses of drapery for expressive exposure; and he only once rendered a female subject in those terms. In 1606, a few years before his death, he painted a half-length weeping Magdalen known from various versions (fig. 46) wearing a chemise, her lower body heavily wrapped, her hands clasped, her upper body swooning back in a tide of white folds. And out of these, one naked shoulder hunches up to cuddle her bare neck and ear.

This poignant image shows how Caravaggio came to add a tragic dimension to the draperies he created out of real clothes. In the earlier picture, he meant us to enjoy the stab of pain that made the lovely boy recoil and expose his shoulder – the lizard's bite fixed the erotic point. But in this Magdalen from a few years later, the same waves of cloth seem to embrace the woman in a cosmic agony, from which only her own shrinking shoulder gives her a touch of physical relief.

We know, however, that Mary Magdalen had long been a figure of female sexuality, and Caravaggio had conveyed this idea in his earlier versions of the Magdalen by clothing her fashionably, as many others had done. By the seventeenth century, however, during the Counter-Reformation, Mary Magdalen's repentant aspect in art had acquired new dramatic force, and she was often shown weeping and praying in the wilderness, clad only in a bosom-revealing chemise or else voluptuously nude, wearing variously revealing rivers of hair – it was Titian who had started this in the 1530s – to represent the wayward Church repenting of her folly. We can see that, for his last Magdalen, Caravaggio still would not expose female breasts, but once again allowed the shoulder alone, swept by folds, to suggest sensual pleasure.

Caravaggio's new way of combining real dress, legendary costume and mythic drapery appears in *The Death of the Virgin* of 1604 (fig. 47). The mourning disciple standing in full view at left wears male biblical costume, the same for a thousand years of Christian art, the long-sleeved gown and wrapped mantle we first saw in the medieval icon (see fig. 3), here even draped to suggest Giotto and Masaccio. Behind him, other disciples show only a few folds, and the painter suggests they are similarly dressed. All are in shadow, with one draped shoulder mildly lit. The light is coming from an unseen high window on the left, its strongest rays falling on three foremost figures, the weeping disciple in the centre wearing a modern jacket, the dead Virgin wearing a modern red dress with no veil – her mantle tossed like a blanket across her stiff legs, her skirt rucked up to bare her feet and ankles – and the mourning Magdalen in front, wearing a modern fitted bodice that shows white chemise-sleeves, modern braided and bound-up hair, and a skirt that falls in simple modern folds that cover her feet.

Caravaggio has closely filled the left and rear space with shadowy figures in traditional costume, gradually increasing the light so that he shines it directly on the ones in modern clothing, especially the Virgin's casually disposed corpse, while nevertheless giving all the fabrics the same abstract, universal texture – not coarse, not fine, not specific – and all the folds the same sobriety. The result is that we are visually persuaded that everyone is clothed in the same style; the difference is unnoticeable. Apostles in old-days robes and principals in ordinary clothes merge under this lighting, all perfectly dressed for this meeting, and it seems right that the Virgin's dead face and hands, spread out above the unique redness of her dress, should get the brightest beams.

The rear figures are punctuated by the traditional apostolic beards and bald heads, the usual beardless, fair-haired Saint John, and a few mourning hands. The disciples' visible feet are also bare, reminding us of Christ's washing of them, as the pan of water near them on the floor also does (see John 13:5). All these elements, too, are shadowy and

47
Michelangelo Merisi da Caravaggio (1571–1610)
The Death of the Virgin, 1604
Oil on canvas, 369 × 245 cm
Musée du Louvre, Paris

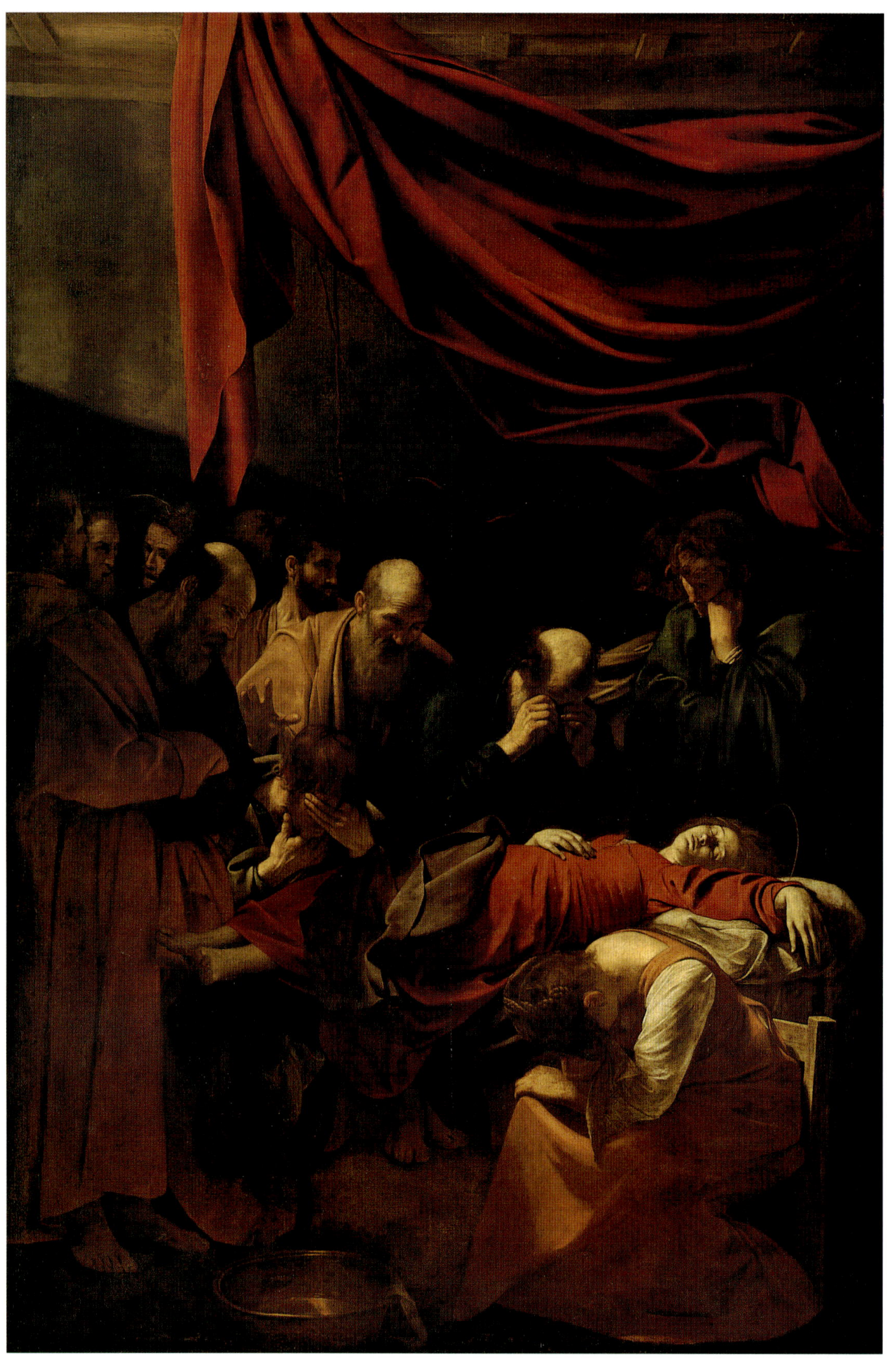

very informally grouped, as though these people had just assembled. But above the figures and dominating the top half of the painting is a colossal crimson drape, also of abstract universal texture and without seams or creases, pouring like an airborne stream of blood across the frame from an invisible source on the right. It swoops up to an invisible fixture in the left part of the ceiling, from which several yards drip downwards over the rearmost disciples' heads, catching some strong light from the window. Its transverse folds, larger and much stranger than any that form the garments, seem to hover and not to feel their own weight.

This great, unprecedented rhetorical gesture echoes the dress and posture of the dead, unifies the group, confirms the sanctity of the event and claims our spiritual attention to it. It can have no practical function in this poor room: it's much too high and full and richly red to be the looped-up bed-curtain for the dead Virgin's narrow cot. Its function is to replace, with visionary fabric, the group of angels or apparition of God the Father that might otherwise inhabit the upper air above this deathbed. With this particular cloth Caravaggio proves that painted draped folds could have their own power to infuse an image with holiness, or any other spiritual or emotional suggestion. It's the more striking because the drapery of the clothing is so simple, the gestures of the figures so muted.

The use of light to fuse a cluster of ancient saints in both current and legendary clothing at one critical sacred moment, all under the tactile blessing of this unearthly red canopy, makes this painting an amazing religious masterpiece. It was, however, not approved by those who had commissioned it, who expected more unified decorum and majesty for such a subject. They might well have preferred something like Annibale Carracci's *Assumption of the Virgin* (fig. 48), an altarpiece painted one or two years before this picture. The lighting, composition and draperies in Annibale's picture represent an opposing view of sacred and legendary painting and an alternative influence on the Baroque painting of the following generations.

Here we see symmetrical grouping, tempered lighting and a notable array of conscious-looking art-historical gestures on the part of the solid figures, together with a multi-coloured set of unspecific but well-harmonised legendary costumes, each with its own set of tastefully mobile and blameless folds. This painter's pictorial rhetoric seems designed to show how art can convey sanctity, but only by the power of art to make a stronger claim on the viewer than the power of the event, which is being skilfully evoked by a painter, not happening. Caravaggio preferred subduing his pictorial sources and conjuring instead the sense of right here, right now. And that sense is what makes his visionary red drape so uncanny.

Within a decade or two after Caravaggio's death, a great deal of pictorial drapery of different kinds had swept heavily into European religious art, swinging, wrapping and falling around figures to reinforce the importance of epiphanies and martyrdoms. The effect of greater amplitude in painted drapery in the seventeenth century mirrored a general fashion for swelling drapery in actual clothing, expressed in full, bunched sleeves, full draped cloaks and very full garments spreading below a high waist for both men and women (see figs. 39 and 40). For sacred subjects, individual painters used various schemes, some of them combinations of what Caravaggio and the Carracci had inaugurated, to create expressive pictorial drapery that would allow similarly abundant shapes for saints.

48
Annibale Carracci (1560–1609)
The Assumption of the Virgin, about 1601
Oil on canvas, 245 × 155 cm
Santa Maria del Popolo, Rome

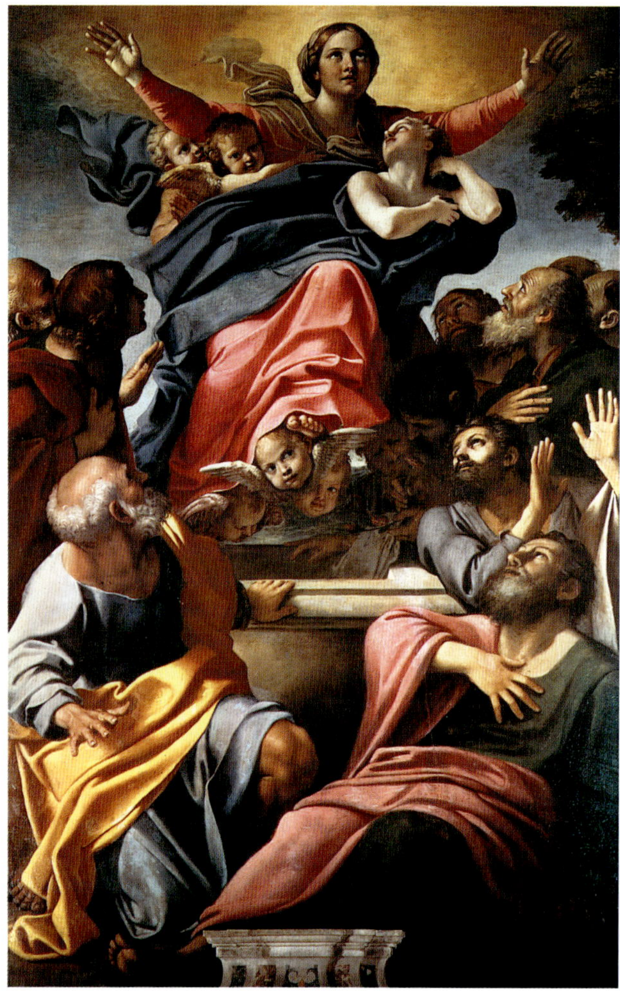

The great Antwerp painter Peter Paul Rubens, who spent the first eight years of the seventeenth century in Italy learning from Annibale Carracci among others, created figures with flesh so pliant and voluminous that their painted draperies could happily complete their postures and gestures without muffling them, as if the painter wished to suggest that the draperies were also alive. Rubens's *Assumption of the Virgin* (fig. 49) of 1626 shows his skill in creating the quality of weightless lift in a composition entirely made of heavy bodies wearing thick stuffs. The soft, lifelike robes and mantles cling eagerly around the bountiful figures, and the Virgin seems helped upwards by her draperies more than by cherubic hands.

In the centre foreground is a female saint in a rosy dress cut in a pictorial fashion both modern and Titianesque, and the real-looking fullness of her skirt seems to have fitted itself spontaneously to the curves of her big body, just as the mantle of the male saint on the right seems to have burst into golden folds to fit around his heroic shape; and Rubens seems never to fail at the steady, effortless invention of new folds to be freshly applied to each gesture of each character. We can see that Annibale Carracci, on the other hand, allowed draped folds to lead their own repetitive life too intensely to permit such a natural-looking agreement between the action of figures and their heavy garments.

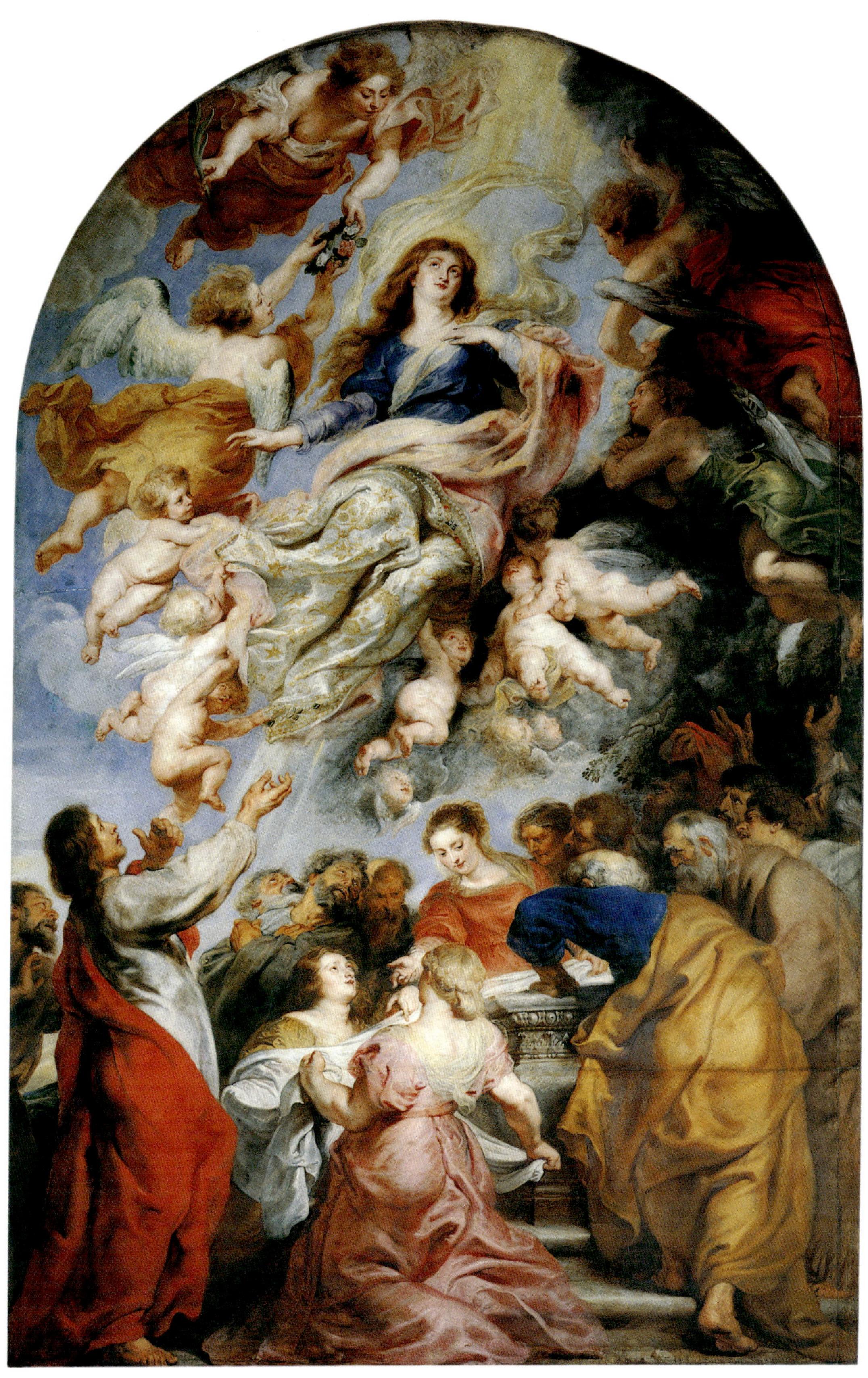

49
Peter Paul Rubens
(1577–1640)
The Assumption of the Virgin, 1626
Oil on canvas, 490 × 325 cm
Antwerp Cathedral

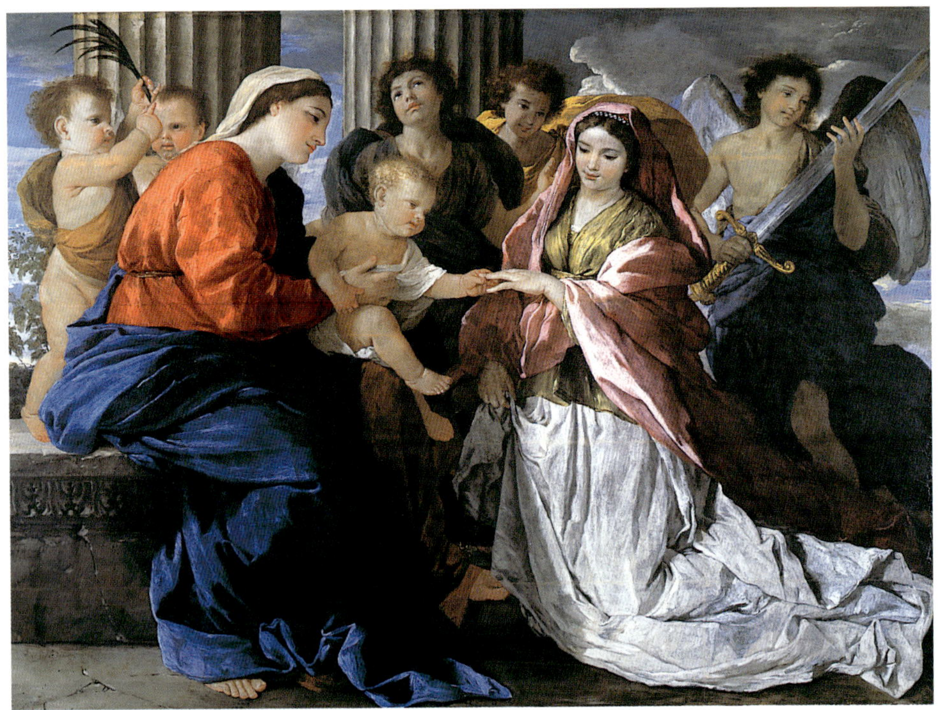

50
Nicolas Poussin (1594–1665)
The Mystic Marriage of Saint Catherine, 1629
Oil on panel, 126 × 168 cm
The National Gallery of Scotland, Edinburgh

During his long career, the French Baroque classicist painter Nicolas Poussin developed his own very personal style for drapery, which he deployed with equal genius for Old Testament, Christian and mythological subjects. His *Mystic Marriage of Saint Catherine* (fig. 50) of 1629 contains many figures in legendary costume, each comprising many folds; but we get none of Annibale's pointed artistry, which reflects the accomplishments of art without respecting the character of cloth, and nothing either of Caravaggio's urgent immediacy or Rubens's dynamic agility. For this event, Poussin has put the row of background angels and the Christ Child into the draped garments of classical antiquity, filling these in as reticent, tinted shapes rather than insisting on the folds or emphasising the antique style. Their shapes look natural, meaning accurately classical, without extra bulk and lift, bright highlights or distracting fabric episodes. Like Annibale's, this Virgin wears her traditional costume, but with full sleeves, since at this date fashion no longer permits the tight ones she wore in Annibale's altarpiece. Poussin's 1629 sleeve is, moreover, set into the dress with a seam, as Annibale's tight ones of 1601 are not (Rubens, too, omitted seams).

Saint Catherine was a king's daughter – we note her small diadem – and the painter has given her gleaming white, pink and gold legendary ensemble great dignity, equal to that of the Virgin's blue classical mantle but further enhanced by the crumpled reality of the huge skirt she must manage as she kneels. The one sleeve we can see of her belted gold silk jacket has both shoulder and arm-hole seams; and Poussin has not refrained from modelling her round breasts with the silk, since the legend says this saint was famous for her youthful beauty. To further that idea, Poussin has deftly given the saint's pictorial costume the fashionable high-waisted, full-sleeved and large-skirted silhouette of the epoch.

As in most works by Poussin, the drapery in this painting has an unequivocal authority. The painter evidently understood the ways of cloth itself just as well as he understood antique sculptured drapery, and he did not sacrifice the truth of either for any picture. For his mythological scenes involving nude figures, his understanding of both live bodies and antique represented ones is equally evident; and the relation between drapery and nudity in those works has the same distinctive clarity and composure.

At this same period in Spain, and in a very different mood, Francisco de Zurbarán was dressing male saints in ennobled versions of heavy monks' robes and sacerdotal vestments (fig. 51). He often made woollen fabric hang around the figure in stiff folds of austere brown, warm white or deep grey, painting the garment so that its own sombre claims entirely replaced the form and weight of the saint's body, leaving bare only his still hands and face, filling the frame with a deep sense of awe uninflected by any vibrations of colour or motion. Jusepe de Ribera was a Spanish contemporary of Zurbarán who made his career in Naples under Caravaggio's influence. His *Saint Agnes* of 1641 (fig. 52) nevertheless shows considerable affinity with Zurbarán's quiet use of non-chromatic drapery. The saint has been imprisoned naked in a brothel for her devotion to Christ. Her hair has miraculously grown to clothe her, and her guardian angel is giving her a solemn, unearthly wrap that will repel all carnal approaches.

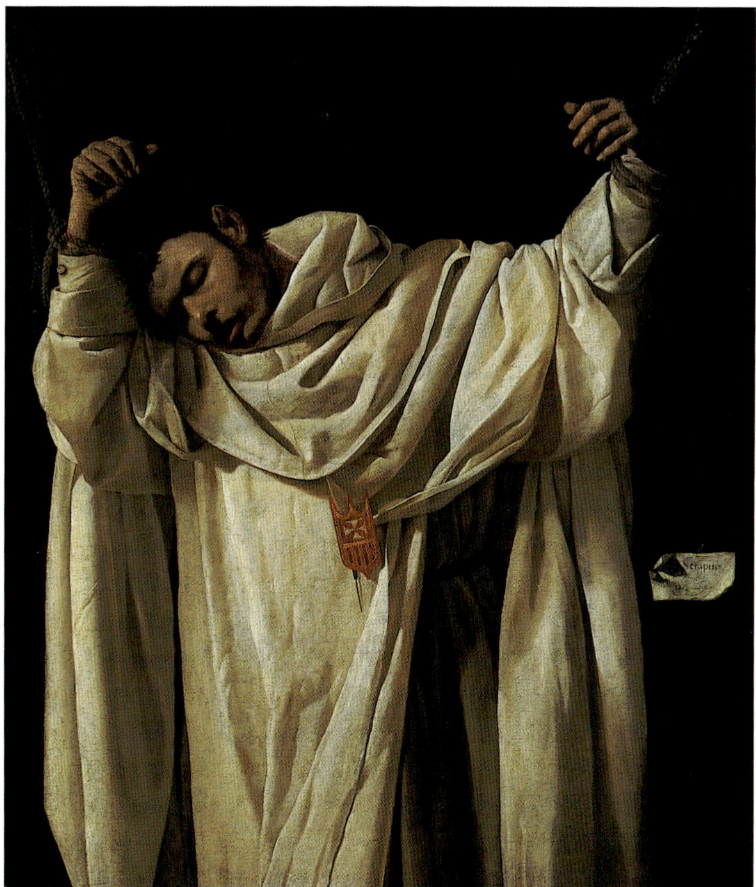

51
Francisco de Zurbarán
(1598–1664)
Saint Serapion, 1628
Oil on canvas,
121.2 × 104.3 cm
The Wadsworth Atheneum Museum of Art, Hartford, The Ella Gallup Sumner and Mary Catlin Sumner Collection Fund

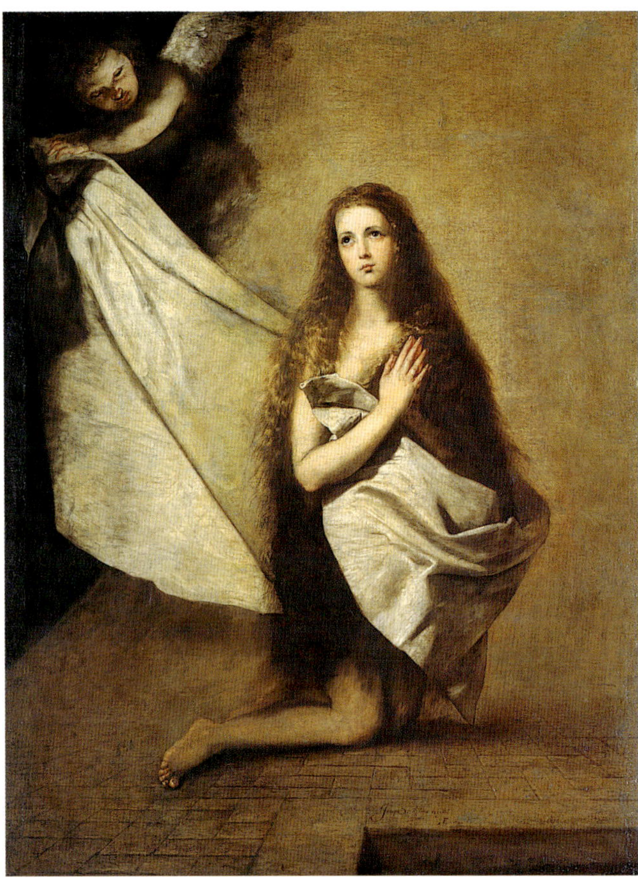

52
Jusepe de Ribera
(1591–1652)
Saint Agnes in Prison, 1641
Oil on canvas, 203 × 152 cm
Staatliche Kunstsammlungen
Dresden, Gemäldegalerie
Alte Meister

Draperies could go to the other extreme for other grim subjects. Judith's murder of Holofernes gave Baroque painters the chance to inject a measure of hysteria into the drama with bright, agitated fabrics, so as to invoke the sexual element in the story without using indecent exposure (fig. 53). The naked flesh in Johann Liss's 1620s scene is confined to the rippling shoulder muscles of both murderess and victim, and the deed is already done. Between Holofernes' shoulders emerges a bloody stump, over Judith's her confirming glance at us as she turns to stow the head and sheathe the sword, her busy sleeves inflating as her arms move.

Judith's shoulders are glowingly set off by the low curvilinear neckline of her feminine chemise: we see she's a woman, and we can read her hilly shoulders as breasts in disguise. Her head and torso are wrapped in a swirling ensemble of brilliant gold, blue, brocaded and pink-trimmed quasi-garments – her turban-like headgear confirms her as a biblical character. The painter seems to have created these silken wrappings to urge on the event, making it seem as if their shimmering tints had distracted Judith's victim while the folds propelled her mind and body into brutal attack. There are tent folds to the right of her, too, swirling in sympathetic rhythm with her garb.

We can also see how a later seventeenth-century artist might unintentionally abuse the liberty of drapery, if he were accustomed to seeing its constant excessive use by his predecessors. The painter Giovanni Battista da Sassoferrato was a latter-day imitator of Perugino and Raphael. He painted many Madonnas with the smoothly idealised faces and

OPPOSITE **53**
Johann Liss (about 1595–1631)
Judith in the Tent of Holofernes, mid 1620s
Oil on canvas, 128.5 × 99 cm
National Gallery, London
NG 4597

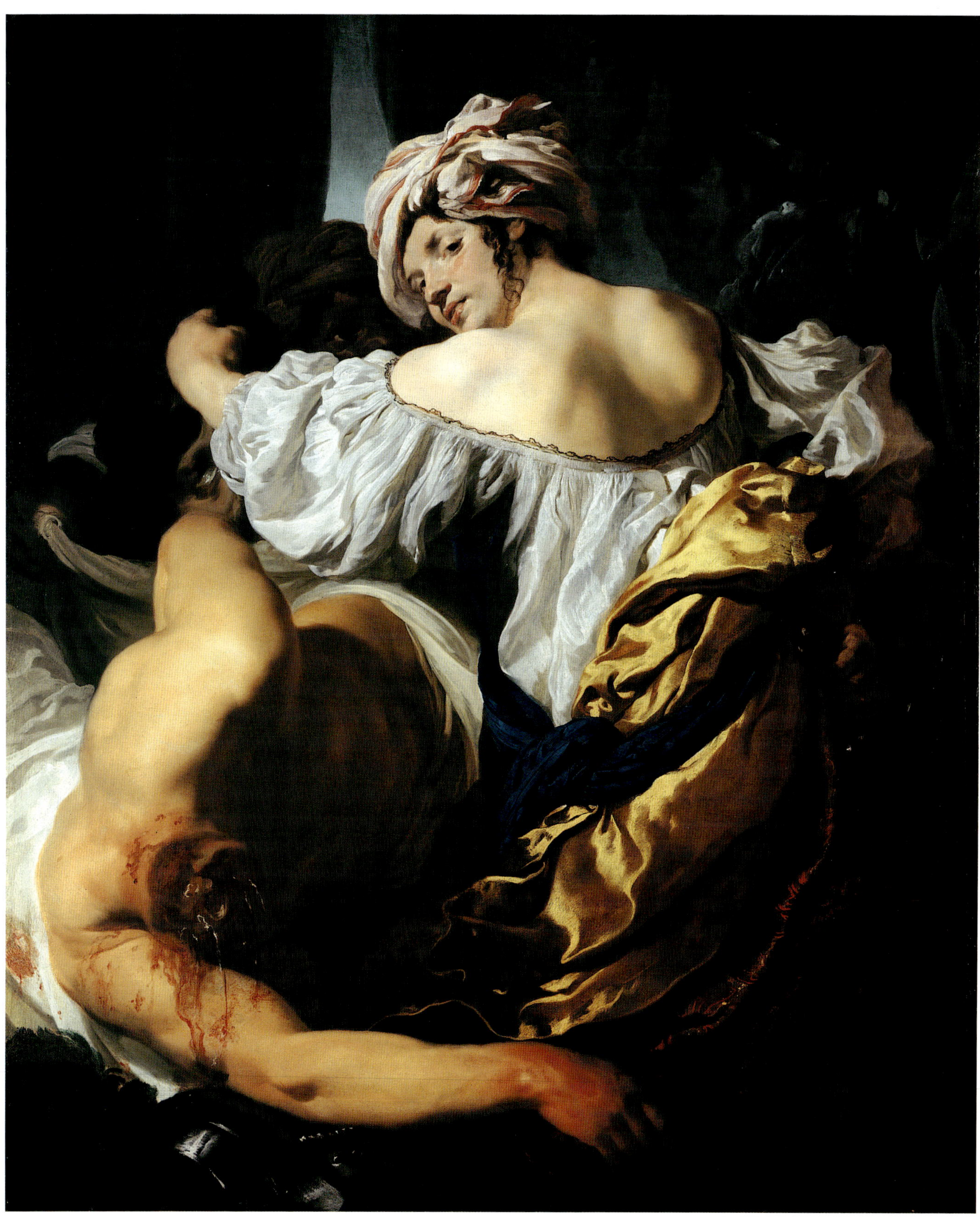

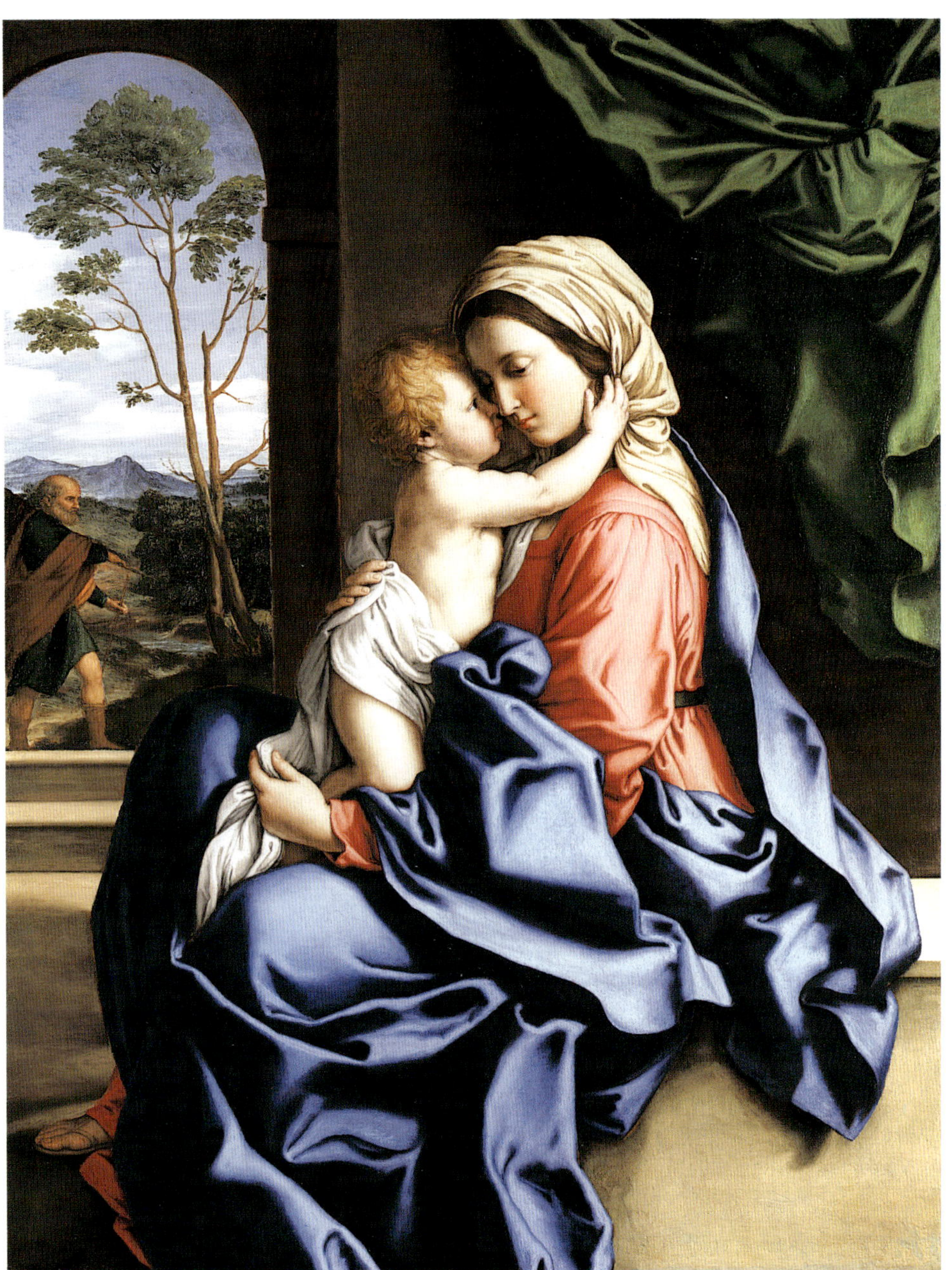

54
Giovanni Battista da Sassoferrato (1609–1685)
The Virgin and Child Embracing, about 1660–85
Oil on canvas, 97.2 × 74 cm
National Gallery, London
NG 740

tempered gestures of the earlier masters, adding similarly calm landscapes. But when it came to clothing the figures and settings, Sassoferrato could not always achieve the continent aspect of Raphaelesque draperies, or we may believe he didn't want to (fig. 54). Pictorial fashion had affected his taste and perhaps his perception, so that his sweet Madonna, although she wears a believable dress, has been swathed in hyperactive stretches of feverishly lit blue stuff. More overwrought green draperies inhabit the upper right corner of the painting, filling the space behind the Virgin with an episode of visual turmoil unsuited to her face and pose, and to the serene view out of the window. The picture illustrates how drapery could become the sign of exaltation without actually providing any.

The difference between the Baroque draperies in this picture, proliferated for their own sake in the late seventeenth century, and the beautiful effects generally achieved for the Madonna's cloaks in 1500 may be understood by comparing this Sassoferrato *Virgin and Child* with the Previtali *Virgin and Child with Two Angels* in Chapter I (see fig. 17). The Renaissance draperies look directly perceived and authentically rich; Sassoferrato's look conceptually rich and theoretically ample, like a formula that's been followed. Previtali's lighting is modulated to integrate the folds with the setting as they drape around the figures; Sassoferrato's brash lighting seems to flatten his, so they stand out as busy patches. Sassoferrato was influenced by Caravaggio's mixtures of real and visionary cloth and by his manipulations of light; but he lacked the resources of such Dutch painters as Rembrandt and Vermeer, who applied their own transcendent vision to Caravaggio's innovations.

To indicate the extremity of his sad Magdalen, Caravaggio notably did not bare one of her breasts, as many painters did. Alluding to the ancient Greek image of the fighting Amazon, Renaissance artists sometimes showed one breast exposed in self-forgetful zeal or fear, in the context of a legendary death struggle, a fight for right, a desperate escape. As the seventeenth century progressed, Italian Baroque painters took up the one-bare-breast motif for penitent Magdalens and suicidal Cleopatras, both characters associated with sensuality. These artists' dramatic skill in rendering folds in motion around a naked breast gave extra charge to the resolve or despair of such personages. Many Baroque painters, such as Guido Reni in his *Lucretia* (fig. 55), were adept at conveying extreme moral crisis and extreme sensuality in the same picture.

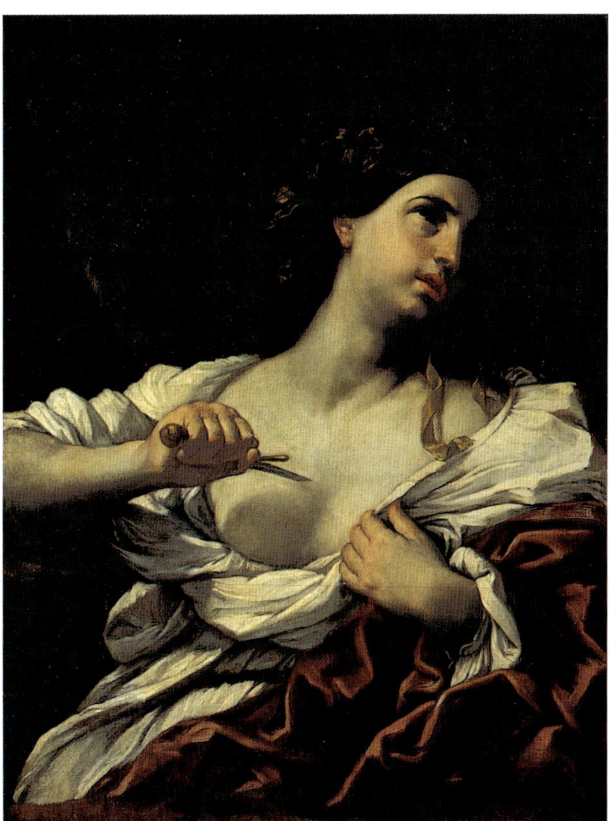

55
Guido Reni (1575–1642)
Lucretia, after about 1620
Oil on canvas, 99 × 76 cm
Dulwich Picture Gallery, London

This combination seemed right for the subject of Lucretia, a beautiful matron of ancient Rome famous for her chastity, who stabbed herself for honour's sake after publicly announcing her rape by Tarquin, her husband's alleged friend and ally. After her suicide, her husband and his followers turned in vengeance against Tarquin and his ruling family of tyrants, drove them from power and founded the Roman republic. The story makes Lucretia an early martyr in Rome's legendary history; but during the tale's afterlife, the suspicion persisted that virtuous Lucretia must have enjoyed the rape and stabbed herself for personal shame. This suspicion had been allowed for in Saint Augustine's discussion of her in *The City of God*, where he condemns suicide, especially by innocent persons. He suggests that one might approve Lucretia's suicide if she had killed herself because she knew she was guilty; and he says that she alone knew her reasons. Later he allows that her pagan religion permitted her to believe that her suicide was the only thing that would make her seem not guilty; but a Christian must find her a murderess, for killing an innocent person, if indeed she was.

She became a recurrent subject for painters, who incorporated the idea of sexual pleasure into her self-sacrificial image, so that Renaissance pictures of Lucretia wielding her knife would sometimes portray her in a disarranged version of the same fashionable finery Mary Magdalen might wear. A seductive full-length nude might bear her name, along with her dagger, when the same model wasn't posing for Eve with her apple or Venus with her mirror. This version attributed to Guido Reni offers thick, unstable folds exposing a vivid breast to the approaching blade in Lucretia's fist, and no other narrative material in the picture except the look of self-conscious despair and conscious sexual appeal.

We can see how the erotic half-length image had changed in the two generations since Titian's calm lady at the beginning of this chapter: a histrionic element had entered into the sensual drama of nudity partly unveiled by drapery. A later example of it is the smiling peasant boy painted in the 1670s by Murillo (see fig. 44), whose appealing nude shoulder we saw earlier as echoing those of Caravaggio' s youths. But whereas Caravaggio's boys, just like Flora, acknowledge their appeal without pretence and seem to wear their seductive draperies for a personal drama, not for an audience, Murillo's boy and Reni's Lucretia each seem to be playing a part, one smiling obliquely with studied charm, one gazing skywards in posed distress. The sense of theatrics comes from the more facile emotional level on which the sensuality is placed, by Lucretia's upturned eyes and twisted drapes, by the sentimental combination of a peasant child's revealing rags and fetching smile.

Artists never abandoned the Renaissance motif of the half-length, half-draped single figure, who may bear a legendary or exotic title but in whom we more easily see the posing model or sitter. Centuries of great art since antiquity had lent prestige to the vision of loose cloth lying or moving against skin, a motif which arouses sensory excitement more elementary than the look of unfastened clothes; and the Renaissance painters had provided a handy close-up format for the theme. Cindy Sherman's vision of herself in semi-dishevelled hair makes a good recent example, with a rosy chenille bathrobe Baroquely draped to expose one shoulder, together with the striking crease between arm and armpit, and one nude ankle (fig. 57). At first glance she resembles a Caravaggio Bacchus more than a Venetian Venus; but in Friedrich von Amerling's 1840s female half-length (fig. 56) we can also see a source in Romantic painting for feminine shoulder exposure like Sherman's: here,

OPPOSITE **56**
Friedrich von Amerling
(1803–1887)
Portrait of a Girl, about 1830–40
Oil on canvas, 64 × 50.5 cm
Residenzgalerie Salzburg

FAR RIGHT **57**
Cindy Sherman (born 1954)
Untitled, 1982
Photograph on paper,
115.2 × 76 cm
Tate, London. Courtesy of
Metro Pictures, New York

OPPOSITE **58**
William Walling Jr (1904–1982)
Dorothy Lamour, 1937
Photograph
The Kobal Collection, London

FAR RIGHT **59**
Philippe Halsman (1906–1979)
Marilyn Monroe, 1952
Photograph
Magnum Photo, London.
Courtesy of CMG Worldwide Inc.,
Los Angeles

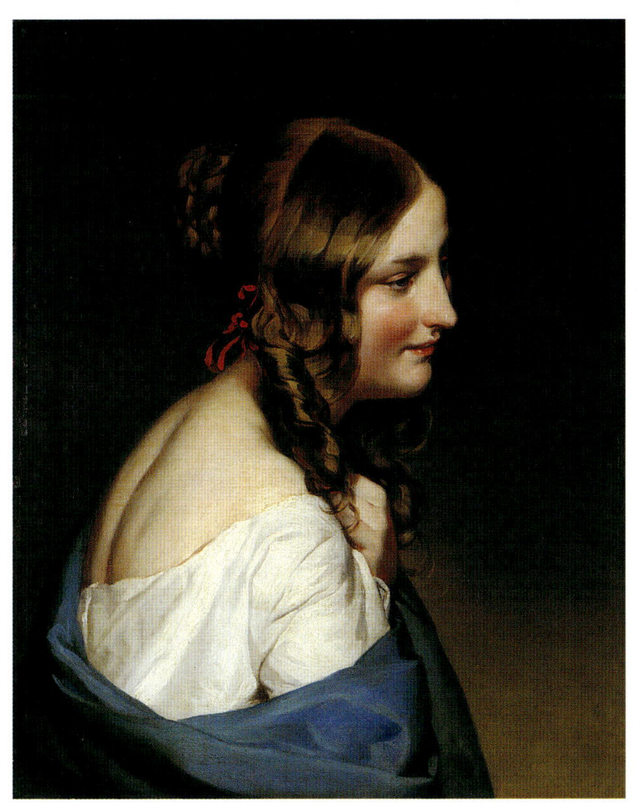
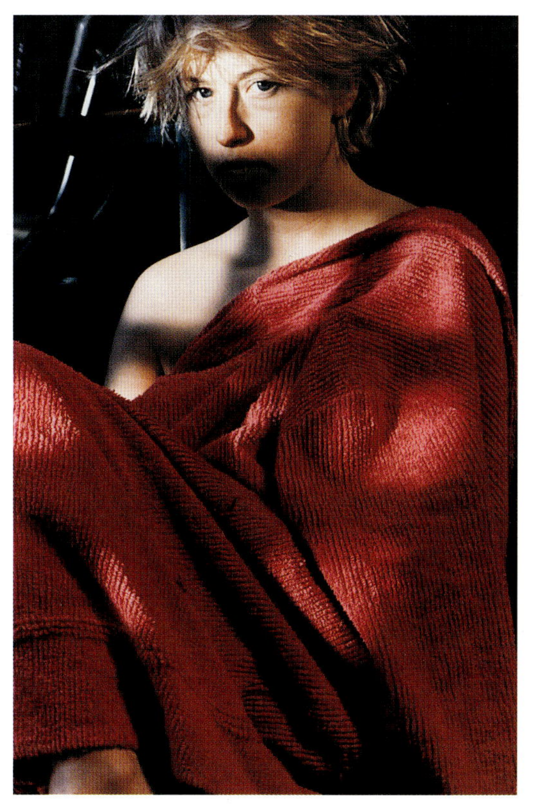
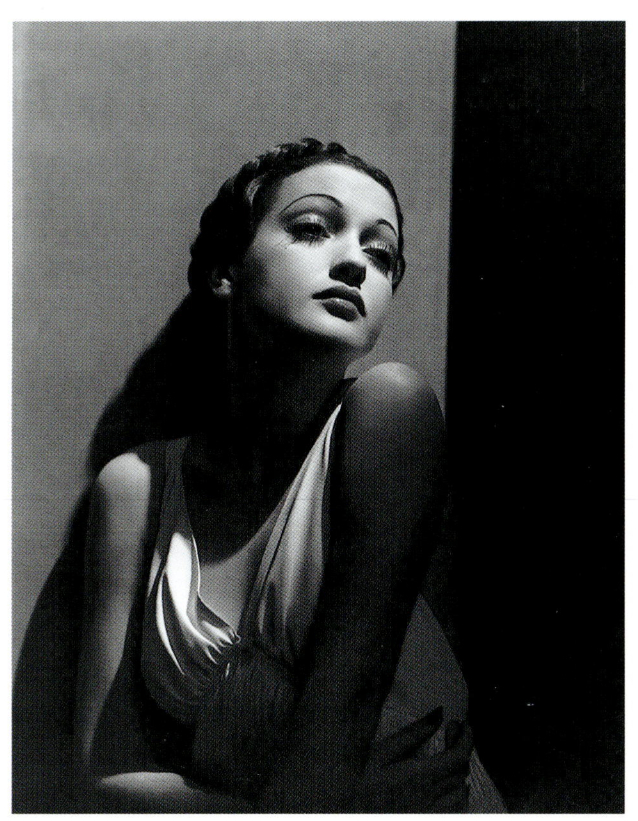
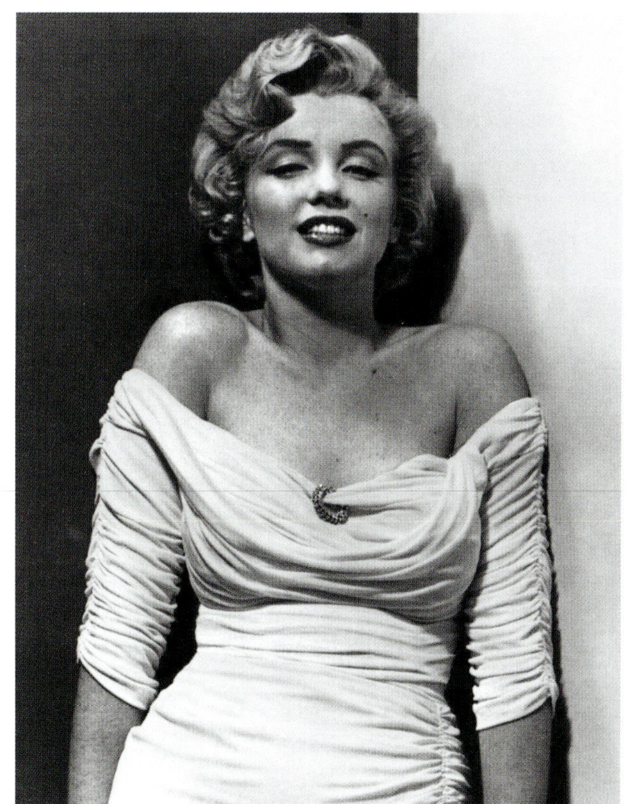

too, the artist has enhanced a bit of quasi bosom-cleavage (now down the back) by using real garments posing as drapery, and including some locks of loose hair.

The great Hollywood portrait photographers, whose female subjects had their own legendary names and faces, made use of the half-draped, half-length theme throughout the twentieth century, deftly adapting it to fashions in draped dresses, often emphasising the upward thrust of bare shoulders (figs. 58, 59). We can see the compelling look of conscious, self-regarding beauty in these images, the look of Venus redoubling her power in the mirror of the lens. Still more than fashion photographs, these dramatically draped Hollywood portraits show how the Baroque spirit has thoroughly held its own in the modern world.

In the eighteenth century, French Rococo painters continued – now with light-hearted zest instead of serious zeal – to celebrate the ancient allure of nude body parts emerging from unaccountable eddies of fabric, and not just in half-length. In his *Dark-haired Odalisque* from about 1745 (fig. 60), François Boucher orientalises the theme, showing the model prone on a low divan, looking up towards us as she exposes her bottom and spreads her legs amid an ocean of crisply breaking folds. Most of this sea cascades heavily down off the wall behind her and surges up between her legs in blue velvet waves, some of it puffs up under her body in a surf of blue and white stripes, the rest foams around her waist and upper arms in white splashes that just might be a chemise. Her foot touches an undertow of rosy carpet on the floor, of which the blue and gold border also bunches thickly upwards as if to join the other waves. Harem-like effects appear in her pearl-decked little turban with a feather, in the low table with an incense pot and more pearls; but the

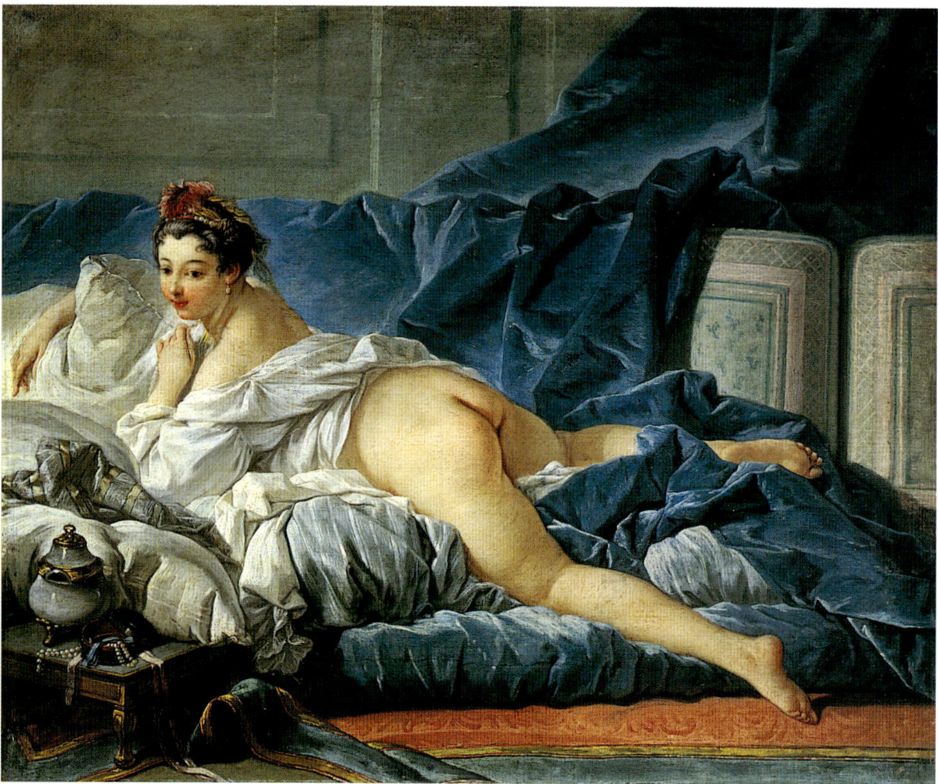

60
François Boucher (1703–1770)
Dark-haired Odalisque,
about 1745
Oil on canvas, 63.5 × 54.5 cm
Musée du Louvre, Paris

61
Jean-Honoré Fragonard
(1732–1806)
A Young Girl on her Bed, making her Dog dance, about 1770
Oil on canvas, 89 × 70 cm
Alte Pinakothek, Bayerische Staatsgemäldesammlungen, Munich

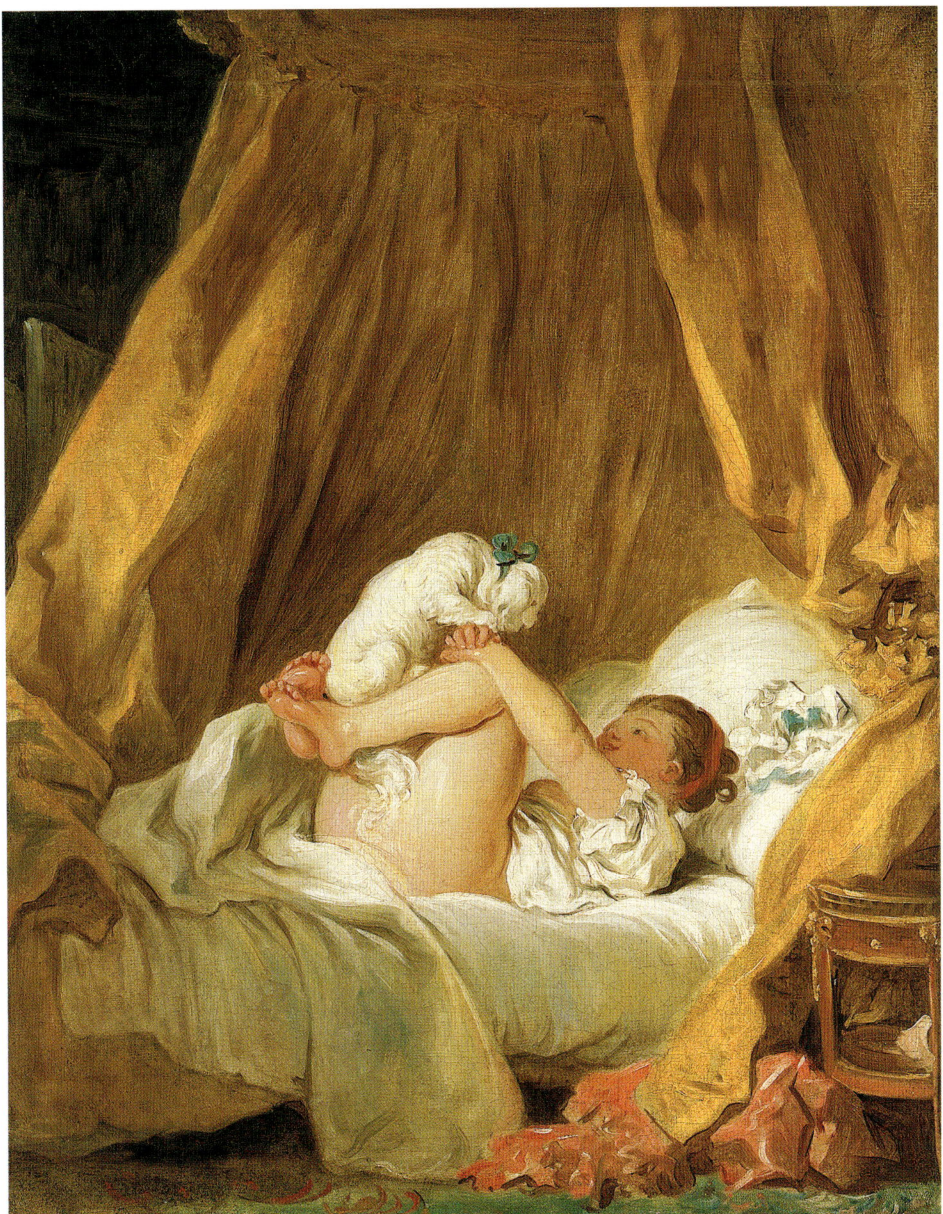

exoticism is mostly conveyed in the undisciplined abundance of fabrics painted only to pour around this backside for sensuality's sake, unconstrained by household function.

In a later image (fig. 61), Jean-Honoré Fragonard spices up the theme considerably by placing the model on her back in a regular bed and applying the fur of a living creature to her exposed underparts. This bedstead, however, is entirely made of draperies that ripple down and bubble up around the action. They seem to be persuading the girl's rucked-up chemise, cast-off nightcap and thrown-down robe to become draperies, too, along with the sheets, so that all may ripple together in high textile excitement about the way this girl raises her naked legs to hold up her lucky dog.

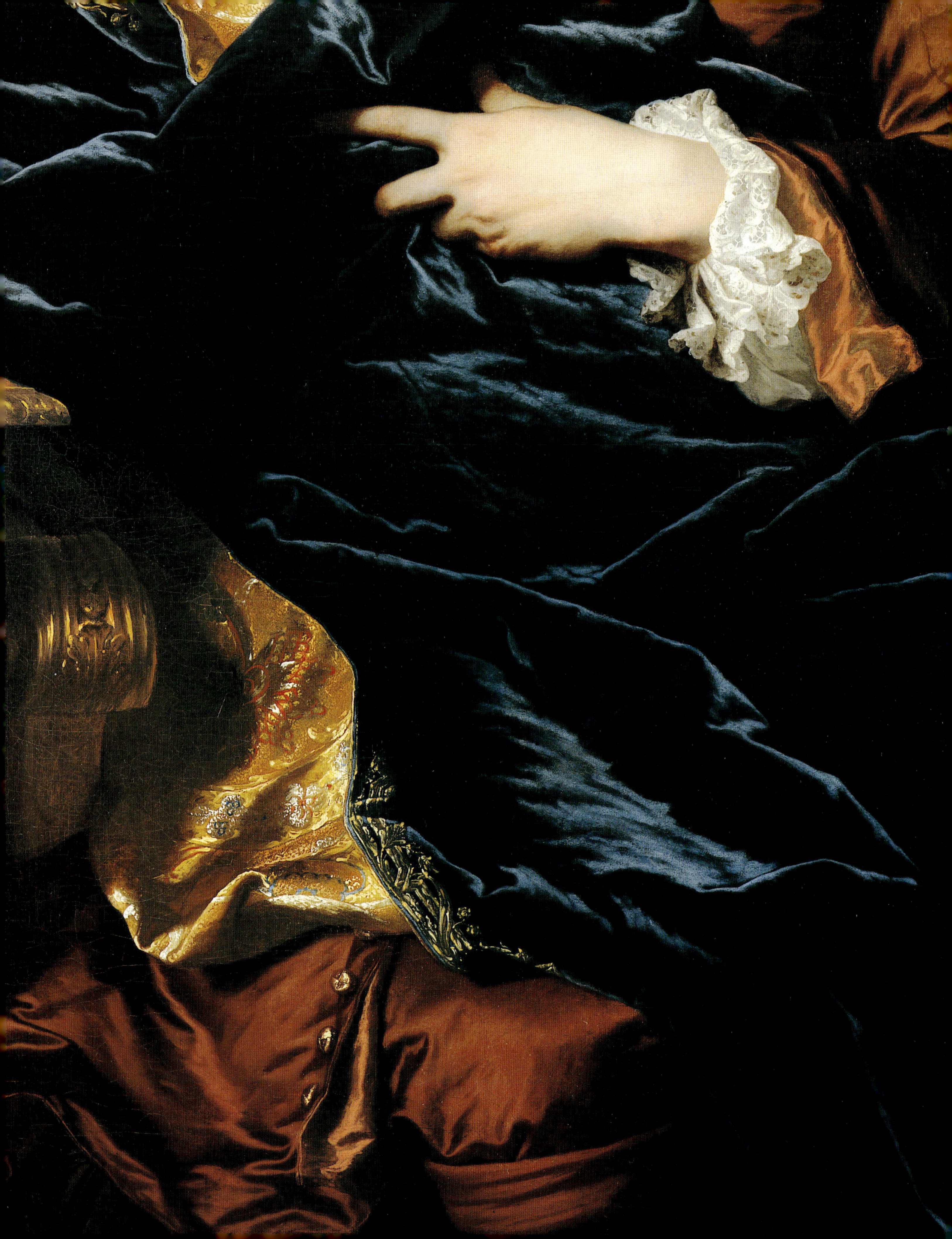

IV High Artifice

BY THE LATTER PART of the seventeenth century, painters' use of actively fantastic drapery had reached a climax, which, with some shifts of tone, managed to last through a good part of the eighteenth. During the period, the straightforward gusto of Baroque pictorial drapery, whether solemn or stormy, gradually gave way to the self-conscious spirit of theatre. Attendant draperies for legendary scenes began to seem more and more like stuff festooned around a stage, while the figures began to look historically or fantastically costumed for a performance instead of appropriately dressed for action or passion. Elegant portraiture might include a large swatch of rich fabric flung across the sitter's clad body, not to serve as a cloak or cape but simply to stand for spectacle, whether the clothes were real or fictional.

By the 1630s, Van Dyck had already initiated this particular kind of effect for his portraits, although, when he put notably fanciful clothing on his sitters, he might introduce suggestions of the costume worn by Titian's subjects – that is, a version of Flora's chemise-plus-drape ensemble, such as Venetia, Lady Digby wears while posing as Prudence in 1634 (fig. 63). She prudently wears two cloaks, one in black to fasten efficiently on a diagonal across her bosom, one in heavy rose satin meant only to wrap and shine mightily across her lap and shoulder. These dramatic drapery effects are nevertheless as straightforward as those in the Rubens *Assumption* of 1626 or the Poussin *Saint Catherine* of 1629 that we saw in the last chapter. For sitters posing as themselves, we also saw Van Dyck creating equally unself-conscious effects both in the sitters' voluminous clothes and scarves and in the ample draperies behind them (see figs. 39, 40).

Van Dyck's portrait of the Countess of Castlehaven (fig. 62), however, shows an extraordinarily non-realistic use of pictorial drapery for its date, evoking Tintoretto but at the same time foreshadowing the more self-consciously decked portraits of the following century. Standing at three-quarter length against a neutral background, Lady Castlehaven first of all wears a generic dress that costume historians have concluded was wholly invented by Van Dyck, apparently to allow the unmediated décolletage of sixteenth-century fashion in his female portraits – Lady Anne Carr (see fig. 40) wears it, too.

Detail of fig. 66

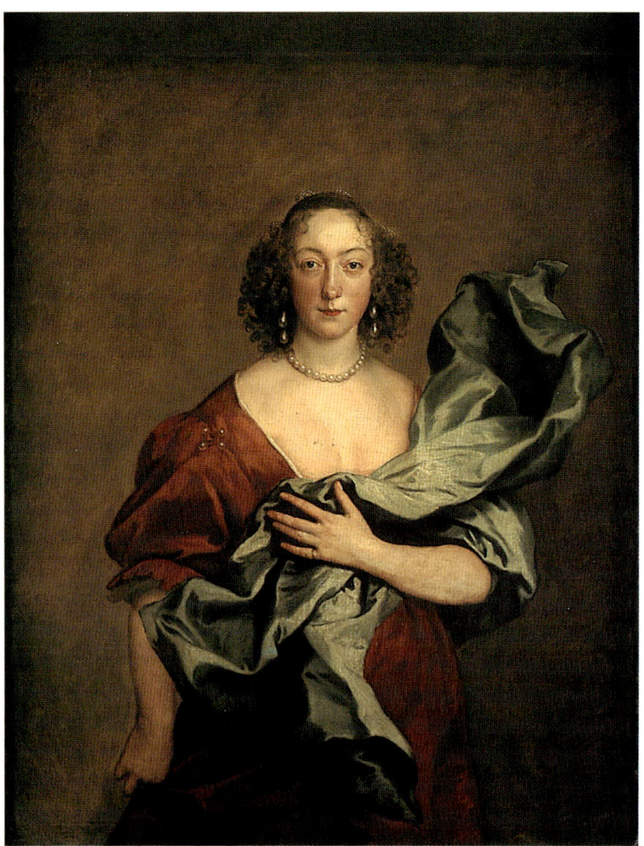

62
Anthony van Dyck (1599–1641)
The Countess of Castlehaven, about 1635–8
Oil on canvas, 133.4 × 101.6 cm
Collection of the Earl of Pembroke, Wilton House, Salisbury

OPPOSITE **63**
Anthony van Dyck (1599–1641)
Venetia, Lady Digby as Prudence, about 1634
Oil on canvas, 101.1 × 80.2 cm
National Portrait Gallery, London

On real-life elegant English dresses of the first third of the seventeenth century, no low neckline would have lacked some ornamental lace, either on the outside against the dress or inside against the skin, or both: Van Dyck himself recorded this in formal portraits of Queen Henrietta Maria in the 1630s.

Instead, the thin white line between Lady Castlehaven's stark neckline and her flesh is an artistic device, like the brooch at her shoulder and the scallops edging her sleeves, to suggest pastoral romance as it had been invoked by Venetian High Renaissance painters. Against her body and into the air squirm two or three metres of blue Tintoretto drapery, tamed for the moment by the lady's hand and arm, clearly struggling to fly upwards towards total freedom in the realm of art. To keep her cool and real, the artist gives a true account of the modern coiffure and jewellery that frame Lady Castlehaven's own strong face.

Active drapery deployed entirely for its own sake, both on and off the figure, had become quite standard in European portraiture by 1700. By that time it was already giving the impression I am calling theatrical, or self-conscious, or stagy, or spectacular, by contrast to the earlier expressive uses I have called dramatic; and this impression was not confined to portraits. I would argue that the difference between such new stuff and that in earlier Baroque works is the spirit in which it is added: it now shows that it is there to signal what I would call the artifice of art. In legendary scenes, the drapery is no longer there directly to enhance the drama going on among the characters, or the internal drama in the soul of a single figure, such as Mary Magdalen or Saint Agnes, or to serve

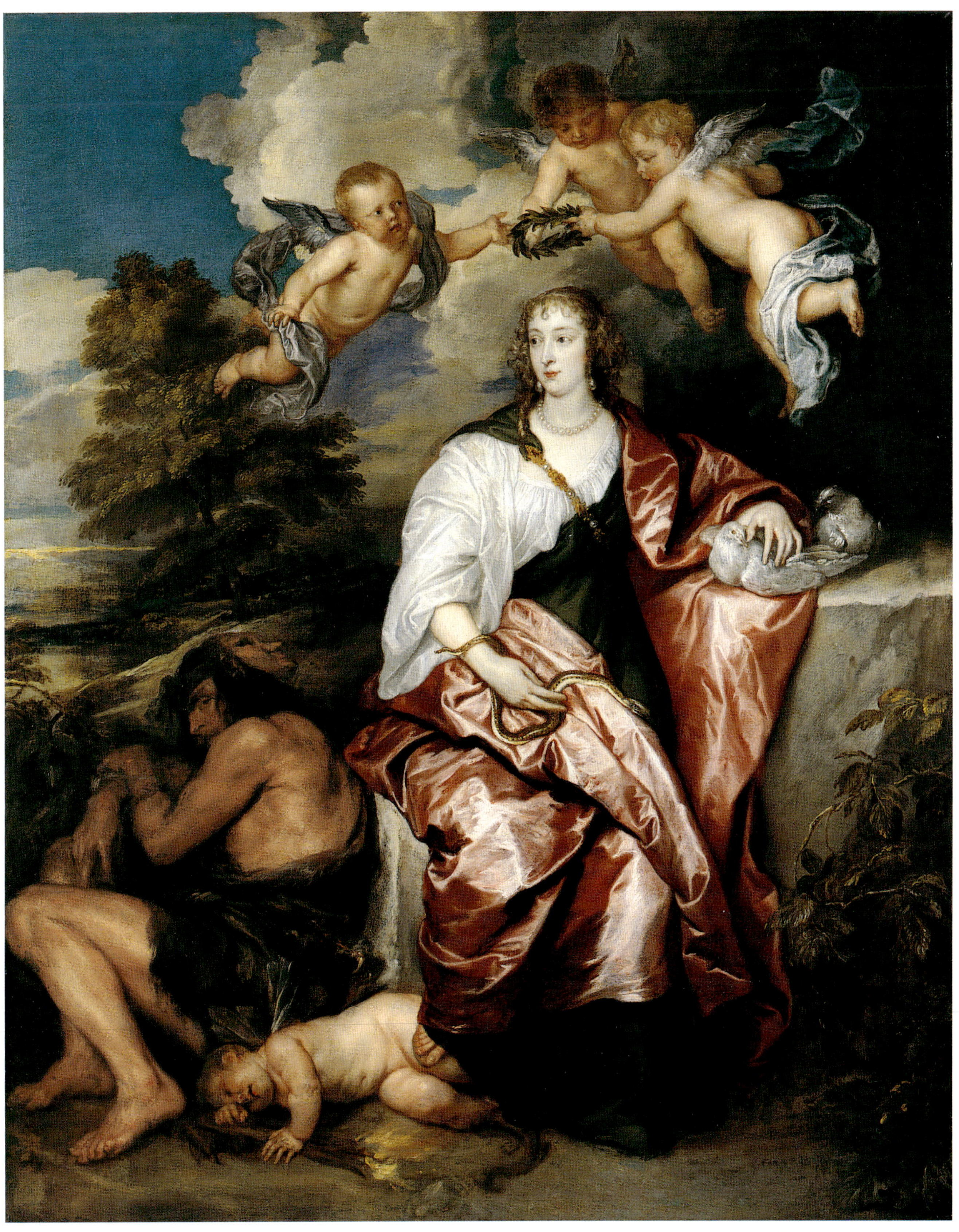

as a foil to a sitter's stiff garments; and it is not there to suggest the work of earlier artists, so as to invoke the power of art. It is there to locate the picture within the realm of artifice, as the drapery around a stage does, and similarly to invite a willing suspension of disbelief in the viewer. It may be used with direct reference to stage practice, or just in a way indicating artifice, but with great realism in rendering the folds, the better to help do away with the disbelief.

A small, sweet example is a portrait about 1700 by the Dutch painter Gotfried Schalken (fig. 64), in which we find the sitter in a contemporary coiffure and contemporary chemise with a wide frill, not at all suggesting Titian or Van Dyck suggesting Titian. But over it the painter has crossed the front of her body with a twisted length of blue silk, one end of which – it's not clear which end – is flying up into the air behind her. Her forearms and hands are invisible, and they clearly have nothing to do with supporting or encouraging the flight of this swatch. Behind her is a real fringed hanging, transmuting at left into a dim bubble of standard attendant drapery. The theatrical element is the serpentine look and flying corner of this piece of pictorial stuff, where there is neither wind nor drama in the image itself. This drapery is decorative, presentational and spectacular in an otherwise gentle portrait.

An imposing example from about 1705 is the portrait of Count Fulvio Grati by the Bolognese painter Giuseppe Maria Crespi (fig. 65). Here the background drapery has been specifically registered as theatrical by the servant-like figure shown swagging it up behind the sitter, who is posed holding a lute on his lap and touching a mandolin on the table, while another servant looks for the right page in a book of music. One

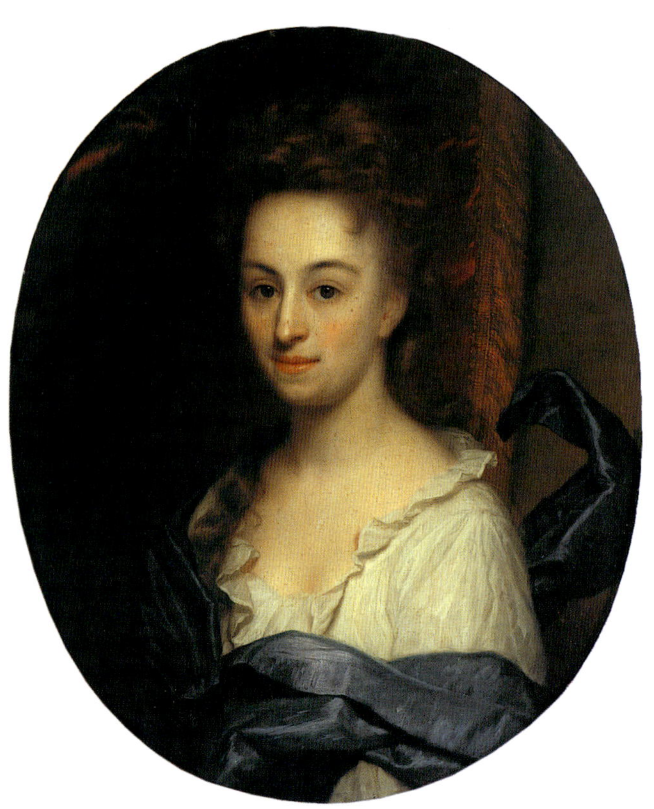

64
Gotfried Schalken
(1643–1706)
Josina Clara van Citters, about 1700
Oil on canvas, 30 × 25 cm
Rijksmuseum, Amsterdam

65
Giuseppe Maria Crespi
(1665–1747)
Count Fulvio Grati, about 1705
Oil on canvas, 226 × 152.5 cm
Museo Thyssen-Bornemisza, Madrid

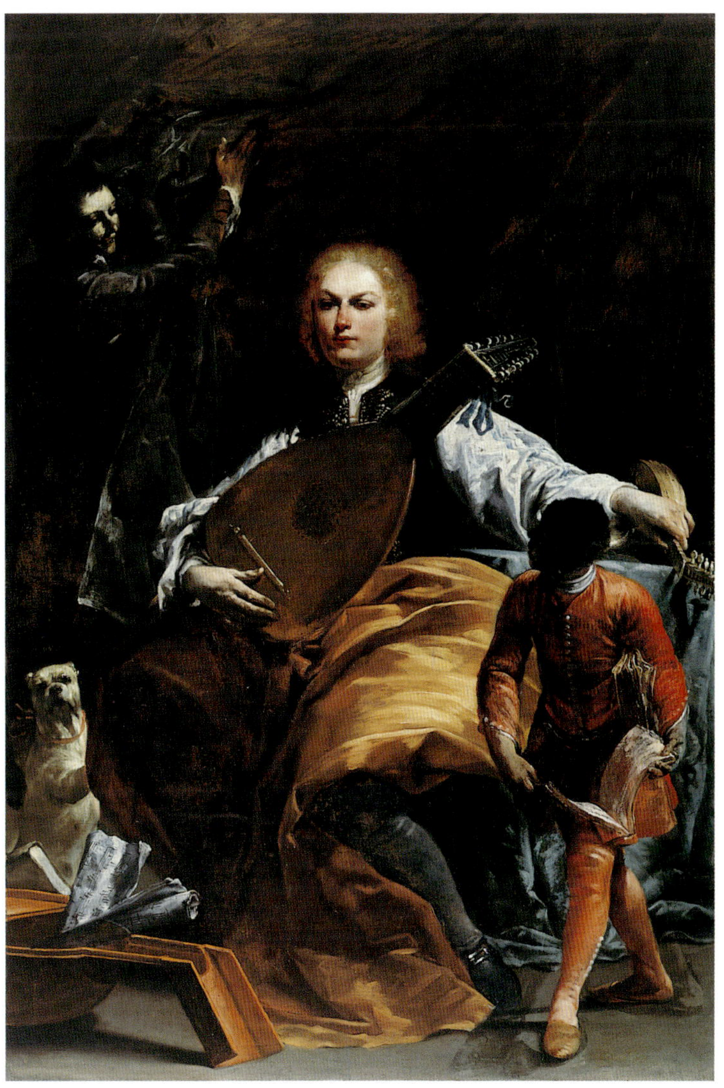

spectacular green drape makes a skirt for the table under the mandolin, but the most spectacular one sweeps under the lute in massive folds of gold silk across the sitter's knees and between his legs, not omitting to make a backdrop for one elegant calf. If this object is a cloak, it's not posing as one here. All these draped folds are there to add scenic textile presence to this portrait of a noble amateur musician, turning it into a visionary *tableau vivant*, offering faint whiffs of imperial Nero fiddling. Apart from all the stuff of artifice, he wears an undress waistcoat with old-days sleeves and a simple shirt with no lace cuffs or cravat, the better to play the lute.

In France, Hyacinthe Rigaud painted Antoine Pâris (fig. 66) in 1724, seated at ease in his library with his lace-trimmed shirt open and his plain brown silk coat unbuttoned, looking quite natural in his vast wig. Against his stomach, however, the sitter is clutching some fifteen metres of bunched-up sapphire velvet, the lengths of which are sewn together with a visible seam, lined with well-rendered gold brocade, and trimmed along the edges with clearly described gold embroidery. This sumptuous object has no beginning

66
Hyacinthe Rigaud (1659–1743)
Antoine Pâris, 1724
Oil on canvas, 144.7 × 110.5 cm
National Gallery, London
NG 6428

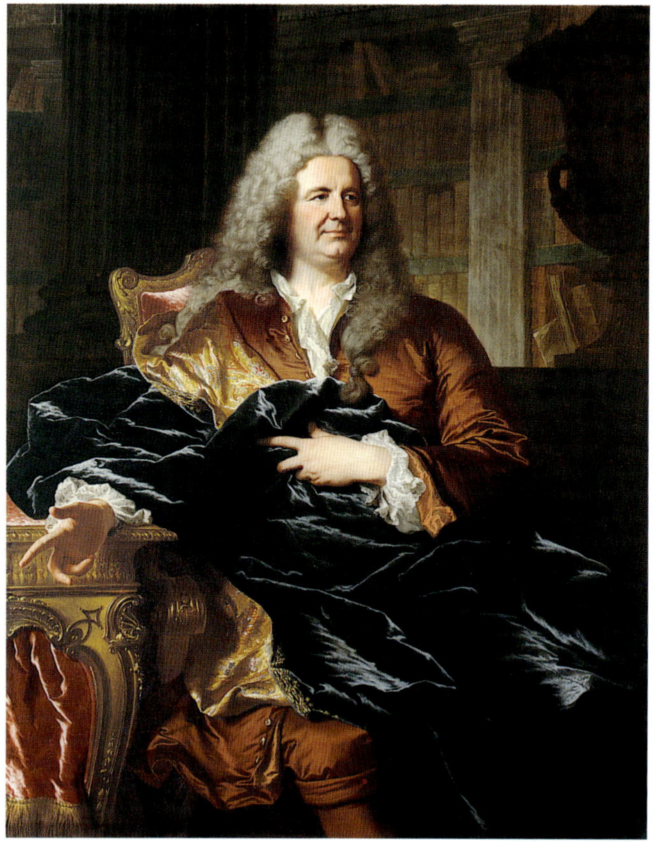

and no end, arriving heavily on to the sitter's lap from somewhere beyond his left knee, then flashing its lining above his right one, finally emerging out of his grasp to billow around his right arm, where it folds over to flash more of its lining before vanishing behind his back, perhaps to continue down off the chair and into the next room. This, no doubt, represents an actual mantle with real dimensions, meant to fall in heavy folds around Antoine Pâris's form on grand occasions. Rigaud has painted it here as a sea of shameless display, a sort of clandestine cloth of honour rippling across the middle of an informal portrait.

Another generation later, in 1749, Jean-Marc Nattier provides an example of an even more artificial style of French portrait (fig. 67). Heavy drapery here, still perhaps suggesting a cloth of honour, is swagged up in forthrightly theatrical fashion, as in the Crespi; but it now adorns an intimate boudoir with a lace-covered dressing table, while at the same time unveiling some improbable classical architecture at the rear. This mother and daughter wear entirely pictorial clothing, vaguely conceived as chemise, dress and large shapeless mantle for each; but the garments have been rendered entirely as draped fabric, more according to the original Titian ideal than to the Van Dyck version, but now crisp and ebullient, and with no hint of allegory or precise classical reference. The theme of artifice is directly stated by the action, which shows the mother adorning the coiffure of the daughter, who kneels beside her holding an open casket of ornaments. The idea is offered that talent for the management of artifice is a virtue, the suitable subject of a maternal lesson and example.

The fancy dress these two are wearing, so puffy and frothy, is related to what we will see later on in the century worn by the sitters for Zoffany and Reynolds, even though by their period Neoclassic ideas about nature and antiquity had assumed their sway, and froth was out of the picture. The value of being dressed up in draped clothing just for the painting, vaguely suggesting an antique mythological character, is already being strongly stated here: we are not to believe that these two aristocratic ladies usually dressed like this, with jewelled bands binding Madame's loose upper sleeves and loosely confining her waist. We know in fact that they both usually wore conical corsets and tight sleeves with elbow frills embellished with ribbons, just like other Nattier sitters of the date, whether or not they added rich, Rigaud-like drapes for a portrait. For other fancy-dress portraits, they might appear out of doors in a Diana costume, with a bow and quiver, a

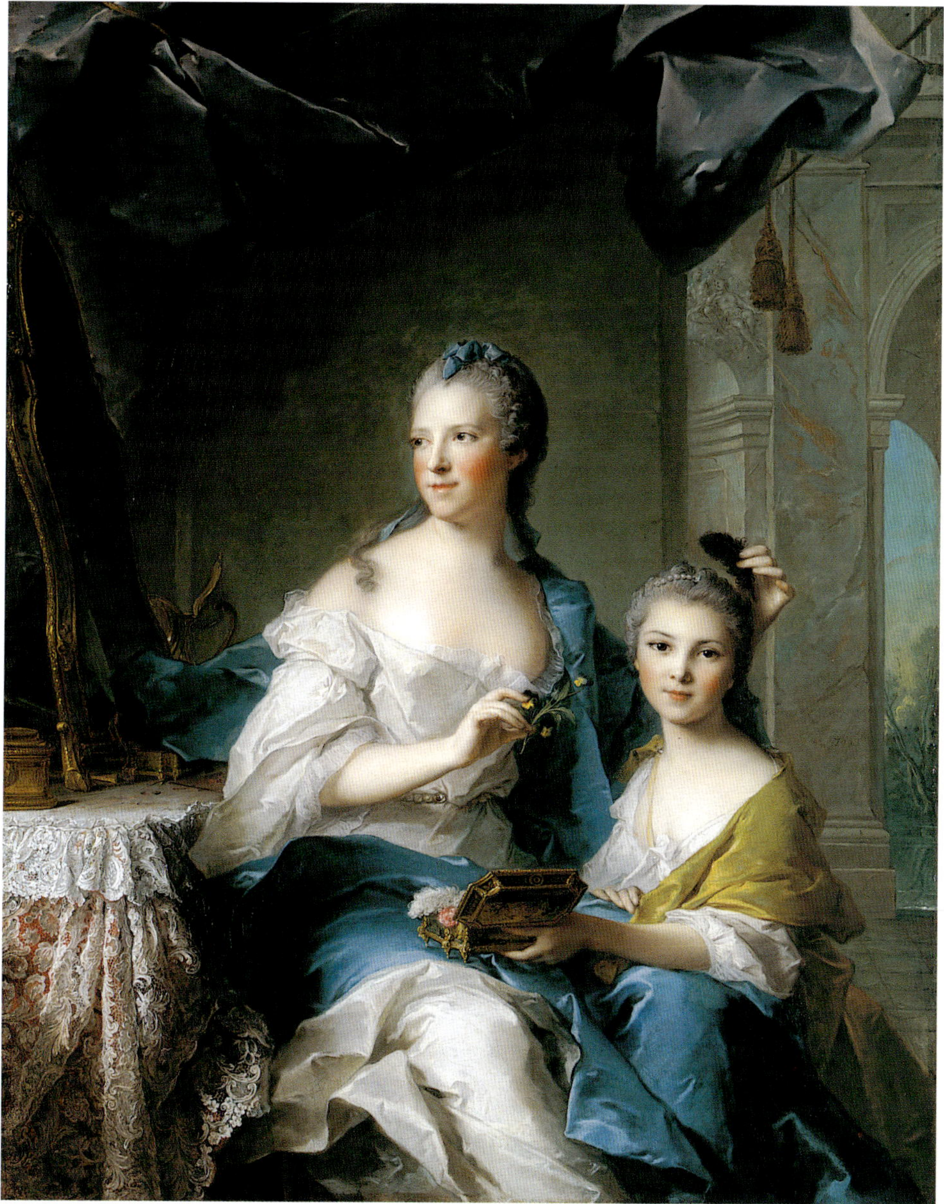

67
Jean-Marc Nattier (1685–1766)
Mme Marsollier and her Daughter, 1749
Oil on canvas, 146.1 × 114.3 cm
The Metropolitan Museum of Art, New York, Bequest of Florence S. Schuette, 1945 (inv. 45.172)

crescent headdress and a leopard skin. For the real-life circumstances shown here, each would be wearing a *robe de chambre*, which these garments do not resemble; but here we can take pleasure in the rich folds of their consciously pictorial, quasi-classical costumes, and in those of their theatrical boudoir décor as well.

This portrait has the character of a genre scene, as well as that of a scene from a romance or a legend; and in those categories works were also being painted with much the same spectacular spirit for draperies and garments. In them we find the spirit of artifice maintained by a new and more self-conscious use of pictorial costume, often portrayed as some kind of conscious fancy dress, even when drapery is not used in the picture.

The specific subject of theatrical costume has long been raised in connection with the general subject of what everybody is wearing in paintings. Evidence suggests that there was much interchange between the clothing worn in paintings and that worn in pageants or on street-theatre stages from the thirteenth to the sixteenth centuries; and I would argue that most of this interchange was quite unselfconscious. Painters were interested in painting clothes that people would recognise not as theatrical, but as appropriate for the character; and stage tailors rarely made clothes copying specific paintings. During any epoch, tailor and painter would agree on the right gear for a particular personage or type, such as what an ordinary angel should wear; and painters sometimes made designs for tailors to use; but the stage did not try to be painterly, nor painting theatrical. They were part of the same enterprise.

Real-life fancy dress has a more interesting connection to painting, because it is invented for and worn by non-actors for special costumed occasions – carnival, court masques, masked balls, festivals; and one such occasion might simply be a painting, with the model dressed up as Flora, or the noble sitter dressed up as Diana, although only by the painter for the picture. We have seen that painters have always had the freedom to add modern stylistic qualities or modern details to the clothes of their sacred or legendary characters, once they have made them recognisable, so that the Virgin in paintings could appear in a whole range of different sleeves, while always wearing what is essentially a Virgin costume; and the goddess Diana, or Cleopatra, or Prudence could wear essentially a classical costume, with the whole ensemble made up by the painter to look like elegant fancy dress on a modern lady, or on a modern model, with torso and coiffure in the right shape.

I am proposing that all European painters tended to do this quite unselfconsciously up until the period we are now considering; and that somewhere around 1700, perhaps a bit sooner, pictorial clothes in paintings – portraits or not – became more intentionally like fancy dress or else actually were fancy dress; and that at the same time any attendant draperies became more patently stagy, even without the painter putting them to specific theatrical use.

The stage and fancy dress both seem to have become more interesting as pictorial subjects in themselves: paintings were made of stage performances, and portraits of professional actors and actresses were frequently painted both in stage costume and in pictorial fantasy clothing, as well as in their own personal clothes. Other portraits in ordinary clothing went on being as common as ever for both sexes, showing a marked difference from the theatrical ones in fantasy garb, while hair styles, as usual, tended to be the same. What was now called 'history painting', meaning that concerned with serious subjects from legend and religion, began to take on a marked histrionic flair, with more pointedly spectacular work for the draperies to do.

The great eighteenth-century Venetian painters Giovanni Battista and Giovanni Domenico Tiepolo, father and son, often painted legendary characters in sixteenth-century costume, no matter when the pictured scene might have taken place – and 'costume' is the only word for what is worn in these works. The detailed and coherent garments on Antony and Cleopatra or on Pharaoh's daughter finding Moses, among many others, although based on the heavy clothes in Veronese's earlier paintings, nevertheless display all the stylistic leavening of stage dress. The quasi-historical high collars are a bit too high, the wide ones too wide, the sleeves are somewhat too swollen, the curled horns of hair too large, so that the whole ensemble has been slightly aerated in the usual manner of historic costume designed for pageants or parades, where the figure need only appear and not act, sing or dance.

In an oil sketch for his great fresco *The Meeting of Antony and Cleopatra* (fig. 68) from about 1743, the elder Tiepolo gives turbans to the Egyptians, as Orientals, and gives the hero Antony a real suit of Roman armour with its helmet and short battle-skirt; but he covers his legs with tight-fitting breeches underneath. All these modes followed stage conventions derived from Renaissance theatre, which were still used on the stage in Tiepolo's own time for indicating antiquity. So, however, was dressing the heroine in a stiff corset and full double skirt with nothing ancient Roman about it: she would always wear a currently fashionable dress, with additional exotic touches to suit the part. But Tiepolo has made the whole outfit into a Venetian sixteenth-century stage costume instead, including Cleopatra's horned coiffure and the slashed rolls around the tops of her sleeves, both of which might have appeared on a stage Cleopatra back in Veronese's time, as fashionable then.

This means that Tiepolo's reference to the stage is not direct, that he's not invoking current stage practice that everyone would recognise. He is, rather, creating a more generic staginess, or what I would call a spectacular way of using historic clothes, a way of emphasising their dressed-up look, without intending to portray something to be seen, now or in the past, on a real stage. This is painterly theatre only, at which he was a perfect master. On the walls and ceilings of palaces, for which many of his scenes were done, framed by stage-like illusionistically painted architecture, such a look of quasi-theatrical spectacle had the perfect place.

We can see a somewhat different sartorial effect in Giovanni Domenico Tiepolo's little canvas of about 1752–3 depicting the marriage of Frederick Barbarossa and Beatrice of Burgundy, an event that occurred in the middle of the gaunt twelfth century (fig. 69). Giandomenico, too, costumed it as if it were happening at the end of the opulent sixteenth, although the hyperbolic collars and sleeves on the bridal pair and their retainers suggest to the modern eye what costume designers of French historical films liked to create in about 1948, much more than what appeared in Veronese's paintings or on the Renaissance stage. The composition, however, is not at all cinematic but entirely art-historical, and it does show, as the costumes do not, the family debt to the great Venetian precursors. But the festive draperies adorning the setting are spectacular in the style of their own date – huge amounts of perfectly credible silk twill, tacked up by stage hands to swing down approvingly over the ceremony, or whip for joy in the mechanical wind.

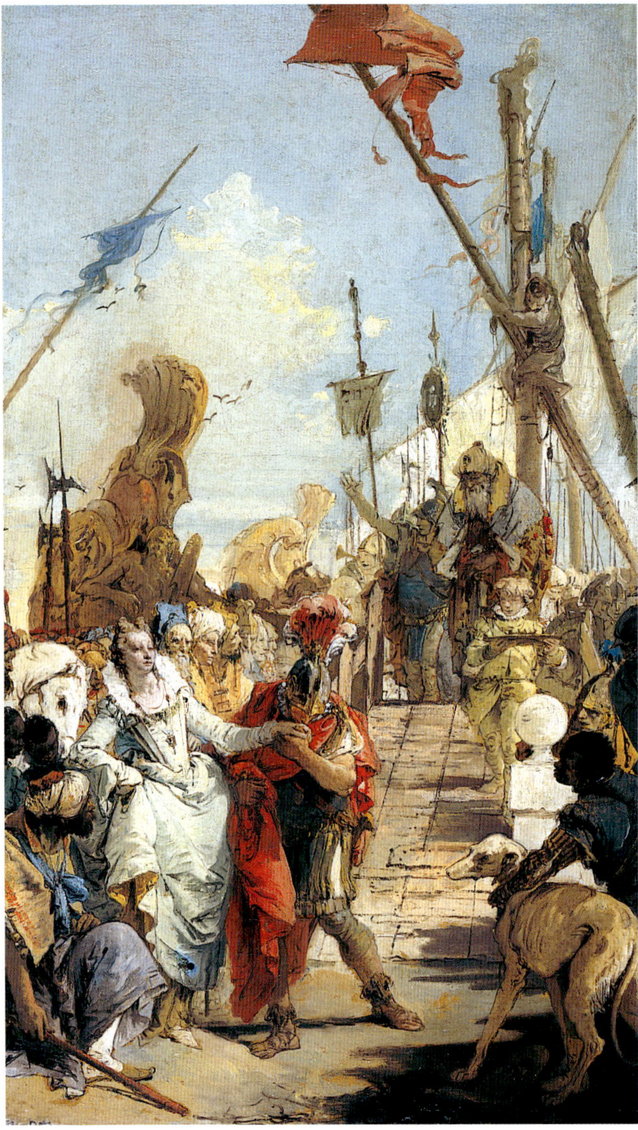

68
Giovanni Battista Tiepolo
(1696–1770)
The Meeting of Antony and Cleopatra, about 1743
Oil on canvas, 66.8 × 38.4 cm
The National Gallery of Scotland, Edinburgh

OPPOSITE **69**
Giovanni Domenico Tiepolo
(1727–1804)
The Marriage of Frederick Barbarossa and Beatrice of Burgundy, about 1752–3
Oil on canvas, 72.4 × 52.7 cm
National Gallery, London
NG 2100

The common Tiepolo signature is the realism of all the fancy dress, its look of having been cut and sewn out of specific stuff, lined, interlined, stiffened, padded and puffed expressly for this production, whether it is a *tableau vivant*, an Allegory of the Four Continents or a drama out of Tasso or the Bible. Seams and fastenings are clearly indicated, as are facings and hems, and the garments fit. These are not imagined pictorial clothes in the Michelangelesque or Tintorettesque vein, where unaccountability is an expressive advantage. They are triumphantly actual, even when they aren't quasi-Renaissance period costumes but invented capes and tunics and bits of theatrical armour worn by supernatural characters in mid-air. As scarves float and sashes flutter among the limbs and clouds, you can see where the airborne garments start and stop, what they're made of and how they stay on.

In France, about a decade earlier than the elder Tiepolo and in an intimate vein, Jean-Antoine Watteau was also specialising in theatrical fantasy, building his own famous

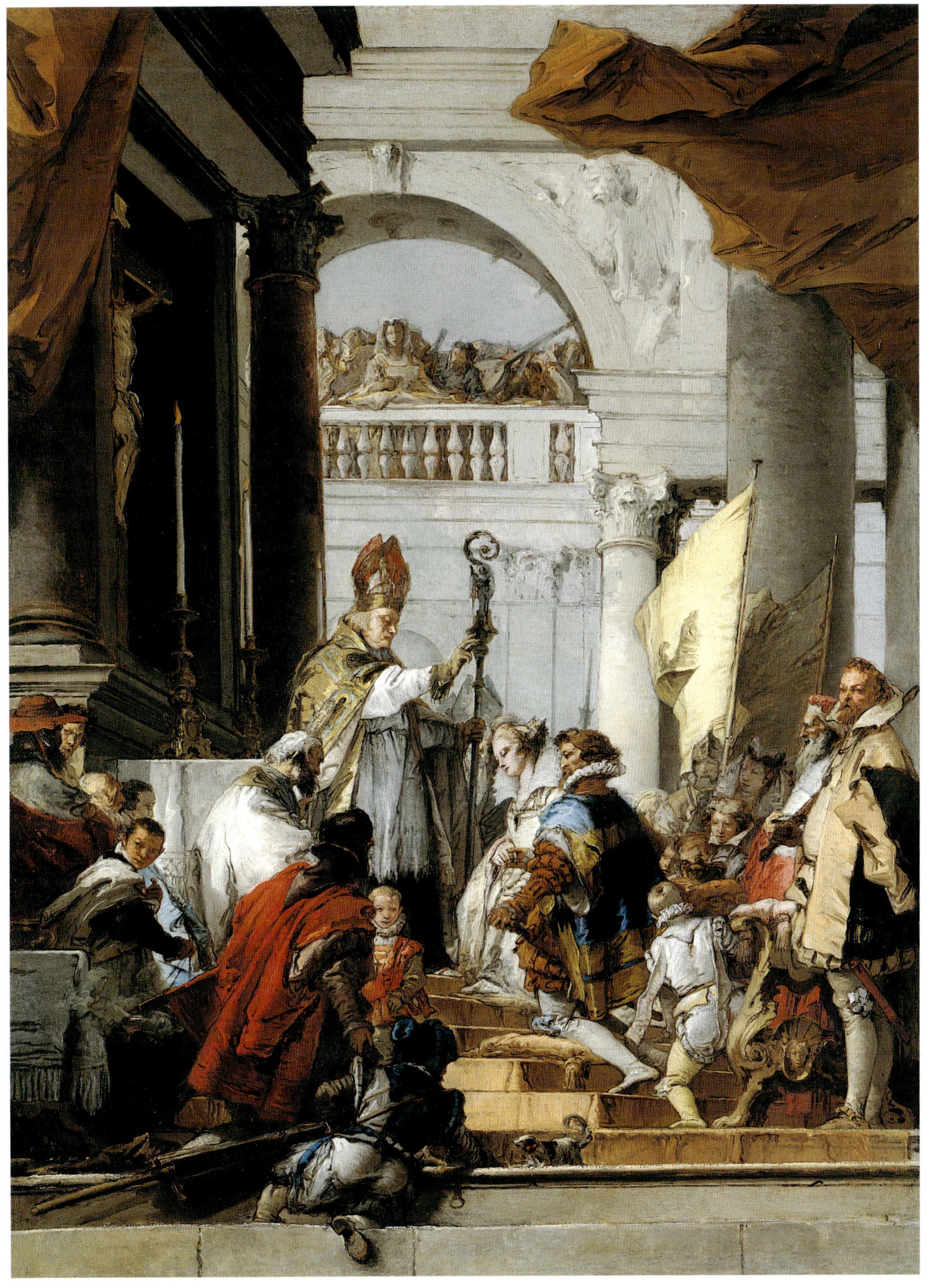

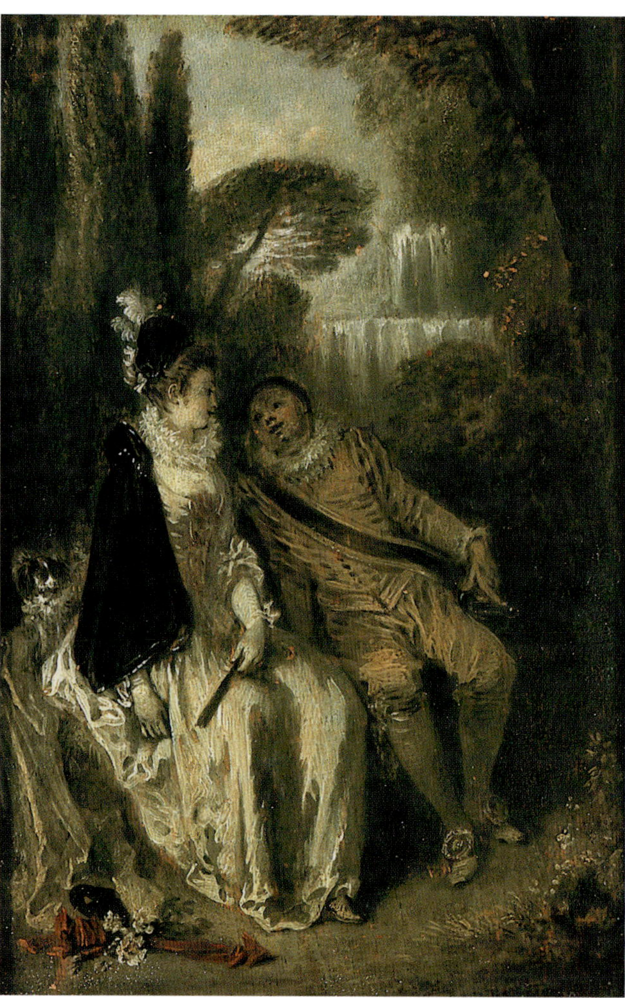

70
Jean-Antoine Watteau
(1684–1721)
Le Repos gracieux, about 1713
Oil on wood, 20 × 13 cm
Ashmolean Museum, Oxford

brand of delicate ambiguity into his precisely rendered versions of late sixteenth-century costume. He, too, had a debt to Veronese, but a larger one to Rubens, partly because Watteau was a Flemish painter, natural heir to the early Flemish way with light, detail and slightly awkward movement. Only some of his characters wear fancy dress, and only some of those refer specifically to the wardrobe of the Italian Commedia dell'Arte, and yet everybody is somehow posing, acting and wearing costumes. There is no epic consciousness or cinematic sweep to these partly mythic but wholly staged scenes, and no very explicit narrative, only layers of atmosphere. Much of this is created by the artist's ability to breathe the shiver of lived experience into his deft arrangements of painted beings wearing costume-like clothing with a natural air.

In the scene from about 1713 entitled *Le Repos gracieux* ('The pleasant rest'; fig. 70), nothing is happening, nobody is playing music or dancing, nobody is even turning around or getting up. The couple seem to be silently communicating while he fingers his sword-hilt, leaning on one arm, and she holds her fan closed, straight-backed in her stays. Behind her, an attentive little dog waits to respond if the emotional weather should change. A mask has fallen to the ground, along with a length of ribbon holding a bouquet and some folds of the domino on which she sits.

The man and woman are both in fancy dress, although it's differently conceived for each of them. He wears a buttoned-up doublet and a ruff, which in England was later called 'Vandyke' costume, and is worn, with knee-breeches and rosette-bearing shoes, by certain gentlemen in Gainsborough's portraits. His black cap makes him a professional comedian, however, and his semi-historical gear is a performer's costume. Her dress is an actual lady's, with a stylish row of bows down the bodice, silk gloves up to the elbow and ruffles trimming the sleeves. Her own ornamental ruff, feathered bonnet and black Spanish cape are the sort of quasi-sixteenth-century additions that would be right for carnival or a fancy ball; we aren't meant to think that her ensemble is intended for professional stage use.

In fact we can't be sure what these people actually are, nor what their relation truly is, other than quite amiable right now. Their dress-up clothes are somehow very moving, the more so since the painter has added no extra rhetoric to their representation. But Watteau has cast extra light on her rounded chin and bosom, and on the sequence of their four knees visible under the silk, one of his almost touching one of hers. These two seem to want their feelings to pierce through their separate trappings, during this quiet moment by the painted fountain. Watteau is showing not just two kinds of disguise – fancy dress and stage costume – but some of their different psychological effects. There is no spectacular drapery in this picture; the delicate erotic balance is all suggested with clothes specifically denoting artifice.

In 1753, near the beginning of his career, Jean-Honoré Fragonard created a very different sort of stage spectacle in his vision of *Psyche showing her Sisters her Gifts from Cupid* (fig. 71). The painter offers this mythological tableau with none of the Tiepolo's and Watteau's exactitude about the texture of stuffs and the structure of garments. Quite the opposite, he conveys his stated theme of classical fantasy – the story appears in *The Golden Ass* of Apuleius, from the first century AD, and in a La Fontaine poem elaborating on it – precisely through the delicious vagueness of the draperies, causing multiple caresses of painted folds to flutter suggestively around, and intermittently to reveal, the elongated bodies of these lovely creatures. They are emphatically not clothes: Fragonard purposely omits any reference to fit or fastenings, mundane textures or gravitational pull. The nymphs' hair, on the other hand, is arranged in the chic styles of the 1750s, and a hairdresser nymph is perfecting Psyche's coiffure. The painter has used the enduring device – also used for the stage and screen – of putting modern heads on fancifully clad bodies, to ensure a quick modern response no matter how strange or ancient the costumes.

Fragonard seems to be offering us a vision of Cupid's divine presence, conjuring him so that he appears in the guise of multi-coloured, flattering and titillating supernatural drapery, which gives instant erotic pleasure to every woman wrapped in it and likewise arouses all who see her wearing it. The stage, too, is decked with a transparent length of it, which is wafting a few chubby putti down from upper right, while other buoyant pieces of the same irresistible stuff are being admired by Psyche's sister nymphs – and all of this is Cupid's bounty, no doubt just as arousing as their own garb. His red quiver full of arrows lies pointedly on the floor in the foreground, to show that these nymphs are in a highly susceptible state. The extremely palpable but shapeless draperies here seem to stand in for caresses – that is, to be producing sexual arousal – in a way akin to those in the explicit 1740s *Odalisque* of Boucher (see fig. 60), who was Fragonard's first teacher. In both, we see the arrangement of their folds made deliberately artificial, the better to do their erotic job.

Very different still is the 1713–4 staging by Donato Creti of a grim ancient moment, *Artemisia drinking the Ashes of Mausolus* (fig. 72), showing the widowed queen lifting a cup from a waiting woman's proffered tray. Artemisia was Mausolus' sister as well as his wife. In the fourth century BC they ruled jointly in the Carian capital of Halicarnassus, where, having drunk his ashes after his death, perhaps to feel still closer to him, she further honoured him by building the immense Mausoleum, which became one of the Seven Wonders of the ancient world. This picture expounds a sombre theme in terms of multi-coloured real stuffs and nothing else, except for the hands, feet and ornamented heads of the two principals. An ornately dressed black servant has sunk so deeply into the shadows at lower left that he barely registers – except for his satin sleeve, which asserts its small claim among the insistent draped components that fill the frame.

71
Jean-Honoré Fragonard
(1732–1806)
Psyche showing her Sisters her Gifts from Cupid, 1753
Oil on canvas, 168.3 × 192.4 cm
National Gallery, London
NG 6445

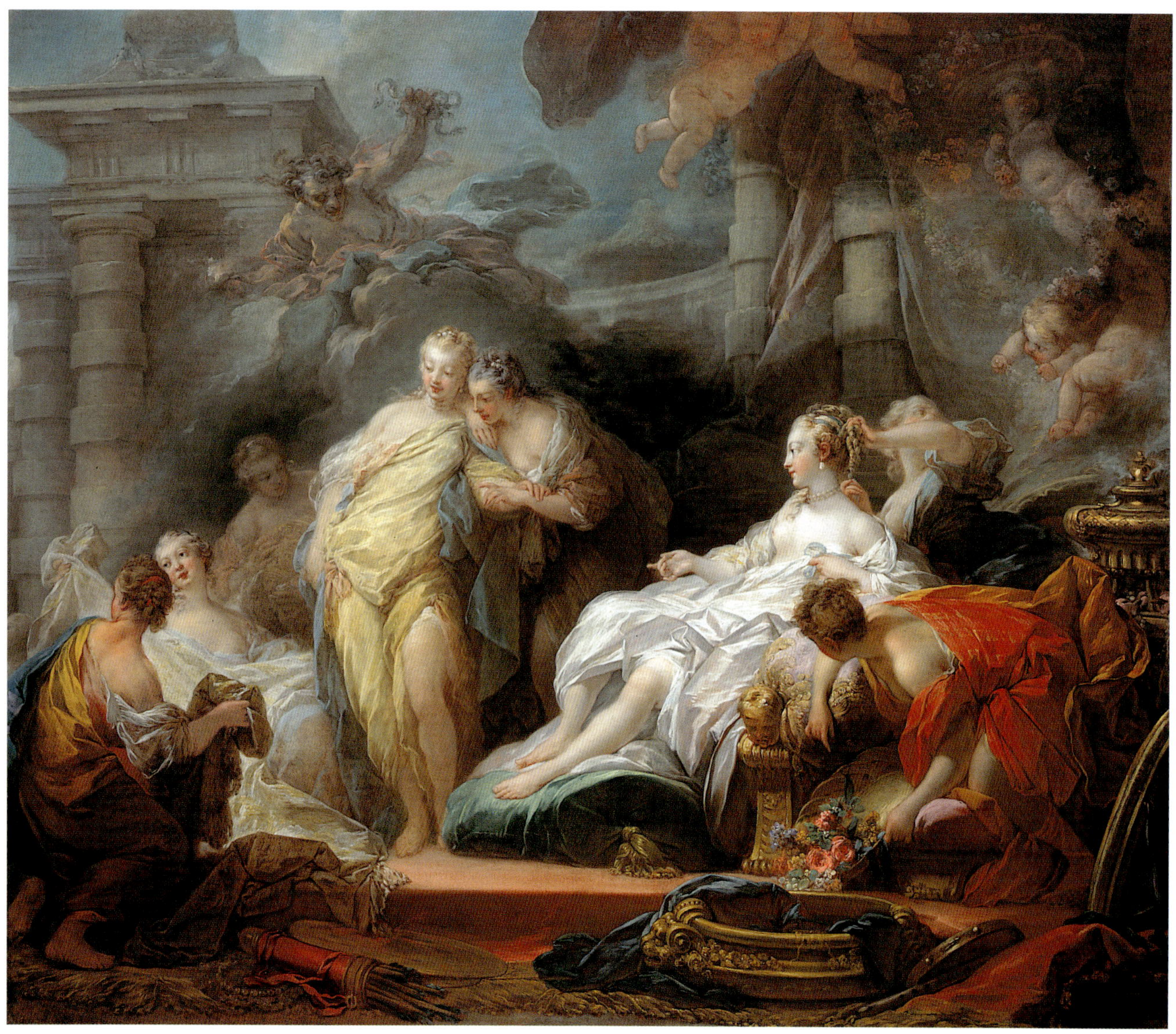

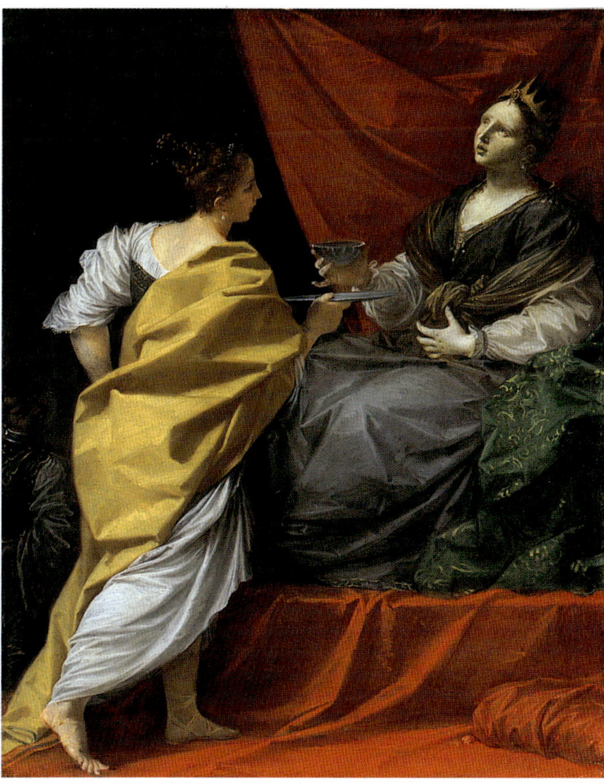

72
Donato Creti (1671–1749)
Artemisia drinking the Ashes of Mausolus, about 1713–14
Oil on canvas, 62.7 × 49.9 cm
National Gallery, London, on loan from the collection of Sir Denis Mahon
L884

There are no pieces of furniture, no architectural elements, no traces of landscape in this picture, as if the sweep, rumple and drag of cloth alone would yield whatever the painter needed to convey the import of this event; and this cloth looks all the more stagy for never being wafted aloft into painterly billows – it all bunches, stretches or hangs. The two female bodies barely exist, Creti has quite subdued them with his tide of folds. He seems to have posed the women first, wearing their shifts and holding their props, and then brought in the contents of a textile warehouse, manipulating different samples around the stage and players, screening or muffling everything irrelevant. Then he set up the lighting and painted the fabric to emphasise the gestures. He made the waiting woman's striding legs look dim below the brilliant swags of white and yellow stuff that rush towards the hand holding the tray, opposing those lighted folds to her shaded face under its exotic hair. By contrast, he cast strong light on the queen's crown, face, throat and stomach-clutching hand, making them emerge from shadowy pools of swirling blue and grey folds; and he showed the whole encounter hung about and carpeted with endless blood-red bunting. This work is an intense exercise in painted drapery melodramatics, perhaps more odd than convincing, but showing how important independent drapery had become for painters to use in obviously artificial arrangements.

Throughout the eighteenth century, artists painted portrait subjects in different versions of fancy dress, as if painter and sitter wished to invoke the spirit of theatre without referring to any actual stage performance. It might be a complete ceremonial costume, such as coronation robes or court dress, more often a fashionable version of period dress such as the 'Vandyke' suit mentioned above, which might be worn to a

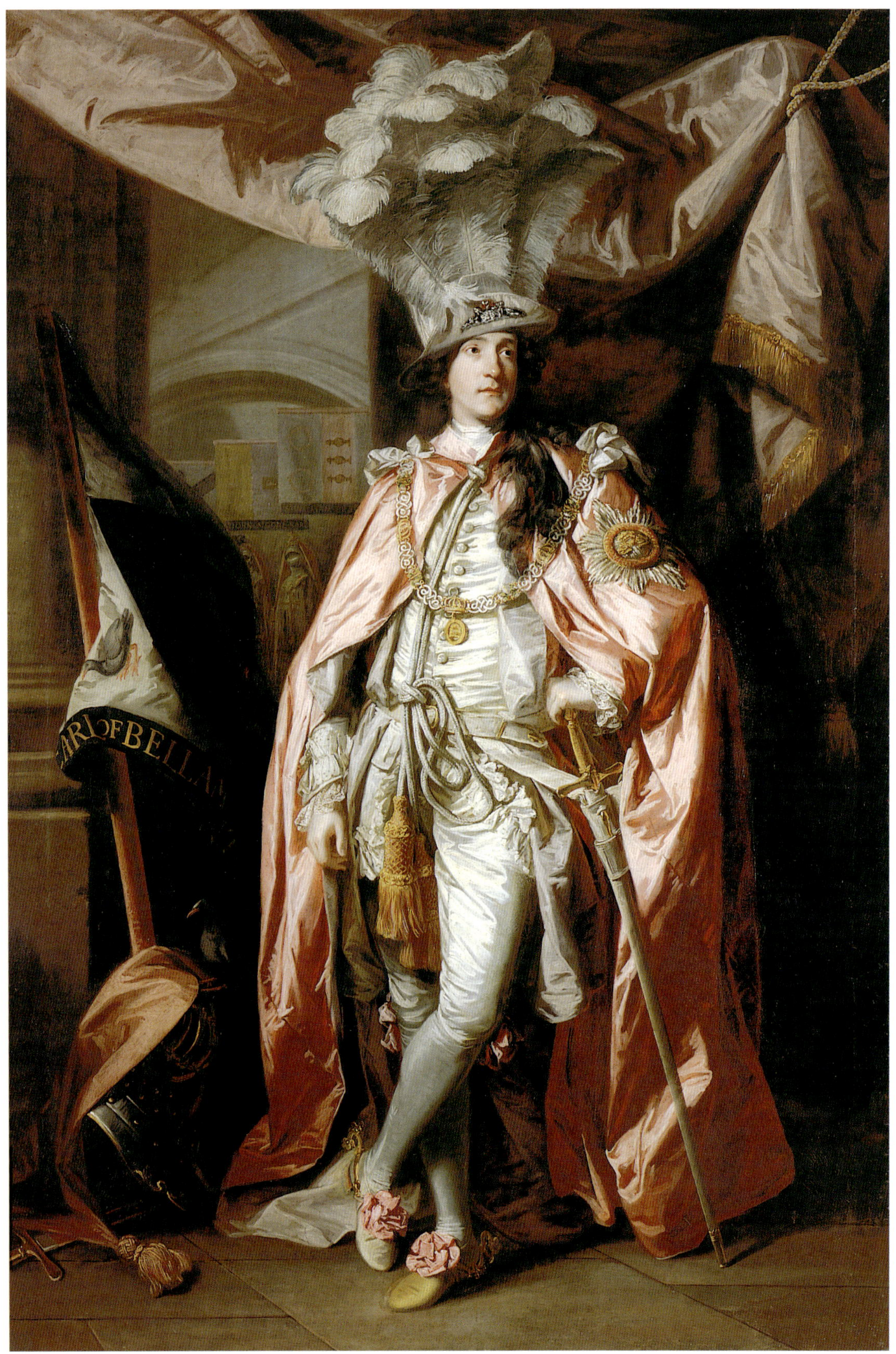

73
Joshua Reynolds
(1723–1792)
Charles Coote, 1st Earl of Bellamont, 1773
Oil on canvas, 241 × 161 cm
The National Gallery of Ireland, Dublin

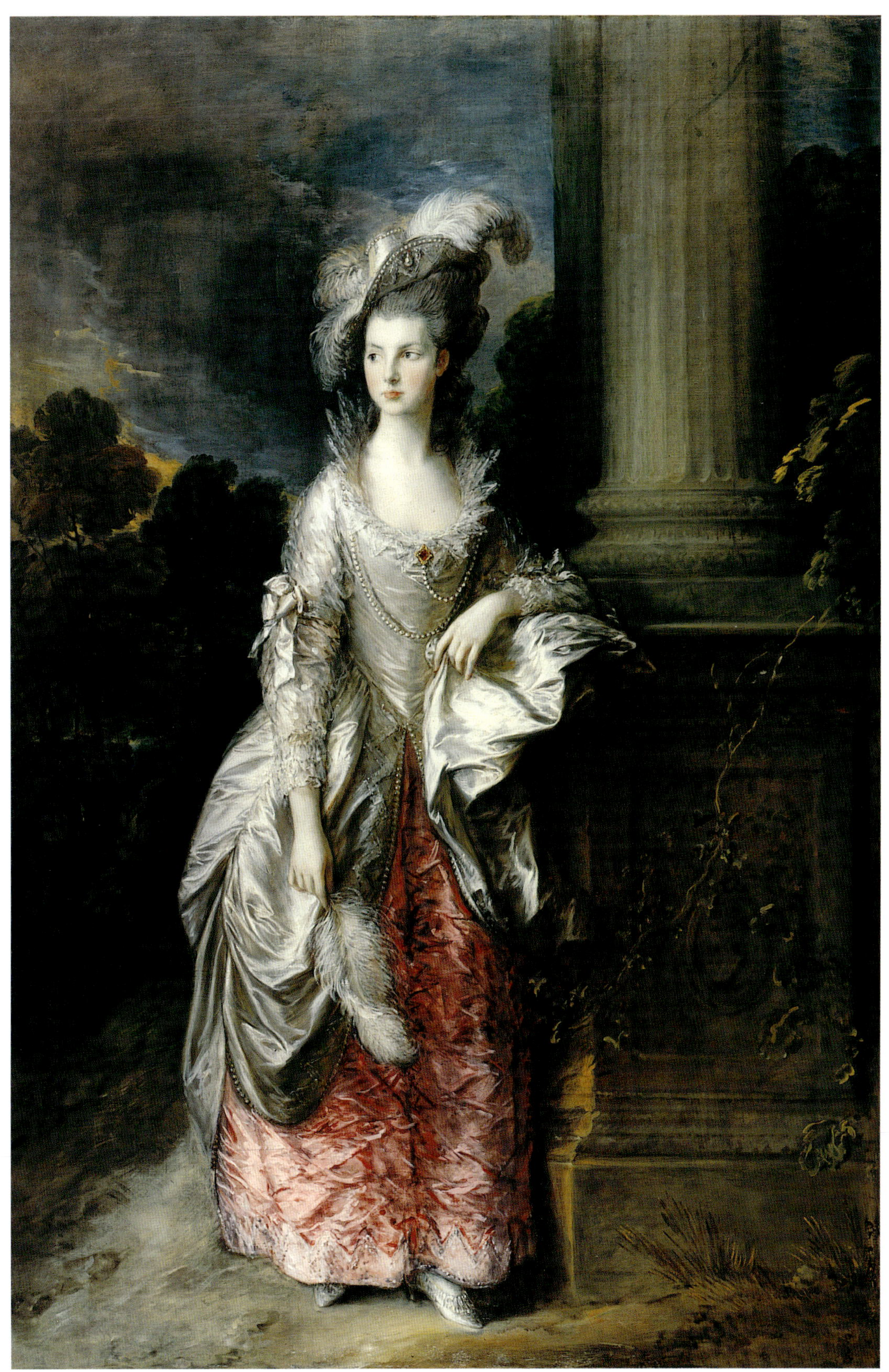

74
Thomas Gainsborough
(1727–1788)
The Honorable Mrs Thomas Graham, 1777
Oil on canvas, 237.5 × 154.3 cm
The National Gallery of Scotland, Edinburgh

costume ball, or an elegantly modernised version of quasi-classical or quasi-oriental garb. Not all such clothes were faithful renderings from life, but many were, and some are documented as having been worn both for the portrait and for the ball. An artist who painted a sitter posing as a legendary person might on the other hand himself supply the appropriate gear, perhaps imitating an earlier master's way with it; but he would certainly oblige a lady hoping to be immortalised in a fantasy costume made at great cost, perhaps for one festive event.

Fancy-dress balls had always been a feature of court and society life, but they had become much more frequent in the eighteenth century. In France, dresses in the *style Henri Quatre*, with the standing collars, looped pearls, full slashed sleeves and looped-up overskirts worn at the very end of the sixteenth century, appeared at fancy-dress court balls in the 1770s and 1780s; and at the same period in England, dresses adapted from Rubens and Van Dyck portraits were extremely fashionable for similar fancy-dress appearances, many of them immortalised in portraits.

Such a dress seems to be recorded in Thomas Gainsborough's exquisite 1777 portrayal of a 'Vandyke' or 'Rubens's Wife' costume on Mrs Graham (fig. 74). This lady's up-to-the-minute corseting and coiffure have been set off by equally modish versions of early seventeenth-century motifs: the string of pearls looped exactly like those in Rubens portraits, along with a Rubensian divide between upper and lower sleeve, here accommodated to modern narrowness; a pearl-edged, divided overskirt, here looped up to form a 1770s *polonaise* on one side and a Van Dyck-like puff of Baroque attendant drapery on the other, exposing a stiff Elizabethan petticoat overwrought with a puffed and jewelled pattern. Mrs Graham's standing collar of lacy spikes, on the other hand, is an example of late eighteenth-century fantasy about days of yore. This detachable artistic motif is found ornamenting pictorial dresses of all sorts in Tiepolo, William Blake and Caspar David Friedrich among others, besides adorning imperial finery at Napoleon's court; but not in the real sixteenth and seventeenth centuries. The hat comes from Rubens, too, now crowning the upswept powdered tower required of elegance in 1777.

Portrait painters had always obliged a sitter who wanted to record the formal signs of his rank. Clearly such a one was Charles Coote, 1st Earl of Bellamont, as painted by Joshua Reynolds in 1773 (fig. 73). This image of the sitter in the robes of a Knight of Bath has an instant theatrical authority, imposed by the lateral swing of the stage drape, visibly held up by stage rope, which forms a background for the earl's immense headpiece – a metre-high array of plumes worthy of Louis XIV playing the Sun King. This hat and its dozen upright feathers is not on the floor or a nearby table, where the overbearing crown or heavy helmet usually sit in ceremonial royal and noble portraits. It rises straight up from the sitter's head as if he were indeed the god or hero in a masque.

His hero's armour is on the floor instead, backed up by a large banner bearing his title in gold letters. Over his shoulders flows the order's double-layered, rose-pink cloak, mantling his figure down to the floor near the armour and the banner. Balancing the upward thrust of the feathers on his head, the thick silken ropes holding the cloak at his neck fall to the waist to form an enormous loosely hanging, double-looped knot, from which two bulbous gold tassels dangle down between his thighs.

Magnificence is at a peak in this portrait, where Reynolds has employed the devices of French artists such as Rigaud, who were recording its glories earlier in the century for Louis XIV and Louis XV, and blended them with Van Dyck's inventions early in the previous one. Cloak, curtain and banner billow pictorially around the young earl, whose dark hair flows forwards over one shoulder in another suggestion both of the Sun King's curls and of the hanging locks on Van Dyck's dandies. The earl's silk suit, however, with its knee-level garter-bows, shoe roses and complete system of bodily wrinkles, is very like the one worn by the comedian in the Watteau painting we saw earlier – its ceremonial, pageant-like function can't help giving it stage associations, emphasised in this painting. Only the earl's Greek-statue pose, often used in England at this period, strikes a modern Neoclassical note.

The overall tone is one of perfect conviction about rendering noble splendour as a theatrical artefact, largely made out of the painterly draping of rich fabric in stagy ways; but such convictions began to subside along with the century. Johann Zoffany's fancy-dress portrait of Mrs Woodhull from about 1770 (fig. 75) might be thought of as a hybrid image. It combines old-fashioned Rococo-like effects with the avant-garde Neoclassic draperies that appeared on many female sitters painted between the 1760s and 1780s by Reynolds, on which those in this Zoffany are clearly based.

Reynolds had invented a quasi-classical style of dress for female portraits far in advance of the Neoclassical fashions in vogue at the century's end, although elements in them were not unlike earlier eighteenth-century versions such as we saw created by Nattier in France. The difference was mainly in the character of the draped cloth, and what that was meant to convey. Reynolds was devoted to what was called the Grand Manner, epitomised by both Raphael and Michelangelo, wherein the sheen and texture of pictorial stuff was purposely subordinated to the dignifying effect of its noble folds. We can see Reynolds already using the idea of classical dignity by 1759–60, for a portrait of Lady Frances Warren, although he is still allowing this sitter some shine for her mantle and an opulent ermine lining (fig. 76). But the folds of the pictorial dress don't shine, and the pose is recognisably classical, even while the dress also maintains a correct Titianesque look of being draped over a large-sleeved white chemise; and her hair is modern. One needs, the painter said, to 'add some modern details, for the likeness', and the modern details were usually in the coiffure.

Zoffany had long specialised in transcribing the details of actual elegance, composing groups of well-dressed figures in which he included every ruffle, button and furbelow and applied no mythological or art-historical rhetoric to their presentation. His work of this kind was very successful, and indeed portraits in ordinary clothing went on being as common as ever for both sexes, always showing a marked difference from the theatrical ones in fantasy garb, except that hair styles, as usual, tended to be the same. Unlike Zoffany's usual clients, Mrs Woodhull here appears as Flora, like many sitters ever since Titian's original nameless model. This time she has stage roses in a basket, pearls in her hair and draped muslin at the bosom, and, like Lady Warren, a one-piece dress with a loose sash and mantle. Also like Lady Warren, she leans on a pedestal out of doors with her feet crossed, and her hair is unpowdered. But, unlike Lady Warren in 1760, Mrs Woodhull in 1770 still seems a Rococo image more akin to Nattier's from 1749 (see fig. 67), because her pose is self-conscious and stiff rather than naturally classical, and so are the too-crisp folds of her dress and wrap. We can see her legs through the skirt, but they haven't the easy sweep Reynolds has given Lady Warren's, and Mrs Woodhull's whole body hasn't the same conviction – she seems uncomfortable without her hoops and stays. Zoffany's

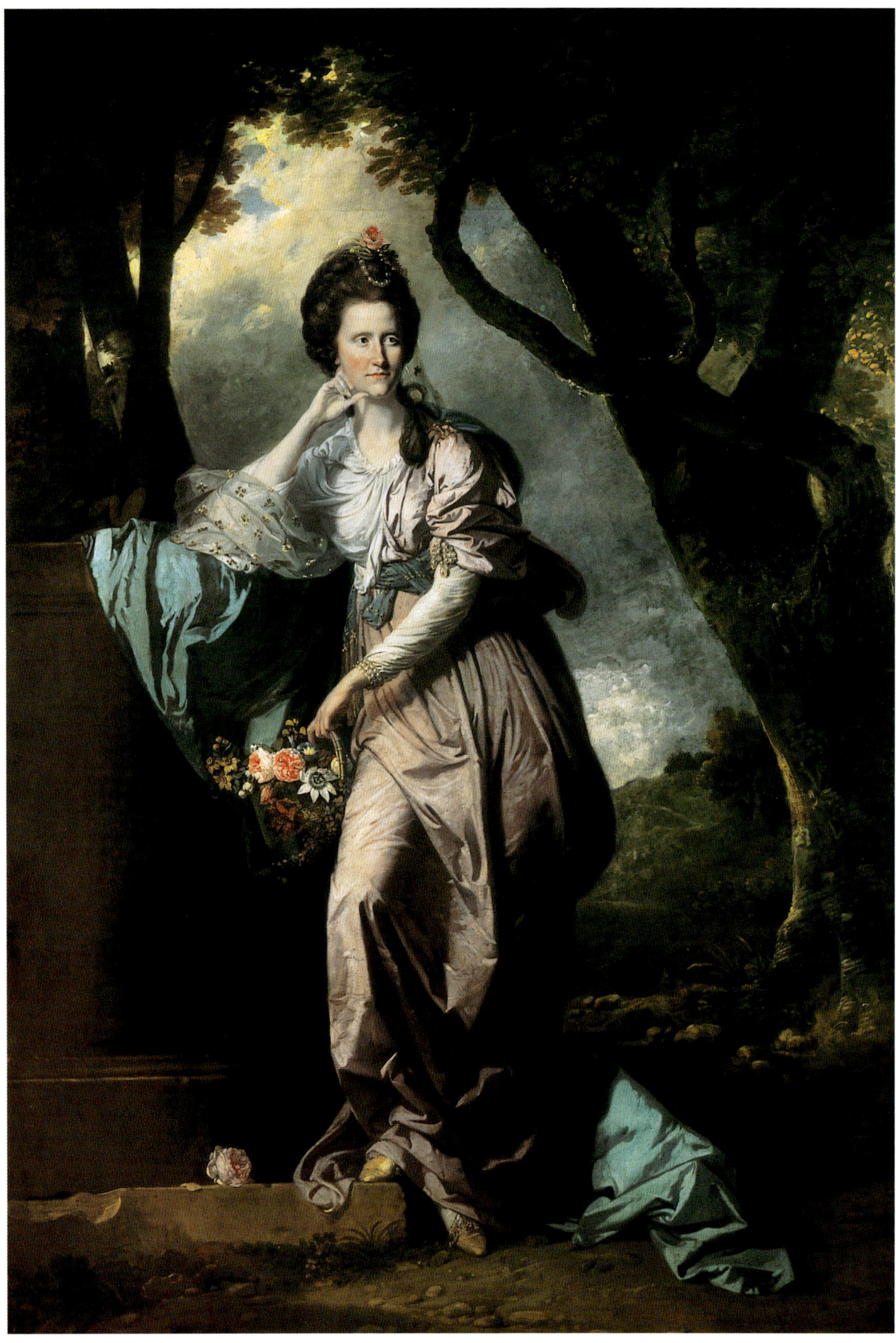

OPPOSITE **75**
Johann Zoffany (1733–1810)
Mrs Michael Woodhull, about 1770
Oil on canvas, 243.8 × 165.1 cm
Tate, London

painting, based though it may be on Reynolds's advanced idea about the natural dignity of classical drapery, nevertheless seems to look back, while Reynolds's earlier one already looks ahead to the end of the century. Reynolds, however, like Gainsborough throughout his own career, also made fashionable portraits with neither classical allusions nor Van Dyck-like accoutrements, and quite as precisely as Zoffany.

The theme of high artifice, so difficult for painstaking and literal-minded Zoffany, for whom the real poetry always lay in the regularity of the taffeta frills, was fundamental to Reynolds. He could move as smoothly as a theatre designer among the art-historical centuries, sometimes seeking the Titianesque sources for Van Dyck's mythological portraits, so as to evoke the self-conscious magnificence of the European past, as with Lord Bellamont; more often trying to find a new way to revive again for portraits the abundant draperies of remote antiquity as Renaissance painters had conveyed them, with a look of timeless nobility. Now and then he copied the subdued dramatic lighting of Rembrandt for a portrait or self-portrait; but quite often he concentrated on the fashionable charm of his own time, perhaps to show the sharp elegance of a black gauze scarf over the shoulders of a white silk dress with many flounces on the sleeves.

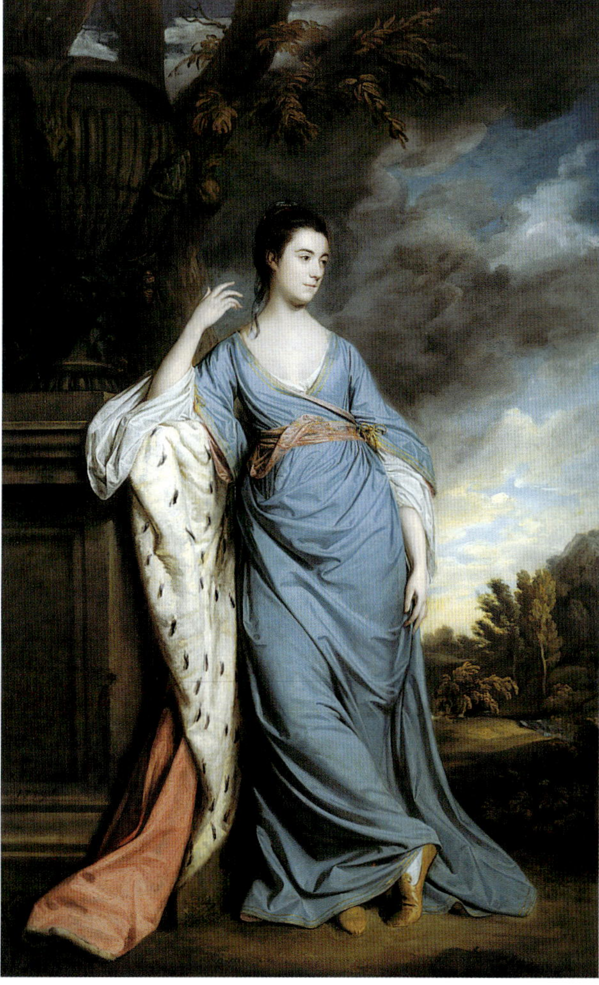

76
Joshua Reynolds (1723–1792)
Lady Frances Warren, 1759–60
Oil on canvas, 238.1 × 148.8 cm
Kimbell Art Museum,
Fort Worth

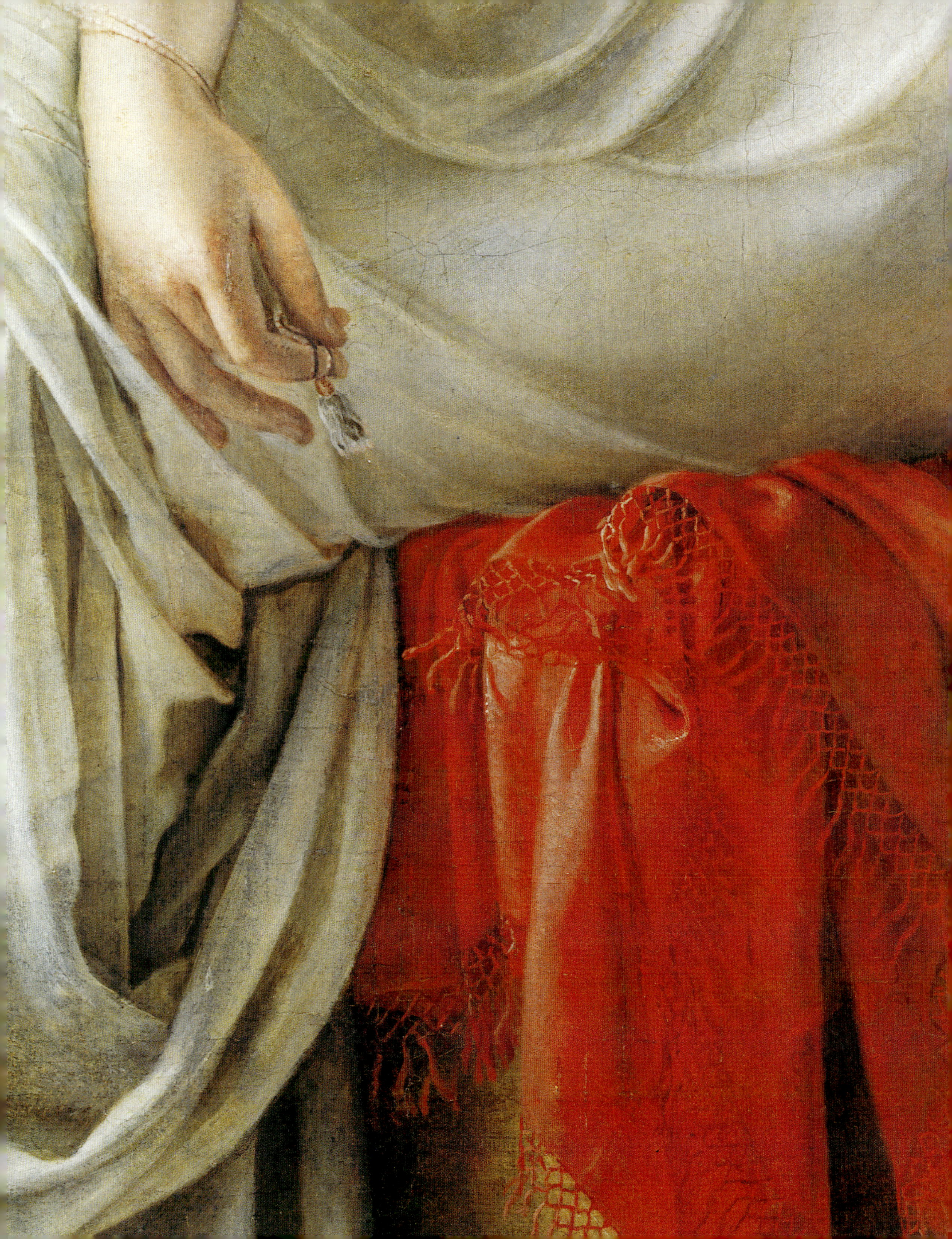

v Romantic Simplicity: Women

The neoclassical movement in European visual art and taste had already begun during the third quarter of the eighteenth century, partly in response to the works of Greco-Roman art being unearthed since 1738 at Pompeii and Herculaneum, of which the engraved images reached a wide public. It has also been attributed to the broad influence of J. J. Winckelmann, the German art historian, whose explanations of the superiority of ancient Greek art began to be published in 1755. A quest was under way to reclaim the classical heritage on what were now seen to be its own terms. Greek art was thought to reveal the clear beauty of natural truth behind the confusing disorder of the world, a truth not just optical but moral. It soon became necessary to look on both familiar and unfamiliar antiquities with enlightened eyes, to see them as mirrors of universal freedom and uncorrupted thought, as well as of unaffected natural form. Ancient sculptures were once again, as they had been in the early fourteenth century, prized for showing modern painters the right way to be faithful to nature, and no longer for inspiring the lengthy tradition of extreme painterly display promoted by their High Renaissance and later Baroque interpreters.

By 1800, modern taste was everywhere rejecting the Renaissance classical tradition, which was seen to have sacrificed fidelity to nature to the expression of worldly grandeur, in a highly theatrical vein. Modern portrait painters were finding new methods for suggesting lack of pretension instead of social importance, and using a clarified figure style representing a closer approximation to the noble works of antiquity. A new respect for clear line, matt colour and stable form replaced the old admiration for flecks of light enhancing rich tints blended into mobile shapes, with hazy edges and vague functions.

This nostalgic impulse to recover ancient simplicity and virtue was part of an incipient Romanticism, not only a yearning for vanished perfections, including a vanished apprehension of nature, but a reverence for individual experience and personal feeling. Such piety and yearning went well with a longing for political and personal freedom, and it could be further expressed in the desire to liberate the individual body in simplified, free-seeming, egalitarian-looking garments. Fashion, in fact, being a safely wordless

Detail of fig. 80

medium, often publicly expresses collective desires in advance of the articulate public statements and risky public actions that trigger change in society. We will see how the Romantic–Neoclassic impulse affected the representations of men and women differently in paintings, besides affecting their actual clothing.

A great difference between masculine and feminine clothing began to appear during the second half of the eighteenth century. Female figures, whether in history paintings, religious works, illustrations for books, fashion plates or painted portraits all came to share a similar classical look. It's moreover very noticeable that, unless it was a man's cloak rendered as a toga in a work of sculpture, quasi-classical costumes created for portraits now appeared only on ladies – and sometimes on children – but never on gentlemen, just at a time when fashion for ladies was itself becoming quasi-classical, and fashion for gentlemen emphatically was not. To account for this, we have to look at the directions fashion had taken since the late sixteenth century.

In the first half of the seventeenth century, male costume became quite loose and mobile and was worn with long hair and huge hats as well as big wrapped cloaks, such as we saw in Van Dyck (see fig. 39). Just as armour itself had became both vestigial and ceremonial, the look of armour in men's clothes was gradually dissolving. By the late seventeenth century it had entirely given way to the ensemble of coat, waistcoat and breeches with stockings that would persist throughout the eighteenth, along with long curled wigs instead of long hair. Buttons, a masculine privilege, except for women's riding habits, were a distinctive feature of the clad male body, on coat fronts, sleeves, pockets, waistcoats and breeches.

This evolving male costume nevertheless remained based on the idea of a complete envelope for all parts of the male body, with no exposure of skin except face and hands; and after its brief period of swashbuckling fullness in the early seventeenth century, it forever lost all the drape and fluidity of ancient dress. But during the second half of the eighteenth century, while men's garments were becoming more and more refined and tightened in shape, women's were being expanded and loosened. Feminine skirts were very soft and voluminous, hair was higher, fluffier and increasingly wide, and large hats were worn on top of it. Men were now carrying their much smaller ones, and their wigs were smaller, too.

We can see from Gainsborough's double portrait of about 1785 (fig. 77) that women at this period took up more space than men, and seemed taller; and here the lady's fluffy white skirt is further enlarged by visual assimilation to the fluffy white dog. Men's coats had tight sleeves, small coat-skirts and no cuffs, waistcoats and breeches were fitted closely to the body, wigs were short and neat. For European men, modern dress in life could no longer pose as antique dress in art, as it had done in Van Dyck's day, when an abundantly draped shirt and cloak could clothe a noble sitter's upper body. Now cloaks were gone; shirts, in life as in portraits, were hidden, and only little frills at neck and wrist might show; the public look was to be firmly covered, with high arm-holes and narrow shoulders.

Women, however, were still wearing some version of chemise, kirtle and gown, although the last two had eventually merged into what would become the dress, after the progressive stiffening of the female bodice during the sixteenth century, in apparent imitation of the armour-like male doublet. By the middle of the seventeenth century, elegant female costume consisted of chemise, gown – with a low-necked laced-up

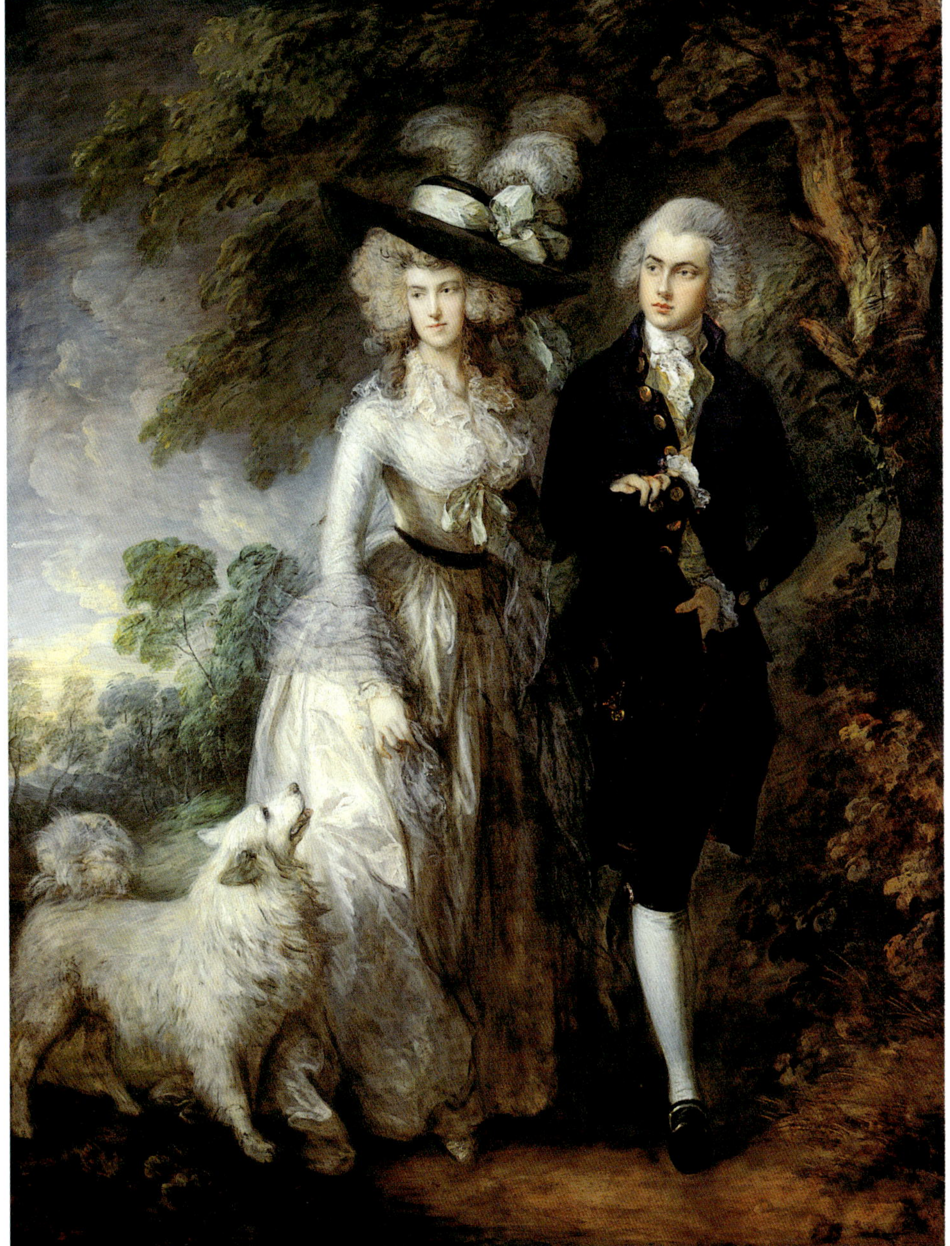

77
Thomas Gainsborough
(1727–1788)
Mr and Mrs William Hallett
('*The Morning Walk*'), about 1785
Oil on canvas, 236.2 × 179.1 cm
National Gallery, London
NG 6209

bodice, stiffened with stays and attached to a long, capacious skirt – and petticoat. This was a shoe-length skirt that usually showed under the parted or looped-up skirt of the gown, although some gowns had skirts that hid it. Sleeves, once long, thick and separate, like those of men's doublets, were now softer and sewn in, like theirs, and might daringly expose the forearm.

Mutable fashions in the shape of the female torso made it expedient that stays should be sewn into a separate, tailored undergarment that could be modified according to changes in the mode, and that dresses should be made to fit the woman's figure as she wore it. And so the corset, after appearing once or twice before, was seriously refined in the late seventeenth century, to shape the chic female mid-section for the next two hundred years and more. It became a staple of female dress, rarely absent under public and festal attire in all classes; and it was usually complemented by some sort of extension of the skirt. Meanwhile the loose, full and low-necked chemise under everything was constant for all women, having changed little for a millennium and a half, the one truly intimate feminine garment and an authentic survival from late antiquity.

Women could always leave off extended petticoats and stiffly shaped corsets so that gowns and chemises both might flow; and then the looseness of antiquity – or, upon occasion, of the Orient, which offered an alternative kind of at-home or fancy-dress wear in the seventeenth and eighteenth centuries – could easily be approximated. Stays might even be left on under the flowing gowns; the customary foundation both looked and felt more natural. Several informal modes of this sort were in vogue during the period before the general Neoclassical reduction in scope occurred at the end of the eighteenth century. Then gowns themselves seemed to be left in the wardrobe, and chemises were worn in public, not just in bed.

The point in all this is that whereas tailored garments had closely covered men's bodies since the fourteenth century, women since then had continued to wear arrangements of long, flowing ones, with various kinds of open neckline. Their mantles and cloaks continued to drape as always, after men had given up theirs, and so did their scarves and veils. Even with stays and full skirts, their shoulders, necks and chests had been exposed, and the loose chemise was always there, often showing its upper edge. Women were always just a step away from antique effects, which could be manipulated by a portrait painter to look even more so; but modern male dress had become very confining and very much non-draped, as non-adaptable to the classical visual idea as women's dress was adaptable.

In elegant portraiture between about 1790 and 1815, women's clothing – even draped clothing invented for portraits – gradually lost all its earlier festive excitement and took on an uneventful simplicity and pallor. Strictly Neoclassic dresses were being made to suggest the thin, narrow-girdled and pinned-together garments found on Greek and Roman statues, now rendered colourless by time, most of which offered vivid information about the nudity underneath. The lately discovered Pompeian frescoes showed how colourful the ancient dresses often were; but for many modern portraits the dress had to be entirely white and the fabric had to fall closely around the whole figure from shoulder to hem. Narrow girdles might certainly be worn, but only very high under the bosom, so as to seem quite unlike the conventional stays that had gripped the ribs and waist.

Unlike the ancient ones, actual Neoclassic dresses could not allow the details of the body to show through, except for an emphatic swell of the breasts (always acceptable) and maybe the thrust of a knee (potentially daring). Certain ladies provoked scandal when they imitated the statues more exactly and wore next to nothing, and many contemporary cartoons show the dirty-minded view of the new mode; but decorum usually prevailed for portraits. We can see in examples from different countries how general was the impulse towards simple-seeming white dresses, and how difficult was the problem of reconciling the effects achieved in antique works of art with flesh-and-blood modern bodies accustomed to modern dress and behaviour. Portrait painters might allow their aesthetic devotion to the classical ideal to gloss over difficulties and harmonise everything in the name of the true art that seeks an ideal nature to copy.

Agustín Esteve's portrait of Doña Joaquina Tellez-Giron (fig. 78) shows how Neoclassical drapery was usually a new form of the ancient chemise, a plain smock of white muslin gathered into a low neckline. Here we see its thick folds pulled in tightly just under the breasts with a narrow belt, from which it flows straight down to the floor in front and ends in a small train behind. Much of the fullness is gathered up between the shoulder-blades at the back, so that the folds fall amply enough behind to mask the buttocks and prevent the train's drag from tightening the stuff against the front of the body as the wearer walks. Completely bare arms are unseemly, so plain tight sleeves cover the upper arms, replacing the voluminous long ones of the old-fashioned smock. Light shines on the face, bosom and free-falling skirt, while the draped green stuff in the background remains shadowy.

The suggestion is made that the young lady is just as free as an antique maiden – although her body is well shielded – because her waistline and ribcage are not defined

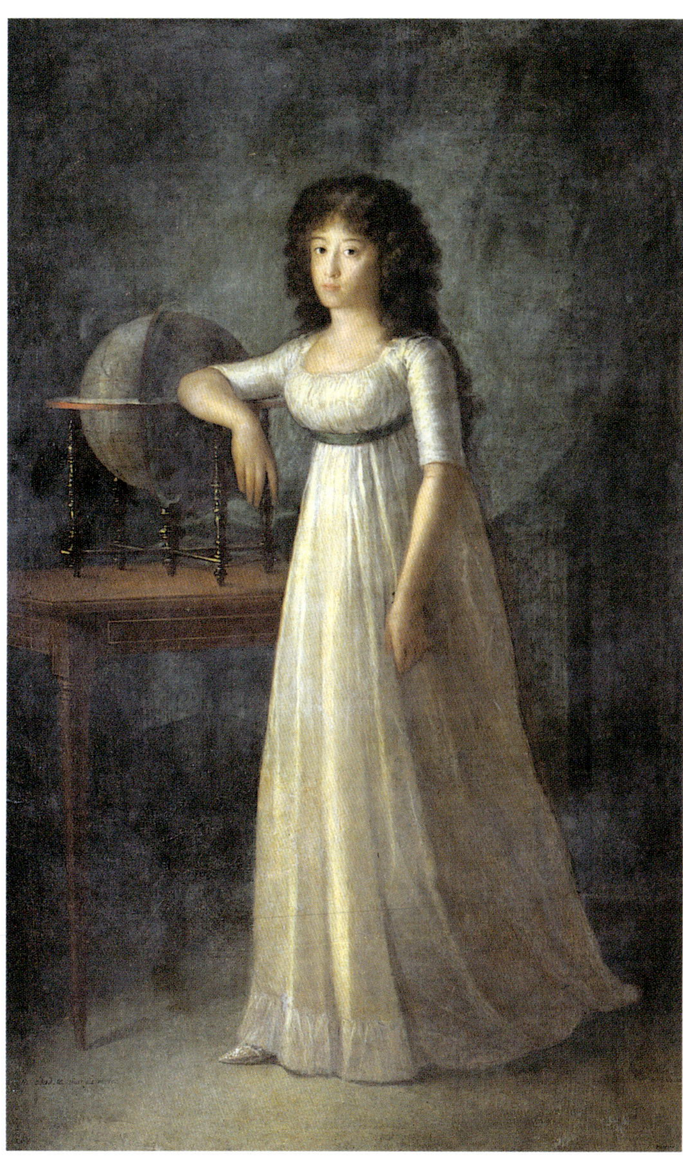

78
Agustín Esteve y Marques (1753–1820)
Doña Joaquina Tellez-Giron,
1798 (before restoration)
Oil on canvas,
190 × 116 cm
Museo Nacional del Prado, Madrid

by stays, her dress is really underwear now freely on view, and its sleeves are very scanty. With her head enlarged by tumbling curls, her ensemble here evokes the freedom of childhood, despite her full figure. One discreet frill thickens the skirt's lower edge, to make it flare and not cling, so that the tip of a shoe must push out to show.

Such dresses look artless in pictures, but the fit and fall were carefully managed. An unseen slip underneath would keep the details of the torso and the motions of the legs invisible, while an idea of natural freedom was conveyed by pronounced breasts, which might be pushed up and separated by newly designed stays that had a short, brassière-like top, and might sometimes – especially in England – have a nearly cylindrical form below that reached down over the hips. The lack of rigid hairdressing, strong colours, accessories or ornaments keeps this young lady's image candid and simple. She is a Spanish duke's daughter: her one prop is the globe on the frame of which she casually leans, as if scorning to be worldly.

A Scottish duke's daughter is portrayed in a much more fanciful manner in J. H. W. von Tischbein's 1789–90 portrait of Lady Charlotte Campbell (fig. 79), who was about fifteen at the time. She, too, is meant to suggest antiquity as well as candour and simplicity; but the painting still has the look of deliberate artifice left over from the previous generation. Tischbein had seen the girl earlier, and said that her fleet movements had reminded him of the dancing girls in the paintings from Herculaneum. For her portrait, however, the

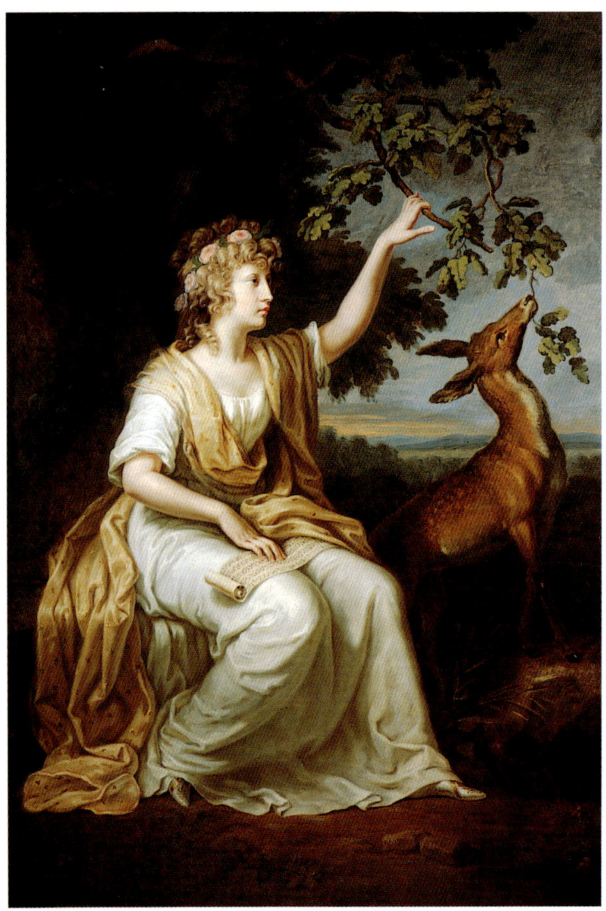

79
Johann Heinrich Wilhelm von Tischbein (1751–1829)
Lady Charlotte Campbell, 1789–90
Oil on canvas, 197.2 × 134 cm
Scottish National Portrait Gallery, Edinburgh

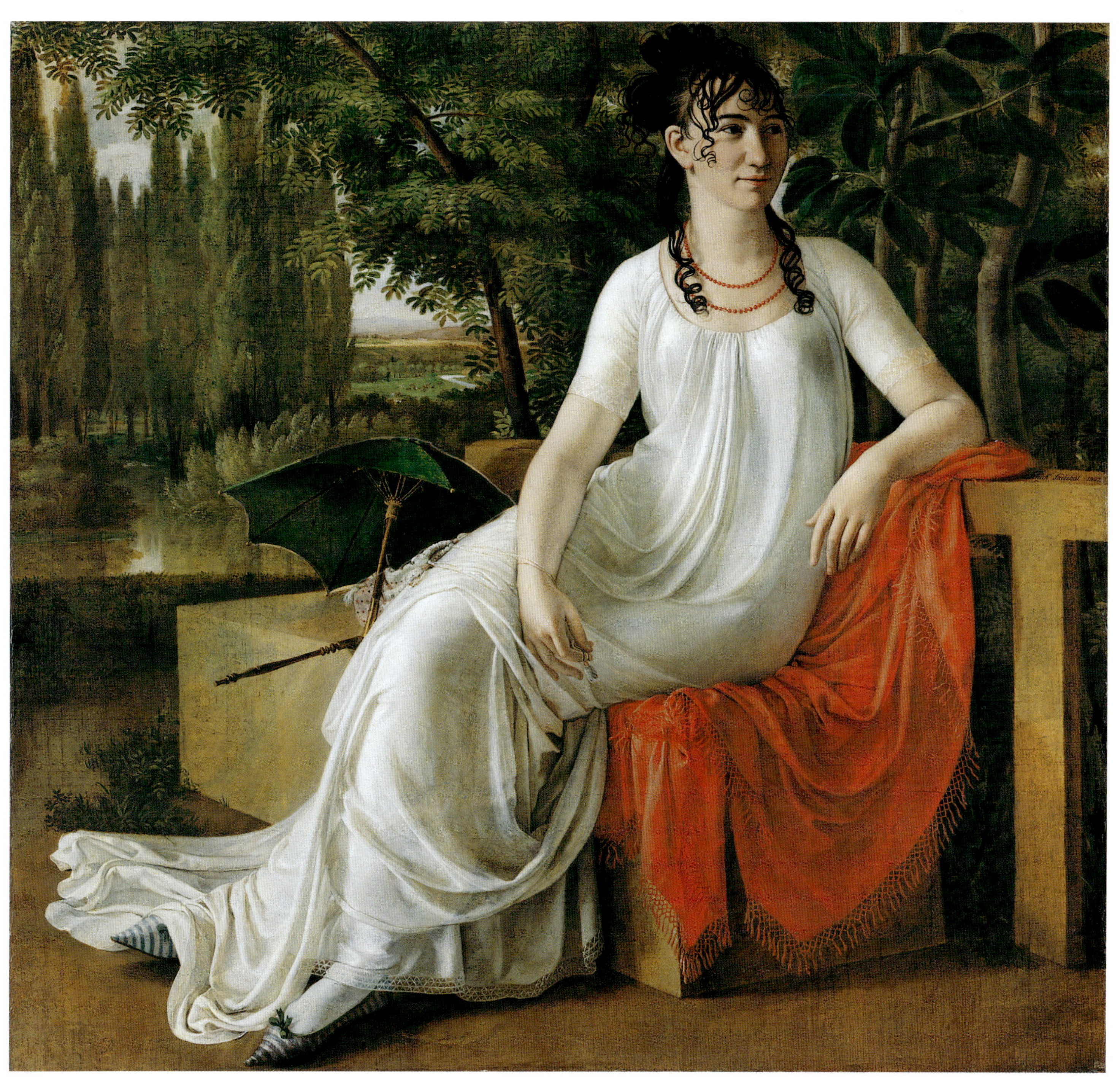

80
Gottlieb Schick (1776–1812)
Frau Wilhelmine von Cotta, 1802
Oil on canvas, 133 × 140.5 cm
Staatsgalerie Stuttgart

painter resorted to an earlier version of the traditional full chemise, with long, rolled-up sleeves and a very long, full scarf wrapped around it, so that the busy folds of shift and scarf serve to distract the eye from her figure rather than to display it, and to quell any sense of its movement or pliancy. Her rose-crowned hair is unclassically full and curly, like Doña Joaquina's; but like Mrs Woodhull twenty years earlier (fig. 75), she is still only a theoretically classical image, a modern *tableau vivant* with no formal resemblance to antique images. She also holds Rococo-like stage properties, a roll of music and a flowering branch for her posed fawn to nibble at.

Gottlieb Schick's 1802 portrait of Frau von Cotta (fig. 80), on the other hand, is a serious effort at suggesting actual classical form; and modern fashion has advanced quite a bit further to support the attempt. This sitter's looks are far more classical than either Lady Charlotte's or Doña Joaquina's; but where they had no frivolous adornments, we can see that Frau von Cotta's red mantle has a fringe, her neck is adorned with beads, her sleeves and hem are edged with lace, she even wears striped shoes with bows and holds a handbag. Her open parasol sits nearby, green enough to resemble a tree. Her setting is uninhabited nature, but she is plainly very worldly, with an amused and sociable air. Schick's Neoclassical convictions have nevertheless made him dignify this woman's image with great success. Her ungirded dress is unevenly gathered on a drawstring, not fixed on a band, and the fullness concentrates between her modest breasts, to emphasise them without showing them. Her seated posture lets the painter compose the front folds into a symphony of graceful arcs that drape her torso, suggesting all her intimate charms without revealing any of them.

Her lack of stays is apparent, but Frau von Cotta follows another modern European mode in wearing a visibly double dress, here a sleeveless, draped and trained one over a shoe-length and short-sleeved one, both close to the body and not very full, to suggest that neither is an undergarment. She seems more nude; and if she were to stand up and walk, her body would show its fine shape but none of its details. Her sympathetic painter has allowed her draped white pose and her hair's dark tracery to dominate the painting, using them to conjure the ancient world and allure us into seeing the modern red beads, fringed shawl and lace edgings as ancient details. He can easily blend the modern parasol and reticule – the latter almost out of sight, her hand virtually empty – into the scheme, because all its clear lines and flat tints lend this vision the dispassionate harmony of a Pompeian fresco.

Things were done differently in France, with an avowed erotic cast. The spirit of French Neoclassicism was fervent, personal and disturbing, as in Jacques-Louis David's celebrated dramatic 1789 rendering of Brutus receiving the bodies of his sons, whose execution for treason he had himself ordered (fig. 81). Its Neoclassicism is insistent, from the shallow, frieze-like composition to the regular festooning of the household curtains, from the design of the chairs to the emotions expressed by the personnel. These are emphasised by the spotlight on Brutus' agonised feet at the left, echoing that on the dead feet of the corpse borne in behind him, and the stronger spotlight on the cluster of stricken females at the right. David shows feminine despair further promoted by agitated draperies that slide caressingly and cling alluringly and turn quite transparent with grief, falling off shoulders, catching between legs and under buttocks, exposing armpits, trammelling up ankles, slithering among the women's limbs in attractive

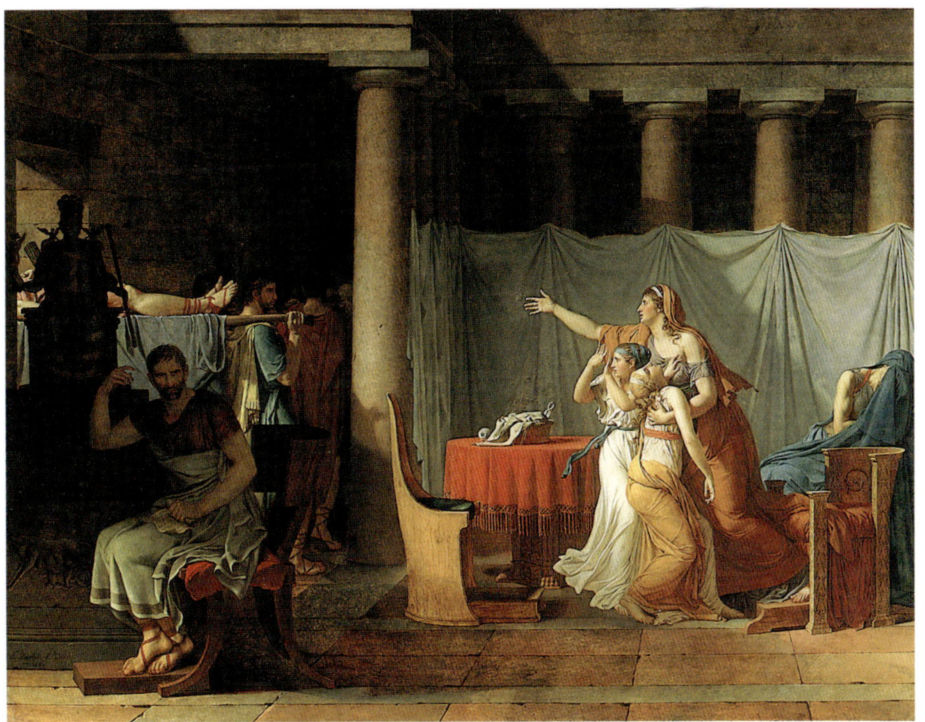

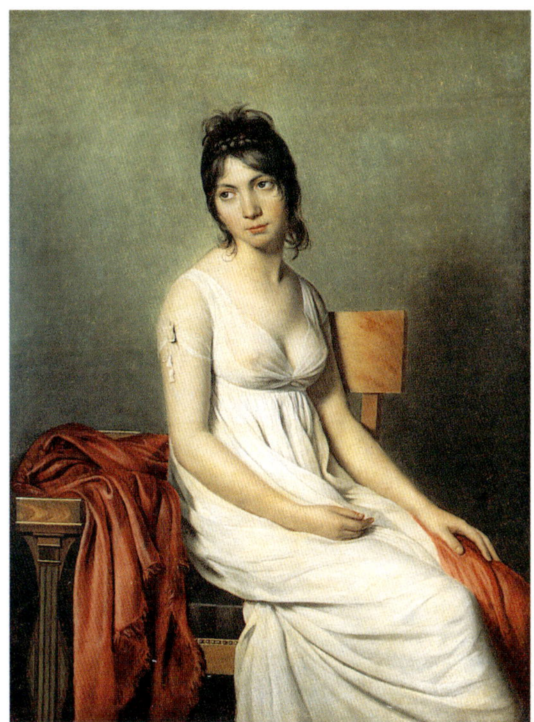

convolutions of woe. Brutus' own expressive antique garb, we may note, wraps his misery firmly and is largely left in the shade with his grim face.

During the ensuing decade, David and other French portrait painters dressed some female sitters in carefully classical trappings resembling those on Brutus' family, including slither, transparency, soft sashes and absence of sleeves; but one portrait from about 1800, attributed to David, shows what an elegant Frenchwoman might really wear in fashionable response to his historical Brutus, not by copying the Roman dresses exactly but by suggesting their sexy emotional effect (fig. 82). The lady's chair echoes Brutus' own, but her clothing only hints at the fluidity of those women's draperies; her dress is a fine study in antique modification, at once stable and highly provocative. It is neither so candidly untrammelled as Frau von Cotta's draped ensemble nor so modestly thick as Doña Joaquina's chemise with its invisible slip, but much more artfully artless.

A symmetrically draped transparent bodice displays her nipples and the upper half of her breasts while holding them up underneath with stout tailoring aided by shoulder straps. To avoid utter sleevelessness, thin stuff veils her shoulders in little drapes caught up with tassels, recalling the drape fallen off Brutus' wife's shoulder. The rest of the dress is opaque and full below its high, narrow belt, quite worthy of Doña Joaquina, although this French portrait is intended to be seductive, as the Spanish one is not. Both ladies, differently conceived and disposed as their images are, have modishly untidy hair and no accessories or jewellery; and, like Frau von Cotta and like Mme Recamier in her celebrated portrait by David, they do nothing with their empty hands.

This hand motif in Neoclassic female portraiture is startling and fairly consistent. It seems to make a deliberate break with past portrait conventions, in which feminine hands – we saw them above on Tischbein's Lady Charlotte – were seldom shown to lie

ABOVE LEFT **81**
Jacques-Louis David (1748–1825)
Brutus and the Bodies of his Sons, 1789
Oil on canvas, 323 × 422 cm
Musée du Louvre, Paris

ABOVE RIGHT **82**
Circle of **Jacques-Louis David** (1748–1825)
Portrait of a Young Woman in White, about 1798
Oil on canvas, 125.5 × 95 cm
National Gallery of Art, Washington, Chester Dale Collection

open, limp and unoccupied, but were given very specific places to rest or things to hold or handle. It's the openness that is striking; earlier subjects might lay one palm against the bosom, or across the belt, or let one palm spread against the spread of the skirt, or ladies would be shown to touch or finger something, unless their hands were actually sewing, reading, putting on gloves, holding a fan or handkerchief, or actively touching the face or costume. In the Neoclassic context, these empty hands seem to be deliberately candid and artless, perhaps related to the look of those female hands in classical sculpture that lie or fall open. The background for this French lady, as for Mme Recamier, is flat and smooth, as if it were indeed the marble wall of an ancient building, and she a work of sculpture, even though her red scarf does have a bit of fringe.

Jean-Auguste-Dominique Ingres, David's most celebrated pupil, interpreted the prevailing style in around 1800 with great intensity, seeming to follow a private Bronzino-like pleasure in serpentine line and glazed shape; but he also used more suitably classic Renaissance sources. His 1805 portrait of Mme Rivière (fig. 83) shows an affinity with Raphael's perfectly composed Madonnas, as well as with his great female portrait, the so-called *Donna velata*. Ingres uses several textures of white fabric and white skin, and many curvilinear drapery episodes in the sitter's costume, along with a constant interplay of gold and tinted ornament among them all, backing up the whole ensemble with lush blue velvet folds that look as natural as the sky. Mme Rivière's background is dramatically dark, the better to emphasise the transparency of her veil; her hands lie against folds.

This is a very rich and sensuous Neoclassicism, with no loss of clarity, decorum and simplicity in the painted image. Like Raphael, Ingres has imposed classical principles on an entirely fashionable costume, without substituting fake-antique elements or flavours.

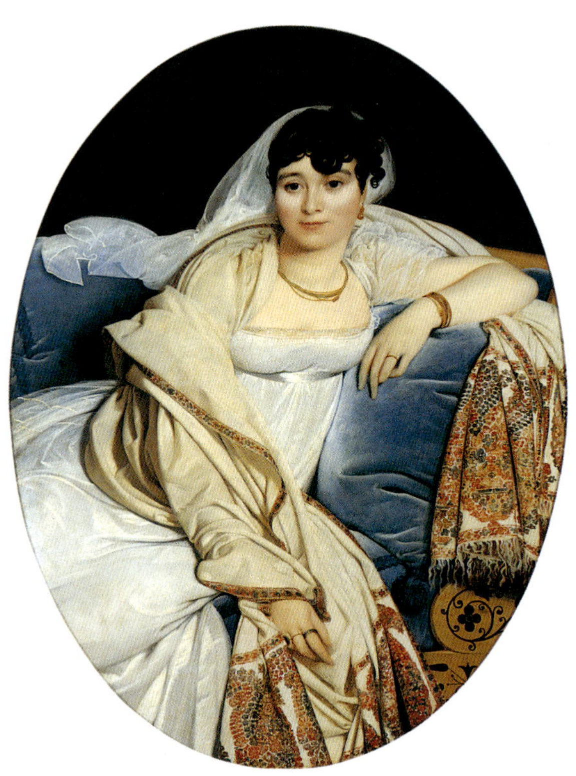

83
Jean-Auguste-Dominique Ingres (1780–1867)
Mme Philibert Rivière, 1805
Oil on canvas, 116 × 90 cm
Musée du Louvre, Paris

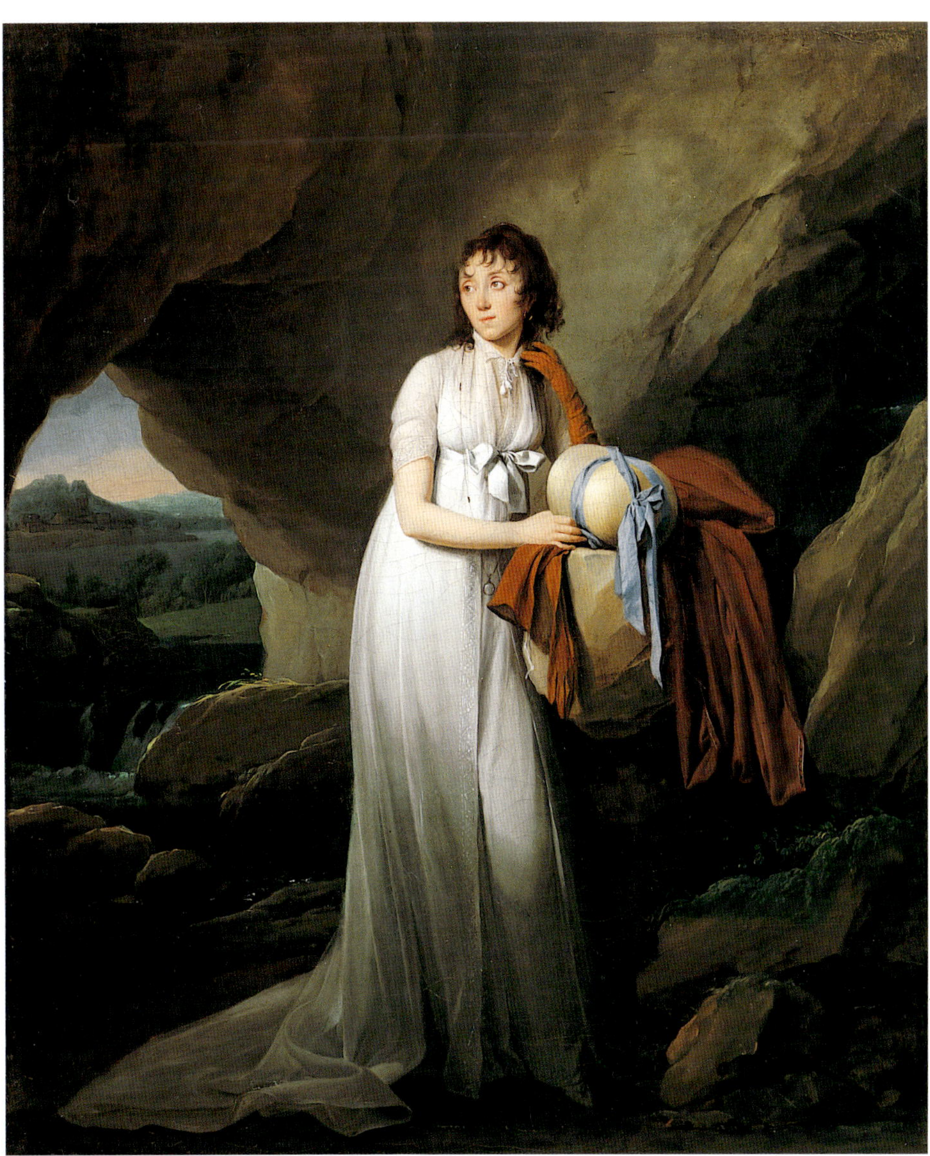

84
Louis-Léopold Boilly (1761–1845)
Mme d'Aucourt de Saint-Just, about 1800
Oil on canvas, 56 × 46 cm
Musée des Beaux-Arts, Lille

He leaves in the jewellery, the chic asymmetrical coiffure, the modish cashmere shawl, the tightly confined bust; and the result is to make the quirks of current fashion look timelessly harmonious – something Ingres never failed to do throughout his long career as a portrait painter. There is nothing either of the fashion-plate or of antique pastiche in this authoritatively composed portrait.

Louis-Léopold Boilly generates a very different sort of French atmosphere in his small female portrait of about the same date (fig. 84). Boilly was interested in fashion for itself, and was one of its most sympathetic recorders and promoters. He was no Neoclassicist ideologue, no purveyor of theoretical beauty, nor a seriously ambitious painter ready to compete with the giants of the past; but he was always eager to stress whichever details carried the sexual appeal in any fashion. This portrait has more affinity with current fashion plates and racy popular prints, including Boilly's own, than do any of the Neoclassic paintings we've so far looked at. Here is another white dress, and a red shawl now edged

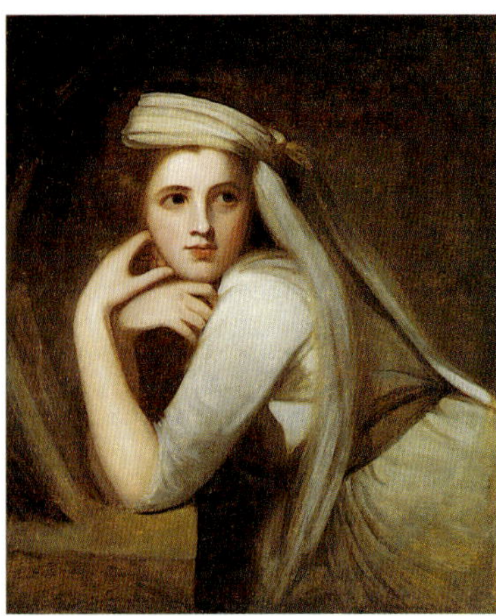

85
George Romney (1734–1802)
Emma, Lady Hamilton,
about 1786
Oil on canvas, 73.7 × 59.7 cm
National Portrait Gallery, London

with gold, and Boilly is happy to celebrate the big satin bow under his sitter's bosom, her turned-over collar held under the chin with a silken knot, her eyeglass on a gold chain and her sizeable gold hoop-earrings. She has long russet gloves (one fetchingly removed, we see its bruised fingers) and a straw bonnet decked with several metres of blue ribbon. Tending her hat with one hand and stroking her locks with the other, she seems to gaze dreamily into an offstage mirror.

This double dress is a short-sleeved transparent coat, edged with bands of glossy white embroidery and fitted over a low-cut sleeveless sheath, through which we can see one knee parting the coat's front opening. Assisted by her pretty eyes and pink bosom under the gauze, this emerging white knee and thigh create the suggestiveness of the portrait. The Romantic grotto in which the lady stands, spreading her fragile finery over the boulders, makes a charmingly absurd background for her appealing figure. Such incongruities between dress and setting have become standard in modern fashion photography.

Boilly's fashion-minded picture makes it evident that some Neoclassical portrait painters, particularly English ones, suppressed the many appurtenances that chic women were really using at the time. Reynolds in his *Seventh Discourse* of 1776 was already preaching that the details of fashion distract the eye and hide the truth in a portrait, and that the rendering of drapery was what really demonstrated the artist's genius and made a portrait timeless, as in Pheidias' day. He overlooked the fact that once fashion prevails over the eye, changing the modish image of what looks natural, draped clothing also submits to fashion, beyond the skill of any painter to resist. In portraits, arrangements of flesh and folds date as quickly as frills and cravats.

In later eighteenth-century England, admiration for classical simplicity was not revolutionary but already traditional, deriving from an earlier taste for Palladian architecture and developed as an alternative to the more elaborate Continental Baroque and Rococo taste. Consequently, despite Hogarth, whose thoroughly anti-classical portrait style flourished at mid-century, simple portraits of English ladies in plain white dresses with classical overtones were already a customary sight by the 1770s, many of them by Reynolds and Gainsborough. George Romney, a successful portrait painter during the same epoch in England, painted similar ones, notably of Emma, Lady Hamilton in quasi-classical garb, in which she had sometimes appeared at social gatherings to perform her famous Attitudes (fig. 85).

This is one of his several portraits of Emma dating from 1782–6, showing modish voluminous hair and pale draperies, arranged somewhat like those in the Tischbein, with no real attempt to imitate classical art beyond using no bright colour or ornament and including plenty of unshiny folds. Her hands, although empty, are arranged in the self-regarding pose of a conscious beauty; and we see the beginning of the short-waisted, short-sleeved white dress that will come into fashion in earnest somewhat later. This is already a far more Romantic image than Tischbein's, or than any portraits by Reynolds and Gainsborough, having the feverish, visionary touch we will see in Romney's drawing and in allegorical or legendary scenes by Blake and Fuseli. The sitter's backward-turning head and gaze, hunched shoulder and asymmetrical head-scarf lend this portrait a narrative flavour, and more Romantic uneasiness than classical stability.

While Flaxman and others were certainly making deliberately classical drawings on classical themes, using carefully accurate ancient dress, William Blake and Henry Fuseli in particular were modelling their figure style on Michelangelo's highly inflected, eroticised version of antique nudity, adding garments in their own idiosyncratic styles. These are sensual and visionary in themselves, not dependent on antique details and just as often suggestive of the Renaissance or Middle Ages as of the Antique.

John Brown's *Family Group (The Rest on the Flight into Egypt)* (fig. 86) of about 1780 shows drapery much simpler than most Neoclassical folds and more reminiscent of the fourteenth century, despite the Virgin's classical chair. With a sweep of curved lines and an abstraction of shapes, Brown adds a mystical cast to this humble subject. Instead of cloaking the Virgin's back, he exposes it, coating her upper torso in a skin-like bodice. In his 1786 sketch *Nature unveiling Herself to the Infant Shakespeare* (fig. 87), Romney creates an allegorical tableau in lush ink strokes, the draperies falling and wrapping with vibrant economy. On the clothed female figures in both drawings, you can see the high waist, sculptured top and long, close skirt of the Neoclassic dresses – and in the Romney, even the short sleeves.

Henry Fuseli shared in the general reverence for Michelangelo, whose works he studied in Italy, and was influenced by John Brown, whose drawing we see here he may have owned. His style was intensely Romantic even when copying classical models, always with a certain suggestive emphasis in the shapes and postures of the figures.

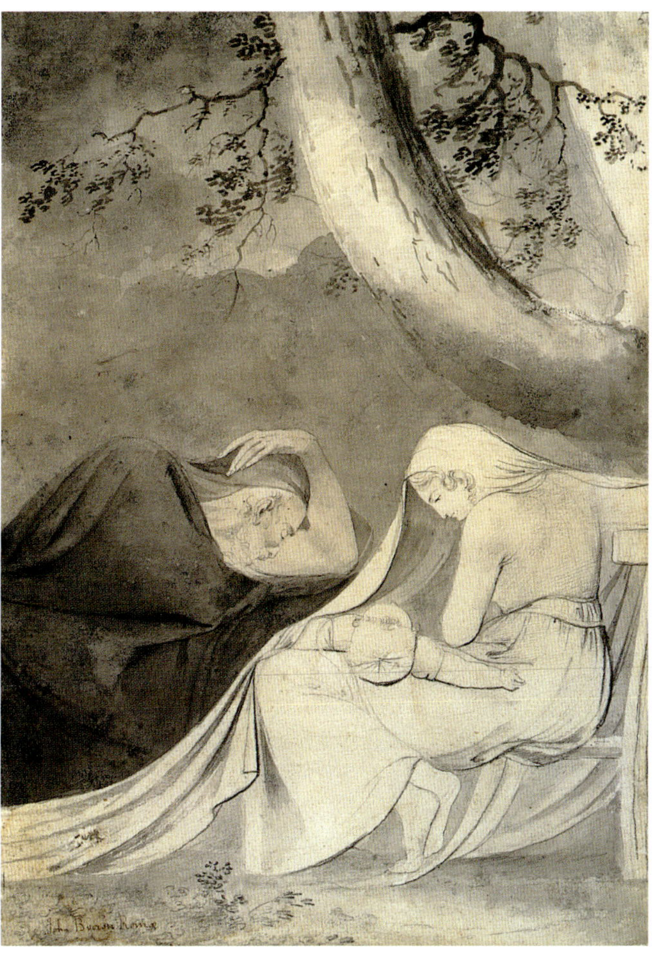

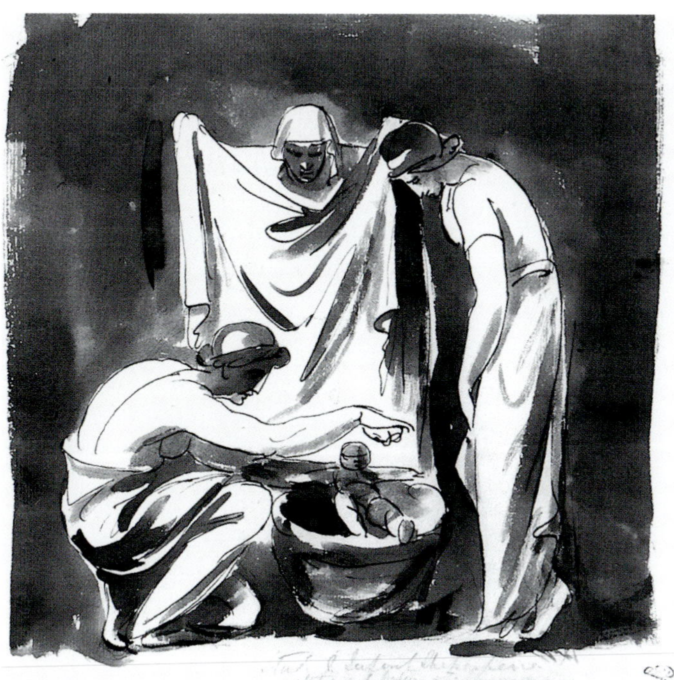

LEFT **86**
John Brown (1752–1787)
Family Group (The Rest on the Flight into Egypt), about 1780
Pen and ink with grey wash, 25.4 × 18 cm
The Royal Academy of Arts, London

ABOVE **87**
George Romney (1734–1802)
Nature unveiling Herself to the Infant Shakespeare, 1786
Ink and wash over graphite on paper, 25.5 × 26 cm
Walker Art Gallery, Liverpool

His 1803 painting, *Thetis asking Hephaestus for Arms for Achilles* (fig. 88) illustrates a scene from the *Iliad* (XVIII, 410ff.), in which we can see two fashion-plate-like female figures with exaggeratedly full necks and long arms wearing modish short-sleeved gowns and chic coiffures, while the limping smith-god Hephaestus with his attendant golden virgins all enter at rear in legendary draperies.

Blake's great watercolour illustrating the climax of *Purgatory*, the second book of Dante's *Divine Comedy* (fig. 89), shows this painter employing the relation Michelangelo proposed between a mythic body and its garments – an example of this on the Sistine Ceiling is the Prophet Jonah, whose upper body seems clad in painted skin. We saw Pontormo making use of this motif in his *Deposition* (see fig. 27), and John Brown for the Virgin's bodice. Elsewhere on the Sistine Ceiling, Michelangelo shows God several times wearing a long-sleeved skin-tight garment that looks as if it grew on him, with only rare ripples below the chest, the lower half of him draped in a swirling wrap. Blake puts just such skin-like garments on Dante's characters as they meet in the Earthly Paradise.

Dante says that the immortal Beatrice on her gryphon-drawn car was dressed in the colour of living flame, under a green mantle and a white veil crowned with an olive wreath. In Blake's watercolour the cloak and veil frame her nude-like figure, which is clothed in flickering reddish ripples that seem to grow out of her skin like an aura, with very little distinction between covering and uncovering it. This seems to express Blake's meta-classical visual idea, borrowed from Michelangelo, appropriate to this moment in Dante, although he used it for many visionary pictures: when we are back not in the classical Golden Age but in a version of the Garden of Eden just after Creation, then

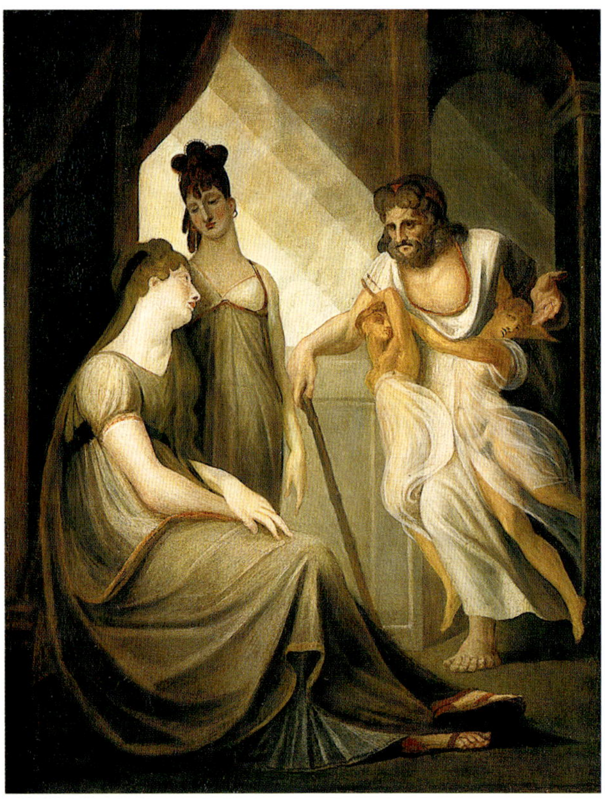

88
Henry Fuseli (1741–1825)
Thetis asking Hephaestus for Arms for Achilles, 1803
Oil on canvas, 91 × 71 cm
Kunsthaus, Zurich

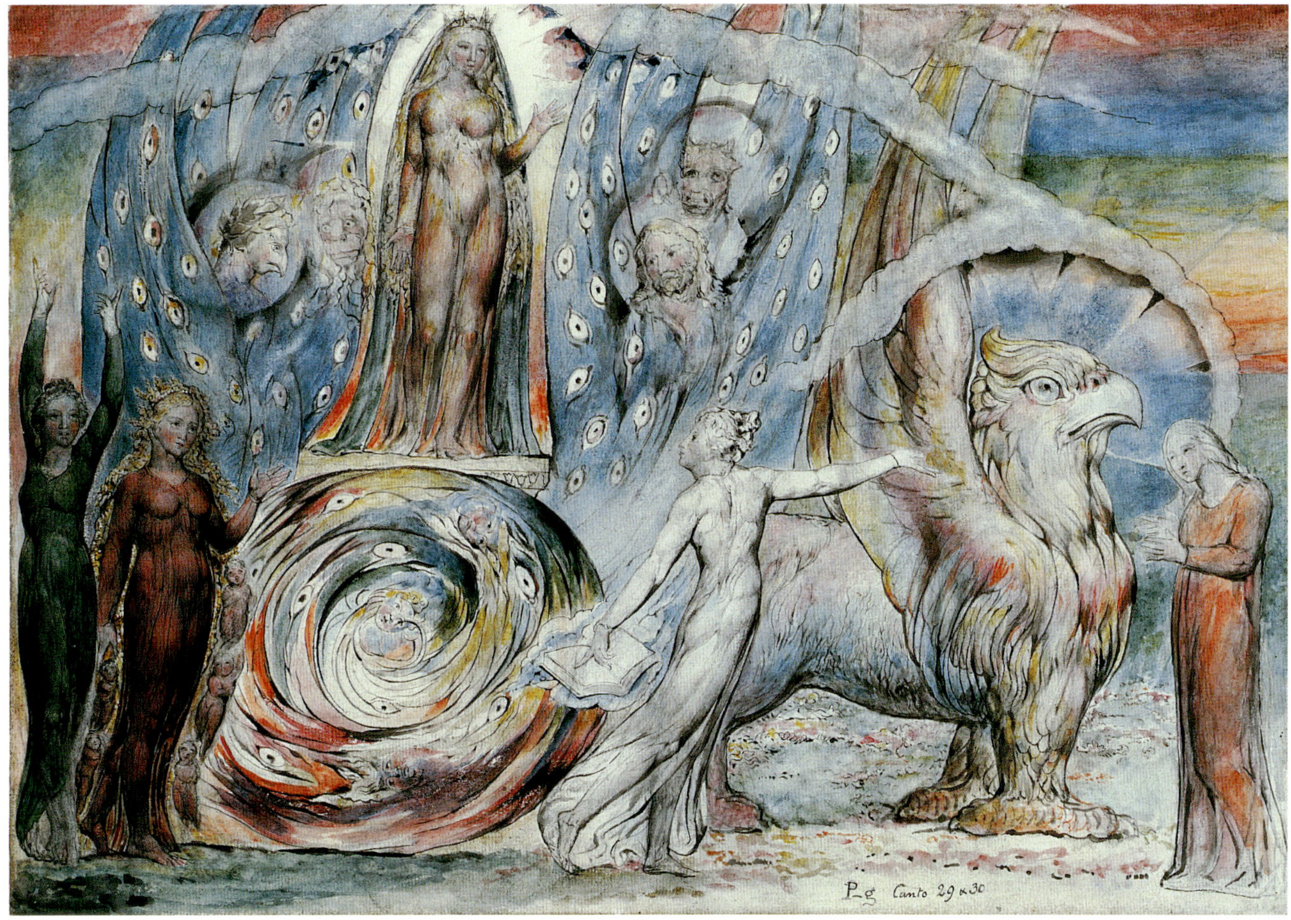

89
William Blake (1757–1827)
Beatrice addressing Dante from the Car, about 1824–7
Pen and ink and watercolour on paper, 37.2 × 57.2 cm
Tate, London

the garment is part of the body, and clothing is as natural as skin. We are then in a perpetually unfallen state, clothed without any prior experience of nakedness or any need for shameful fig-leaves.

Beatrice's attendant green, red and white allegorical females have similar single garments that seem generated by their bodies, with indefinite skirts neither hiding nor baring their legs and feet, and with a supernal cling beyond the abilities of any real stuff. Dante, who carefully described Beatrice's body as dressed only in colour, tells us these figures had *bodies* that were green, red and white, not clothes; and so Blake solves the nudity problem with his standard ineffable non-garments for all four. The long-sleeved gown worn by mortal Dante on the right is real and medieval, falling straight and hiding his legs and feet. We see only the bend of one leg, just as in the works of Giotto or Daddi.

We may note that this male figure, like Brown's Joseph and David's Brutus and Fuseli's Hephaestus, is wearing legendary costume nothing like the male gear of the artists' own time, whereas all the visionary ladies' dresses, like the Roman ones on Brutus' female relatives, do bear some resemblance to the close-draping feminine fashions of 1800. Female dress at that moment had a costume-like Romanticism built into its Neoclassic, figure-revealing simplicity, a nostalgic and even primitive character – since it was based on the ancient shift – that was easy for painters to promote as attractive in various styles and genres. Male dress in real life, except for actual fancy dress, did not

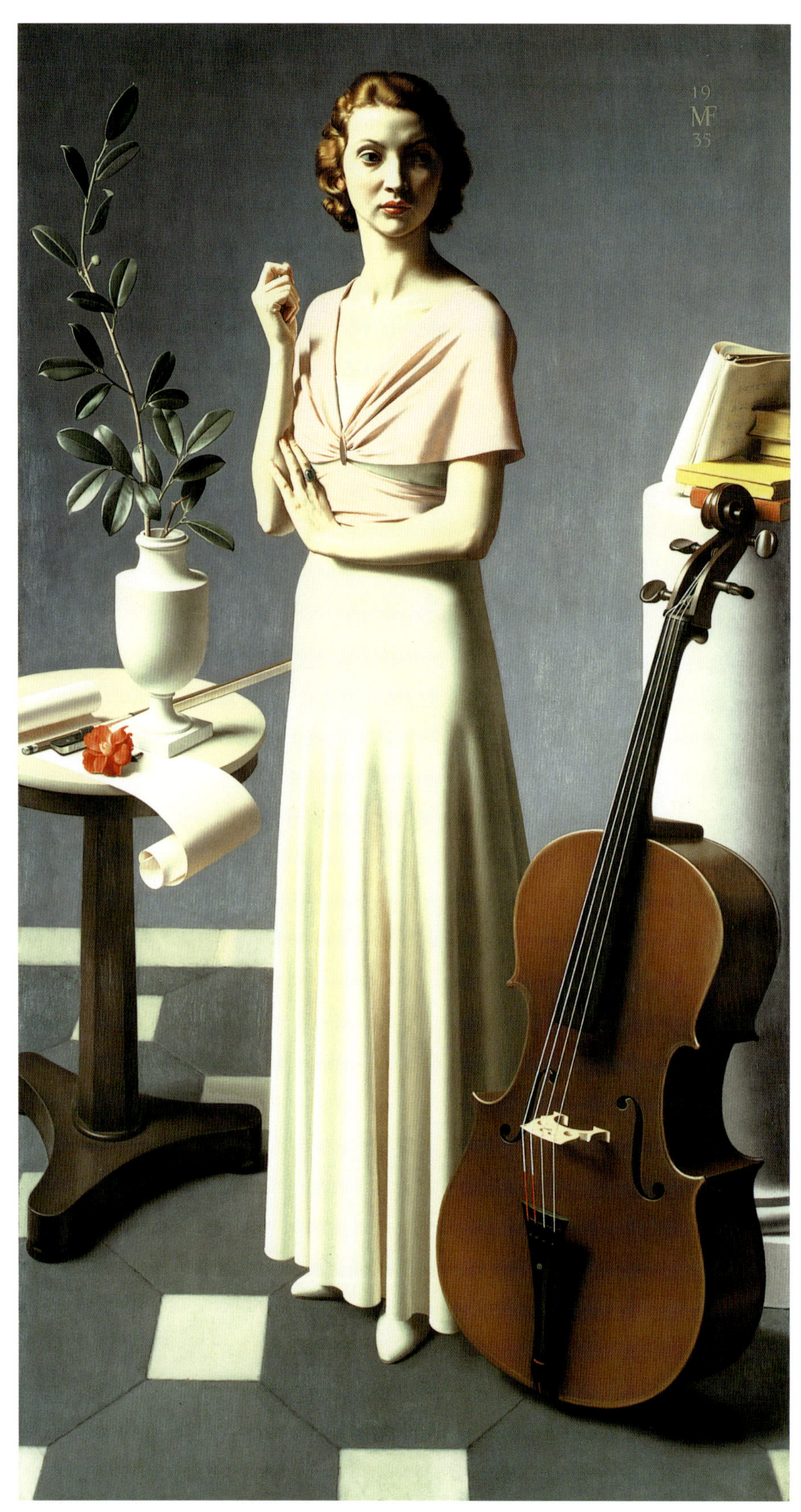

90
Meredith Frampton (1894–1984)
Portrait of a Young Woman, 1935
Oil on canvas, 205.7 × 107.9 cm
Tate, London

develop such a Romantic, Neoclassically nostalgic costume-like dimension to match women's; and so, in visionary or legendary scenes, painters had to put men in versions of pictorial legendary costume, while women could wear versions of already legend-like modern fashions; and then the whole composition would look harmoniously antique. In real life their clothes by this time looked wholly different.

Meredith Frampton's 1935 *Portrait of a Young Woman* (fig. 90) demonstrates the enduring aesthetic vitality and feminine appeal of Neoclassic drapery, and was painted at a time when Neoclassic principles were anyway informing much Modern art, design, music and architecture. For this portrait, however, nostalgia for antiquity has been expanded to include a nostalgia for several Golden Ages in the history of painting.

An idea of order governs this picture; nothing is permitted to seem casual, and there are references to several artistic traditions associated with order, clarity and emblem. Its vibrant stasis has the richness of Ingres, the floor and the cello suggest Vermeer, the tipping of the floor Van Eyck. The leaves in an urn and the curl of the scroll invoke the Renaissance in Italy. The marble-topped table, the play of light on the subject's face and her smoothly brilliant hair suggest the Pre-Raphaelites. The white column, sliced off to support books and a musical score, refers to the abiding simplicity of classical architecture. Then there is the sitter herself, embodying the modern Neoclassical woman in her simply draped white garment. She is the new ideal woman, whose body is sensual because of being functional, not in spite of being so. The painting suggests the pleasure she gets from living in her body, rather than that taken by others from looking at it.

Like previous Neoclassic ladies, this sitter is empty-handed. The salient cello, together with the discreet bow and score, suggests she is an active musician; but her hands and arms convey only conscious femininity, with one hand touching the other forearm, the other hand folded like a flower on a stem. Like the one worn by David's sitter, her draped top is symmetrical and covers the upper arms, but it subdues her bosom instead of enhancing it. The bias cut of her skirt is wholly modern, and the emphasis is now on her smooth pelvis. It's when we look there, not at the breasts, that we're meant to believe she wears nothing under the dress, in the antique fashion. The silk is very sleek over the visible hipbones flanking the flat abdomen, below which we see the folds begin their rhythmic, slowly deepening fall. Her two shod feet stand squarely, keeping her hem level as it hangs clear of them. The self-caressing arms invite us to consider how her dress feels to her, how she will feel the skirt swing around her when she walks. She is self-sufficient, not artless, as classic as you like but disciplined, alert and ready, like a white-clad modern dancer.

There is no attendant drapery anywhere in this picture. In general we have seen no drapery in Neoclassical female portraits that was not part of the sitter's costume, except for the dim green draperies behind Doña Joaquina, left over from earlier convention. The beauty of rampant drapery was clearly no longer believed to enhance the beauty of women, neither to suggest their sexuality, quasi divinity, high rank or great wealth, nor to suggest theatrical artifice as a positive aspect of their appearance in portraits. When they do occur, attendant draperies in Neoclassic portraits, as in the history paintings of the same period, show that painters had gone back to the fifteenth-century principle of accountability. Fabric can be seen hung up as it might be in reality, serving as a domestic curtain to close off an archway, or to create a room out of two colonnades, as in David's *Brutus*, with believable fixtures holding it in place.

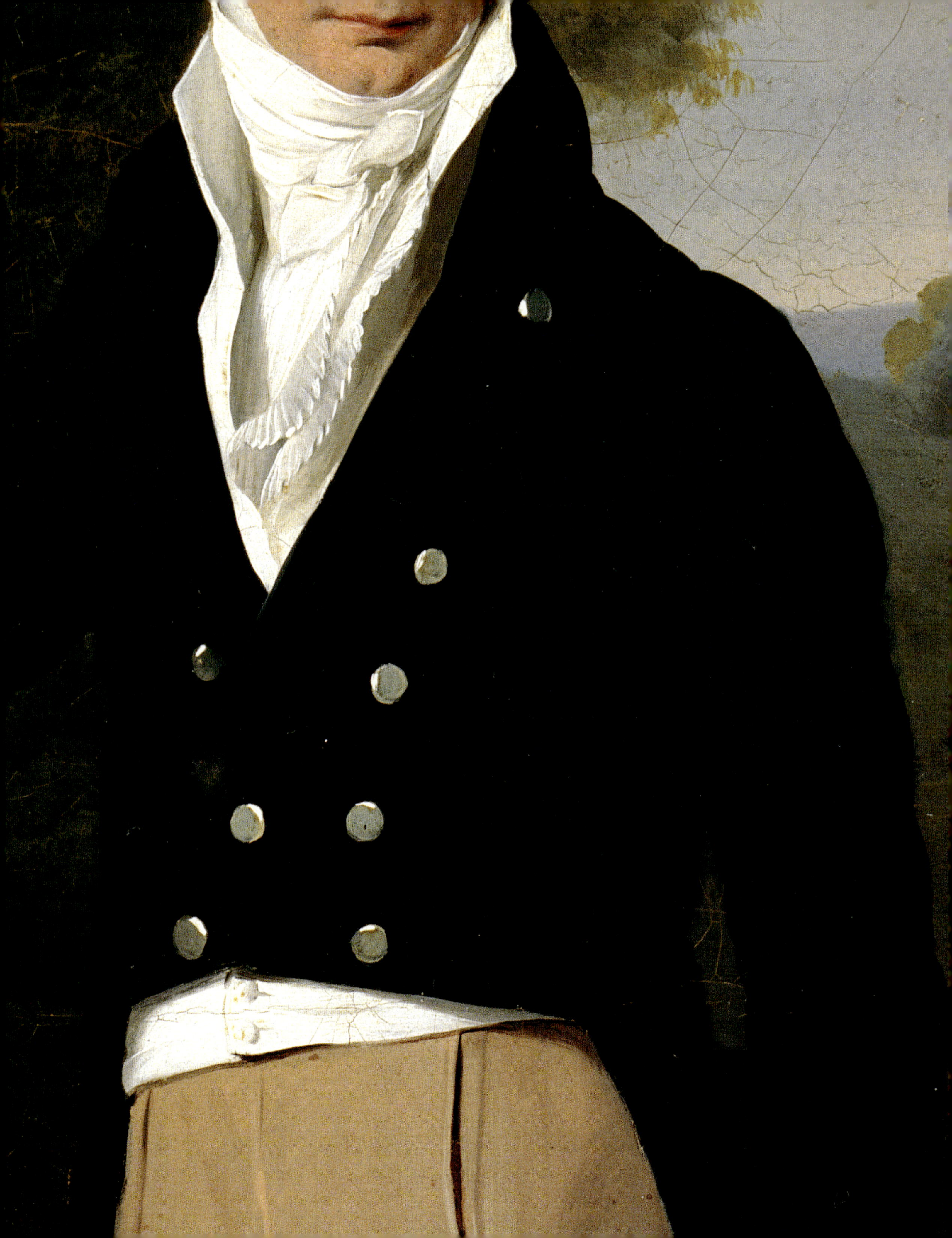

VI Romantic Simplicity: Men

In the history painting and other illustrations by David, Fuseli, Blake, Brown and Romney that we saw in the last chapter, the female figures wore clinging garments not unlike those in Neoclassical portraits, whereas the male figures wore purely legendary gowns and mantles. Other Neoclassical renderings of heroic Greek and Roman scenes showed men entirely nude, just as the ancient Greek statues did, perhaps with a cape or drape. But we have noted that real-life masculine dress had been required for centuries to articulate the sections of the male body and cover it entirely; and that the long gowns and mantles worn by Romans in late antiquity had gradually become priestly or ceremonial in real life. Meanwhile public male nudity – except for bathing – had become purely pictorial and sculptural.

Except in classicised portrait sculpture, men in 1800 could never appear in true classical garb – draped togas, long gowns or tunics that bared sizeable expanses of leg, arm and chest – because, during centuries of European custom, those features of dress had become feminine. Women's clothing in all classes had permitted exposure of the neck and chest since the fourteenth century, of shoulders and the lower arms since the early seventeenth, and of ankles in the mid eighteenth. Women had always worn versions of tunic, gown and mantle, and their clothing had never divided their legs. At the beginning of the nineteenth century, we have seen how easily live women could re-make themselves in Neoclassical earnest simply by re-designing their hair, re-modelling their underwear, and making their gowns and mantles of thin fabric with no surface ornament.

We have also seen how simple gentlemen's suits had become in the 1780s – or at least how simple one might seem in an informal English portrait, by comparison to a lady's dress (see fig. 77). We may now contrast Mr Hallett's figure-hugging black clothing with the ebullient costume worn in William Hogarth's 1741 portrait of the future 4th Duke of Devonshire, with its pale colours, many folds and busy edges moving away from the wearer's body so that it seems to expand (fig. 92). The duke's coat is collarless, its shoulders very narrow, unpadded and not very well tailored – the garment is designed to emphasize its surfaces, not its shape. Encrustations of gold embroidery engulf his gold

Detail of fig. 93

buttons and button-holes, the coat's very lining is exuberant, the waistcoat is of multi-coloured brocade, and Hogarth shows the duke thrusting out his stomach to increase the efflorescent frontal display. At lower right, the painter includes the beginning of his deep, gold-trimmed cuff.

In even sharper contrast to this courtly Rococo image is Henry Raeburn's portrait of James Hutton, from the mid-1780s (fig. 91). This cool vision of informal male seriousness seems like a prophecy of the masculine sartorial future. The untrimmed, three-piece suit in dim, matt wool, allowing a touch of white at neck, stomach and wrists, worn in seated nonchalance with smooth natural hair and a meditative expression, expounds a new gentlemanly ideal. We will find it achieved in the nineteenth century and sustained throughout the twentieth.

In the closing decades of the eighteenth century men urgently needed a shift in elegance, a way to re-clothe their bodies without effeminately denuding and draping them, something to fit them visually into the new political and social climate and the Neoclassical aesthetic scheme. This scheme demanded a candid and simple aspect, indicating respect for enlightened political views as well as for natural virtue and feeling, and not for the outward magnificence that once denoted superiority of rank. In a definitive departure from the deeply cuffed silk coats, embroidered waistcoats and knee breeches that had evolved out of the padded Renaissance doublets, slashed jerkins and tight hose – often worn with lace neckwear, wrought shoe-buckles and plumed hats – men's elegant clothes were gradually re-conceived and re-made into modern suits. These fulfilled the articulation-plus-total-coverage requirement, but they looked quite different from traditional finery.

This time they were modelled not on noble armour, but on a combination of labourers' gear, French Revolutionary street-wear, and the sober wool coats and black hats worn with leather boots and plain linen by English gentlemen in the country. For the superior modern man, muted colours, plain fabrics, simple cut and neat but flexible fit took the place of the elaborate embroidered upholstery and the shiny silken wrinkles of earlier times. It was a kind of nudity, a stripping away, a clarification, a modernisation. To reinforce the idea, powdered locks and curled wigs gave way to natural hair, of the right length to show the real shape of the head and ears, besides deftly suggesting the antique busts and statues.

Part of the change was already under way by the 1780s in the monochromy and fashionable close fit we remarked in both Mr Hallett's black velvet suit and Mr Hutton's dull wool one. These two new elements already show a certain impulse to imitate the unity of form to be found in the classical nude male figure, which was not at all recalled by the spreading and vari-coloured coats and waistcoats of the century's first half: the ideal body underneath those garments seemed to have a long, round-bellied torso, narrow chest, broad hips and short legs.

Making the plainer masculine style desirable would first require raising the aesthetic credit of male sartorial simplicity, to establish its distance from servility or crudity: it was going to be necessary to romanticise it in art. The portrait of plain Mr Hutton does not make him look especially attractive for his plainness, whereas Hogarth made the gilded duke a treat for the eye. A freshly compelling visual quality had to be created by artists to enhance the look of the new simple male modes.

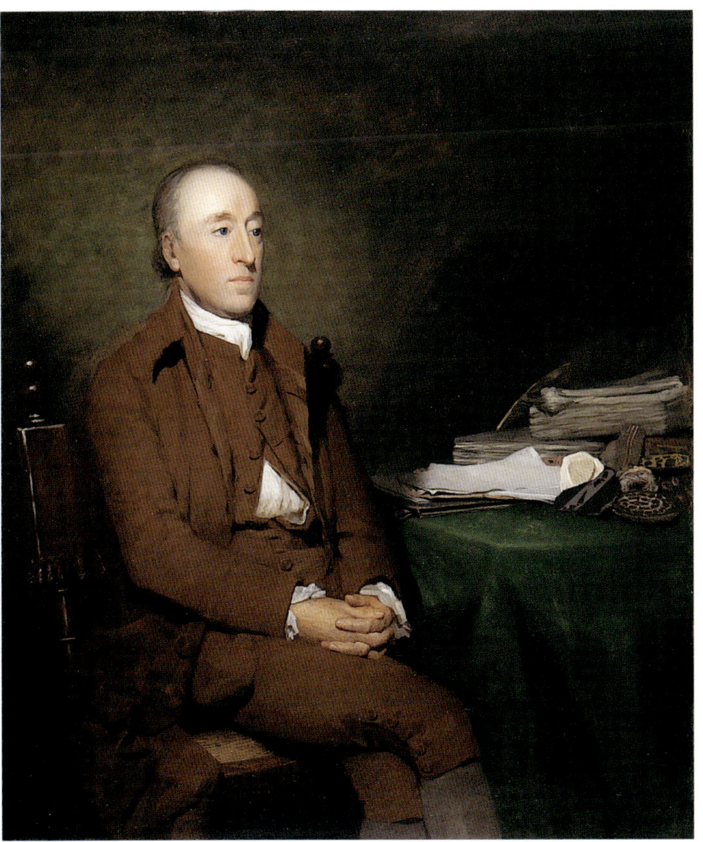

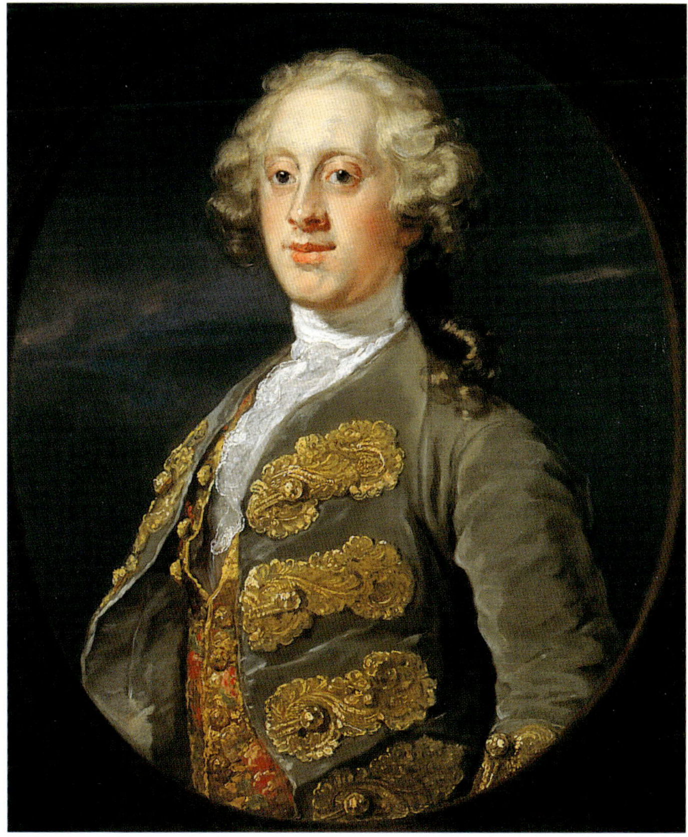

ABOVE LEFT **91**
Henry Raeburn (1756–1823)
James Hutton, about 1785
Oil on canvas, 125.1 × 104.8 cm
Scottish National Portrait Gallery, Edinburgh

ABOVE RIGHT **92**
William Hogarth (1697–1764)
William Cavendish, Marquess of Hartington (later 4th Duke of Devonshire), 1741
Oil on canvas, 75.9 × 63.5 cm
Yale Center for British Art, New Haven, Connecticut, Paul Mellon Collection

These were already being romanticised in real life by the famous Beau Brummell, who, as dandy-in-chief of London society at the turn of the century, was renowned for his perfect clothes and figure, but also known for his utterances – for example, 'to be well dressed is to be unnoticeable'. More significantly, anecdotes circulated about his numerous rituals for preserving the perfect cleanliness of his perfect body and its linen, and others about how many artisans and craftsmen were needed to achieve the perfect fit and condition of his simple garments, gloves and boots. There is in the tone of Brummell's celebrity a Romantic and erotic intensification of the Neoclassical theme, with its emphasis on the purity of the linen folds and the clarity of their arrangement, the beauty of the body, the preservation of the smooth line of the figure and its extremities. It suggests the creation of classical nude sculpture out of the clothed male form, to be accomplished by tailoring and grooming.

The English country costume was portrayed in its original fairly shapeless form in paintings of the 1760s by George Stubbs, who showed men with dogs and horses in fields, wearing plain garments rendered in an entirely non-Romantic spirit. By 1800, the costume was being remodelled as if to clothe a Romantic Neoclassical statue, one suitable for essentially urban appearances, though Nature was its theoretically correct milieu, and it reflected an original Adamic and Arcadian nudity of the body under it. During his many long visits at noble country houses, Brummell never concealed his distaste for exercise, stables, horses, coaching, hunting, shooting, anything that might involve dirt and dishevelment. Dressed essentially for those activities, he much preferred being a statue in the drawing room.

There are no painted portraits of Brummell in his smooth and simple envelope, only a few undistinguished prints in which he looks ordinary, as he (surely falsely) said he preferred to look. But the Romantic–Neoclassic ideal began to come alive in other men's portraits from the decade following 1800, and persisted until the 1830s. The Brummellian sartorial scheme became international, visualised by European portrait painters as part of the Romantic masculine image at the highest level of elegance, according to the new perception of the classical male figure, which Neoclassic theory considered to be the truly natural one.

Portraits of men, no less than those of women, had always had natural scenery in the background, but an outdoor setting now became more common and was presented more as surrounding than as backdrop. A new custom, moreover, arose of using a void and shallow background, some version of ambiguous nothingness into which the viewer could project meaning and feeling, instead of the drapery and architecture that had long served as signs of the sitter's importance and the painter's artistic good faith. We saw such a background suggesting a marble wall behind a draped statue-like lady in the last chapter (see fig. 82), and we can already see it behind Mr Hutton, perhaps suggesting calm thought and unencumbered judgement.

Louis-Léopold Boilly, in this masculine companion-piece to the female portrait we saw in the last chapter (see fig. 84), makes the simple components of modern tailoring on his male subject's figure blend very well with the landscape (fig. 93). His array of warm, natural tones accented with white and black form a counterpoint to the similar spectrum in his outdoor background. The sitter is even shown acting upon nature, seeming to pause while trimming the branch he has just sawn off, to finish the railing of a rough wooden bridge he has just constructed. We are to believe these are his own acres, that he is not above working on them, and we see that his country clothes with their immaculate linen look comfortable and becoming, correct for both public appearance and physical effort.

No trace here of the exquisite accessories, the attractive narcissism, the dissonance between the rocky cave and the gauzy dress that makes Boilly's female sitter look like an apparition in a dream, or a performer on a stage. Whereas the lady gazes away, just as the Earl of Bellamont (see fig. 73) did from under his plumes, this man looks straight at us. Fashionable women, we are bound to notice, are still keeping up the theatrical spirit, the consciousness they once shared with richly clad men of being the embodiments of fantasy. Elegant men now seem to be abandoning the look of obvious artifice for the look of theoretical honesty, wearing a costume here acknowledged to be a suave idealisation of plain country gear, with the sitter not just holding the appropriate props for rough work, but making as if to do it.

The idealisation emphasises the body under the clothes, as the original version shown in Stubbs did not; and this painter encourages the effect. He shows us how the waistcoat, formerly buttoned over the dome of the belly all the way down to a double point at crotch level, has become much shorter, so that it cuts straight across a raised waistline and thus seems to lengthen the legs. These are now clad in smooth, pale doeskin breeches that allow the painter to give considerable emphasis to the genital region,

OPPOSITE **93**
Louis-Léopold Boilly (1761–1845)
M. d'Aucourt de Saint-Just, about 1800
Oil on canvas, 56 × 46 cm
Musée des Beaux-Arts, Lille

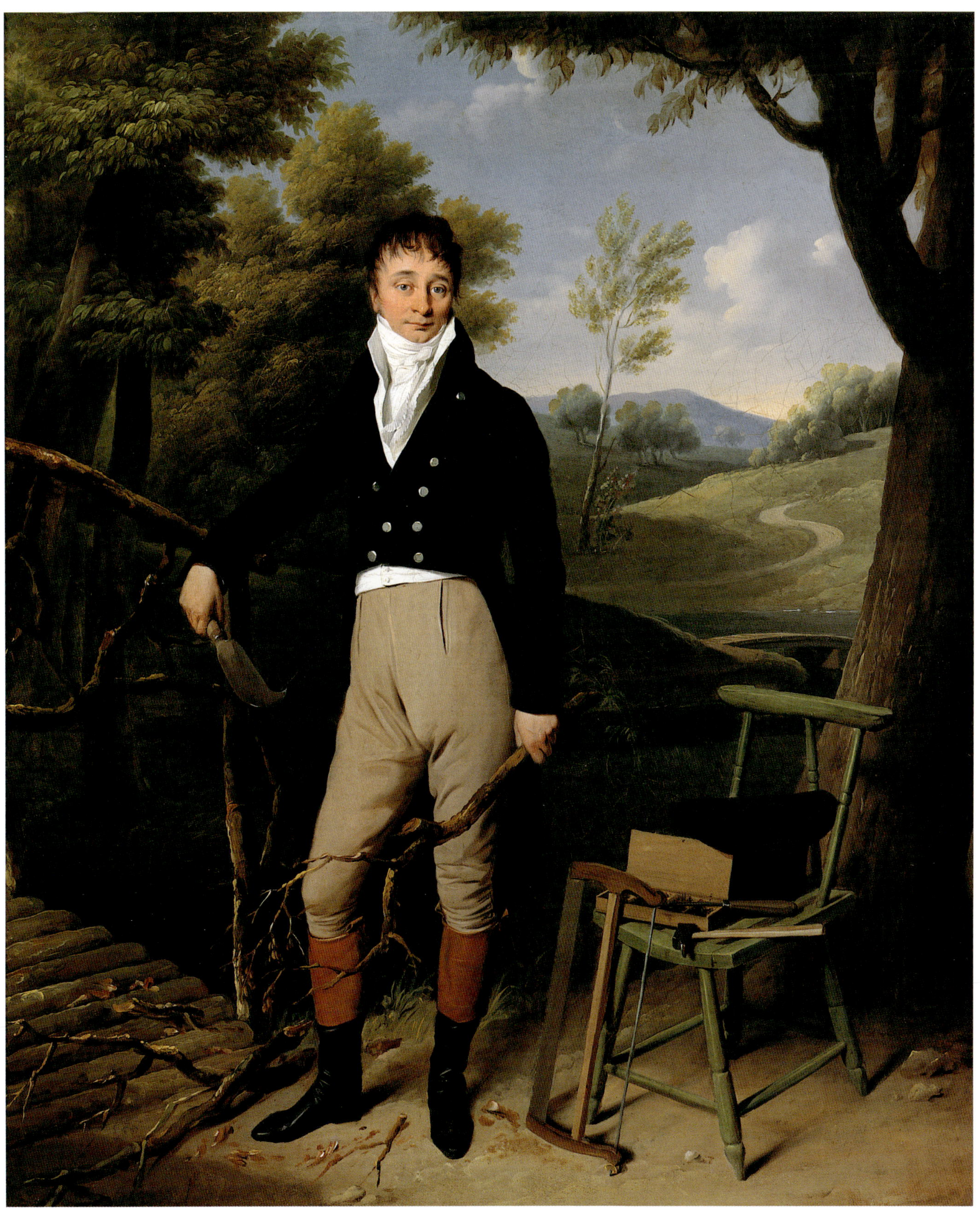

formerly masked by the long waistcoat, and to give the sitter a quasi-nude look above the smooth, tight top-boots.

The country coat, once a loose garment with a floppy collar, is shown crisply arching across the high waistline in front, fitted and buttoned around the ribs but opening laterally across the broader-seeming chest, its shoulders, now assisted by padding, also made to seem broader for the coat's shortness. Its blackness is made to delineate the sitter's trim figure, and its neat coat-tails fall straight behind, leaving the vertical line of the body uninterrupted by any outward swing that might widen the hips. The coat collar is now shaped and stiffened to rise and open below the open collar of the waistcoat, both collars spreading outwards to display the perfectly sculptured knot of the white cravat and the discreetly pleated shirt-frill. Above it the shirt collar, wrapped in cravat, forms a high white pedestal for the candid face, topped by its tousled hair. On the seat of the crude chair at right sits the gentleman's elegant hat, retreating behind the hammer, saw and box of nails.

Some fifteen years later, in 1815, Ingres gives us the same costume more thoroughly refined and brought indoors. Here a greatcoat adds another layer of opening collar and a more dramatic backdrop for the sexy display of skin-tight doeskin, now adorned with dangling seals, along with a nearly Herculean spread of classical shoulders (fig. 94). The coat is wide open, the gentleman's whole fine figure is on view, now without bright coat-

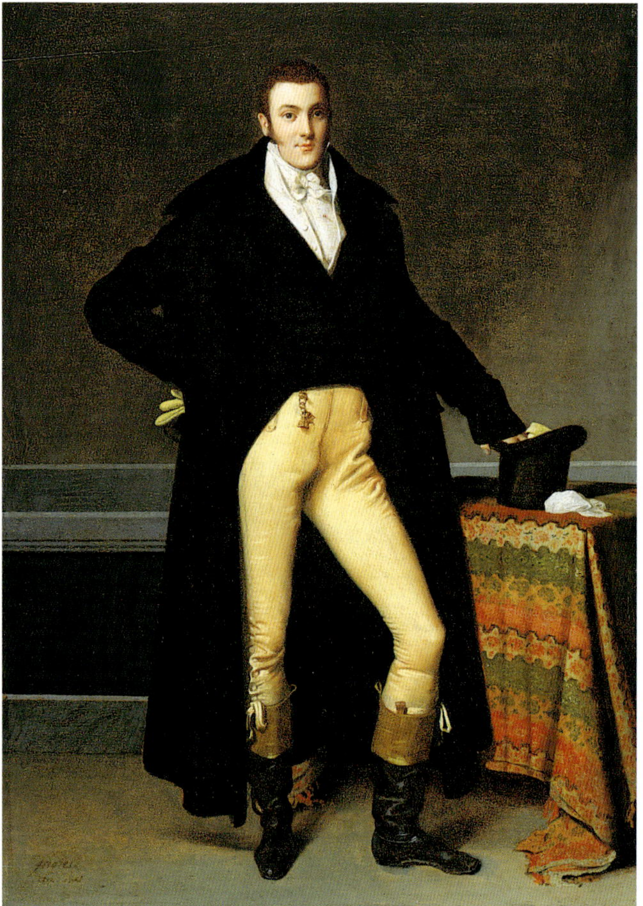

94
Jean-Auguste-Dominique Ingres (1780–1867)
Joseph-Antoine de Nogent, 1815
Oil on wood panel, 47 × 33.3 cm
The Fogg Art Museum, Harvard University Art Museums, Cambridge, Massachusetts
Bequest of Grenville L. Winthrop

buttons to interrupt the sculpture. This hat is at hand, along with gloves, and the sitter is attended by a table covered in a slightly draped exotic textile.

Behind him is another empty wall, such as we saw behind Mr Hutton, although distance now permits a view of the wainscotting, so that classical suggestions are made by the combination of moulding and drape. We can also see how the idealised figure of the classical nude hero, impossible for real men's lives, is sketched by a clever shaping of tailored wool, tight leather and doeskin – all unworked textures, like human skin. The clothed man acquires a newly articulated bodily beauty that echoes the muscular shoulders, lean flanks and long legs of the Homeric warriors in contemporary history painting.

By the 1820s, the modern masculine ensemble had further evolved to add neat wool trousers below the unadorned and fitted wool coats, to balance the tubular sleeve with the tubular trouser-leg. Trousers were the last and most thrilling element to complete the ensemble forming the modern suit, because they derived from the crude and loose cotton trousers worn by common seamen and slave labourers on colonial plantations, and by the ferocious *sans-culottes* of the French Revolution. In reality they had long been adopted under informal circumstances by the owners of plantations and the officers of ships, for comfort and ease while managing in hot climates – their life in elegant circles had begun as very casual private wear. Since the original connotations of trousers were lowly, alien or terrifying, they could strengthen the attractive virility of modern suits once they became part of the scheme.

The early Romantic and still Neoclassic proposition for male dress, requiring that artless country garments be recut to fit Apollo, was then further homogenised to create a High Romantic version in the form of a full-length suit. Eugène Delacroix's 1826 standing portrait of twenty-one-year-old Louis-Auguste Schwiter (fig. 95) offers a beautiful example of the male classical figure unified by clothes instead of nudity. This young man's ideal body is carved by the painter out of soft black suiting, his shoulders shown delicately augmented by padding, his neck strengthened by a standing collar, his mid-section flattered by the curves of a smoothly fitted coat and waistcoat, his legs lengthened by the continuous black modelling of his trousers. Delacroix has painted this figure with a caressing tenderness absent from the strict male images of Boilly and Ingres; he shows how painters' imaginative perceptions of male tailoring were expanding to allow for broader emotional suggestions.

This is a Romantic Parisian dandy, not a romanticised country squire; his look at us is guarded and faintly smouldering.There are no buff breeches and boot-tops to qualify the perfect shape of his inky figure. He is outdoors, but not engaging with Nature; he stands on a stone terrace strewn with leaves and flowers, facing, we must think, a sumptuous interior through high windows behind us – who is he waiting for? He is in evening dress; and while his soft hair is lifted by natural breeze, his feet are shod for the ballroom. Behind him are steps leading down to the park – there are even distant mountains against the light-streaked sky. This is a Balzacian image, made of sharp social observation infused with mystery and sexuality.

The complete blackness of the baron's evening suit was a recent innovation, including the long black trousers, a Brummell invention. Knee-breeches had been required with dress coats throughout the second decade of the nineteenth century, and many dress suits were then still in colours. Delacroix shows the baron's evening black striking a new

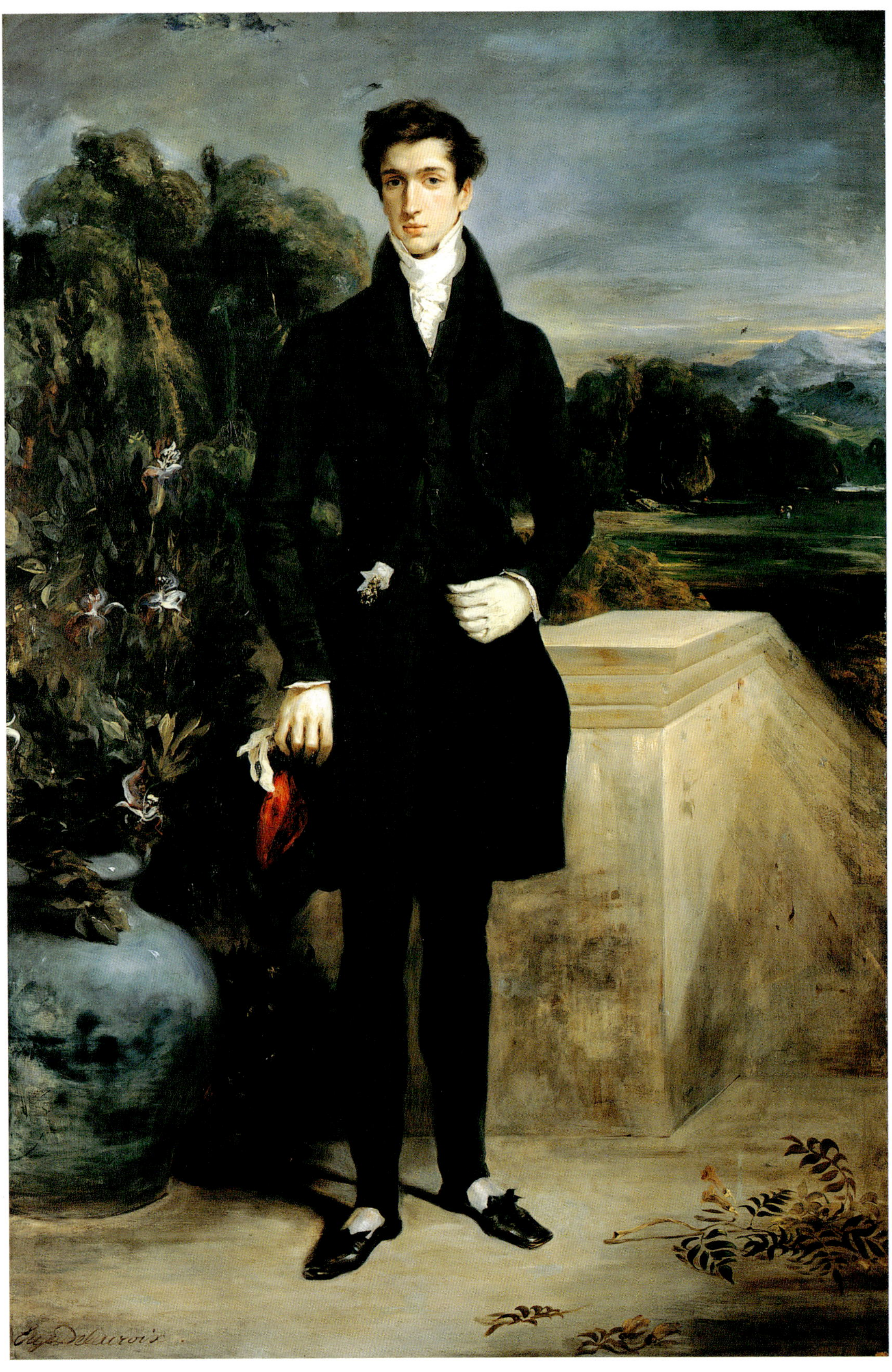

OPPOSITE **95**
Ferdinand-Victor-Eugène Delacroix (1798–1863)
Louis-Auguste Schwiter, 1826–30
Oil on canvas, 217.8 × 143.5 cm
National Gallery, London
NG 3286

and resonant emotional note, initiating the Romantic allure of black clothing that has affected all fashion for both sexes with enduring tenacity ever since. Its celebration here by Delacroix foreshadows his various versions of *Hamlet and Horatio in the Graveyard*, especially the one in the Louvre from 1839, where the black-clad Dane even resembles the baron.

Black clothing has existed ever since fast black dye was invented in prehistoric times, but its symbolic importance and psychological effects have varied greatly in society. Several of those variations were expounded by great European portrait painters – Memling, Holbein and Hals, Bronzino, Titian and Velázquez – as well as by the poets, playwrights and novelists who inspired generations of history painters. A tradition of portraits in black, begun in the fifteenth century, has since then fed on itself, allowing painters to render any current modish black in ways that either suggest earlier masterpieces or deliberately oppose them – either way, the effect has been to foster the continuation of the fashion for black. Romantic painters made liberal use of it, often when painting themselves or other painters, as in Géricault's famous *Artist in his Studio*, also in the Louvre.

Henri Lehmann, a pupil of Ingres, painted his three-quarter-length portrait of Franz Liszt in Rome in 1839 (fig. 96). We can see that Lehmann's dramatic use of line and lighting romanticised the image of male tailoring more thoroughly than Ingres's clarified eroticism had done. The setting here is another flat, shallow and void interior wall with peripheral intimations of classical panelling, wainscotting and a corner. There are no meaningful objects, no supportive pieces of furniture, no spaces opening behind the figure. As the only object against the cool wall, the outline of Liszt's figure is the more striking in its high-buttoned, double-breasted near-black frockcoat with its closed velvet collar and flaring open cuffs – we even see the delicate silhouette of two black buttons, one on the chest and one at the waist behind, and we note that his straight hair just fails to touch the collar – there is something of Bronzino's black-clad and slope-shouldered youths in this picture.

Liszt's intense face turns towards us, half of it catching the spotlight that also strikes his beautiful fingers, the nails glistening against the darkness of his upper arm. No white linen distracts from this glowing hand and head, where the famous pianist's lank hair and gleaming eyes crown the sombre shape of his torso. The dedication of genius is suggested by this painted garment, which demonstrates that unadorned dark tailoring is suitable not only for businessmen and gentlemen but for men of exceptional creative gifts – the artist is shown as priest and prophet. Liszt's tight-waisted, pitch-dark coat is seen here as the funnel of a molten musical talent, but its blackness gives it an air of religious commitment. We see the pianist's folded arms defending his flame against the world, his coat his tower.

Despite its distinguishing function in the picture, this painted frock-coat resembles real-life modish coats in the late 1830s and early 1840s, some of them worn with black silk neckwear covering all whiteness of shirt. The classical body was now out of fashion, and the Romantic body looked shaped by its garments, not the other way round; the Neoclassic impulse of early Romanticism that gazed back to a Golden Age of man, art and nature was over. Mystery was in: frock coats were cut to cross over and veil the crotch completely, and trousers, even with daytime cut-away coats, were no longer clinging. Natural bodily charms were concealed, but hair was again worn rather long.

A sharp sartorial definition was imposed on the male body, to increase a new look of deliberate drama. Tailored shoulders were steeply sloped, chests were padded out in a

96
Henri Lehmann (1814–1846)
Franz Liszt, 1839
Oil on canvas, 113 × 86 cm
Musée Carnavalet, Histoire de Paris, Paris

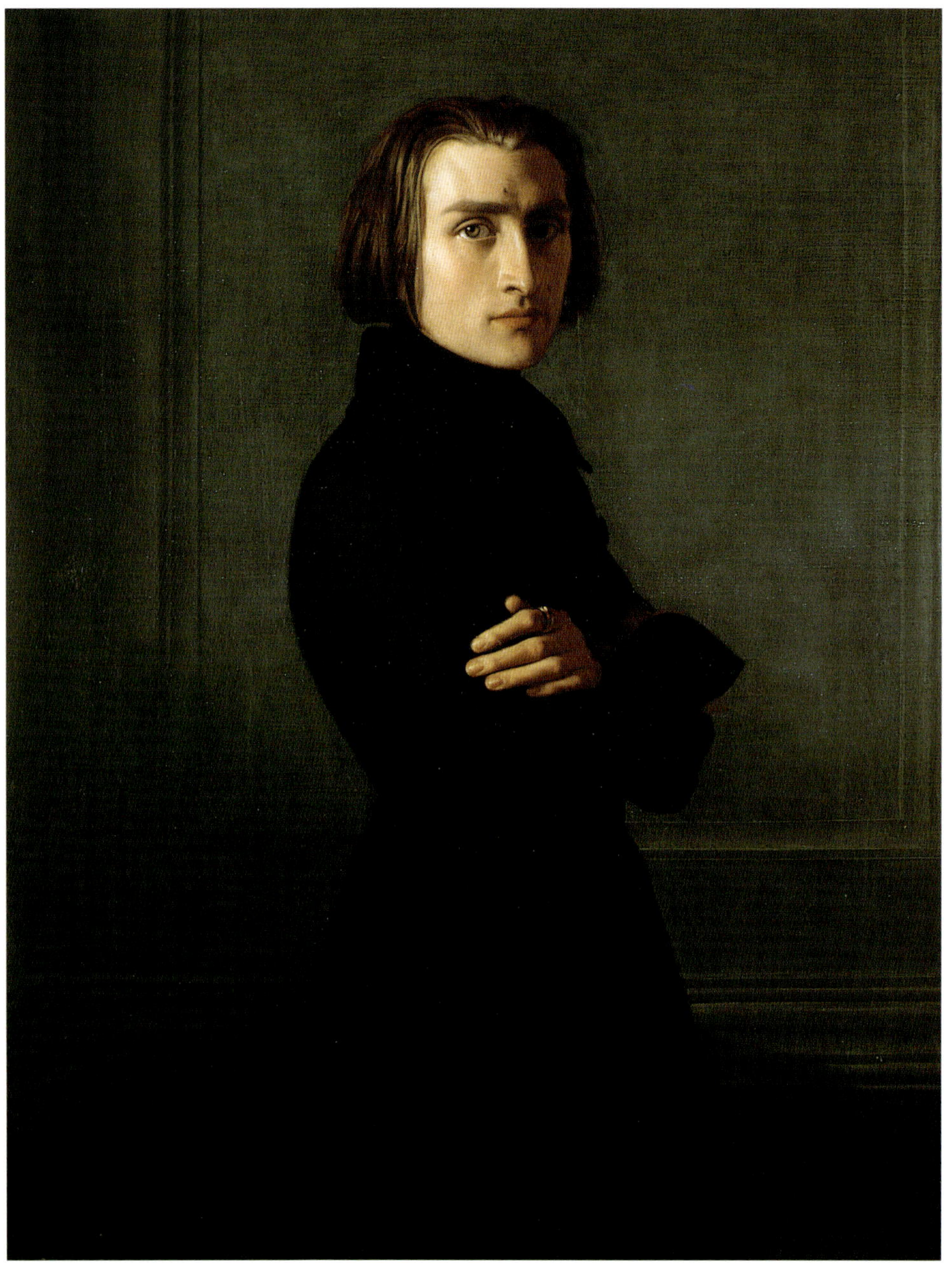

curve, waists were very tight, coat-skirts flared out below and reached the knee, except in full evening dress, for which a tight-waisted black tailcoat and trousers would be worn, with white waistcoat and white neckwear – as ever since. This newly ritualised black-and-white evening costume sharpened the Romantic masculine look as we saw it in the Delacroix in the 1820s – at once sexy, serious and a little sinister – specifically for dress occasions, when ladies would sharpen their femininity with more extreme décolletage, more feathers and even frothier garments.

Breeches were outmoded, reserved for ceremonial use or worn by the old; and by this time white cravats were worn only in the evening. Black and coloured ones appeared in the daytime, waistcoats were often fancy and colourful again, coats might be blue or green or brown, trousers and coats were usually not of the same colour and fabric. Some Romantic portraits and genre scenes from around 1840 show the rich range of these combinations, as do fashion plates; but Lehmann has kept all trace of the current variety of colour and texture in male dress out of his Liszt portrait, so that the pianist is seen as if clad in a single stark garment. Indeed, black frock-coats became predominant a decade later and remained so until the end of their reign at the end of the century.

Different expressive qualities for the modern masculine suit were expounded by each of these four different Romantic portrait painters from the first half of the nineteenth century; but their sitters share a strong look of wishing to engage personally with the viewer. The expression on each man's face and the pose of his body are intensified by the close-fitting shapes and unadorned surfaces of his non-chromatic clothing, which emphasise any wearer's individuality, force of personality and physical charm. Absent is the old idea that the male sitter's portrait is enhanced by signs of power or beauty that include draped fabric behind him or the ripple of his rich silk garments catching the light – the important things emphasised in all four costumes are a lack of shine, a limited palette and above all a fit that makes the man's expressive figure stand out.

If we look back again at the Gainsborough double portrait of the Halletts out walking in the 1780s (see fig. 77), and again compare the male Boilly portrait to its female pendant (see figs. 93 and 94), it is evident that the Romantic spirit, already alive in the last quarter of the eighteenth century, was urging painters to render dressed men and women as different sorts of creature. Men are displayed wearing clear-cut dark tailoring that candidly outlines the whole of the living body, women are veiled in waves of ambiguous white gauze manipulated to prevent the display of their true shape, to allow only certain charms to catch the eye; and they still wear their feathers and delicious knots of ribbon, while men have austerely abandoned theirs. In these two pairings, although the pictures differ in style and show different fashions, the man's dress suggests a new virile simplicity and restraint, the woman's clothes maintain a traditional blend of artifice and excess, an appearance gradually coming to be thought of as wholly, even naturally, feminine. The Romantic revolution in dress was essentially masculine; and it has had lasting effect.

In the second half of the nineteenth century, plain wool tailored suits gradually became standard for men of all classes: farm labourers and factory workers wore them when off duty as well as to fêtes and to church, while clerks and shop assistants as well as merchants, politicians and princes wore them to work every day. Students and artists were doing the same in a Bohemian milieu. Among all these groups and others, the formal scheme was the same; the nuances and quality varied greatly.

The envelope of smoothly tailored coat and trousers – the coat collar steamed open and flattened down, forming lapels to show a V of shirt and cravat; the shoulders and upper chest shaped with padding, the body not at all – became a levelling uniform like an animal's hide, the definitive outer skin of the Western human male of every genus. The character of the tailoring scheme was so basic that it proved infinitely flexible, like the classical orders of architecture, so that its form could stay new by changing slightly, expressing new cultural nuances instead of decaying and being extinguished by the advance of social change.

Kinds and qualities of suits multiplied and metamorphosed for varying purposes at any one time, and suit fashions shifted in shape and bodily proportions throughout the course of time, as they are still doing. Painters were also changing their ways of showing men's clothes and making them expressive in paintings, in line with the changes in art itself.

In Claude Monet's *Man with a Parasol* of 1865 (fig. 97), we can see elements of the basic costume that Baron Schwiter wore forty years earlier (see fig. 95), but quite altered in painterly, social and emotional character. Painting itself has changed, and the Impressionist idea has been set in motion. A new sense has arisen that imitating nature means imitating the effects of light, that deploying pure colour in an array of visible and variable brushstrokes might be a painter's means of transmitting immediate optical experience, as if that were a common pleasure to be shared, a direct natural gift, unfreighted by the painter with any narrative task or moral import beyond its miraculous self. The constant theme is still freedom, now starting with freedom to see. Here Monet's untitled subject is essentially in motion, not posing. Monet produces the feeling that we've been watching the man walk the length of the dappled path towards us, and that he'll pass right by in a moment, intent on the bench where he means to sit under his parasol and read his magazine.

The scene's contingent quality is matched by the ease of the man's softly coloured, loosely fitted informal suit – the pliant blue trousers different from the coat and wrinkled waistcoat, the shirt checked, the cravat yellow and flowing, the tipped-back hat pale behind the dark head, the gloveless hands full of journal and parasol. The Impressionist method here serves to demonstrate that the range of light colours possible for men's informal suits and their accessories is as variable as that for sun-struck leaves and pathways. The suited man is not set up in a special relation to the park, he is part of it, and we can see it's a public place where other people may amble into the frame at any moment, all of them dressed as what this artist would see and transmit as a variety of similarly light-created, paintable creatures.

Impressionism here permits the medium itself to convey one aspect of the life of suits, the relaxed, multi-coloured and rumpled version of simplicity. Delacroix had set up his baron in the all-black, close-fitting, white-accented and long-tailed version of this suit, as the vividly Romantic shape of urban elegance silhouetted against a country sunset. In Monet's generous non-Romantic image, black and white are elegantly worn by the dog .

Black clothing was nevertheless in the ascendant in the last third of the nineteenth century, certainly black coats. Male tailoring continued the suit formula of coat, waistcoat and trousers, but the coat's shape was now unfitted and boxy, trousers looked as stiffly cylindrical as top hats. The look of a body made of thick, unshaped sections was desirable; various kinds of overcoat were like bigger boxes. Frock coats buttoned high on the chest, hiding the waistcoat and showing small, coloured cravats neatly knotted around lower collars. With their (usually black) skirted frock-coats and their cut-away morning coats, men wore their stovepipe trousers in another fabric, often striped. These ensembles were respectable formal day-wear, but many varieties of jacket and coat and also knickerbockers were invented, all with slightly different uses, for men engaging in varieties of sport and leisure. Evening dress stayed all black with a white waistcoat, shirt and cravat; the fitted, open tailcoat kept the wearer shapely and still Romantic.

In the 1860s, however, entirely informal gentlemen's suits all of one fabric, called

97
Claude-Oscar Monet
(1840–1926)
A Man with a Parasol (*M. J. F. Jacquemart*), 1865
Oil on canvas, 99 × 61 cm
Kunsthaus, Zurich

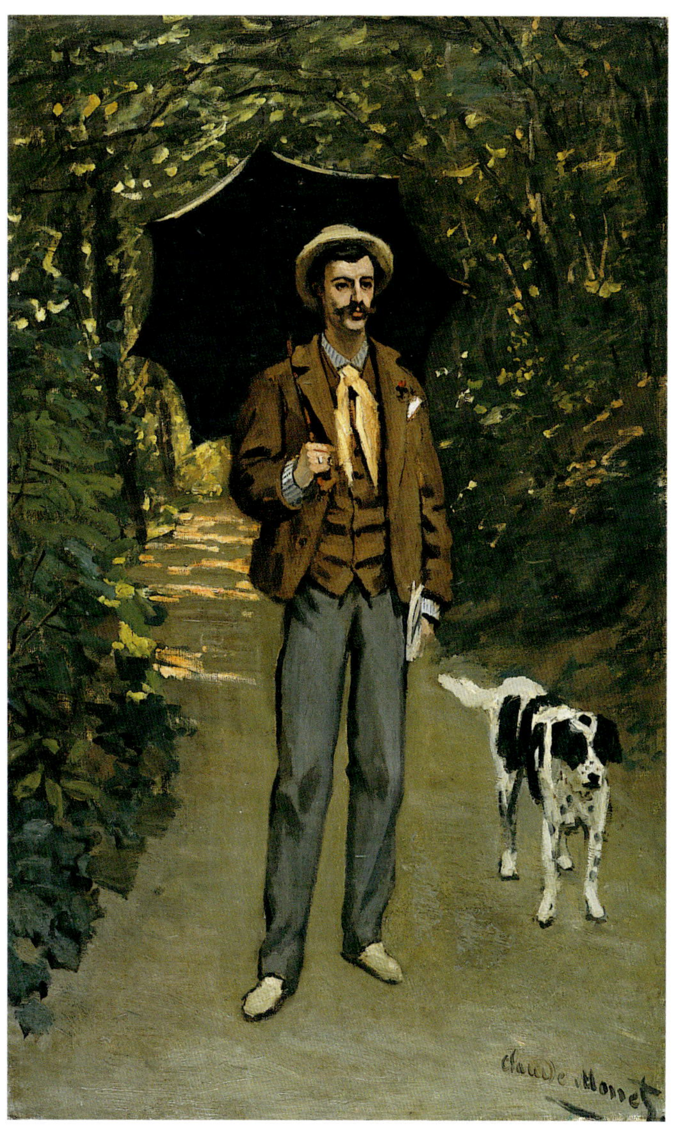

lounge suits, began to be made in softer and more colourful stuffs and worn with softer and lower hats, although the cut was still boxy. Most important, the lounge coat had no waist seam that could create a skirt or tails out of the lower half – those indicated old-fashioned formality. The short-coated lounge suit, originally appropriate only at private leisure in the country or at home, was eventually acceptable as public urban wear – we see its coat and waistcoat on Monet's stroller – and later on became the most elegant and formal daytime suit, the frock coat of the twentieth century.

For the aforementioned farmers of the later nineteenth century, such lounge suits were made for festive dresswear, often in thick black wool for practicality, and also boxy – you can see one on the man in Renoir's *Dancing at Bougival* in the Boston Museum Fine of Arts. From the late 1860s to the end of the century, not only the surface but the shape of Everyman's body was now quite hidden by his well-tailored but loose-fitting tailored clothing. Painters were rendering it in a variety of expressive ways: we'll look at a couple of examples.

Gustave Caillebotte was a friend and supporter of Impressionist painters, but his own style remained much more personal and more atmospheric, less devoted to a completely chromatic surface. He painted many men in black or blackish modish suits, sometimes in a black that has been greyed or blued or browned to contrast with another black texture or to blend with neighbouring objects, sometimes in a colour, but always dim. Caillebotte's *On the Pont de l'Europe* (fig. 98) of about 1877 is one of several views he painted of people walking on this lately built Parisian bridge, which spans not the Seine but the many railroad tracks emerging from the Gare St-Lazare, itself painted again and again by Monet. The station, tracks and bridge were great feats of the modern engineering now everywhere evident in recently demolished and reconstructed Paris.

This picture offers a fine contrast to Monet's park view with its genial, colourfully dressed character arriving along a receding sunny path under a leafy vault. It's also strikingly different from another one Caillebotte painted of this same bridge, showing full-length views of diversely clad people, including a man and woman in conversation, and a dog. In that picture he used the receding steel bridge to form a sharp perspective component for the setting, and he put a bright blue sky behind it.

Here the beams and railing fill the frame, no dogs or women are present. The three independent male figures are only partially visible, turned from us and each other and bunched into the left half of the foreground. The other half is occupied by the intersection of steel girders, which expose more distant steel structures, some sky and some smoke. The nearly hidden man leaning on the rail is a labourer, the wrinkled sleeve of his workman's smock providing the streak of natural blue not present in this blighted sky. Two other men, one leaving and one staying, wear top hats and frock coats in what seems to

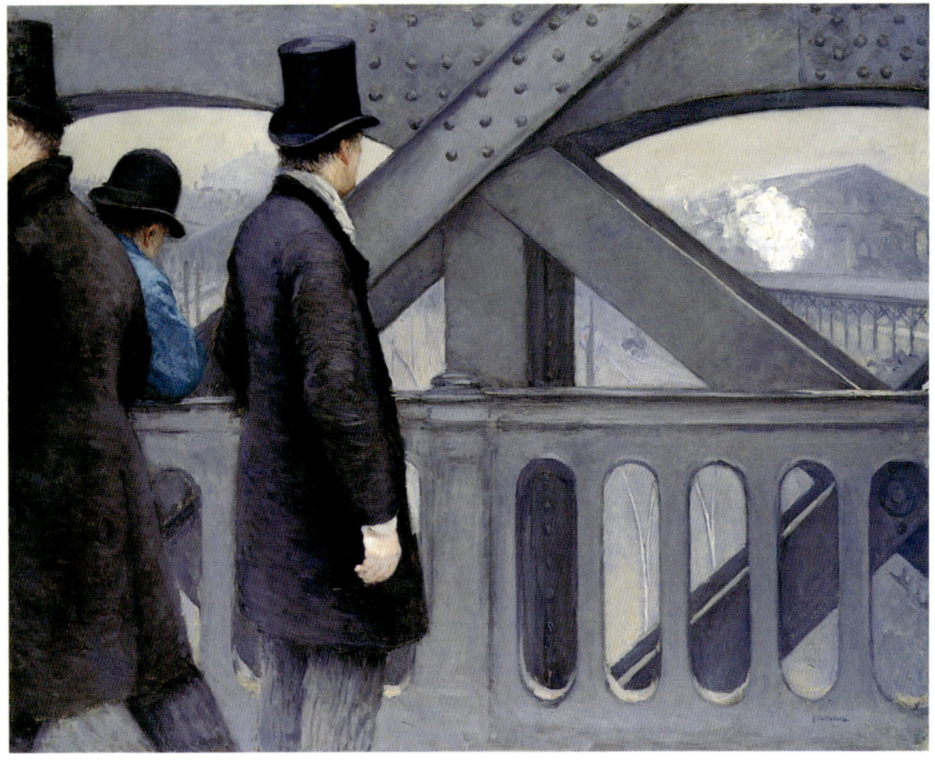

98
Gustave Caillebotte (1848–1894)
On the Pont de l'Europe,
about 1877
Oil on canvas, 105 × 131 cm
Kimbell Art Museum, Fort Worth

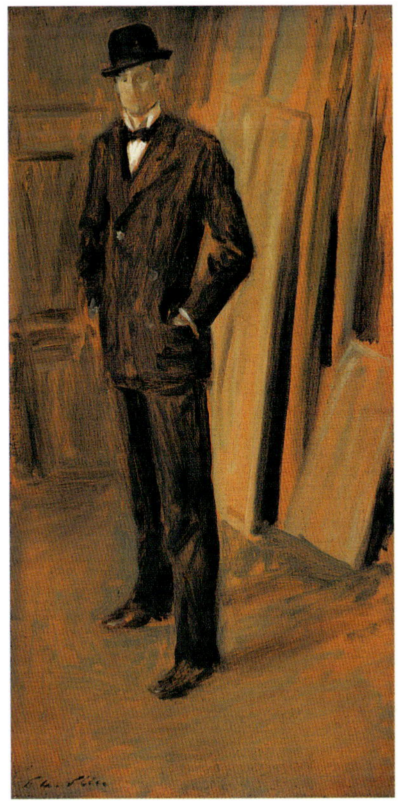

99
Philip Wilson Steer (1860–1942)
Walter Sickert, 1894
Oil on canvas, 59.7 × 29.8 cm
National Portrait Gallery, London

be black, with greyish touches painted to connect them to the grey bridge. But it's possible that the painter has put them in stiff grey coats that can more closely identify them with the stiff grey steel, to give them the same strict, precisely constructed nature – the visible rivets in the bridge looking like the displaced buttons invisible on the coats – and the same impersonal quality. Then the picture can suggest that the two faceless, smoothly coated and hatted men have themselves been cast in the same modern mould as the steel beams, each indistinguishable from the other, intersecting quite mechanically in a new industrial world, their stiff coats forming the structure of modern life; and that the one who stands still and looks out may have been seized for a moment by this thought.

A different painterly spirit can present a similar tailoring scheme as a different kind of phenomenon. Philip Wilson Steer painted Walter Sickert in 1894, when both painters were thirty-four (fig. 99), showing in his portrait how Impressionism had affected non-French painters in the generation following its inception. The painting resembles some of Whistler's, as well as those of Degas, in its muted palette, tilted floor and feathery film of mostly vertical strokes that integrate figure and ground. This pictured suit is not the boxy frock-coat with striped trousers which Caillebotte painted to make the man look straight and dense. This is the boxy lounge suit in one fabric, now more formal than in the Monet; and this painter sketches it so lightly that the suited man seems saturated with the roseate painted atmosphere. Sickert in his suit appears as a loosely defined, unshaped man-like form, floating slightly upwards to the left, seeming to have an uncertain existence among the stacked works in his fellow painter's studio.

Steer emphasises the looseness of the suit itself, its ability to bend and be dented, even to open its pocket to the distorting entrance of a hand, without losing its look of tailored integrity. At the same time, Sickert's suit is painted to be bigger and stronger than he is. His delicate head and evanescent face are disproportionately small, and the hat, collar and cravat are more sharply defined than they are; the coat and trousers and even the shoes are disproportionately long and large. This obliquely illustrates one of the most appealing ideas about the modern suit – that it's a kind of refuge and disguise, a flattering, roomy container to hide in.

And it's not really a box. In a later development of its original Romantic–Neoclassic aim, the suit seems to reproduce the man's body in a better form than it has. A suit like this looks comfortable and unassuming, not tight and stiff and imposing; but it really does impose a new body on the man, one that also seems to add something to his mind and spirit. The weaknesses of any kind that the man may have are replaced by the strength of his suit's suave, flexible and harmonious design, so that he seems suave and strong and flexible; and his privacy is guaranteed by its unrevealing shape.

At the end of the nineteenth century, we may remark how distant is the above idea from the one illustrated by Boilly at the beginning of it, when shape-revealing tailoring was designed to expose and celebrate the wearer's individual form, face and feelings. The Romantic Neoclassicism of that epoch is just as far from the steely and sturdy 1870s idea we saw in Caillebotte's man on the bridge as this is from that one; but the same elements of tailoring have persisted through all these variations in suits, partly because of the expressive qualities painters have seen in them and given to them, all suggesting that the suit improves the man. The frock coat on Lehmann's Liszt is not different in

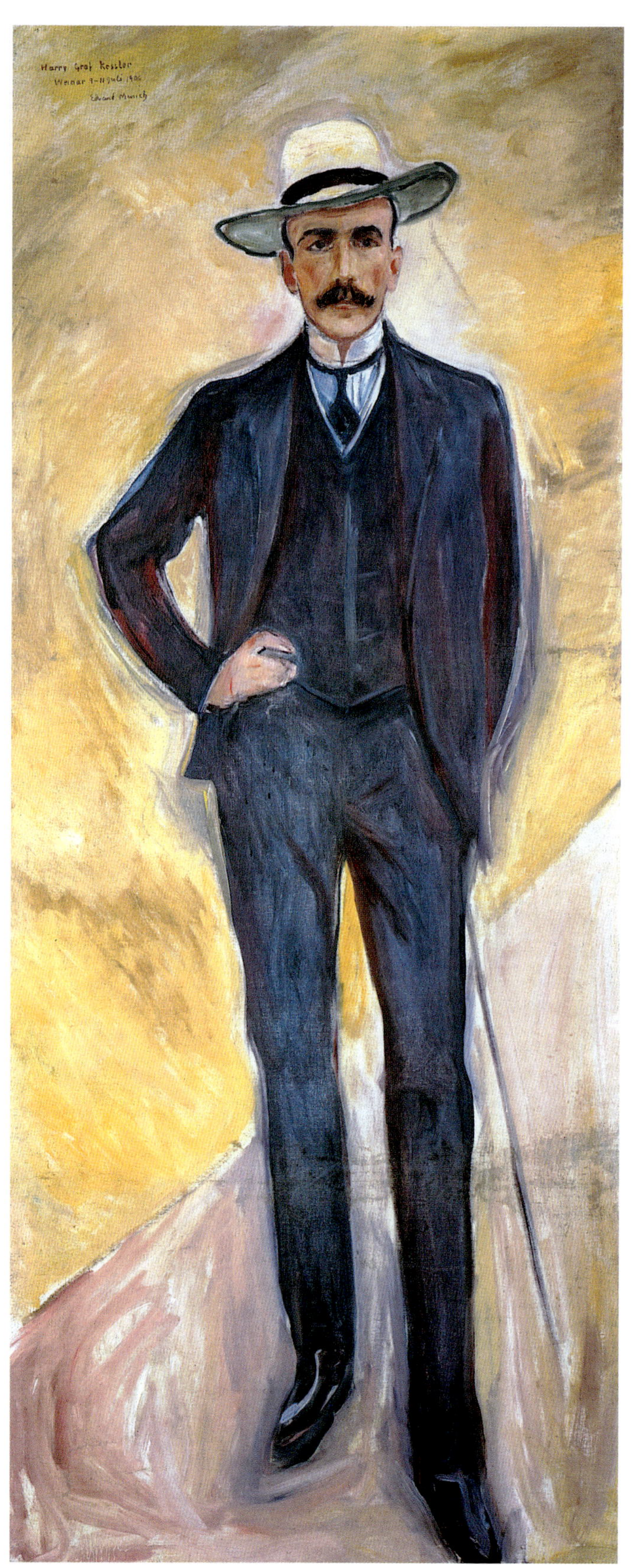

100
Edvard Munch (1863–1944)
Harry Graf Kessler, 1906
Oil on canvas, 200 × 84 cm
Staatliche Museen zu Berlin,
Neue Nationalgalerie

basic construction from the one on Caillebotte's passer-by. The shift from a small waist, sloped shoulders and flared skirt to a straight skirt, big waist and straight shoulders is a technical matter, noticeable but not huge; whereas the shift from sharply lit and delineated Romantic drama to subtly shaded psychological and empirical observation is a huge one. It is the force of pictorial imagery that makes these different qualities cling to the tailoring of these different epochs, as if they were intrinsic to it.

Now we move into the twentieth century, to find out how the lounge suit looks, forty years after the man in the Monet wore his early version to walk in the park. In Munch's 1906 portrait of Harry Graf Kessler (fig. 100), the suited man is again transformed by the style and character of a painter's work. The lounge suit is now called a walking suit, here in a shape fashionable in about 1900, when the colours were still frequently pale and the textures rough. At this date what was once informal and even Bohemian is correct and elegant. What has changed most about suits since the one worn by Baron Schwiter in 1826 is the neckwear: Delacroix showed the baron in the Brummellian folded white linen cravat, Monet gave his Bohemian a colourful knotted scarf, and Munch's count now wears the thin twentieth-century necktie, the final, formal abstraction of all past folded and knotted neckcloths. The look of boxy bulk is out of fashion, but the body of the coat is still straight, here quite short with curving cut-away fronts, so the narrow trousers can appear even longer. Fashionable suits were about to get wider and fuller again in the next decade; but at this moment Munch can show the suited count as a formidably slim creature.

He also shows his suit as smooth and solidly dark, which may well have been the count's personal taste; but the painter here makes it an unlikely blue-black against the yellowish void that forms a background not urban, not rural, a luminous cloud with a tilted plane for the count to stand on. We can imagine and project a setting on to this; but nothing is there except a feverish glow. Against this lurid screen the painter makes the suit's black outline extra-vibrant by painting the yellow strokes against the black edges and letting a few overlap it, as if the backlight were bouncing off the figure, and this helps remove all sense of ease or flexibility in this suit's function as bodily covering; it's again like armour.

Fashion requires that this coat not curve in at the waist, but the painter has given the waistcoat no kindly wrinkles such as Monet gave his subject; these long trousered legs are extra-angular and the body proportionately shorter. Encouraged by the glaring backdrop, this painted suit is like a black beetle's carapace with coppery glints, and the strokes that form it are dense and tight. The count's red cheeks look choleric, his curving green and yellow hat seems sinister, the shine on his shoe more menacing than elegant – these same touches might seem light and cheerful in another painter's work. Shirt collars are now stiff, the edges and corners may cut into the neck and jaw instead of caressing their sides; this narrow black necktie is like a noose, the narrow black hatband a warning, the sting-like walking stick a semi-concealed threat. Bare hand on hip, the count seems braced to challenge a murky destiny. This is a modern Expressionist version of Liszt's forbidding Romantic suit; this painter now uses a male figure in a fashionable urban costume to create an atmosphere of unease and psychic danger around him. Munch has even borrowed the pose common in current fashion plates to add a further eerie effect to this image.

Masculine evening dress, having become permanently cast in the Romantic mould early in the nineteenth century, was clearly in great need of modernisation. After the invention of the daytime lounge suit in the 1860s and its gradual acceptance as urban daytime dresswear, the next step was to make it in black for the evening; and so the dinner jacket or tuxedo, originally called the dress lounge coat, was invented in the 1880s. The Americans claim to have invented and named this modern costume at a country club in Tuxedo Park, south of New York; but the British, unchallenged emperors of male tailoring since Brummell's time, naturally claim to have invented it first, at more or less the same date. The form required a stiff white shirt and collar like the full-dress costume but with a black tie, and the coat was originally worn open to show a black waistcoat. This costume was meant for cosy evenings in a club-like or private-house atmosphere, and throughout the rest of the nineteenth century and the first quarter of the twentieth it remained improper for elegant restaurants, formal dinners and balls, the opera, the theatre, or any other public occasion requiring evening dress.

In Max Beckmann's *Self-portrait in a Tuxedo* of 1927 (fig. 101), however, we see a highly individual modern painter's vision of modern informal evening dress, the black lounge suit with both coat and waistcoat cut low to expose more white shirt, stiffened for the evening.The lapels would have been faced with silk, not indicated in this picture, to distinguish this elegant coat still further from an ordinary black suit – the one those farmers had been wearing to the dance since the 1880s. The picture has a background like the Liszt portrait, another flat interior surface with wainscotting below, possibly a plate-glass window with no view, its vertical edge a possible curtain. This is more nothingness, but less psychologically suggestive and more to be appreciated for its geometric and non-chromatic design, which sets an abstract, Modern tone for this portrait.

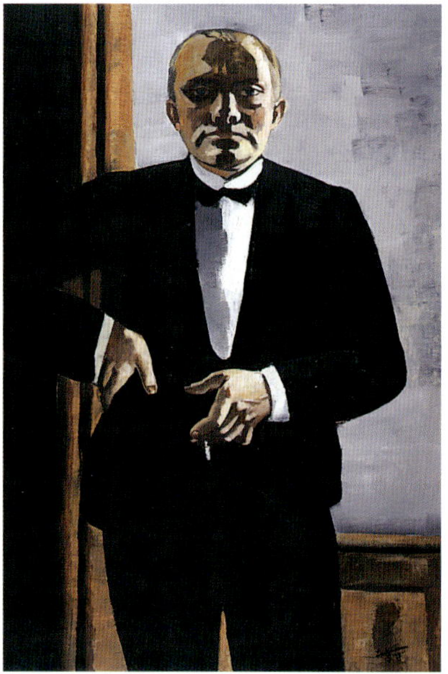

101
Max Beckmann (1884–1950)
Self-portrait in a Tuxedo, 1927
Oil on canvas, 139.5 × 95.5 cm
Harvard University Art Museums, Cambridge, Massachusetts
courtesy of the Busch-Reisinger Museum, Association Fund

The spotlight hits one side of the stern face, finding the frown as it does on Liszt's brow, striking half the white shirt-front, both the white cuffs and both the painter's hands. The point is made that this severe but casual costume interlocks with the individual personality of the man, as its blackness and whiteness act out an intimate drama with his expressive hands and face. But the graphic formality of the painting, suggested to the painter by the tuxedo, is what originates the drama.

The painter presents himself as Graf Kessler does, with one hand on his hip and his weight on one leg; but the cigarette in the other hand, along with the artist's closeness to us, makes this version of the suit more conversational than the full-length portrayals we've been looking at. It's as if the smoking man were indeed at his club, where we are also members – talk is candid, gloomy silence respected, and the costume is shown to strengthen rather than mask the humanity of the man, as in its original conception at the end of the eighteenth century. Beckmann is careful to delineate his two black thighs before cutting them off with the bottom edge of the frame, so that the suit's balance won't be destroyed. The two sleeves need their two counterparts below, as arms need legs for a balanced nude.

The suit gradually lost its obligatory waistcoat during the twentieth century, and so did the tuxedo, although both may still have one. The two-part costume now called a suit – that is, with the coat and trousers of the same stuff – has come to occupy a smaller area of the masculine sartorial realm, as a range of clothing for active or dangerous sports and for the more physically taxing occupations have come to be adapted for male urban wear.

Suits remain comfortable, flexible, subtly various and becoming to everybody, however, and they still have not gone away. Several painters in the last quarter-century have done them ample justice, never finding in them any constraint on the visual imagination.

Suits appear frequently, for example, in the work of Lucian Freud, their shapes and textures always as richly rendered as the human skin and hair. *Man in a Chair* of 1985 (fig. 102) is a fine study in the mobility of modern tailoring, a lovely assimilation of a suit's wrinkles to the wrinkles of the hands and face, with both infecting the intense wrinkling of the neighbouring rags. This is the waistcoatless suit, here relieved of all straightness – pliable and attractive, gaping happily above, between and below the buttons, its light-coloured stuff alive with possibility against a dark nothingness background. The red and gold chair makes a good intermediary between the pinched corner and the big-handed big man in his humane-looking suit. Although this picture has an affinity with Raeburn's portrait of Mr Hutton (see fig. 91), this painted suit has enough Rococo overtones to rouse the ghosts of earlier painted draperies among these modern flannel folds.

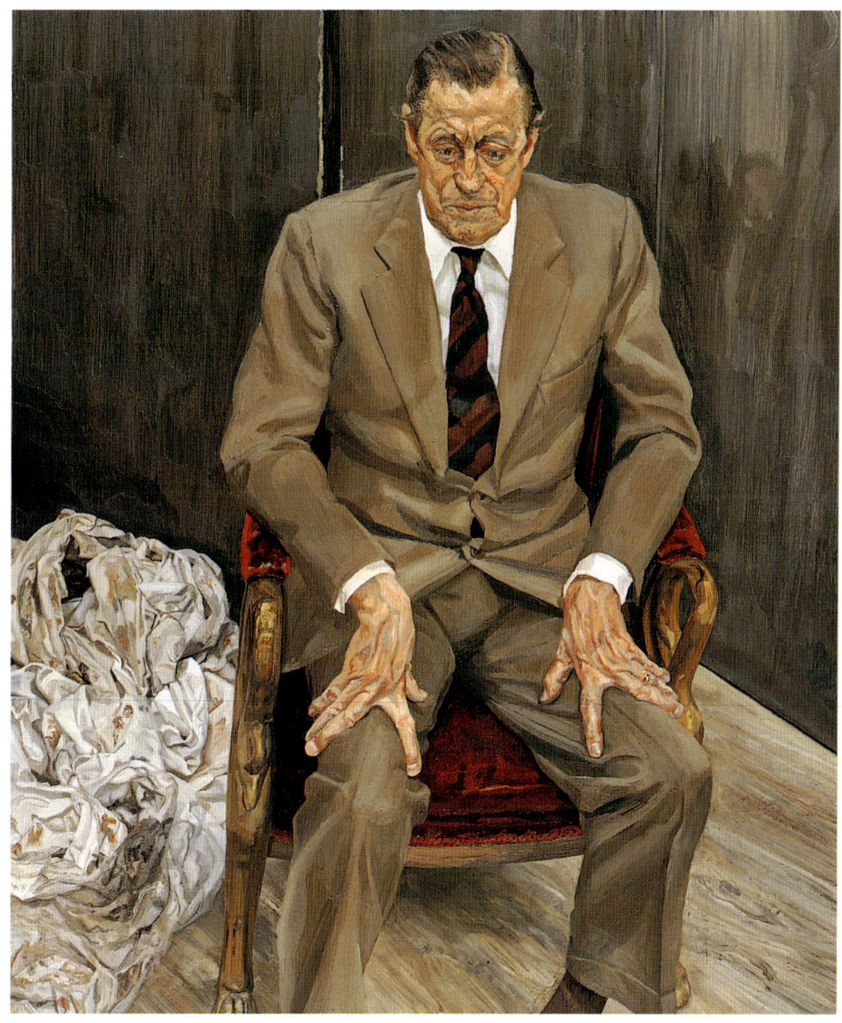

102
Lucian Freud (born 1922)
Man in a Chair (*Baron H.H. Thyssen-Bornemisza*), 1985
Oil on canvas, 120.5 × 100.5 cm
Thyssen-Bornemisza Collection, Lugano

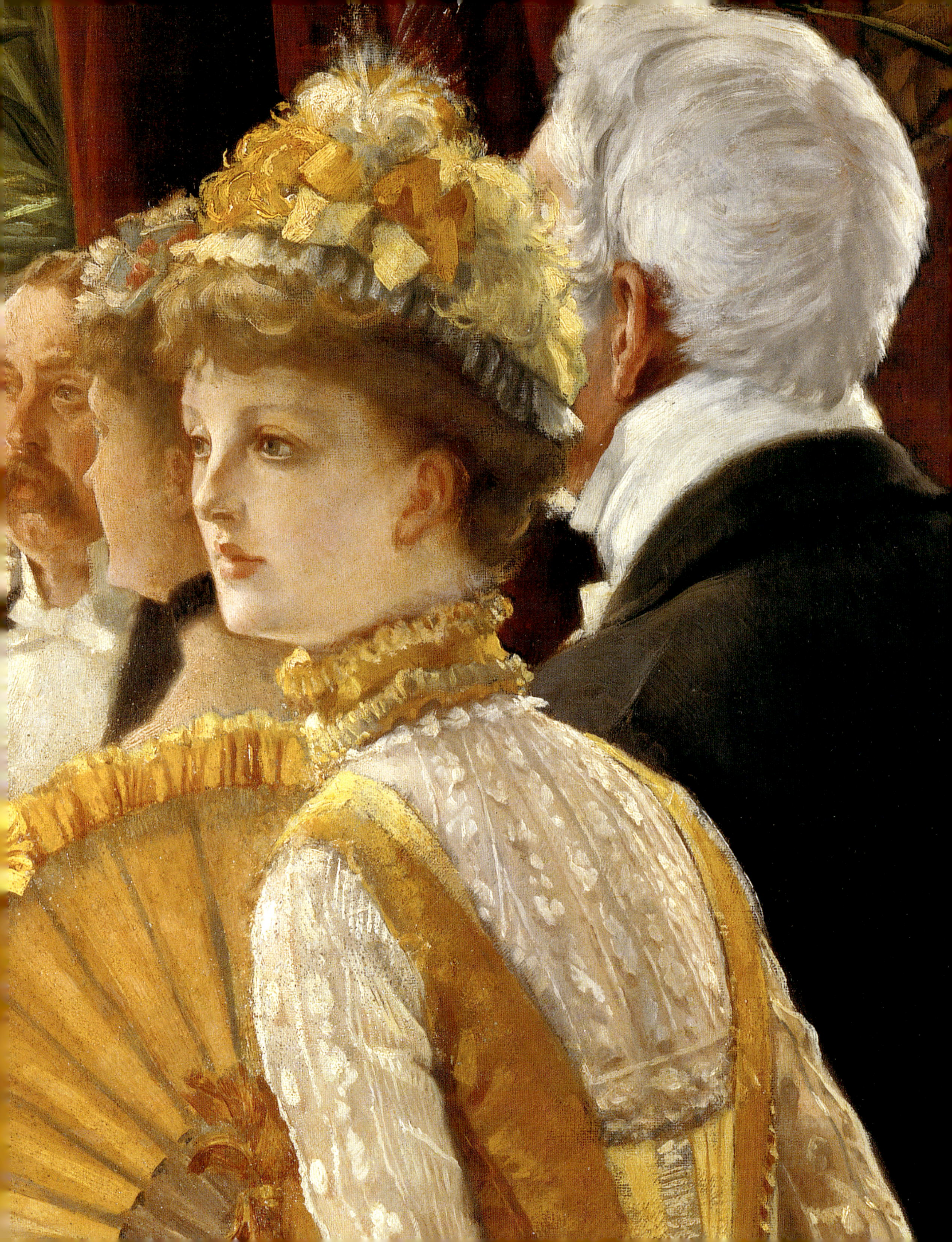

VII Restraint and Display

After 1800 the feminine vogue for columnar white dresses with high waistlines lasted less than twenty years. Towards the end of that time, stays were being designed to shape the female torso like an hourglass, fashionable sleeves and skirts were spreading out again and beginning to carry more and more ornamentation. The Neoclassic fantasy of the statuesque Greek maiden was over, and the Romantic apparition of the buoyant sylph took its place – notably under the influence of the innovative Romantic ballet *La Sylphide*, with its tutu-clad supernatural heroine – to be followed by other apparitions, often based on other fictions both literary and theatrical. Nineteenth-century modish dress for women became the vessel of mixed visual fantasies, played out with bright colour and multiform detail on shifting shapes of considerable volume. Painters taking couples as their subject emphasised this trend, letting the man's clothes look recessive and dim by comparison to feminine brilliance and scope.

It should be noted that much nineteenth-century women's dress was plain and sober and was often rendered so by painters in portraits and genre paintings, and we've already seen that painters could make male dress convey a great range of feeling; but it was often the case that in paintings of couples the woman's dress became the visible focus for the emotion and sexuality of both characters, whatever their relations were. In such pictures, male dress seemed to stand for fact, female dress for feeling and imagination.

Arthur Hughes's 1850s painting called *The Long Engagement* (fig. 103) shows a faded affianced pair, their faces worn with virtuous waiting, surrounded by burgeoning nature. The light falls strongly on her shining golden hair, on the many shining folds of her violet velvet cape, on the shimmering violet veil hiding the blue-feathered hat hung on her arm by its blue ribbons, and on the pleats of her glistening blue damask skirt, also catching the white lace frills at her wrists and neck, and the brilliant red flower at her bosom; the silky dog is another of her many adornments. She is pressed close to her lover, her pale face lifted to catch its own important share of light. The man meanwhile is dressed in a drab pair of brown trousers and an even drabber brown coat, his hair and whiskers mousy brown, his hatted head, shoulders and face in shadow so that his linen is invisible,

Detail of fig. 105

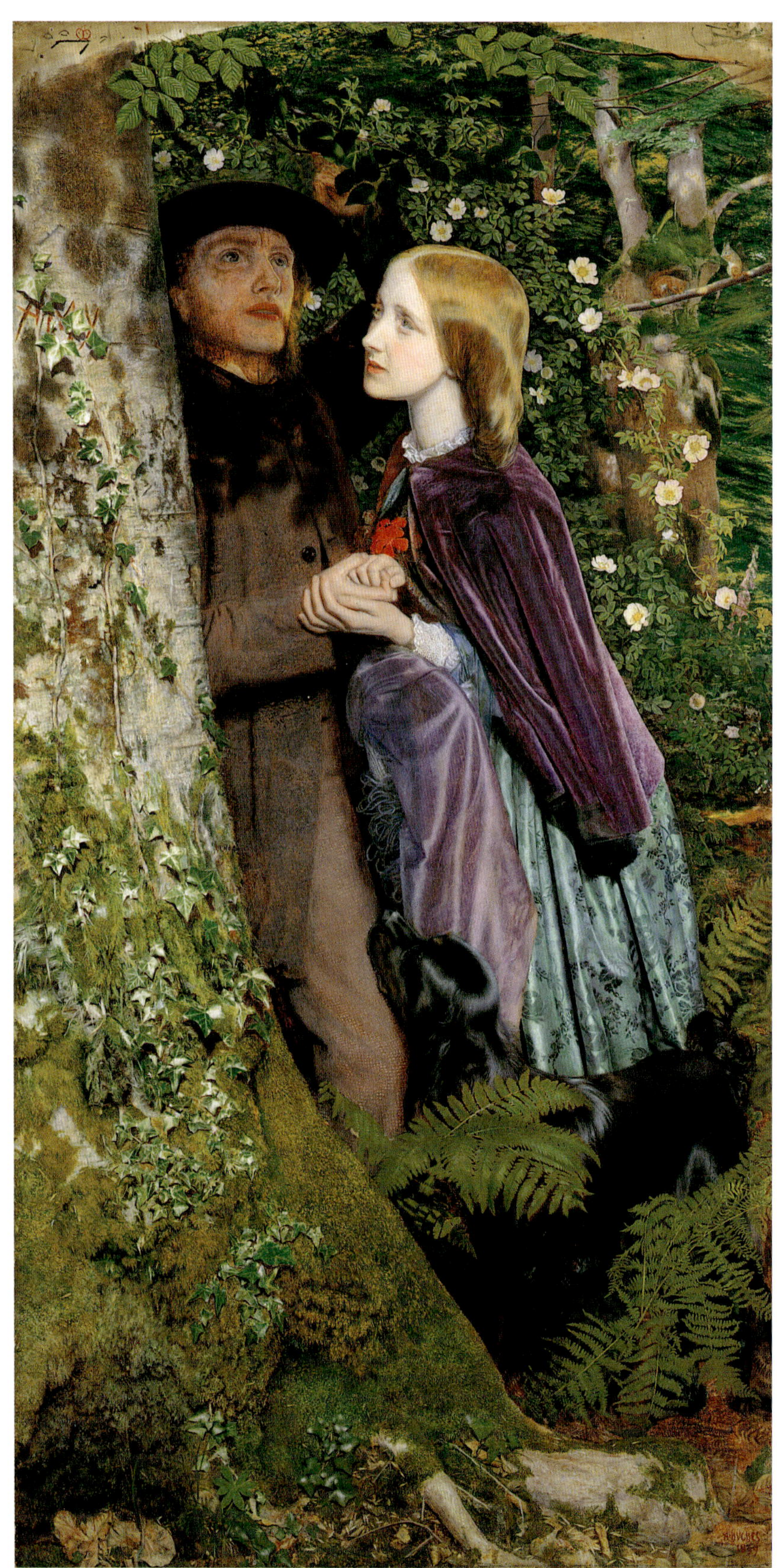

103
Arthur Hughes (1832–1915)
The Long Engagement,
about 1854–9
Oil on canvas, 105.4 × 52.1 cm
Birmingham Museums and Art Gallery, Presented by the executors of the late Dr Edwin T. Griffith

and no details of his costume show except one button. His right hand is spot-lit only because she holds it between hers.

The man seems like a boulder next to the tree against which he leans; she is poised like a big rainbow version of the small white flowers in the background. Why should she be so flamboyant, he so dim? Why should they not both be in sad drab fabrics, feeling the strain together, or both colourful, fighting gloom together? He might have been dressed like the man with the parasol in the last chapter – Pre-Raphaelite painters such as Hughes often did paint colourful male gear in great detail. It is alleged, however, that this young man is a curate: that excuses his dull garb. But this Victorian example of correct dress for fraught encounters between the sexes supports the Romantic standard for visualisations of men and women that was already in force in 1800. We glimpsed it in the Gainsborough of the 1780s, in the difference between the two Boilly portraits, and between David's renderings of Brutus' garments and those of his women (figs. 77, 84, 93, 81).

This woman's painted clothes suggest female affinity with the fleeting aspects of nature, not just flowers but moving water and changing skies; her feeling are quickly expressed, she may swoon or weep; but she also cares how she looks, she chooses and perfects the details of her appearance. His painted figure suggests masculine steadfastness and lack of surface tremor, the immobility of stones and the trunks of oaks; his spirit lies deep, though it can be stirred. He stands firm, never weeps, and never looks in the mirror. She will weep for both of them, just as she will shine in pomaded hair and well-selected coloured silk.

The same sartorial concept governs Alfred Elmore's *On the Brink* of 1865 (fig. 104), although the emotional and sexual circumstances are entirely different. Here again the rich, expansive costume of the lady takes visual responsibility for the emotional atmosphere. The tempter behind her is in shadow, like the dim fiancé in Hughes, and his dark garments have no details, although a red glow outlines him and lights his neck and jaw. Instead of the fresh leaves and flowers in the earlier background, wicked gaming among the depraved is rendered in detail behind this pair, most sinners being women in bright dresses. Her full skirt fills the foreground with rivers of flame, her silk cloak flows in billows of smoke, her velvet hat is a cap of embers – she is burning with shame, with desire, with doubt, with gambling fever. The villain tempting her may feel some warmth, but his aspect is cool as the moonlight that strikes her, searching out the furrows on her distressed brow, finding her weakness.

James Tissot's *The Ball* of 1878 (fig. 105) makes an even sharper pictorial distinction between male and female appearance, but it invites a cynical response in the viewer, as the earlier Romantic pictures do not. Here the dim male is faceless – already among the dead, you might say – his snow-white hair enough to define him, along with his evening costume of absolute black and absolute white. Her costume is more ornate than those of the last two mid-century ladies, made more erotic at the end of the 1870s by an elongated hourglass torso and big bedizened rear. The painter has precisely inventoried her feathers, ribbons, ruffles, lace, hat, gloves and bracelet, remarking the huge fan that screens most of a neighbouring lady's dress from our notice. Her form-fitting yellow and white ensemble with its feathery crest and ruffly tail now turns her into a non-human, bird-like creature, and so does her expressionless face.

The meaning of this Maupassant-like scene does not lodge in her feelings, as in the previous two scenes, where the female face and dress expressed concordant emotions.

104
Alfred Elmore (1815–1881)
On the Brink, 1865
Oil on canvas attached to panel,
114.3 × 83.2 cm
Fitzwilliam Museum,
Cambridge

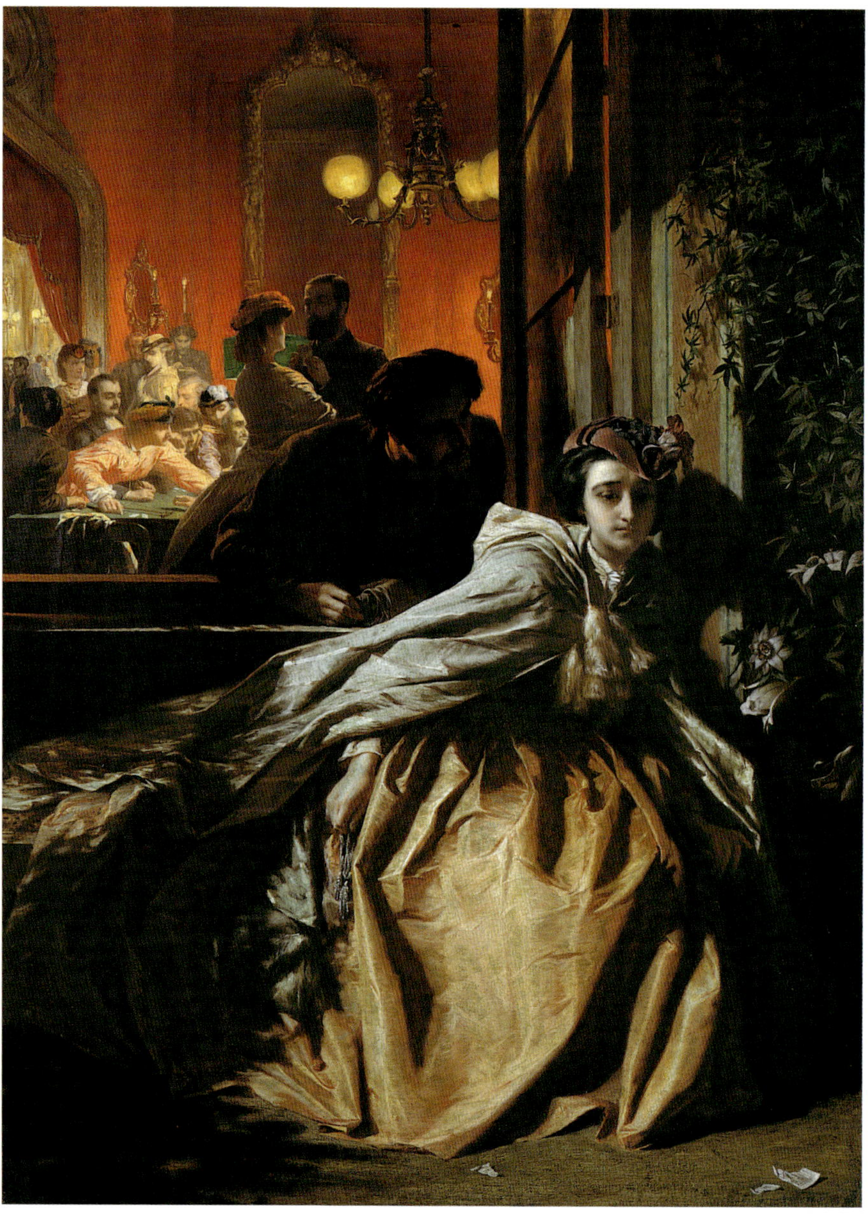

Here there is no emotion in the picture. Meaning emanates directly from the lavishly curved and clad specimen of blonde female youth that fills the centre of the painting, blotting out others, and it is we who do the feeling. The character with whom the sight of this vision might make us identify – in mockery or pity or envy or embarrassment – is the hoary gentleman on whose arm she enters the ballroom, and whose identity we see her obscuring with her costly fripperies as she sweeps her train across a foreground chair.

Precedents exist in the history of art for genre scenes containing dim men and shimmering women, especially in seventeenth-century Holland. Dutch painters specialised in figuring eroticism through the material terms of comfortable bourgeois life, especially its clothes. Many scenes have the same elements as Victorian paintings, but the narrative is more generally amorous, often showing straightforward courtship, sometimes straight-

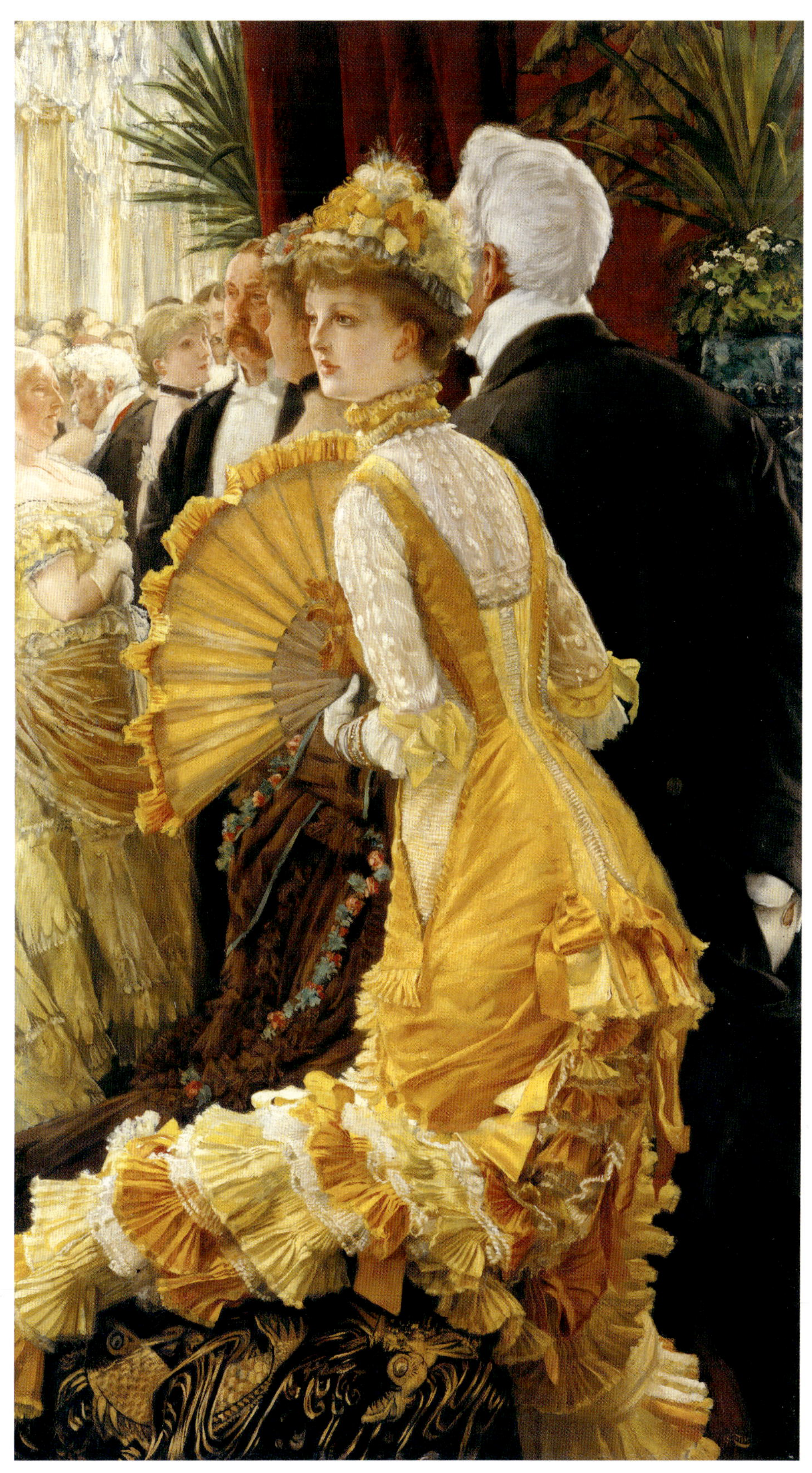

105
James Tissot (1836–1902)
The Ball, about 1878
Oil on canvas, 90.2 × 50.2 cm
Musée d'Orsay, Paris

forward venal transaction with money being offered. The exact circumstances are not specified in Gerard ter Borch's *Woman playing a Theorbo to Two Men* of about 1667–8 (fig. 106), but the painter deploys shiny satin skirts and sleeves to illustrate the woman's attractions, which are further enhanced by the music she's playing. Her thick layers of expensive silk, linen and fur are shown as even more delectable than nudity would be. They are not signs of prosperous domesticity but directly rendered extra levels of physical and material pleasure, in the manner of the heavily clad and ornate Venetian beauties of the previous century.

The men's clothes in Ter Borch's painting are likewise bulky and sumptuous, despite their blackness and the men's shaded placement behind the table. Right now the men concentrate on the song, not the girl; but the still dimmer object behind them at the right is a bed, which only points up the compelling shine of the full-length seated woman at left, her knees fashionably parted under the satin, to whom they will turn when the music stops. The customary dog enters attentively, maybe soon to nose out the playing-card on the floor. It's worth noting that many double portraits or family portraits in mid-seventeenth-century Holland showed prosperous husbands and wives both dressed in equally expensive and

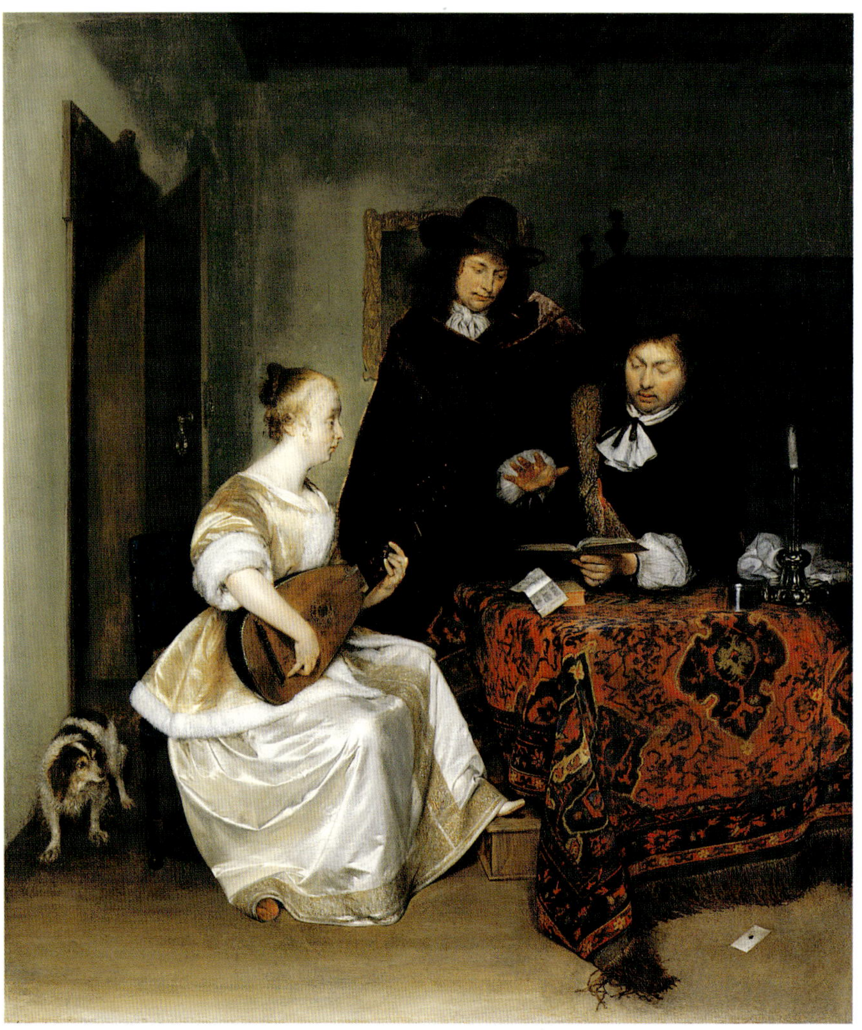

106
Gerard ter Borch (1617–1681)
A Woman playing a Theorbo to Two Men, about 1667–8
Oil on canvas, 67.6 × 57.8 cm
National Gallery, London
NG 864

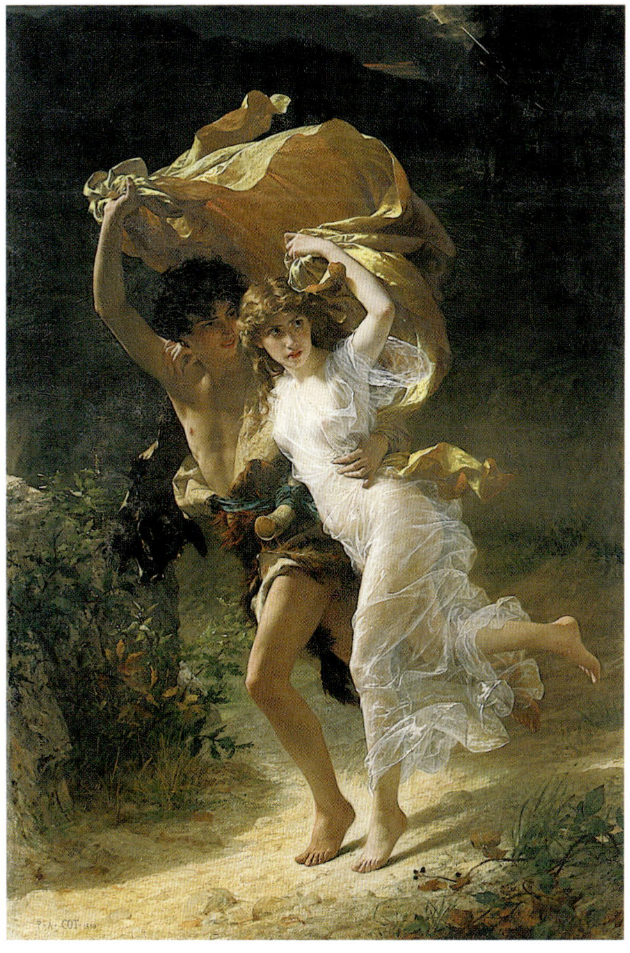

107
Pierre Auguste Cot (1837–1883)
The Storm, 1880
Oil on canvas, 234.3 × 156.8 cm
The Metropolitan Museum of Art, New York, Catharine Lorillard Wolfe Collection, Bequest of Catharine Lorillard Wolfe, 1887 (inv. 87.15.134)

ornate black, with the submerged suggestion that bright, shiny colours on ladies were not appropriate for portraits expressing domestic stability. Genre scenes, then as always, might on the other hand show dim men and bright women whose specific relation was unspecified, and whose appearance and behaviour were open to more than one interpretation.

When Tissot and other later nineteenth-century painters chose to show unromantic scenes from modern life, their pictures were more in line with Ter Borch than with Hughes. Some Romantic painterly clichés about the sexes might still appear under the rubric of history painting, which included invented genre scenes set in antiquity. In 1880 Pierre A. Cot painted *The Storm* (fig. 107), showing a quasi-antique young couple posed as if fleeing together before a threatening sky. He is dark, she is fair; he wears dark, rough skins, she wears thin white gauze; his face is in shadow and he looks at her, while her face is lit and she looks over her shoulder, rather like the couple in *On the Brink* (see fig. 104). It doesn't take much effort to see that the fantasy dress of this Arcadian pair suggests the current fashionable conventions for clothing the sexes: the blue sash fastening his brown pelts and hunting horn suggests a blue cravat with a tweedy, brown informal suit, while her busy white non-garment seems to be a see-through version of an elaborate dress like the one on Tissot's blonde. Some of the transparent stuff even produces the effect of a bustle extending the rear of a tight-fitting dress, prominent in the painting and catching most of the light.

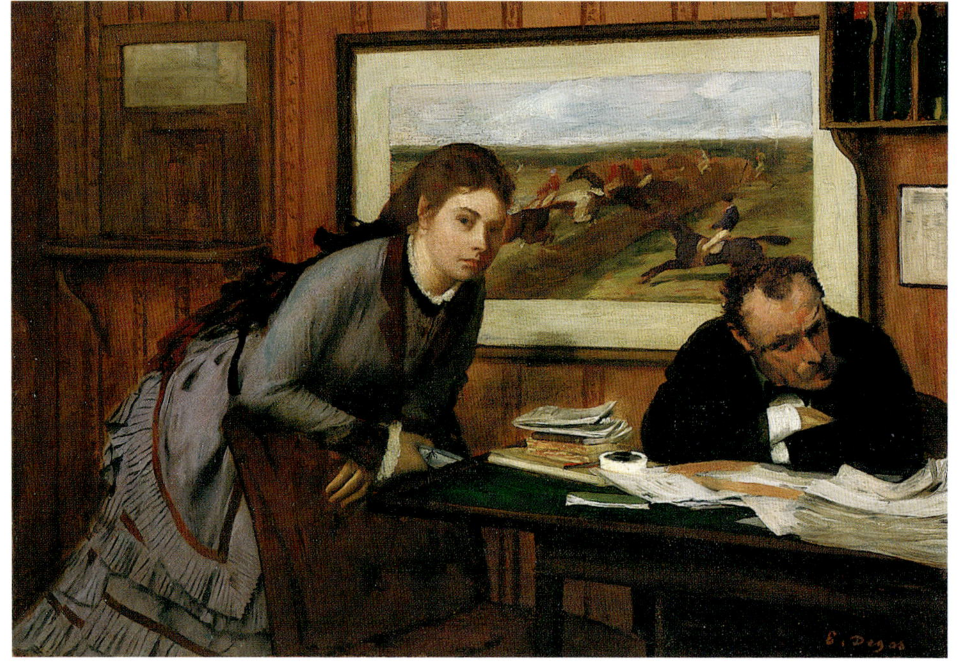

108
Hilaire-Germain-Edgar Degas
(1834–1917)
Sulking (*The Banker*), about 1870
Oil on canvas, 32.4 × 46.4 cm
The Metropolitan Museum of Art, New York, H.O. Havemeyer Collection, Bequest of Mrs H.O. Havemeyer, 1929
(inv. 29.100.43)

Looking at this 1880 painting we can also catch up with the latter-day use of pictorial draperies. By this date, any painter's skill at rendering the free action of stuffs had most of its exercise in fantasy compositions like this one. Painters such as Leighton and Burne-Jones in England developed personal styles of fantasy drapery to rival Mantegna or Tintoretto; Gérôme and Cabanel in France, like Cot, invented draped legendary clothes with a precise, academic character. Puvis de Chavannes's draperies for antique or utopian fantasy have a pallid, stiff, unearthly look just like that of his figures, especially in his large mural compositions. Conventional sacred art was in decline, and we have noted that portraits no longer required drapery. This meant that apart from academic painted nudes with or without narrative subjects, which usually needed draperies somewhere in the picture to mark them as serious art, fantasy recreations of ancient or medieval days were the only pictures in which draped fabric was vital to the composition. Impressionist or Realist artists might scrupulously record its role in current female dress, but that had become a matter of small swags of surface decoration.

Feminine skirts and cloaks, such as we saw flowing and billowing in Elmore and Hughes, stopped flowing and became weighty and complicated in the second half of the 1860s and for the rest of the century, just as women were seen increasingly as more complicated themselves. Tissot's scene was one extreme vision of such finery, offered purely as plumage. Edgar Degas, however, used feminine dress of the epoch much more effectively to convey a non-Romantic, psychologically interesting view of the sexes in his painting from about 1870 called *Sulking*, sometimes simply called *The Banker* (fig. 108). The painter makes a woman's forward-leaning posture show the bodily effect of a complex dress with an elaborate heavy bustle, letting it suggest the weight of the woman's complex state of mind and contribute to the ambiguous atmosphere, which is the chief sign of this pair's low-keyed dissatisfaction and disharmony.

Degas's admiration for seventeenth-century Dutch painting is evident here as elsewhere; and he has insisted on a Dutch-like ambiguity in the theme of the picture, even adding a significant-seeming background picture within the picture to increase it. He shines more light on the colourful woman than on the sombre man; he shows more of her, placing her in the centre with her eye on us; but he gives no sign of the specific relation between the two, or of what has caused their obvious emotional disconnection. Without any Romantic rhetoric, the painter coolly observes that this man's sulks, like his seated and retreating pose, closed face and dark coat, are more contained and less outwardly articulated than those of this woman with her raised face and exfoliating blue frills.

Henri de Toulouse-Lautrec explored the look of Parisian cabarets and music-halls throughout his short career, sharpening his eye for bizarrerie in dress, which embraced modish and show-business trappings for both sexes and the working clothes of prostitutes. *The Englishman at the Moulin Rouge* of 1894 (fig. 109) gives an example of his keen eye for the contrast between gaudy women and formally dressed men, again not unlike some Dutch versions of the theme. Here, however, as seldom in Holland, Lautrec has avowedly made the man the focus of the picture, giving strong texture and detail to the painting of his black garb and pale face, and making the faces and clothing of the fluffy lady and her friend much more sketchy and insubstantial.

The scene is a low-life milieu where the women are all the more attractive for being faintly grotesque, parading their wicked distance from slumming gentlemen in perfect

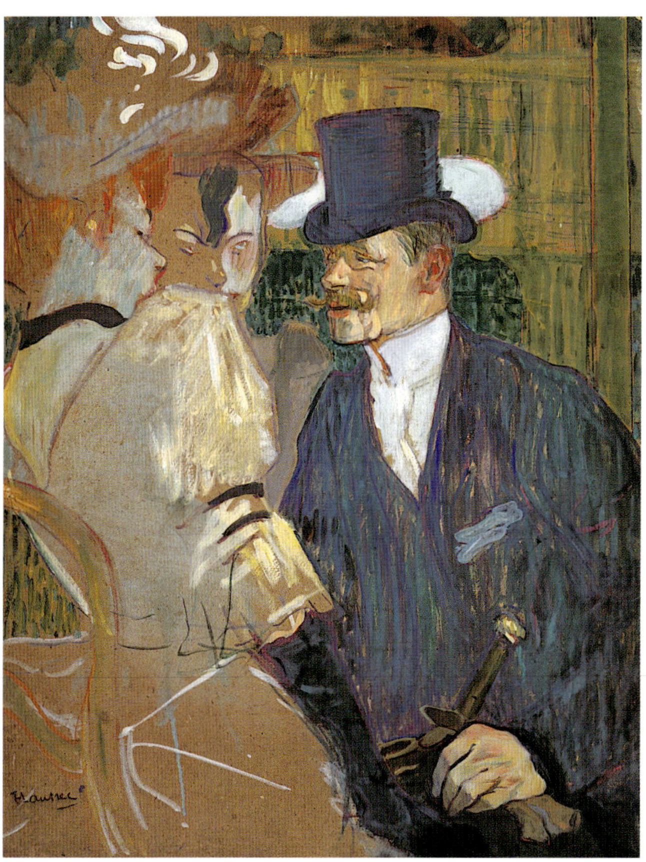

109
Henri de Toulouse-Lautrec
(1864–1901)
The Englishman at the Moulin Rouge, before 1894
Oil and gouache on cardboard, 85.7 × 66 cm
The Metropolitan Museum of Art, New York, Bequest of Miss Adelaide Milton de Groot, 1967
(inv. 67.187.108)

evening dress. The lightness with which Lautrec suggests the central curl of black hair down the brow of the middle figure, along with the orange hair and frothy gear of the other one, contrasts with the serious clarity with which he has rendered all the Englishman's accessories, dwelling further on his moustached mouth, florid ear and finely modelled hand, and not omitting the decorative handkerchief against the rich black of his coat – this is a solid portrait. The women are ephemeral winged creatures of the night, two versions of the same riotous idea, and their funny finery is comprehended in a few strokes. One gloved hand is a blur, not quite feeling the gentleman's knee, and their eyes and mouths hardly show.

A more intensely riotous idea appears in Ernst Ludwig Kirchner's *Red Cocotte* of 1914 (fig. 110). The twentieth century is well launched, various modern expressive methods now dominate painting. Going beyond Lautrec's explicit *fin-de-siècle* Parisian scenes, Kirchner gives us a harsh Expressionist vision of the prostitute's presence. He paints this woman as an explosion of fireworks that tilts the purplish street, flaunting her red wrap and hat before a phalanx of burnt-matchstick men, who collectively demonstrate their herd-like fixation on the flame-like creature. The one at lower left is the witness, perhaps

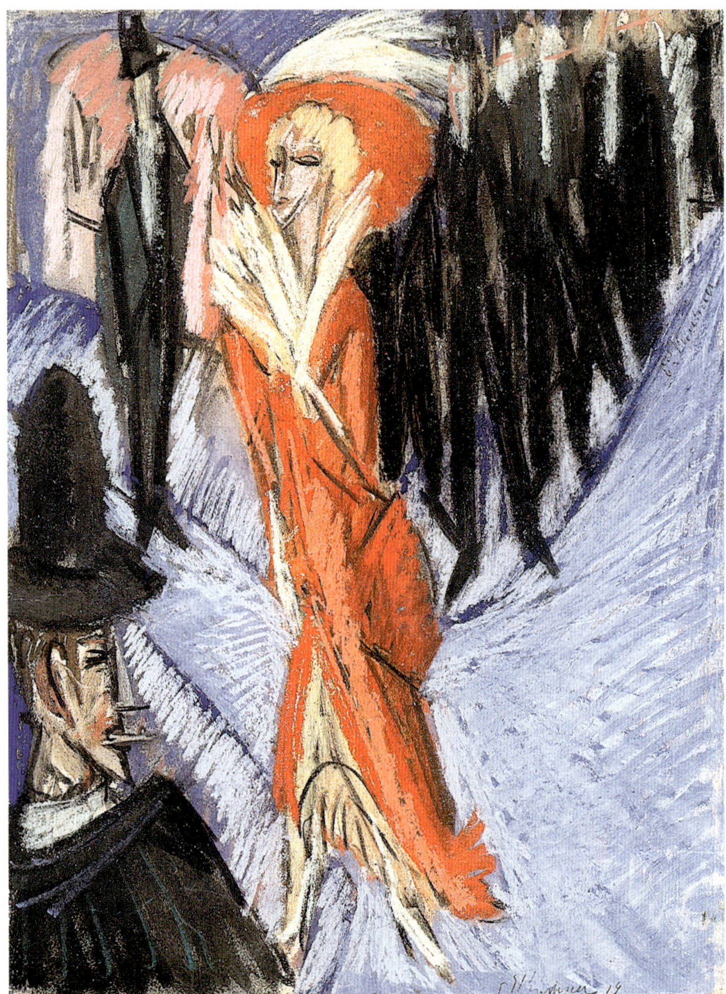

110
Ernst Ludwig Kirchner
(1880–1938)
The Red Cocotte, 1914
Pastel on paper, 41 × 30.2 cm
Staatsgalerie Stuttgart

the pimp or the mark of the moment. The artist has organised the painting so as to insist on the pinched uniformity of the men and the large singularity of the scarlet woman flashing her white frills and plumes, her fringed skirt and pointy shoes.

In 1914, women were still taking up more room with their clothing than men were, most of the spread created by the large hats and extravagant wraps of which Kirchner shows examples. The early twentieth-century trend for women's clothes was nevertheless towards a parity of silhouette with men, sleek in their coats and trousers and neat hats. By the mid 1920s, painters tended to portray the female body as a single unmodulated shape, as did fashion illustrators. Actual dresses were supposed to hang straight from the shoulder to a hemline somewhere on the calf, eventually rising to the knee before subsiding again. Underwear was again being remodelled, this time to suppress all shapeliness, and flesh-coloured stockings were emphasising exposed legs.

Frits van den Berghe's 1924 double portrait shows the conventional subject of a married pair in festive dress (fig. 111). The painter has nevertheless arranged their modern bodies in a Romantic composition that emphasises the differences between them and

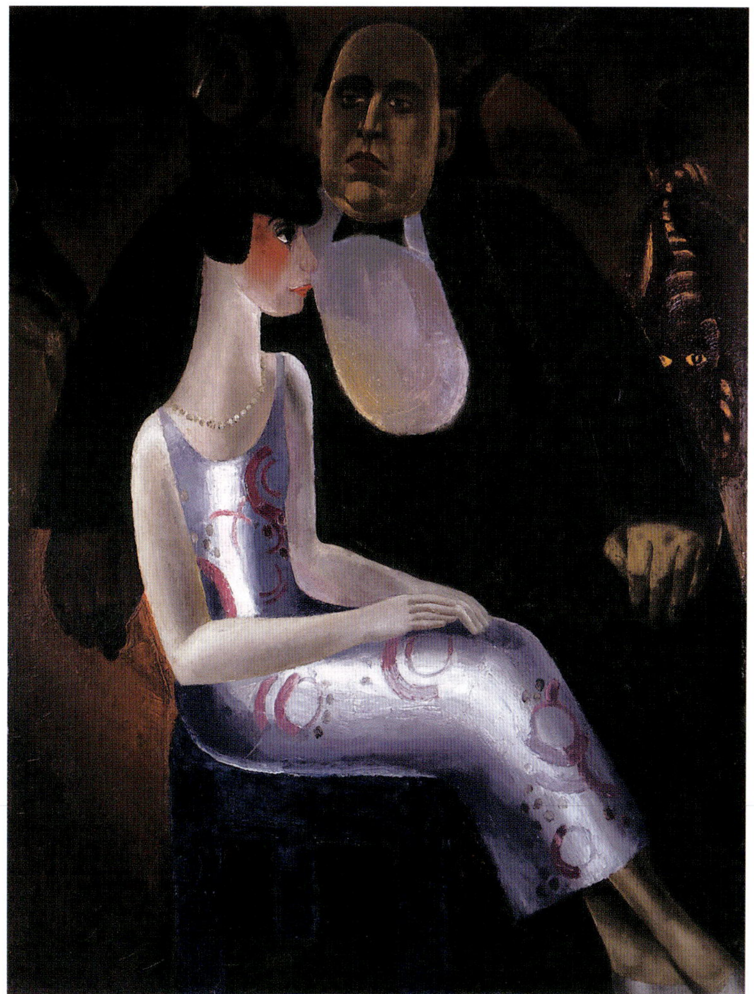

111
Frits van den Berghe (1883–1939)
Paul-Gustave van Hecke and his Wife, 1923–4
Oil on canvas, 160.6 × 120.4 cm
Koninklijk Museum voor Schone Kunsten, Antwerp

creates a tension again reminiscent of the extreme scene in the Elmore picture. The shadowy man is huge in his tuxedo, his small silvery wife seems to exist entirely inside his silhouette. His heavy face has dark red lips, and his lids lower as he looks past us over her head, scanning the horizon for possible threats. Her profile is doll-like with its helmet of hair, insistent rouge and bright eyes staring out of the frame. These two have the air of Svengali and his victim – his body seems to loom, hers to shrink. She sits next to him on a bench with black legs, but the composition suggests that she is sitting on his lap, and that the legs are his short gorilla ones. Appositely enough, on the background wall are the partial images of wild beasts and part of a female nude.

The brightest light in the picture slides in one band down the wife's metallic dress to her calves, making two bends that give her the rigid body of a seated Egyptian statue, hands on knees. Her hands are one-fifth the size of his, which seem to barricade her like

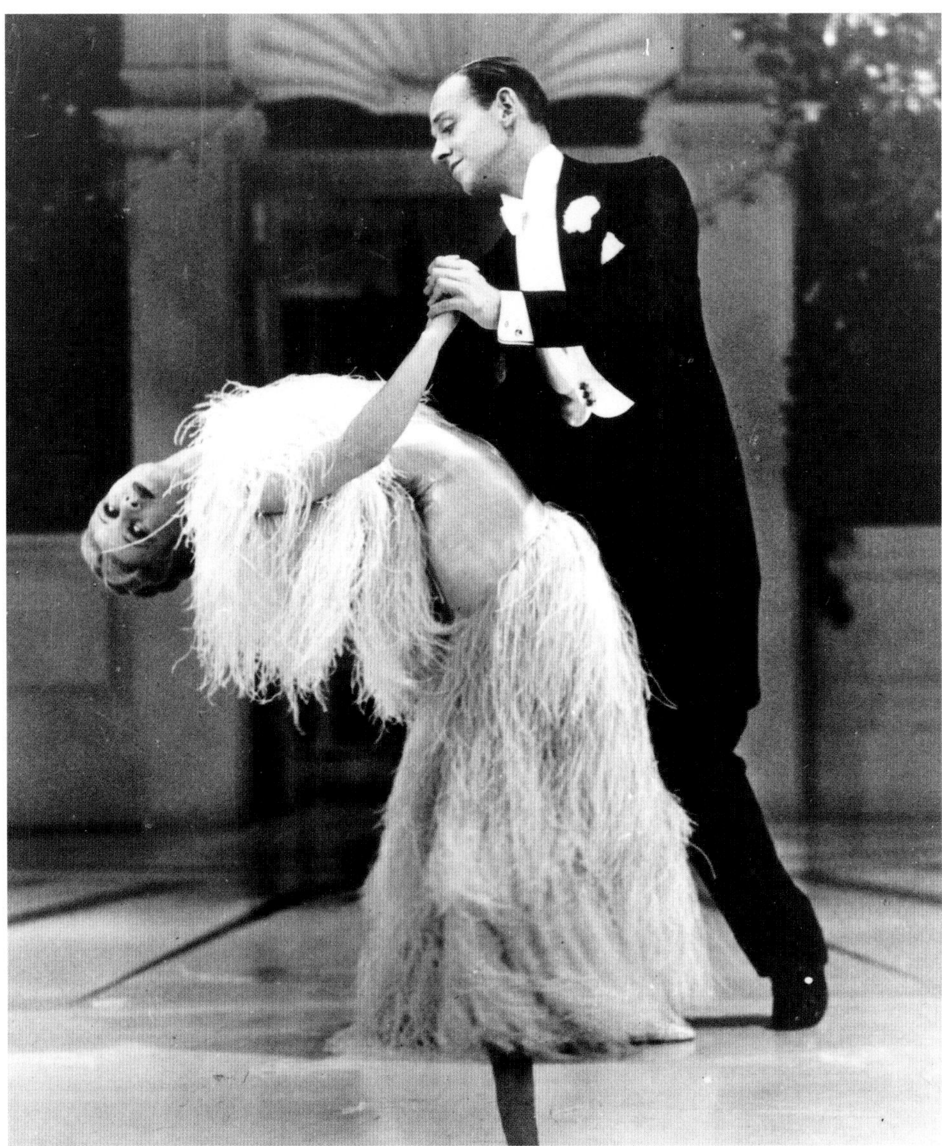

112
Publicity still for *Top Hat*, 1935: Fred Astaire and Ginger Rogers
Private collection
The appearance of Mr Fred Astaire has been arranged through a special licence with Mrs Fred Astaire, Beverly Hills, California.

Courtesy of RKO Pictures, Los Angeles

two gates at the right and left of the painting. Her strength is clearly in her long, strong neck; we can think she has magic of her own to counter his dark bulk.

The painters have generated drama in these nineteenth- and twentieth-century pictures by the opposing ways the male and female figures are painted in their clothes. Common to them all is the sense that men and women are fundamentally different creatures, especially when they meet. It's not only that their plumage is different, but that colour refers to them differently and light strikes them differently, just as ideas do. They are painted to be seen differently by us, and to be seen in the act of finding each other different. In all these paintings, the men and women do not meet each other's eyes; their minds are shown to be working separately.

The painted clothes express the idea that men in their simple tailoring and sober colours have stopped wishing to be fantasy apparitions themselves, as European courtiers of both sexes had once wished to be, according to the old conviction that high rank required personal display. Instead all men have taken on the discreet, functional, quasi-clerical look of persons who are interested in imaginative thoughts and unseen acts, not imaginative appearances and flamboyant acts. While the women's clothes in the paintings were suggesting flowers and water, birds and smoke, butterflies and fire or painted statues, all being the repositories of emotion and fantasy, the clothed men were portrayed either to suggest natural stone and wood, perhaps man-made ramparts and buttresses – or powerful black-and-white masculine creations such as diagrams and columns of figures, written histories and written laws.

In the film still of Fred Astaire and Ginger Rogers dancing (fig. 112) we can see that things are changed within this same convention, partly by the arrival of a new medium in which to render it. At this epoch, the beauty of all evening dress was most impressively expounded by modern photography and especially by the black-and-white cinema. The beautiful tailcoats and dinner jackets and the perfect white shirts and ties worn by male screen actors became one of film's keen visual pleasures, along with the fabulously fluid and shining evening wear of female stars; and the same pleasure could be found in publicity portraits and stills.

We are now in 1935, a good moment in the relations between the sexes as represented in the cinema, where witty repartee between men and women often flourished, and where it was understood that women had education, employment, effective contraception, careers and the vote. Men and women were still known to be entirely different, but they were felt to be less incomprehensible and opposed to one another than they had been in dread Victorian times. The dance we are watching is a true partnership of equals, he suavely proposing, she fluently disposing, both committed to giving a perfectly integrated joint performance. The feathery satin and the white tie and tails submit equally to the graphic beauty of black-and-white cinematography, whirling together in a single harmonious spectacle; it's a transcendent fantasy of harmony between the sexes, achieved with no sacrifice of delicious sartorial difference.

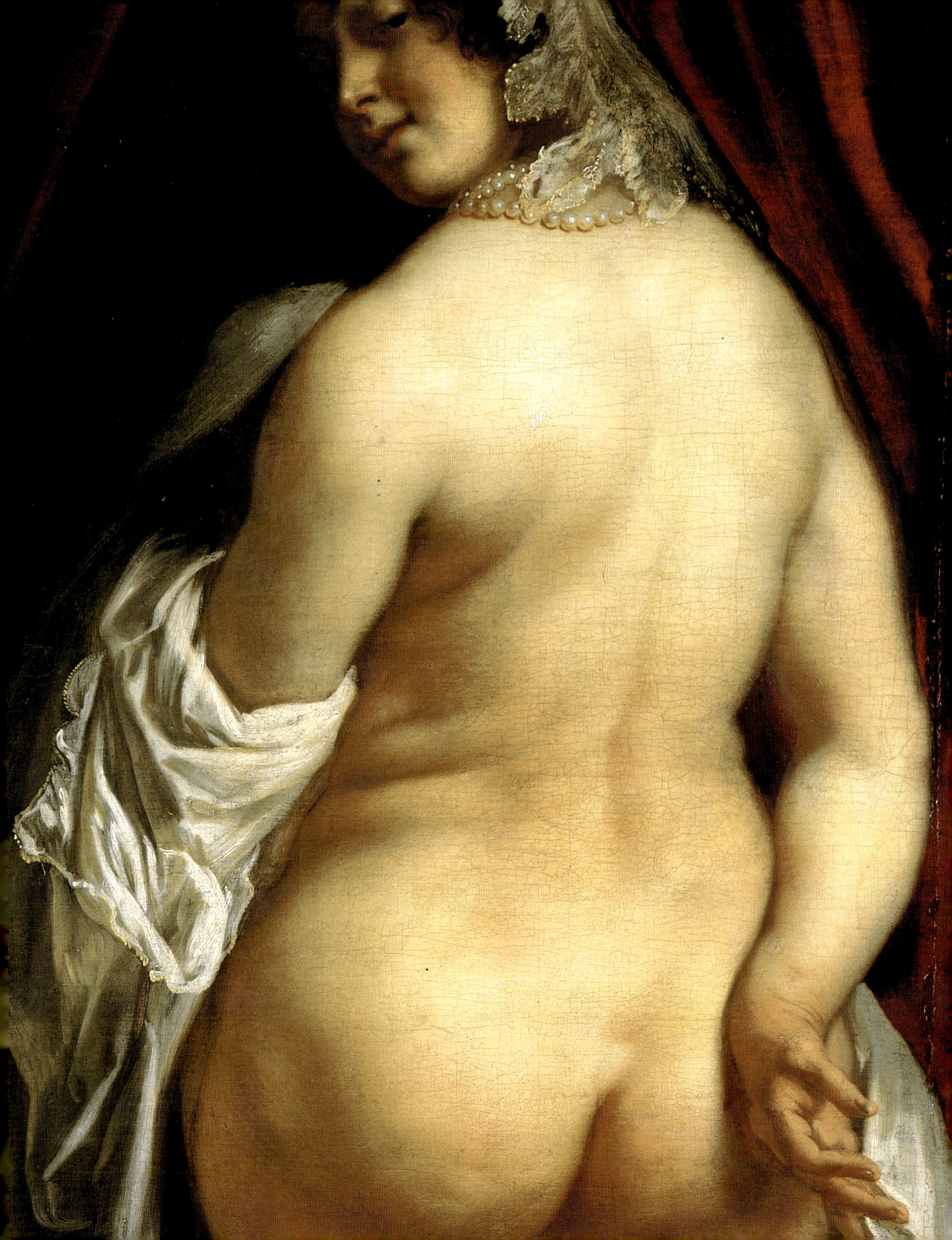

VIII Nude and Mode

SINCE ITS BEGINNING in the late Middle Ages, images of the female nude in painting have shown the unmistakable influence of fashion. Its influence appears in nudes by artists devoted to classical ideals, such as Ingres, no less than in nudes by painters committed to a personal manner, such as Tintoretto, or to a realism unaffected by classicism, such as Rembrandt and Courbet. Although painters committed to ideal truth may think they are immune to the mundane vagaries of fashion, and painters devoted to optical truth may think themselves immune to the impulse to idealise, both will be susceptible to the normative power of fashion, which affects all eyes, even the sharpest. We can see in painted nudes how feminine fashion has shaped a temporarily ideal vision of the nude female body and, at the same time, made that ideal shape seem temporarily natural.

Preparatory sketches done from the living naked model may show the unmediated accuracy of the artist's eye and hand, before the need to turn the sketch into a work of art impels him to make the nude look either more natural or more ideal, in either case more satisfying. Then the look of the body shaped by fashion tends to take over, since it's the one most sexually desirable at the moment, the one most often used in current imagery, and therefore it looks right. It looks right because the fashionably dressed body itself was, and still is, offered most persuasively in pictures, not directly. Today the camera media do this; but when fashion started, painters and printmakers immediately began interpreting it, exaggerating it, demonstrating its most acute contemporary charms – and rendering it in nude form. Both sexes were included in these uses of fashion in art; but we are now considering only the female, from the middle of the fifteenth century to the middle of the twentieth.

A French miniature from the 1460s, showing a poet presenting his volume of verse to a lady, gives an artist's very clear vision of French feminine fashion at its date (fig. 113). We see how the painter has made the proportions of the body conform to a desired look for the clothes in wear. The large head is further enlarged by its towering headdress and veil; the bare chest, bosom and shoulders are made to appear very small, and they are very precisely modelled, as if they were delicate adornments; the wide belt tightly

Detail of fig. 118

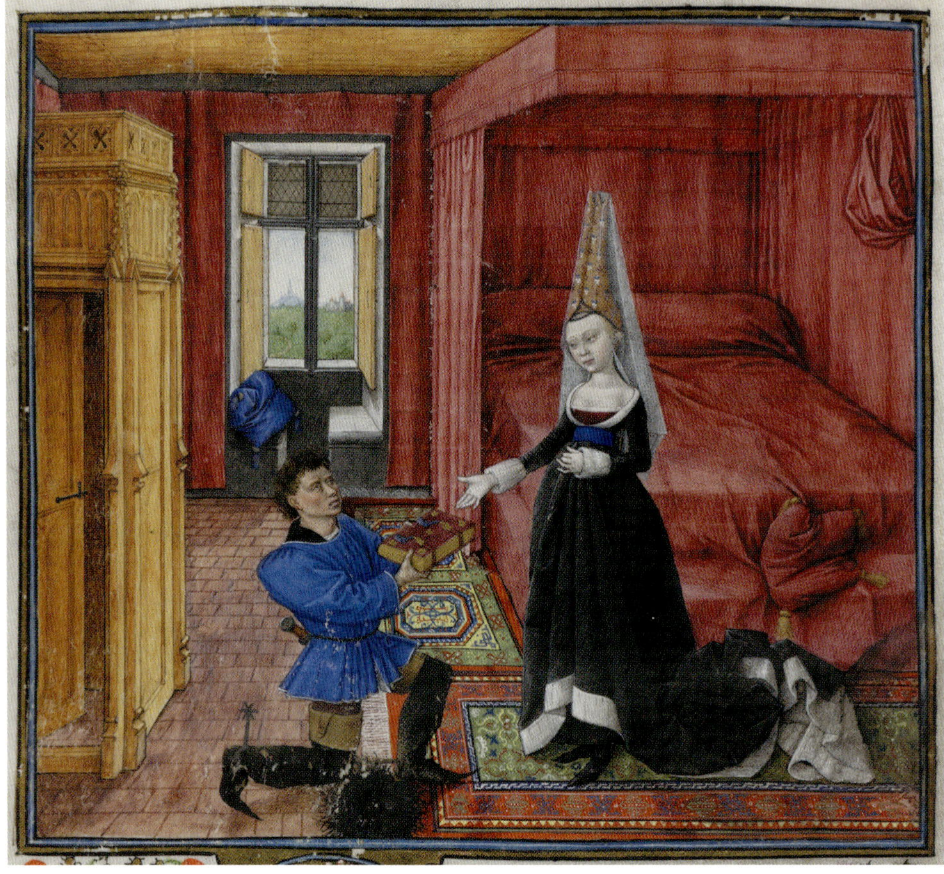

113
Barthélemy van Eyck (active about 1440– about 1469)
A Lady receiving a Book from a Poet, from *La Teseida* (French translation) by Giovanni Boccaccio, about 1460–9
26.6 × 20 cm, parchment
Österreichische Nationalbibliotek, Vienna, codex 2617, f. 14v

constricts the ribcage above the waist, further shrinking the volume of the upper torso; the tight sleeves with high arm-holes insist on thinness for the arms, with flaring cuffs that make the hands look larger.

The lower torso is much augmented and lengthened by the heavy folds of the skirt, which are held up in front to enlarge it further. The posture is tilted back to balance the weight, and the lengthy train piles up behind to balance the posture. The lifted skirt shows that the look of feet is important: they are deliberately revealed wearing long, pointed shoes that make them seem bigger. We may note that the general surface of the costume is smooth and its lines clean, the sleeves and belt fitting without wrinkles, the skirt folds falling as straight as the veil. No hair shows, no jewellery is worn, but the lady's ear appears as an ornament. The serpentine mass of ermine trimming on the train heaped far behind the lady and the gold and gems on the hat rising high above her give the only ornaments to her costume, each situated well away from her body.

When we look at a painting of *Eve* by Hans Memling (fig. 114), who worked in the same tradition at the same time, we can see the imprint of an elegant lady's clothed figure on the nude body of the original temptress. There are the large head, large hands, and large, squarely planted feet, the small, delicate breasts and shoulders and the small, cylindrical ribcage, of which the narrow arms allow us to see the slim outline. Below are the swelling and elongated belly, thrust up and forwards as the upper body tilts back to support the absent folds of skirt, and the low rear that slopes out to allow the backward

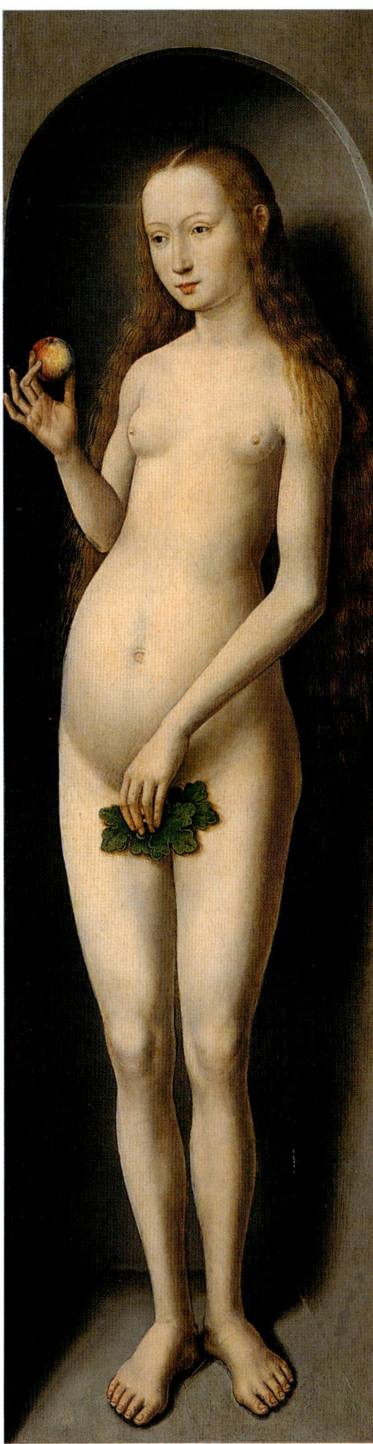

114
Hans Memling (active 1465; died 1494)
Eve, reverse of the right wing of *The Virgin and Child Enthroned* triptych, about 1485
Oil on oak panel, 69.3 × 17.3 cm
Kunsthistorisches Museum, Vienna

drag of an absent train. Here, too, the surface of Flemish Eve's body is as smooth and its lines as clean as those of the French lady's dress. The Flemish painter's close attention to Eve's delicate knees, toes and shimmering hair correspond to the French illuminator's close attention to the clad lady's jewelled headdress and ermine-trimmed train. Eve's ear also appears, a natural jewel among her long tresses.

A century later in Venice, nobody has a slim ribcage or thin arms, nobody has a large head, large hands or large feet, and everybody has big shoulders. Paolo Veronese's 1560s portrait of an unnamed lady in red (fig. 115) shows that an elegantly dressed woman's arms are now thickly upholstered and best seen to advantage when held well away from the body with elbows out, the better to display the equally thickly upholstered cone of her bodice, and to extend the spread of her pale chest and shoulders above it. Nobody now has two noticeable breasts, either. The distinctly rounded small ones of the fifteenth century have been spread out to fatten and unify the smooth expanse of chest and shoulder, and only a slight dent behind the neckline shows they exist.

Her big upper body makes the lady's head look quite small, and her tight coiffure preserves that effect. If we attempt to estimate her body's vertical proportions from the size of her head, we can see that her thick bodice ends at what must be hip level, and that her skirt therefore begins too far down to fall gracefully; but we know that Venetian courtesans at this period lengthened their legs with high platform-soled clogs, so that their skirts might hang longer, covering the clogs and trailing behind, balancing their long bodices. The whole ensemble made them look very tall, and their public appearance was imposing, especially since they had to walk slowly.

Veronese carefully describes the decorative elements of this woman's clothed figure, beginning with the three rings on her one small visible hand, which loops up the long chain of her jewelled girdle. He wants us to appreciate the magnificent openwork of the red velvet sleeves with their rich lace cuffs, we must admire the embroidered gauze covering her shoulders, the lace bordering her wide neckline, the pearl earrings gleaming against the dim background, her two pearl necklaces and the vast jewelled brooch attached just below the central shadow. Finally, we must watch the open edges of her gold-laced red bodice plunge down and converge at navel level, exposing her chemise in a narrow white V.

Jacopo Tintoretto provides a nude version of this heavily charged vision. In the canvas attributed to him called *Proserpine and Ascalaphus* (fig. 116) we find a nude female figure half reclining amid some shrubbery, being approached by a male figure shrouded in drapery. The shape of this mythological bare body shows its debt to current fashion, especially in the small size of the head, the large size and bright smoothness of the chest and shoulders, the elongated legs and torso, and the posture of the heavy arms. Like Veronese, Tintoretto angles the arms away from the body to lay stress on its thick shape, which is embellished with nipples to show where the breasts are. As if to suggest a modish bodice, Tintoretto permits no kind of marked roundness or indentation to interrupt the flow of the nude torso's long, padded form, which eventually divides into long, fleshy legs ending in minimal feet. We see her navel marking where a skirt might start.

For all her nude abandon, this allegorical figure looks stiff in her pose, as if she still wore her big invisible dress; and even her nudity needs decoration. Besides her nipples, standing in for earrings, she has bracelets instead of lace cuffs, gauze above her head instead of over her shoulders, a drape over her thigh to stand for a skirt. To fix the veil to her neat coiffure, she wears a little brooch on top of her head, instead of a big one at the bosom. These are obviously not Tintoretto's conscious responses to Veronese, but the expression of similar tastes in female shape and adornment that both shared with many contemporary painters and patrons.

115
Paolo Veronese (1528–1588)
Portrait of a Woman,
about 1565
Oil on canvas, 106 × 87 cm
Musée de la Chartreuse, Douai

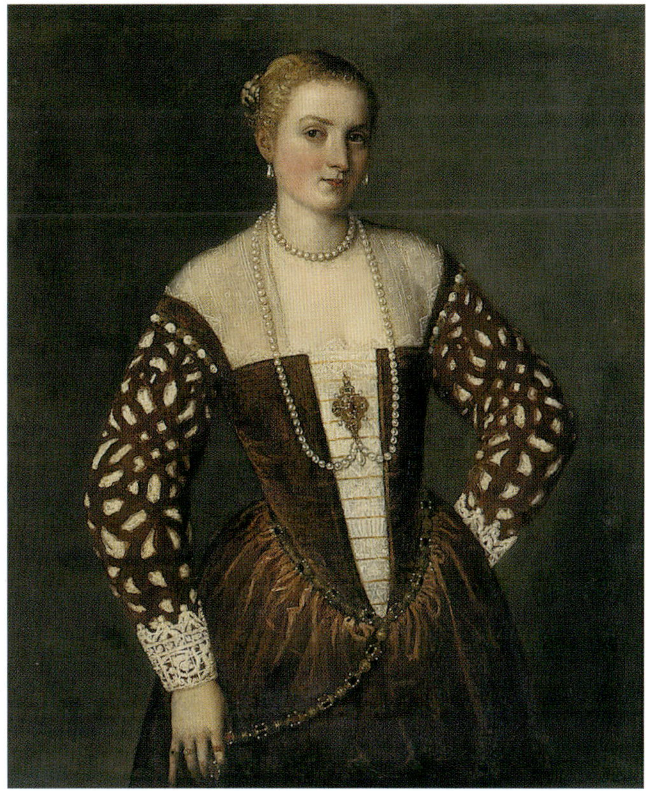

116
Attr. to **Jacopo Tintoretto**
(1518–1594)
Proserpine and Ascalaphus,
about 1578–80
Oil on canvas, 101.5 × 128.5 cm
Courtesy of the Marquess of
Bath, Longleat House,
Warminster

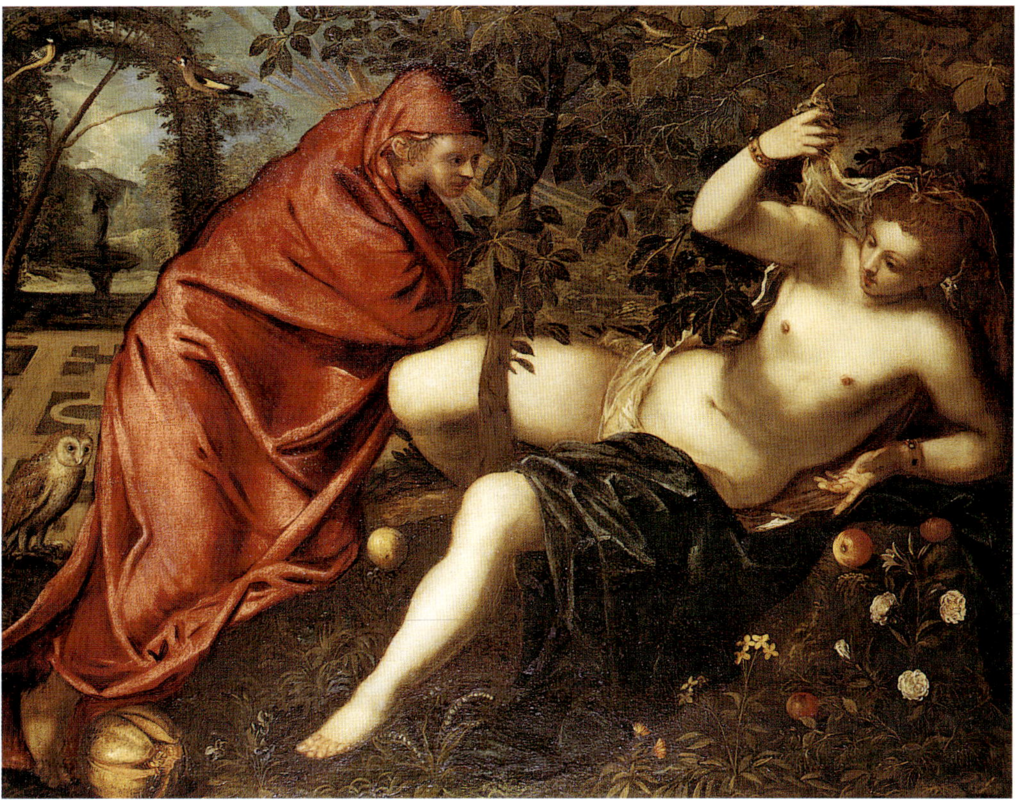

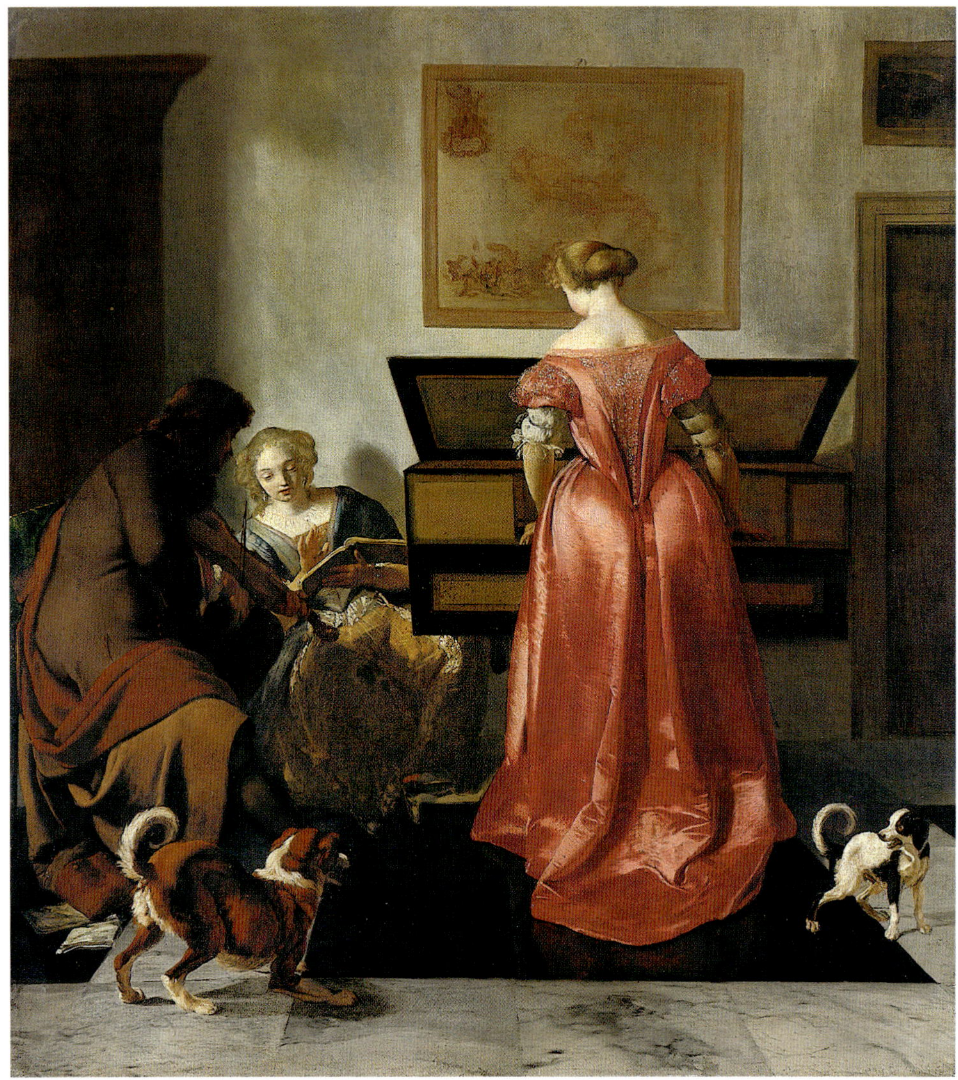

117
Jacob Ochtervelt (1634–1682)
A Woman playing a Virginal, Another singing and a Man playing a Violin, probably 1675–80
Oil on canvas, 84.5 × 75 cm
National Gallery, London
NG 3864

Another hundred years later, in the Netherlands, the emphasis had changed again. Jacob Ochterveldt's 1670s painting (fig. 117), similar in theme to the Ter Borch we saw in Chapter VII, now focuses the eye on the rear view of a brilliantly dressed lady standing at a virginals. The painter has sharpened the focus by concentrating the light on the huge double dome and central channel of apricot satin that form the back of the skirt and its train. Her chignon and bare shoulders contain visual echoes of the same double shape, so we see its resonance as the chief element of her costume. Curved blades of satin swoop down her back to converge at her sacrum, forcing our eye to follow the dark chasm between the shining domes – is that really her shape? Imagine how it moves when she walks!

The erotic appeal of this picture is made directly to the viewer through the lady's satin-clad rear, which she is not thinking about as she strikes the keys, and which nobody in the picture can see. We are not meant even to consider the other players. The face and bosom of the singing lady are of limited interest, her clad body is in shadow, the fiddling

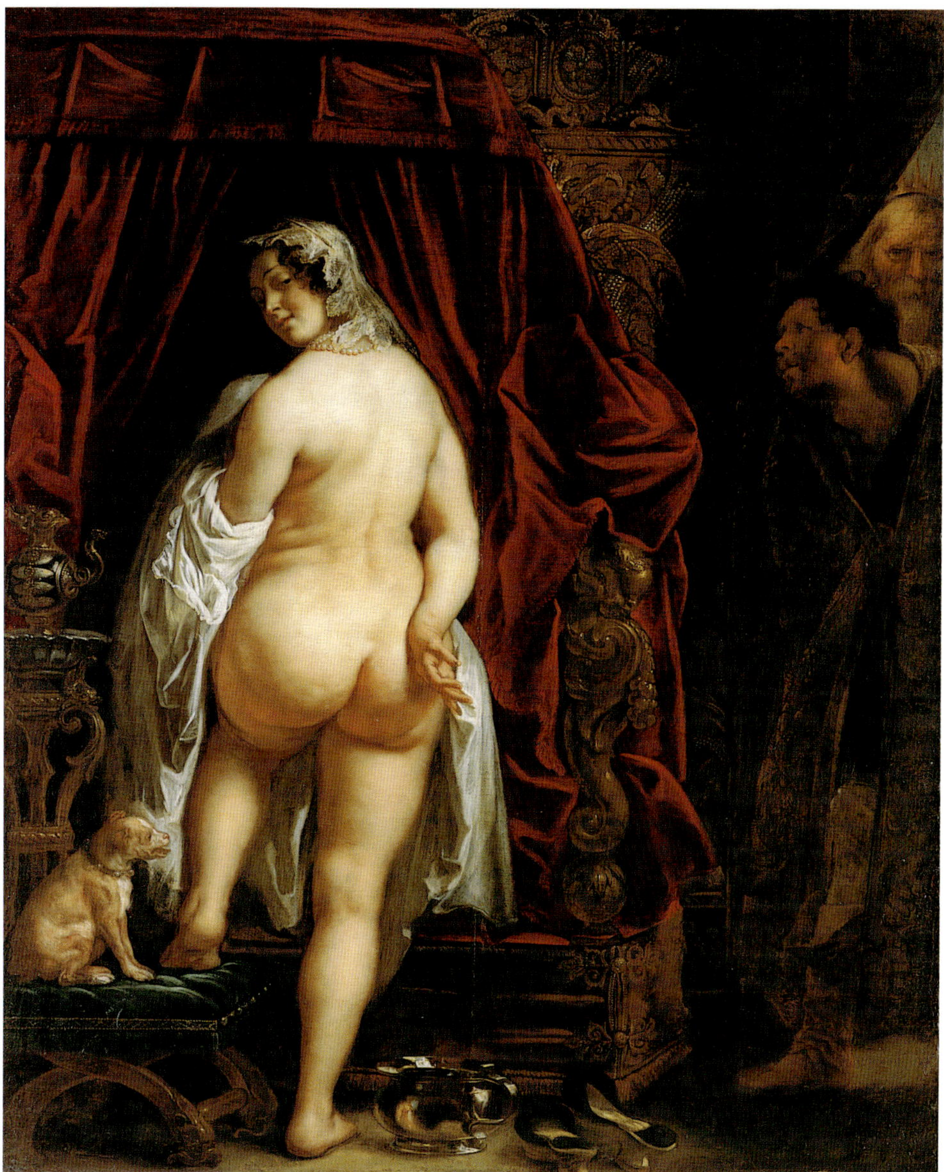

118
Jacob Jordaens (1593–1678)
King Candaules of Lydia showing his Wife to Gyges, 1646
Oil on canvas, 193 × 157 cm
Nationalmuseum, Stockholm

gentleman of course wears dark clothes and hides in deeper shadow, both are concentrating. But the painter, knowing that he arouses us with the colour, shape and behaviour of this big skirt, makes two dogs play a flirtatious game around its richly suggestive cascade.

The fantasy aroused by looking at Ochterveldt's lady seems to be illustrated by Jacob Jordaens's painting depicting a scene from Herodotus that was a common subject in the Netherlands at this period (fig. 118). The tale concerns a Lydian king proud of his wife's figure, who allowed his servant to watch her undress for bed, with radical consequences; and here we see the peeping man, the king and the very consciously disrobing queen. Voyeurism is the theme of both Ochterveldt's genre scene and Jordaens's legendary illustration, since what we are being offered is a desirable woman's rear view, the one she can't see us looking at. Awareness of a clandestine eye is nevertheless included by Jordaens, whose nude queen turns to look at us while she sheds her skirt and shift, brushing her buttock with one hand to show us she knows – and we can go so far as to note the chamber pot just below. Her dog admires her, too, sharing his excitement with the eager spy.

The queen's naked body seems to fill out the shape of the dress in the Ochterveldt, her vast hips and buttocks supporting a solid nude superstructure, its sloping shoulders and plump arms matching the bulky bodice with off-shoulder sleeves worn by the keyboard player. We can feel the weight of this female body, its big bones, thick muscles and massive fatness, as we feel the weight of the music-maker's dress, its folds thickened with padding and canvas, its upper shapes maintained with starch and metal stays. The painters of these two pictures have made no effort to lighten the effect of either – weight is part of the erotic pull of each, and overlapping folds of flesh echo those of satin.

We noted in the last chapter that elegant women abandoned the high-waisted Neoclassical look during the first third of the nineteenth century and began to adopt an hourglass shape for the torso. Emphasis on full and wide-apart breasts became even more marked as the ribs and waist were artificially indented, and painters hastened to allow this mode to show their sitters to best advantage. In his portrait of Mrs Scott Moncrieff (fig. 119) from about 1814, Henry Raeburn places his beautiful sitter in half length against a black background and drapes her shoulders in a dark red cloak that hides her arms and hands completely. He turns her head away from the strong light, keeping half of her face and neck in shadow and shading both eyes with the big dark curls on her brow.

Raeburn turns her body away from her head, however, so that the light may strike full on the offered plane of her bare chest and on the widely separated upper slopes of her breasts, traversed by the straight, plain neckline of her white dress. The painter puts a dark shadow under each breast to indicate its individual shape and models each with a few caressing folds, and then he shades the thin white ribbon that crosses her body just under them, to set off both.

Below that her dress fits closely, showing one side of her indented waist against the dark interior of the cloak, and the painter makes the cloak reduce her waist more by hiding the other side. At chest level, the cloak's white lining is momentarily turned outwards to make the wide whiteness of her bosom even wider. Nothing else, no eloquent eyes or hands, no pretty sleeves, no shiny earrings, brooch or necklace, no feather in the hair, curl on the neck or lace on the dress distracts the eye from the double glory of these breasts, offered in this portrait as the beautiful sitter's chief adornments.

William Etty's nude *Venus* (fig. 120) from a few years later shows a fantasy response to the same emphasis in current fashion, and asserts the mode as natural in the nude. To keep the light from Venus's face, this painter lowers her head, raising her arms up and out of the way in the Venus Anadyomene pose, instead of hiding them. The effect of these devices is to make nothing so important as the fall of light on brunette Venus's big, wide-apart breasts with their dark nipples, and the corresponding shadows and reflections under them. She even seems to look down at them herself.

On the lighted side of Venus's body, we can see her waist indented like Mrs Moncrieff's, marked with a little crease in the flesh, and Etty reduces its size by deepening the waist-level shadow on the other side. The continuing line of Venus's figure shows the flared shape her skirt might take over her full thighs; but we can see it would still be narrower than a Raeburn-like bosomy bodice. Compared to his careful modelling of Venus's figure and her breasts especially, the rest of Etty's painting is a sketch. The draperies, the background and even Cupid get minimal attention, so we know what he most wants us to look at.

The twentieth century had its own Neoclassic period roughly in its second quarter. Modern taste began to find more beauty in objects with a clear unadorned structure than in those with wrought embellished shapes, and modern painters were subjecting the protean swarm of natural phenomena to simplified form and arrangement. The clad female body became such a reduced shape in real life, rendered by fashion into a smoothly unified object for eyes now being taught to see the world in terms of simple visual components. The female face became another such component, to be rendered as a mask with sharply delineated lips and eyes. Cosmetics were now being used to re-create the face as if it were a contemporary work of art, not to emphasise the look of its natural charms.

BELOW LEFT **119**
Henry Raeburn (1756–1823)
Mrs Scott Moncrieff, about 1814
Oil on canvas, 76.5 × 64 cm
The National Gallery of Scotland, Edinburgh

BELOW RIGHT **120**
William Etty (1787–1849)
Venus and Cupid, probably 1820s
Oil on millboard on panel, 80.8 × 39 cm
Russell-Cotes Art Gallery and Museum, Bournemouth

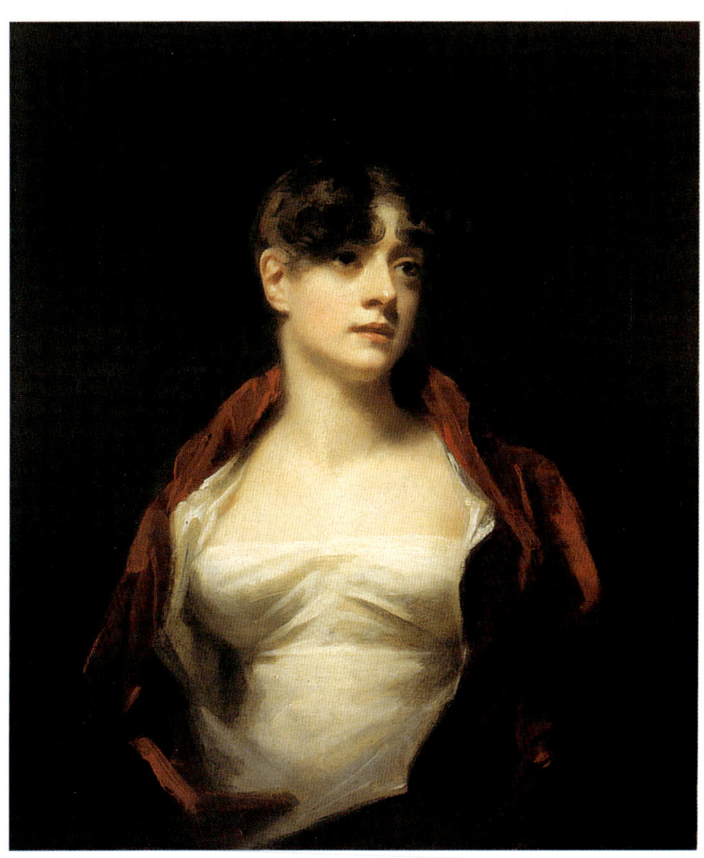

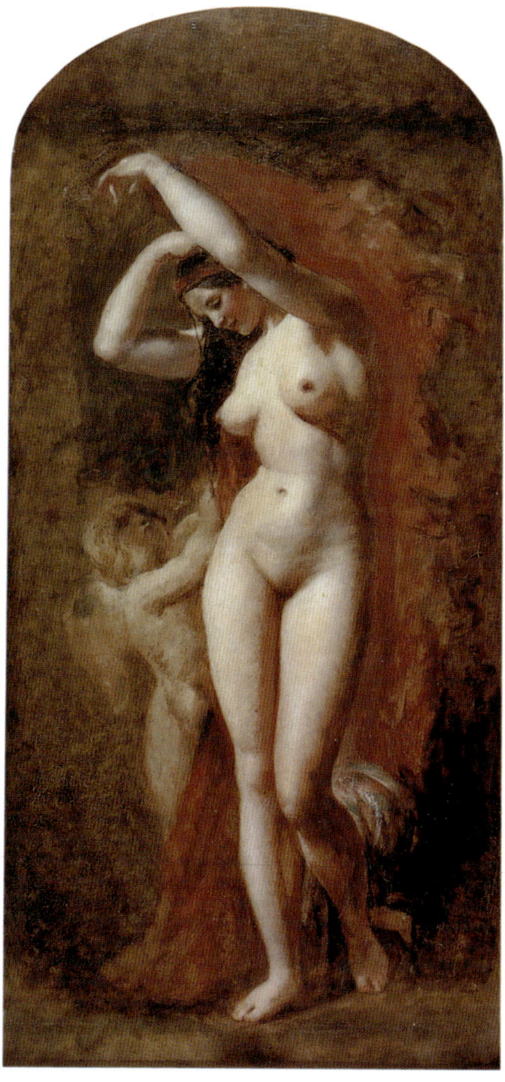

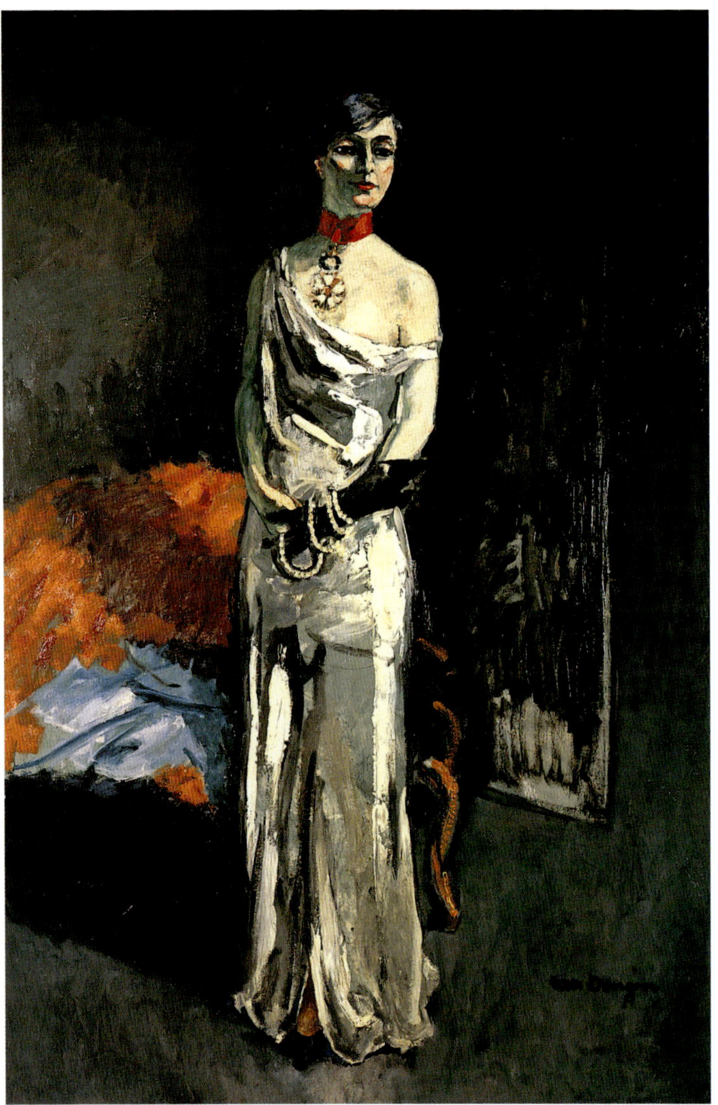

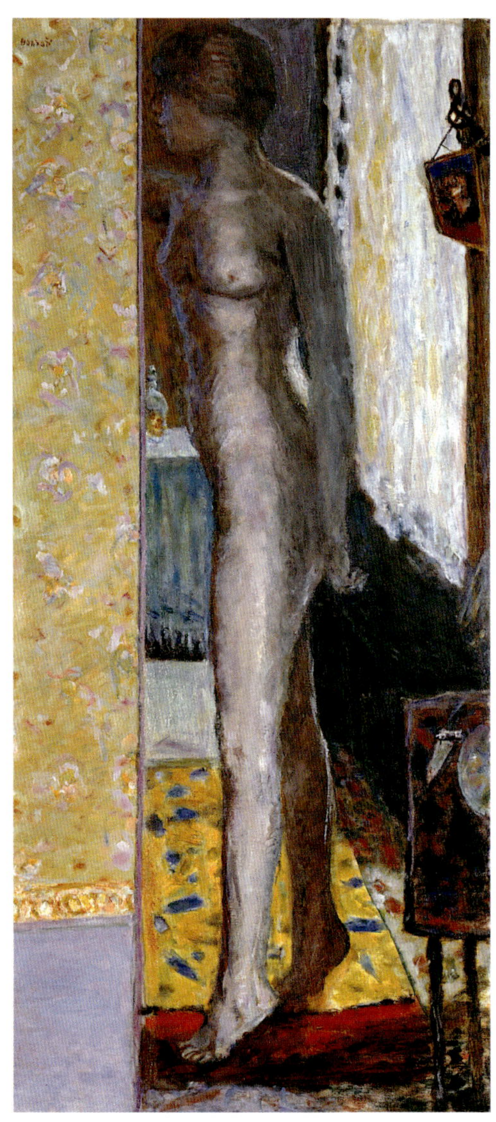

ABOVE LEFT **121**
Kees van Dongen (1877–1968)
The Comtesse de Noailles, 1931
Oil on canvas, 196 × 131 cm
Stedelijk Museum, Amsterdam

ABOVE RIGHT **122**
Pierre Bonnard (1867–1947)
Standing Nude, 1920
Oil on canvas, 122 × 56 cm
Private collection

In female portraits, painters would fuse the individual's image with the rightly designed female shape, which was not unlike that of a living pillar. We can see an example in Kees van Dongen's 1931 portrait of the Comtesse de Noailles (fig. 121). This painter has shown the lady in a modern version of traditional finery. She wears mobile white satin, prominent jewels and extreme décolletage, and she shows one shoe, as did Rubens's sitters, or Nattier's, or Ingres's or John Singer Sargent's. Van Dongen has notably not posed her in candid neo-Neoclassical purity, as Frampton did the cellist (see fig. 90): his mode of painting refers to the traditional kinds of bravura brushwork that once praised satin in similar terms even on saints – as in the work of El Greco, for example – or on the elegant ladies of Baroque days, as in that of Velázquez and Frans Hals.

This countess is eccentric: her one evening glove is black, her bracelet is a necklace loosely quadrupled around her wrist, her pendant is a medal, its wide ribbon her choker. A Neoclassical reference is the dropped shoulder of her draped dress, the ancient sign of licence, here exposing armpit cleavage and almost a nipple; but the modernity of the image abides in the columnar shape into which it all fits, and here there is a resemblance to the Frampton. As in that picture, no hip, knee or elbow is thrust out, the figure's posture is strictly upright. No projecting breast, belly or thigh interrupts the vertical line from shoulder to floor, while several gleaming downward streaks define her standing legs under the satin. She is the same width the whole way down; but while keeping within this strict, pillar-like outline the painter has nevertheless found a way to drape the folds of her dress in Baroque painterly strokes, and he gives her a dark Baroque background. In this portrait, as in others of his, Van Dongen shows the modern made-up face that we saw in Chapter VII, fig. 111, as well as the modern unshaped body.

Pierre Bonnard's *Standing Nude* of 1920 (fig. 122) shows the painter responding to the new clothed silhouette Van Dongen endorses. Bonnard does not abandon his visual appreciation of nude female bodies in their ripe succulence; but he adds his personal version of the current delight in the look of unripeness. We can first see how fashion has affected Bonnard's eye by noting the model's tiptoe feet, imitating the effect of high-heeled shoes. At this date, the look of female shod feet was more striking than ever before, because daytime skirts had become irreversibly short enough to expose them at all times. Nude beauty had to include their increased erotic value, along with that of legs.

Next we notice how the model's falling left arm seems to flatten her buttocks, forcing a straighter line for her torso; and finally we follow the band of light that falls right down the centre of the model's body and floods her foreground leg, leaving a thin tributary ribbon of light down her rear one. This beam guides our view of the figure as a narrow column, half of it consisting of leg. The model does have small round breasts and a little stomach, but Bonnard shapes those curves in the darker colours and dimmer light that also shape her face. Comparing Bonnard's vertical streak of bright light with the glittering strokes straight down the skirt of Van Dongen's countess, we can see Bonnard's streak as an appreciative gesture towards fashion's power over the nude.

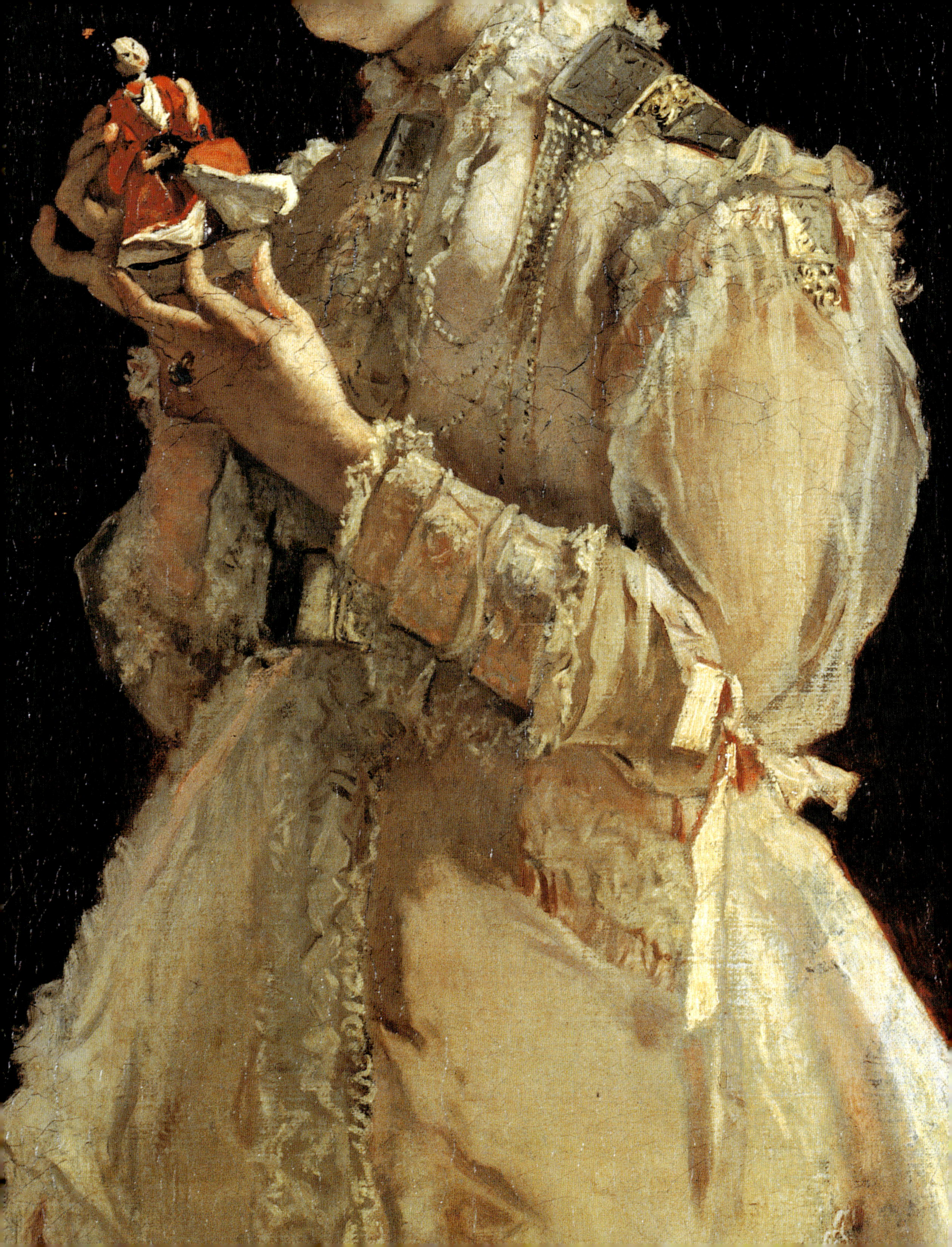

IX Woman as Dress

In the previous chapter we explored the idea that painters are likely to render women's nude bodies as if they had been formed by modish clothing. Exploring another facet of the same theme reveals that some painters, especially during the later nineteenth century, might render a woman wearing an elegant dress as if the dress had created her – as if she had no body separate from the modish clothed one in the picture. This seems especially true in paintings that show a solitary, reflective woman at one with her elegant costume, looking as if the painter were not there and nobody else were looking at her. What she wears is shaped by the painter according to the fashion; but by showing her in reflective solitude, he also shows that fashion has shaped her body into a natural-feeling thing, something in which she feels at ease while alone and unseen, free to follow a train of private thought. The painter thus further suggests that her fashionably dressed body is inseparable from her private turn of mind, as if the woman in the picture had no need of a private nudity, of a private body without its fashionable clothes; this is the one in which she really lives. These examples thus offer yet another pictorial suggestion that fashion is natural to women, even the sense that it is what makes them natural.

These female images tend to fend off the idea of the social grace or social context of an elegant dress, partly because the woman in them does not meet the viewer's gaze – doing that would call attention to herself, her garb and her situation. Sitters for portraits and models for non-portraits of dressed-up women have often met our eye, as in Vermeer's paintings of ladies playing the virginals but looking at us, surrounded by a carefully stocked milieu that contributes directly to the effect of the gaze. When Vermeer's subjects do look away, they are pouring milk, writing and reading letters, holding a guitar, a balance or a pose; he never painted a woman doing nothing but thinking. By contrast, these late nineteenth- and early twentieth-century pictures present a modern apparition, one that expounds the existence of female inward states in much the same way that modern fiction does – there is a Henry Jamesian scent about them. Surrounding objects seem irrelevant to the pensive figure, not expressly required for our understanding of her, not necessarily pertinent to her thoughts.

Detail of fig. 123

Similarly modern is the absence of the kind of surrounding narrative context which was so common in the Romantic first half of the nineteenth century. Artists in those years usually painted well-dressed solitary women contemplating someone's portrait in a boudoir, or reading a black-edged letter in a drawing-room, or actively seeking spiritual enlightenment outdoors, as in Caspar David Friedrich's *Woman before the Setting Sun*, where the woman, seen from the back in a fashionable dress, coiffure and earrings, stands directly between us and the sun, outlined by it and spreading her arms, as if inviting it to irradiate her with meaning before it sinks. In many cases, the clothes might be an explicit part of the narrative – mourning, a wedding dress or travelling costume. The picture would be a scene with one character, implying at least one other, often with an explicit title. Some French ones were called *La Parisienne*, the subject dressed elegantly for the street, perhaps not meeting our gaze but manifestly inviting the world's gaze, dressed to tread the world stage. In a different spirit, lasting into a later epoch, certain painters would leave out all explicit narrative circumstances or titles, insisting on the image only of the dressed woman as a self-sufficient phenomenon. Her eye doesn't challenge ours, only the shape and aura of her dressed self and its own ambience suggest – to the artist, and through him to the viewer – her possibilities.

In Alfred Stevens's 1866 painting called *The Lady in Pink* (fig. 123) the subject stands holding close to her face with both hands a small figurine – a Chinese porcelain? a Japanese doll? – we can't identify the object. She is dressed to perfection for that year, the level of waist, tilt of coiffure, trim and shape of skirt and sleeve are worthy of a fashion plate. The painter, however, has imparted depth to her chic image by means of adroit lighting. The better to see the object she holds, the woman turns her back to the light, which comes from the right to strike the fullest part of her foamy skirt and the most decorated part of her double sleeve. It also puts a high shine on her rounded jaw and neck, carefully outlining her pink ear and fingers, but it leaves her face in shadow.

The shadowed face is an old device indicating contemplation, and this lady seems to brood over the object she holds so carefully, of which we don't know the meaning – we can't confidently say she broods about it, but we perceive her thoughtful state. We are given no clue as to the content of her thought, only that she seems to feel her fine public costume blending easily with her private ideas. We also can't identify any specific or coherent setting, although some isolated Far Eastern objects share the frame with her Western European figure against a dark background. Stevens invites us to see the lady as a precious object herself; but her absorbed face and pose forbid us to think that she sees herself as one.

The rich and numerous details of her dress do not appear to be on her mind at all; she is not dressed to be seen. It seems rather that the comfortable completeness and integrity of her clothed body encourage contemplation in her. It's as if she were not a woman, wearing a dress with all its supportive underpinning, and naked under it; we are rather meant to perceive this elegant clad state as her only one. We must think: her body consists only of this costume, no wonder she seems so at home in it. The nudes in the last chapter illustrated the same idea from the other side – there the nude body in the picture has been created by an absent dress, from which it derives its only reality. In the picture of the perfectly dressed lady, there is no separate body under the dress to be considered, either by her or us. This dress is her body.

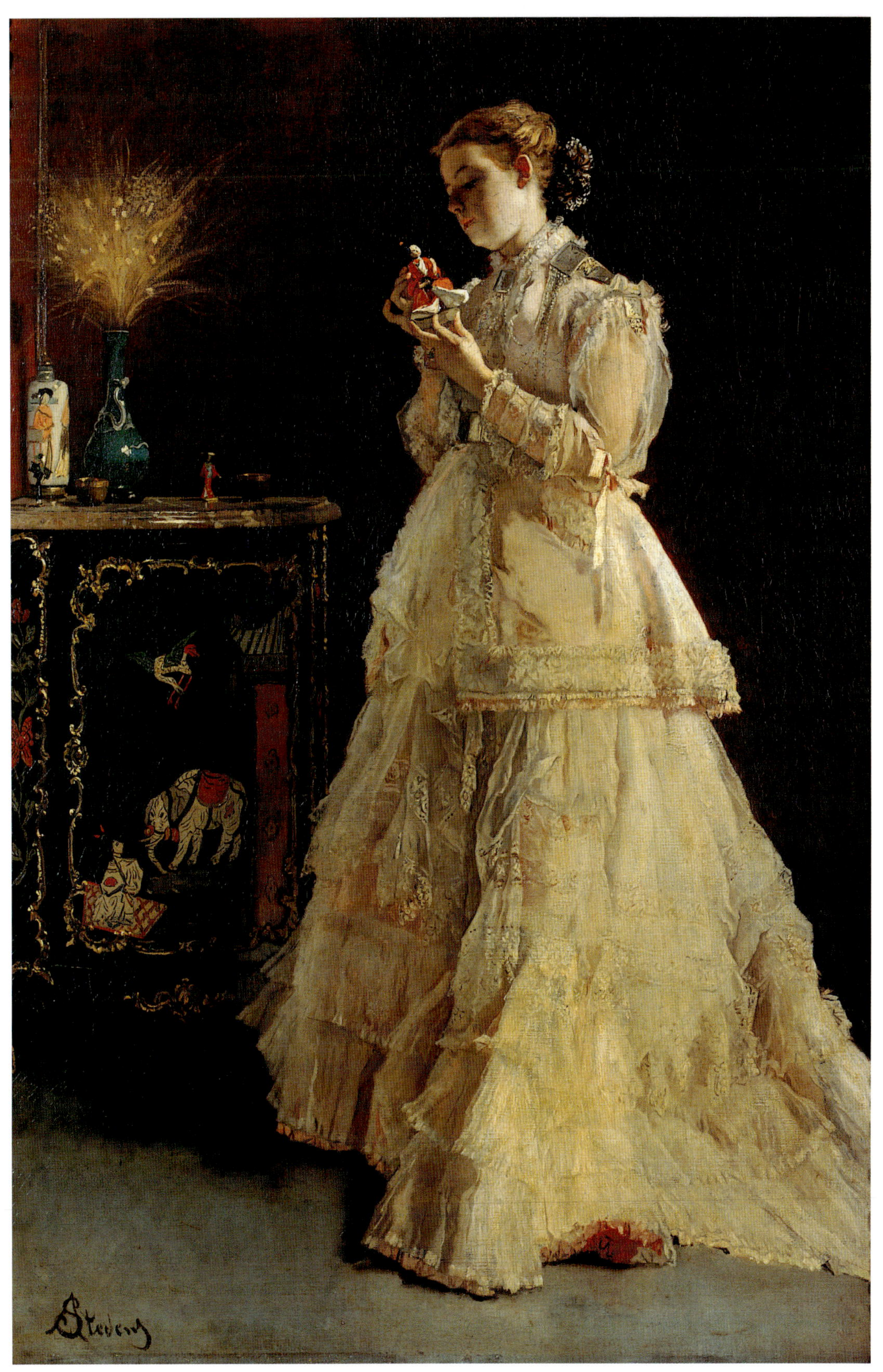

123
Alfred Stevens (1823–1906)
The Lady in Pink, 1866
Oil on canvas, 87 × 57 cm
Musées royaux des Beaux-Arts de Belgique, Brussels

A much more ambitious and truly ambiguous statement of this theme appears in Camille Corot's 1874 painting entitled *The Lady in Blue*, sometimes (significantly) *The Blue Lady* (fig. 124). This woman holds a closed fan loosely in her left hand, and leans against a mysterious piece of furniture on which lies a mass of fabric, just at the right level for her to rest her elbow on it and support her chin with her closed right hand. Her blue costume is quite of its moment: the degree and angle of the bustle and its drapery, the stripes on the skirt, the train, the waist level, the coiffure are all modish. But her setting is the artist's studio, not an elegant room – we can see an easel on the left; and her widely cut arm-hole, which shows her whole shoulder and would permit a view of her downy armpit if she stretched out her arm, is a usage unknown to fashion at the time. In 1874, modish décolletage would display the bosom and back, but the point of the shoulder would always be covered, and bodice arm-holes were cut high and tight-fitting so that armpits stayed invisible. A bodice revealing shoulders and armpits such as this one could only be worn with a chemisette under it; but none appears here.

It would seem that the painter has insisted on this open arm-hole in order to lay stress – right in the middle of showing a heavily clad woman – on the nudity of the smooth, strong shoulder and the nascent armpit, deliberately including the whole of the bare arm that aids the lady in her reflections, as if she were a classical Sibyl. The style of this painting also has some of the dim surface coolness of a Poussin, in which such a pensive antique character might indeed appear.

The light strikes the elaborate back of her blue dress as well as her arm and temple, nape and fan-bearing hand, but it leaves her thoughtful face in the shade. The sign of contemplation here is the chin on the hand, to which the lovely, bright arm leads our eye. Her eyes are deep in shadow; what is she thinking? The dress, which creates the only body she has, seems to suggest the character of her thoughts – heavy and convoluted, full but plain, unexpectedly erotic, and all of one colour.

Corot painted many brooding women, most of them in strange garb that seems to combine normal European clothing with local peasant dress and studio properties; perhaps some of these ensembles were invented straight on to the canvas as they were being painted. In these pictures, the women look disconnected from their clothing, as the models probably felt. Their costumes are unplaceable by the viewer, being heterodox and heterogeneous, and their serious thoughts similarly lack reality.

This brooding woman is one of the few painted by him in a modish dress, and it's one of the most compelling for that reason. Dresses like this one appear in quite different contexts in works by Renoir and Degas (see fig. 108; see also Renoir's *M. and Mme Sisley* in the Wallraf-Richartz Museum in Cologne for a chemisette under a sleeveless bodice) – we recognise it. But here we can see the woman and her clothes in their true unity, daring bare armpit included; we therefore perceive her individuality more clearly, and we can feel more involved in her unknowable state of mind.

Forty years later, Thomas Wilmer Dewing's 1912 painting on the same theme is called *Lady in Gold* (fig. 125). Dewing painted many pictures of well-dressed women, sometimes two or more together, sometimes moving around in a luminous outdoors, sometimes sitting motionless indoors, always in strongly atmospheric but unclear circumstances. By these means, Dewing seems to have sought to evoke their inner life as the true subject, not their appearance or activity, while nevertheless insisting on their contemporary

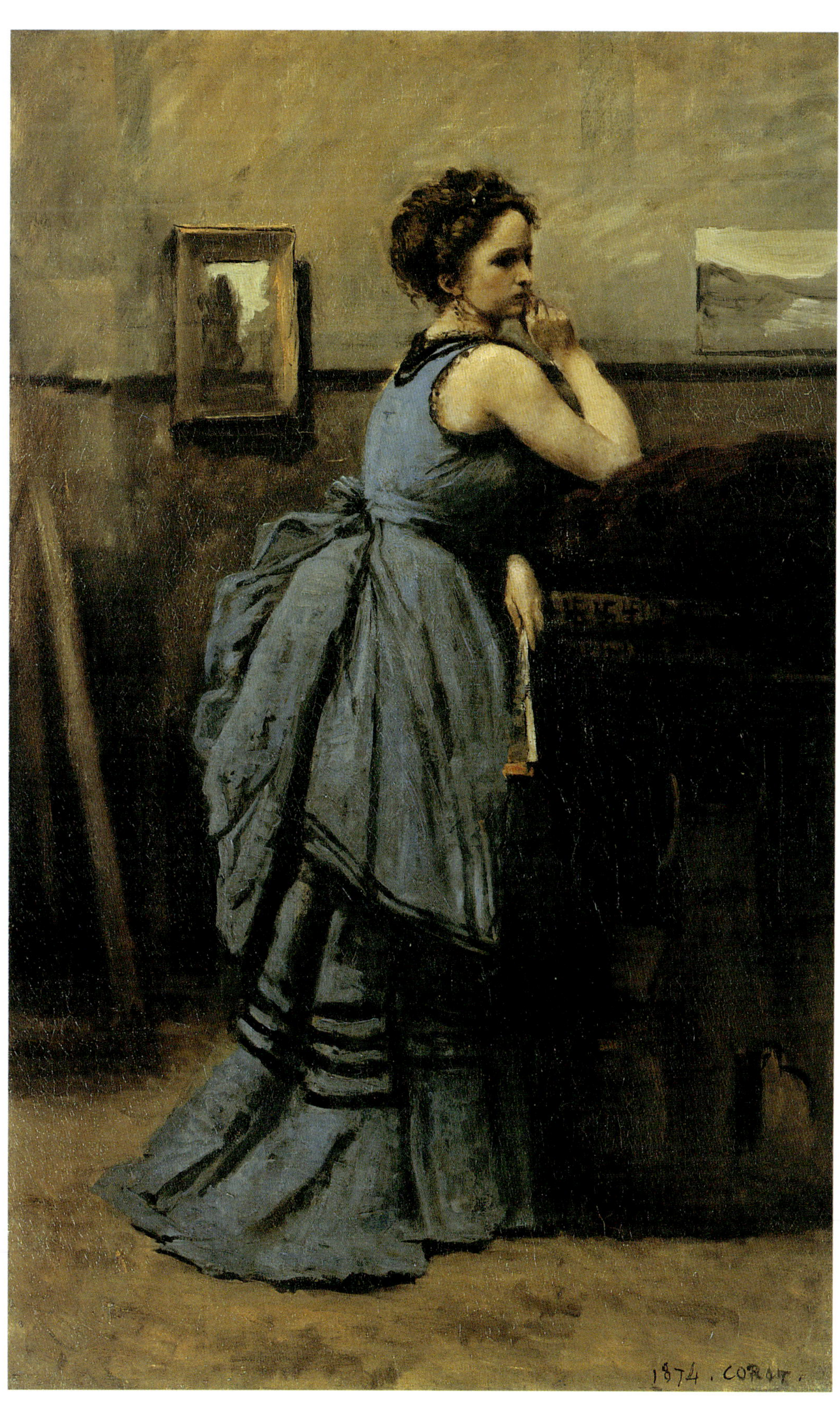

124
Jean-Baptiste-Camille Corot
(1796–1875)
The Lady in Blue, 1874
Oil on canvas, 80 × 50.5 cm
Musée du Louvre, Paris

elegance as part of their mood and their unknown thought. For this particular image he looks back to Rembrandt, to find the way to dim the light for a scene of quiet pondering.

The lady sits back in a nearly invisible wooden chair, dangling one hand down into the shadows, and holding an inactive fan on her sloping lap. Her eyelids are lowered; she looks past her lap towards her invisible feet. This is a mature woman, not a girl; her dim-coloured evening dress represents her arrival at a stage beyond blushes. Precious objects are near her, but they sit on an arbitrarily placed table, where they have been assembled neither for obvious display nor for obvious use; and she ignores them. There are pearls in the picture and a porcelain vase, but no mirror, and this is not a toilet table. Just as in the Stevens, the background is undefinable.

Her dress slides diagonally in a shimmering multi-fold blur to create an almost shapeless and unbending body for her, with a broad, low mono-bosom and narrow hips, so that her outline is full above and tapers down. Her hair is piled heavily and fuzzily on the crown of her head, its puffed-out fullness lower down revealing only the lobe of her ear. All these details constitute the height of chic in 1912, as do the deep curving décolletage showing a blank expanse of chest, the sleeves covering the upper arm, the

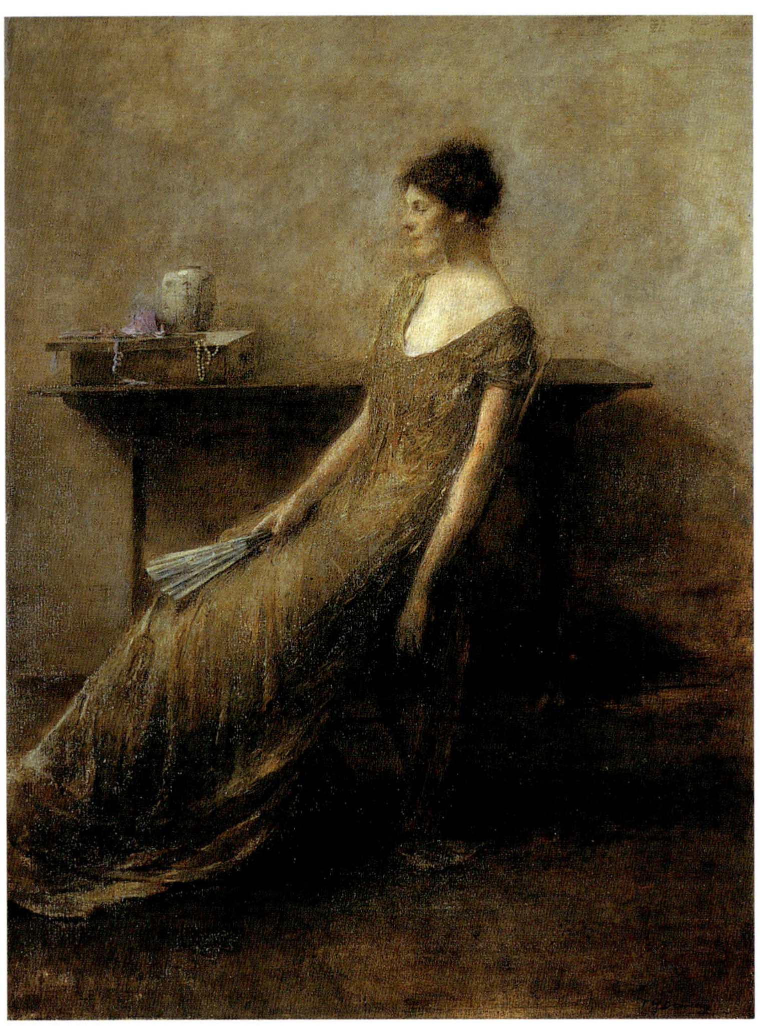

125
Thomas Wilmer Dewing
(1851–1938)
Lady in Gold, about 1912
Oil on canvas, 61.3 × 46 cm
Brooklyn Museum of Art, New York, Picture Purchase Fund

muted iridescence of the gown's colour, the general lack of definition in its cut – you can see the same mode on ladies by Klimt, for example, with an entirely different effect at the same date. Like all the others we're looking at, this dress has a train, here swept up and back over the seat of the chair without display.

Dewing has skilfully used these chic elements in a way to conjure an ambience of reverie for the seated woman, as she takes the light full on her unadorned chest as if to let it strike inward, and allows her brow and cheeks to take some, too. Instead of shadowing it, however, the painter has ambiguously blurred the lower half of her face, suggesting that a sequence of fleeting expressions is crossing it as she meditates. Nothing in this picture makes plain what her thoughts are; and her blurry face further indicates that we can't follow them, and that maybe neither can she.

But the modish costume, like those in this painter's other works, and like the others we've been looking at, is a prominent part of the mood of the picture. Again, the painter shows the dressed lady merging with her finery in contemplative solitude. Here, her thoughtful body consists of one long dimly iridescent shape sloping away from the gleaming skin above it; she is like a mermaid in her seaweedy scales, pausing in thought against a murky underwater outcrop, not noticing the bits from a shipwreck lying nearby.

Portrait in the Open Air is the title of Giacomo Balla's 1902 version of this theme (fig. 126). It shows very clearly the influence of Impressionism, not least in the snapshot composition. The lady in a white dress is apparently walking out of the frame, turning her back on the sunny view, staying in the shade, gazing at something we don't see, leaving us – she seems not to know she's in the painting, or perhaps she's escaping from that possibility. We can't know; but her focus is certainly away from the sun-drenched street the painter has so freshly recorded, and from the green and flowering plants that frame it, and from the painter himself.

The trained skirt gathered to the side and lifted off the ground with one hand for ease of walking is a signature gesture for the date, present in many painted and photographed street scenes of the time. The gesture causes the skirt's fullness to outline and increase the lady's rear, just as the ruffles low on her bosom augment it in front. She walks with a fashionable forward-tilted posture, the famous S-bend characteristic of the Gibson Girl, a creation of popular illustration and the popular stage at the turn of the century. The painter lets us catch sight of her chic, white-clad figure just as it's very clearly outlined against the purple and green boards behind her. Her eyes are melancholy, but again her lower face is ambiguously painted, so that we can't see her expression as fixed.

Her thoughts are urging her into motion that displays the elegance of her walking shape, although she seems unaware of it, and of us. Her dress, like the one in the Dewing, is painted in a network of sparkling brushstrokes, here in summer white on white, as if the garment were a source of energy, an intimate element in her purpose, part of what prompts her desire to leave. This is another case of the surroundings seeming irrelevant to the figure, as in the Corot; and we even seem to see her think so, too, as she moves out of them. Led by a black shoe, her dress goes with her, and with her thoughts.

This sequence of paintings shows a progression in styles of painted elegance between 1866 and 1912. Stevens and Corot both show a respect for the look of immobility that did justice to the multiple details of modish dress in the 1860s and 1870s – the clad woman is

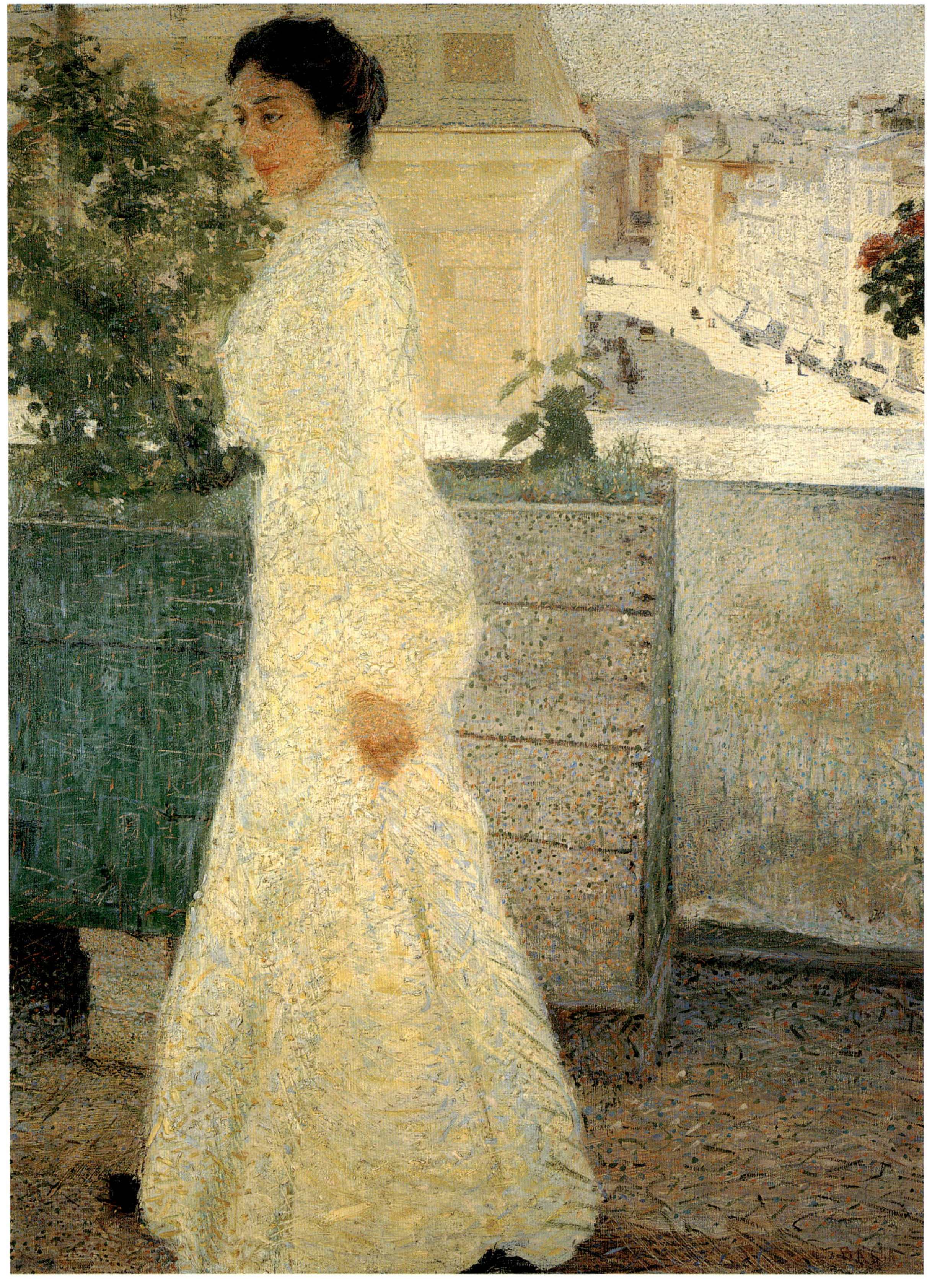

OPPOSITE **126**
Giacomo Balla (1871–1958)
Portrait in the Open Air, 1902
Oil on canvas, 155 × 113.5 cm
Galleria Nazionale d'Arte Moderna e Contemporanea, Rome

like a richly flowering tree or an elaborately upholstered sofa; the trains of the first two dresses are spread out to stay where they are. After the turn of the century, the sense of motion, if only that of light over surfaces, has become integral to feminine elegance, and sharpness of detail matters less than the right general outline. Balla and Dewing both show a fashionably clad woman with an integrated, smooth shape, and with the train incorporated into the sense of its flexible mobility.

The fashionable clothing on all these women emphasises the primacy of their dressed shape, rather than suggesting that underneath these elegant public folds they have non-modish, personal bodies that belong to their true lives. By presenting them in an obviously private state of mind, the painters stress the idea that these women feel free to be alone and brood comfortably, at one with these clothes. All the pictures suggest that the chic dress is identical with the body of the woman, not something imposed on it, which she might wish to escape in order to relax and think. On the contrary, the pictures give the sense that she has assumed the finery in order to be free; that she has put on her true body to become her true self. Once free in her costume, she can do her thinking in any surroundings.

As we have pointed out, the creative power of a fashionable dress is so strong that painters of the nude seem to perceive nudity only by means of its mediation, as if female bodies had no true visual reality other than the one such dresses create. In this group of pictures, we have found painters seeing a woman's elegantly dressed body as if it were the only one she has. In these pictures she has no other nakedness. The absent look of these women, moreover, keeps the pictures from seeming to be portraits of women whose public names and connections we might wish to know, although the Dewing and the Balla may well be. They all seem determined to remain anonymous, indifferent to both the painter and his public, as if they certainly had not put on their finery in order to be painted.

Such pictures as these have echoes later, in the classic fashion photography of the 1940s and 1950s, where an anonymous model in a grand dress is posed looking away from the viewer, perhaps at something she holds or sees outside the frame (fig. 127). This example by Norman Parkinson shows how painterly lighting adds drama to the photograph of a solitary dressed-up woman doing nothing. Here the outdoor sun floods the front of the figure so brightly that we can see the details of the dress only as it sweeps back into the dimness inside the fine room – the moth-like lady in her ballgown seems to have sought the light. She rests her face against her folded hands and leans against the window-frame, gazing downwards from the empty salon at the sunlit world. There is again no narrative – why is she dressed like this? She has something of Dewing, something of Corot, something of Stevens – all these pictures show a perfectly modish dress not as part of a woman's milieu, where something is happening at some time of day, but simply inseparable from herself.

This dress, too, is of its own moment, showing the most startling innovation for ball-dresses in the middle of the twentieth century. The entirely strapless bodice had not been thought of before 1938, when the underwear to support it was being invented; and this image from about a dozen years later shows it fully developed by Christian Dior. The modern décolletage entirely frees the arms and armpits, so that they now join the shoulders, bosom and back to make a single exposed element, crowned by the head. Here the photographer shows all of this to great advantage. The dress seems to sweep upwards, concentrating its spread flounces closer and closer together, gradually narrowing and tightening to whittle the waist, and finally producing the bust, arms and head as one extravagant flower at the top, balancing the big petals below.

The dress is photographed more for such atmospheric effects than to show its exact structure. Only its fusion with the woman wearing it is patent and perfect and suggestive, along with the fusion of her shoe and foot in the left foreground – no other aspect of the picture is so potent. The result produces not a desire to own the dress, but to be the woman in the photograph, capable of arousing fantasy in spectators – that is, to be the imaginative achievement of an artist, who has given dimension to the practical

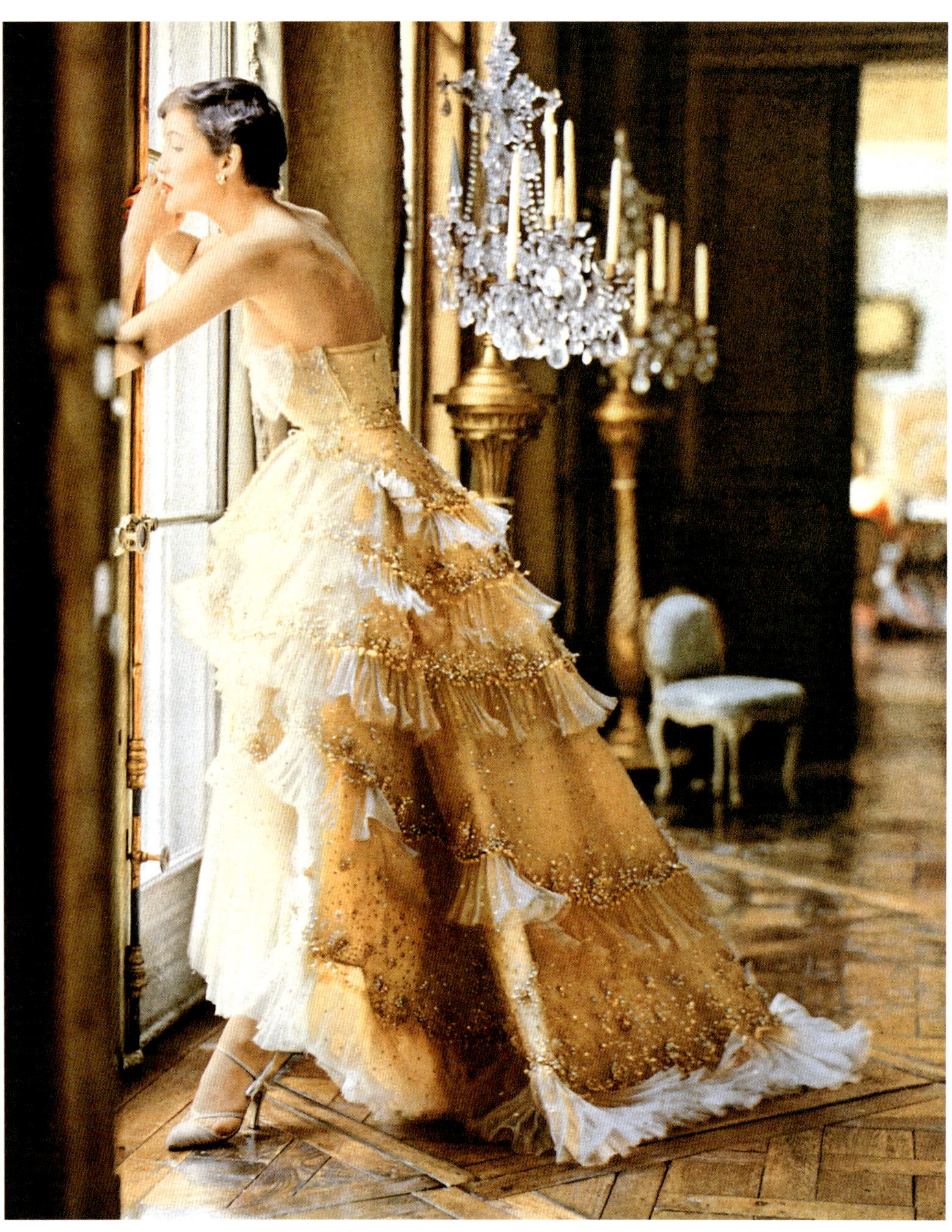

127
Norman Parkinson (1913–1990)
The 'Mozart' dress by Dior, from *American Vogue*, April 1950
Photograph
Condé Nast, New York.
Courtesy of Norman Parkinson Ltd./Fiona Cowan, London

achievement of a dressmaker, and produced this image of a woman whose being, of unknown scope, is identified with her elegance.

Superior fashion photography such as this depends on women's continuing belief that such dresses can rightly create them, can free them to be themselves, as Cinderella became her true self at the ball. In such a photograph, it wouldn't have to be a ballgown – it might be a perfectly chic, perfectly fitting suit, also shown perfectly creating the woman, and so freeing her to act and think, her body invented by enabling, present-perfect clothing. In a world where vigorously visible details of fashion are felt to apply mainly to women, artists have noted their power and imaginative function in women's inner lives – in paint and on film – and so have the many writers, both during the period covered by this chapter and on into this century, who have dealt with female subjectivity. This is the subjective view of fashion that feels it not as tyrannical but empowering.

This power is distinct from the impact of the dressed-up woman on masculine sensibilities, also explored in depth by other painters we have considered, and by writers all the way back to Homer. There, too, perfect feminine trappings are seen as powerful – but chiefly as having the power to seduce. Pictures expressive of that view are more likely to show the woman looking at us, or looking self-conscious, as Boilly's lady does (see fig. 84). In both views, however, the power of fashion to create the female body remains crucial. For men, it seems to enhance the attractions of what's really there; for the woman inside, it replaces what's there with something better, the fusion of two kinds of substance into one creation superior to either.

In all these images, we can also see how the picture of a woman in a fashionable dress can go beyond the straightforward display of surface elegance to produce a suggestion of obscure restlessness, of submerged longing, that seems to underlie the hidden thoughts of the well-dressed women we've been looking at – and that even seems to lie at the core of fashion's endless movement. You could say that it lies behind the flow of modernity in general – a subdued need for something always different, something maybe better, something new in life and art, some fresh form in which to feel free. These fine dresses are all different, current only for the moment. Each has given a certain provisional emphasis to the body, as a change from what was provisional before. The freedom they denote is the one fashion itself denotes – that of constant forward movement, the chance to be forever shifting, to resist stasis and stagnation, to seek other ways, to find more arrangements to subvert and re-make.

The woman, fixed in a picture, nevertheless feels part of the flow. In this array of pictures, we can see artists making modern discontent manifest as the need for constantly new shapes for dressed female bodies, figured as one thoughtful woman in a momentarily chic dress. They show her fused with it, as if she and the dress together were brooding on their combined, endlessly unresolvable future.

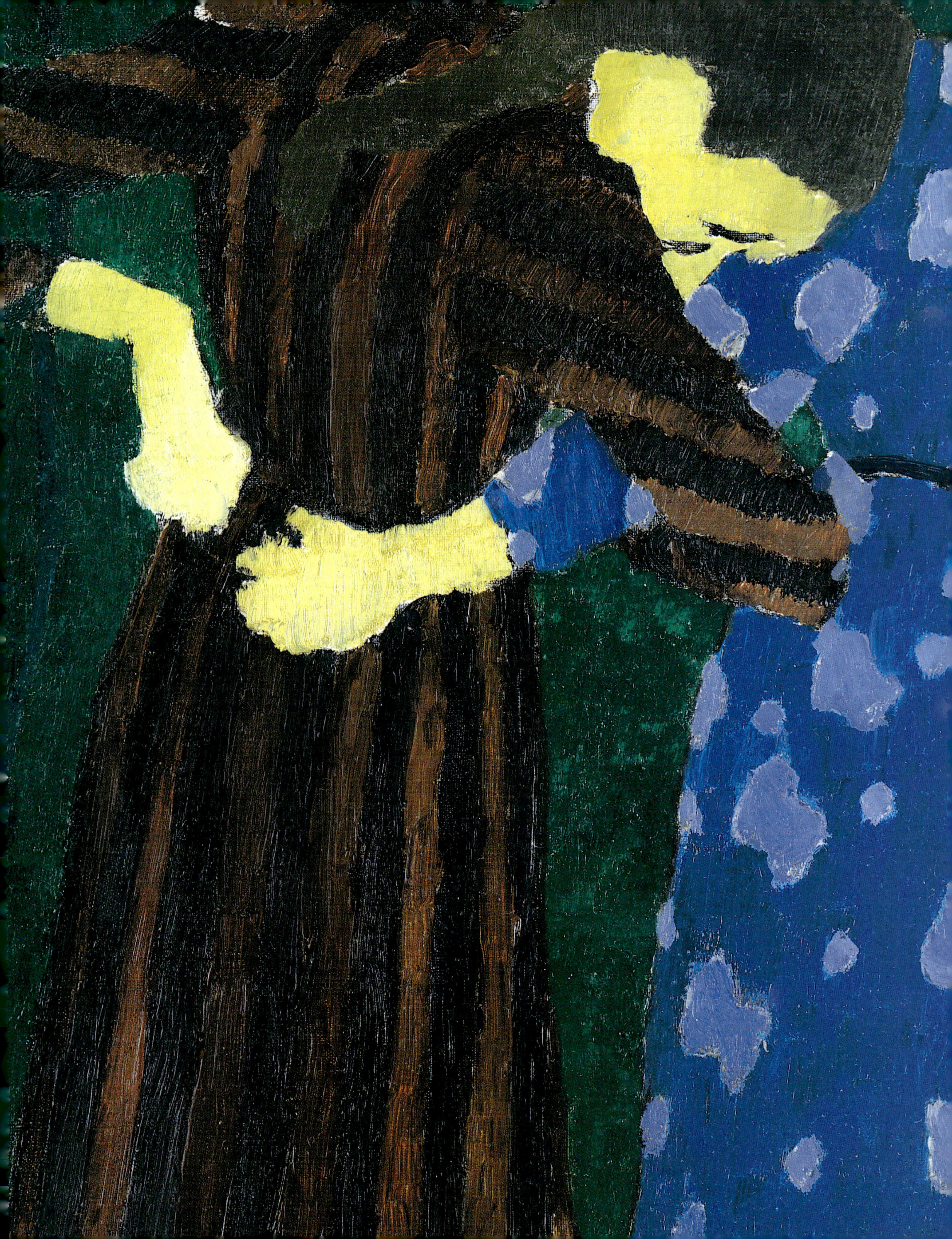

x Form and Feeling

By 1900 European painters were reminding viewers more and more emphatically that the clothing and any other phenomena in their pictures were parts of an organism made only of colour on a flat surface. They began openly making new uses of very old artistic strategies, the kinds visible on the painted vases of Archaic Greece and the painted tombs of ancient Egypt, as well as in the vivid colour prints of eighteenth-century Japan. They took new note of traditions – including those current in late antique and medieval Europe – where artists presented garments and bodies as part of an overall style for everything, and all lifelikeness was achieved only in terms of the formal system. Modern painters developed new forms of stylisation for its own sake, each in his own way, and many of them felt free to draw on examples from civilisations remote in time and place from modern Europe.

The image of dress was to profit hugely from the Modern dispensation. Curved or jagged edges, punning shapes and spaces, uninhibited colour spread in precise, harsh or nebulous strokes – all could patently be manipulated to add sensory and emotive depth to new renderings of clad bodies, their postures and gestures. Since artists now felt free to re-invent the world, they seized the right to infuse it with personal vision and idiosyncratic formal invention, to see and re-make it again and again according to individual drive and need.

On the new terms for painting, parts of clothes could be rendered as odd patches, which might resemble similar patches representing hands or noses, or flowers or leaves; the appearance of a body-part detached and posing as an element of dress, or of a detached garment posing as a part of nature, could thus be generated to add a stronger emotional web over the picture's surface, especially a deeper erotic level under it. Such arrangements could further alert the viewer's eye to such similarities in real life, or in the illusionistic pictures of the past where no such connections were apparently being made. Dress could appear in art for what it was really worth in aesthetic and emotional life, with no separation in its value from bodies and faces, no sense of its being any more deceptive or frivolous, any less or more interesting than any other aspect of material life.

Detail of fig. 131

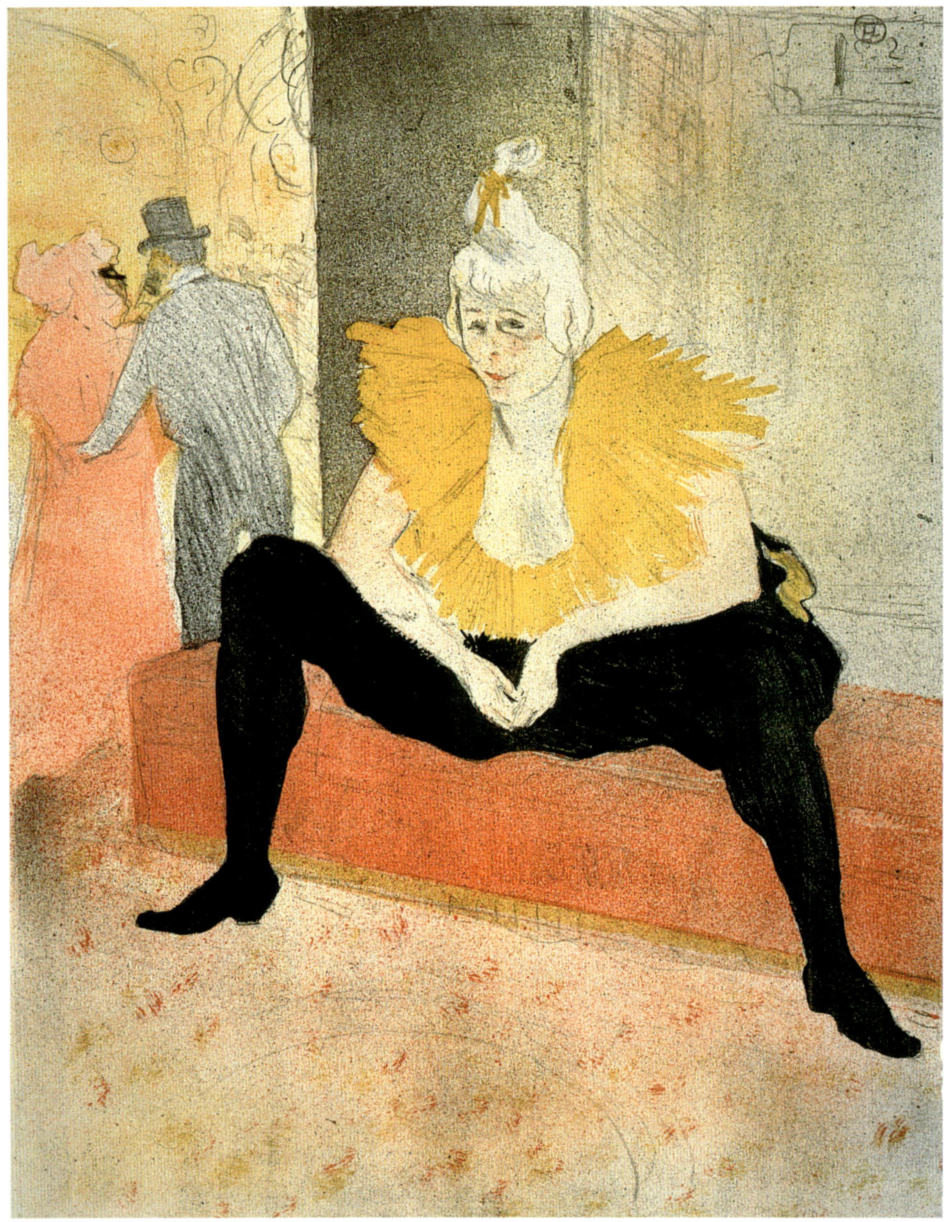

128
Henri de Toulouse-Lautrec
(1864–1901)
Seated Clowness, from the album *Elles*, 1896
Crayon, brush and spatter lithograph in four colours, 52.5 × 40.4 cm
The British Museum, London

In Henri de Toulouse-Lautrec's 1896 lithograph *Seated Clowness* (fig. 128) the formal excitement aroused by the rippling black shape of the performer's spread legs, her angled bare arms and the exploding edges of her immense yellow frill creates a large part of the picture's erotic cast. Because of the sharp juxtaposition of spiky yellow, spidery black and blurry ivory, the charge is more electric than a detailed naturalistic rendering – a photograph, say – of the same figure in the same place could carry, all the more since nothing but planes of cool rose and brown provide the set and one ephemeral couple provides the background action.

In the centre the clown's folded hands create a black triangle at her crotch, a false pubic bush which adds a pungency to the wry, sketchy face engaging us under the grotesque white topknot. The intensity of this image is a product of sharp formal contrast and economy of composition – Lautrec learned much from Japanese printmakers – exploiting the costume to give an exaggerated depravity to the pose. Through Lautrec's magical synthesis, we can see that this milieu is banal and sordid, this costume is vulgar and unfunny, this woman is ageing and ugly; and that this picture of all three is sexy, exhilarating and beautiful.

Another example of sartorial drama created by form is Félix Vallotton's 1897 painting called *The Lie* (fig. 129). The erotic intensity is smoother, the milieu is bourgeois, the matter probably adulterous, and we don't know who's lying. The black and red shapes of the man and woman mingle amorously, a black and a red foot stick out, his fingers clutch her red waist, hers decorate his black shoulder, their other hands make one fist below their close-together faces. He bends forwards, she bends back, his black legs flank her red skirt – both sets of sartorial shapes have clear edges, reflect no light, and have no detail, so that only the fact of their intertwining is specific and insistent. One tiny black buckle on her red shoe at lower left balances his one black shoe in the centre – we note they have only two feet between them – and echoes the black-red roses against the bright-red chair on the right.

Chair, table and sofa form a billowing sea of flat contiguous shapes across the middle of the picture, moving without a pause and with no details from the plum sofa under

129
Félix Vallotton (1865–1925)
The Lie, 1897
Oil on artist's board,
24 × 33.3 cm
Baltimore Museum of Art,
The Cone Collection, formed by
Dr Christabel Cone and Miss Etta
Cone of Baltimore, Maryland

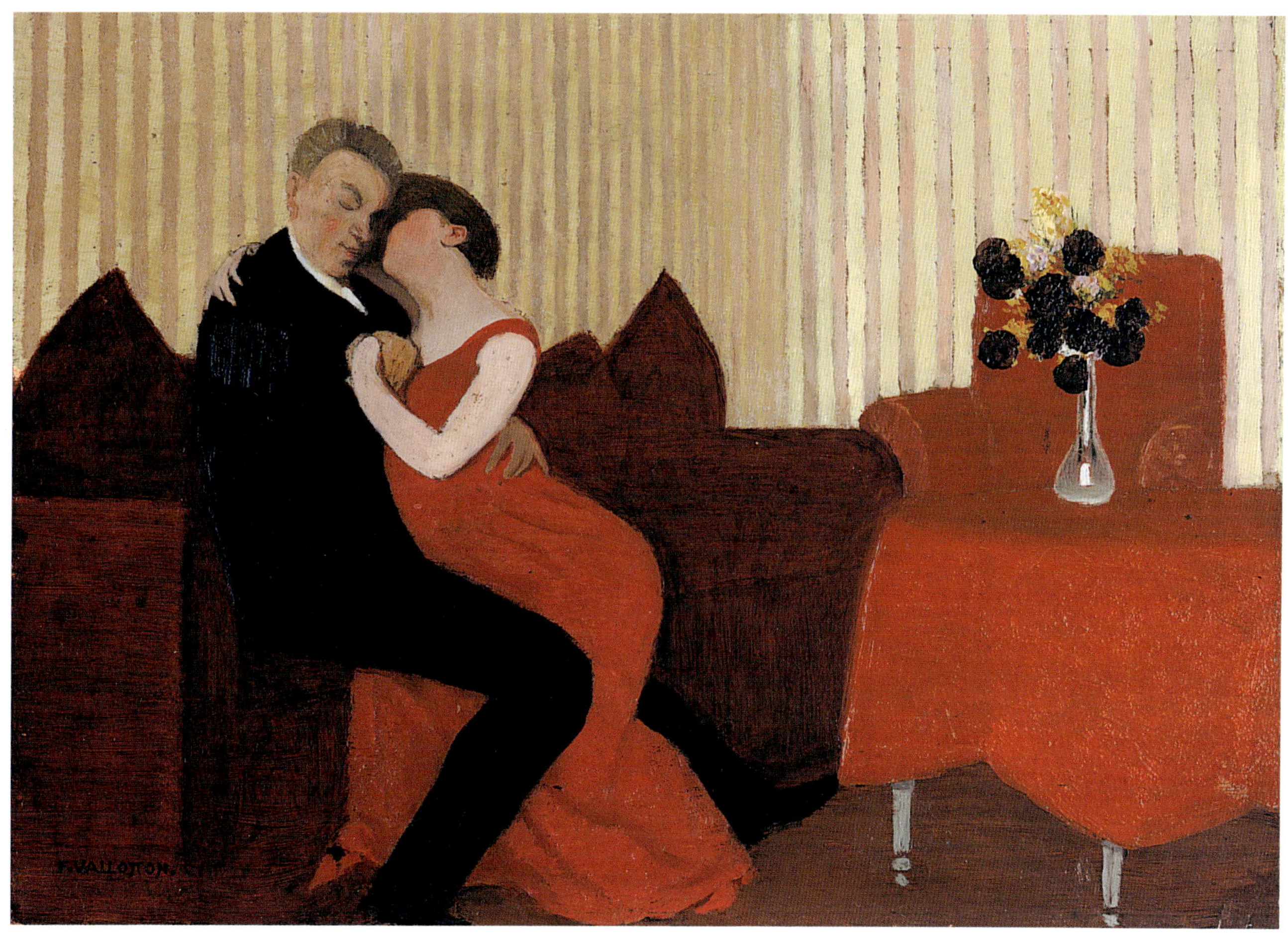

the pair to the bright chair and table. Two pale table-legs part under their lifted skirt, to answer the parting of his two black ones. The colours in the room go from dark plum through rich red to bright red to pink and white; and all of these versions of red in curvilinear shapes and insistent vertical strokes, which involve flowers, furnishings and wallpaper in the flow of the drama, support and intensify the unqualified redness of the red dress. We feel it's very much the red lady's room, the stripes pulsating with the uneven beat of her heart; and we see that the suited man is the black problem in it.

Painted relations between the sexes have changed since the middle of the nineteenth century. This dark-clad man does not seem recessive, like the ones we discussed in Chapter VII; he and the red lady vibrate like *yang* and *yin*. A fashion plate from about fifteen years later shows a still more radical shift in attitude, along with a new elegance in the graphic art devoted to fashion (fig. 130). This plate looks much more like a modern painting than any had ever done in the 1880s and 1890s, when fashion illustration bore no resemblance to avant-garde painting – although avant-garde artists had been stealing visual elements from banal fashion plates since the 1860s.

Modern fashion and modern art were demonstrating a new accord during the period just before 1914. Modern painters such as Vallotton gave a freshly vital importance to dress in pictures, showing the psychological power that formal stylisation could lend it. Their work encouraged a modernisation of fashion art and helped to raise fashion itself on the aesthetic scale. The display in painting of stylised form encouraged the idea that dresses and chairs, or automobiles and suits, might themselves be designed according to analogous visual principles, as works of art now represented them. As part of this combined interest in the way the look of all things natural and artificial might be similarly stylised, the design of actual clothing came to require serious aesthetic consideration; and fashion designers were becoming publicly famous for the first time in history.

Fashion illustration had long been a minor commercial graphic medium with no connection to advanced movements in either art or design. Its unregarded status doubtless contributed to the marginal aesthetic consideration long given to fashion itself – in its quaint plates, fashion could be seen not to take itself seriously. During the first quarter of the twentieth century, French fashion illustrators began to adopt themes and forms from avant-garde painting and printmaking, and their work – with fanciful titles given to the dresses as if they were works of art – appeared in new prestigious magazines devoted to the arts, along with images of avant-garde stage-sets and costume designs. The great couturier Paul Poiret, who cultivated his celebrity, encouraged the renewed marriage of art and craft by hiring the celebrated painter Raoul Dufy to design printed fabrics especially for him, and made a point of hiring Ecole des Beaux-Arts graduates to render his designs in stylised modern lithographs, which he published in elegantly produced booklets. Abstraction in form was affecting art, fashion and design all at once, changing the look of actual objects and real clothing together with the look of their various representations, and changing the public perception of both object and image.

One result was the creation of a new visual harmony between dressed men and women, who, as we can see from this French plate, began to be portrayed as similar long and narrow objects, both not dissimilar to the graceful stone urn on a garden wall. It dates from before the First World War, however: the man and woman are equally elegant and their clothes are equally demanding, no ideal of comfort and practicality invests these figures. There is no idea of equality of the sexes; theirs is a visual similarity deriving entirely from the momentarily fashionable imitation of the unchanged male silhouette by the female one.

Nevertheless the sexes are here in great aesthetic rapport, having the same physical shape and size, the same visible feet (with spats) and the same gestures and props. They share the same dark colours as they gaze together at the bare branches. She still wears fur trim, a velvet hat and curved heels, as he does not, but her skirt is now like a single trouser-leg. He still has distinctly separate legs, as in the Vallotton; but the couple in that 1897 picture, ardently dissembling in their *yang-yin* embrace, would never want to adopt the air of cool fellowship illustrated in this fashion plate. It was a new fantasy, not to be realised for several decades.

This 1913 plate further indicates how fashion, especially when purveyed in its image, often anticipates social change. At this date Mrs Pankhurst, the famous English crusader for women's suffrage, was frequently being gaoled for her vigorous activism; and English women were granted the vote in 1926, American women having got it in 1920. This

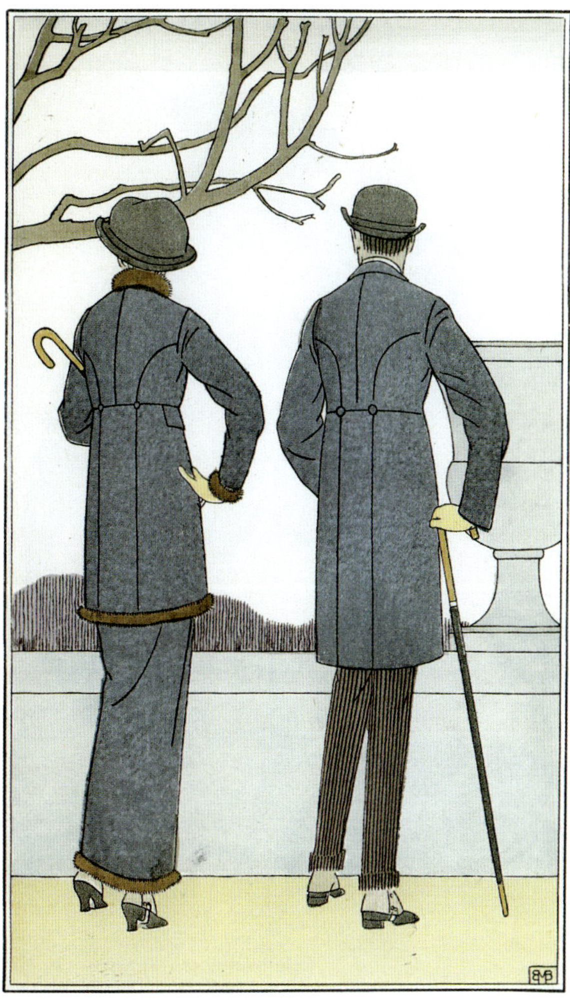

130
Woman's Suit, Man's Suit, 20 Nov 1913, from *Journal des Dames et des Modes,* December 1913, pl. 121
Thomas J. Watson Library, Rogers Fund, The Metropolitan Museum of Art, New York (inv. 231/J82)

picture, however, is a French fashion plate, reflecting French notions of the sexes, and French women did not get the vote until 1946. The similarity in the design of men and women manifests the new appeal of a certain androgyny in sexual matters, not an interest in their political equality. But it looks prophetic.

Edouard Vuillard loved fabric, having grown up among lengths of it in his mother's home-based dressmaking establishment. He used its printed or woven patterns in many paintings, and not just for clothes; he even seems to have absorbed a sense of these first elements of dress as fundamental elements of nature, as if a field of flowers took its looks from a yard of daisy-printed cotton. Here the painter's *Young Girls walking* (fig. 131) shows a green bush sharing the frame with two girls in differently patterned dresses. This is another tight composition emphasising the flatness of the plane with flat patterns, another entwined couple expressing intimacy, now devoid of sensuous flow, full instead of the abrupt motions of adolescence. Both girls' clothed bodies share the modern tubular look with the raised and slightly indented waist that we can see on both figures in the fashion plate; but here their dresses are placed in an intimate surface relation with both outdoor phenomena and their own youthful bodies, on purpose to carry considerable psychological freight.

Vuillard puts blue flowers on the darker blue dress, which gives the doubly blue girl the chief role in this greenish scene, her leadership confirmed by her smiling cheek, lifted blonde head and encouraging arm around the other girl; but he also assimilates her whole clad body to the body of the neighbouring bush, which he shows dressed in green leaves that seem printed on a darker green ground; and he compares her pale hand to the few pale leaves printed on the grass below the bush, while comparing the vertical stripes on her stockings to the vertical stems supporting it. Blue girl, green bush, leafy grass and the unidentifiable white-spotted patch at upper left at which the blue girl gazes all combine as happy, fabric-like patterned phenomena, akin both in nature and in this picture. They leave unassimilated the awkward brown-and-black-striped girl with dark hair, who bows her uneasy face and sticks her elbows out, her stockings fettering her ankles in horizontal stripes. But the four black-booted feet that are entering the frame and hurrying these two pubescent girls along the path nevertheless unite them in their swift passage through this uneasy moment. Clothes here set the emotional tone in the contrasting disposition of their printed textures, which separately relate their wearers' spirits to the world around them.

Children's clothing in art has a long and complicated history. How it looks always depends on how the children in the picture are being perceived, not just by the painter but by the world. In noble portraits before the second half of the eighteenth century children were usually being perceived dynastically, which meant that their condition as children was less important to the way they were dressed than the fact that they would inherit and were marriageable. Since then, however, the fact that they are in a state of childhood has been of first importance in their painted clothes, whether in portraits or genre works. Actual children's clothing has always had its own fashions, which have had differing relations to what adults have worn, sometimes resembling it closely, sometimes not, usually with some indicators of childhood status and of the child's sex, but not always. In art these customs have been complicated by the fact that fancy dress has been worn by children in portraits even more often than by adults.

OPPOSITE **131**
Edouard Vuillard (1868–1940)
Young Girls walking, 1891–2
Oil on canvas, 81.2 × 65 cm
National Gallery, London
on loan from a private collection
L652

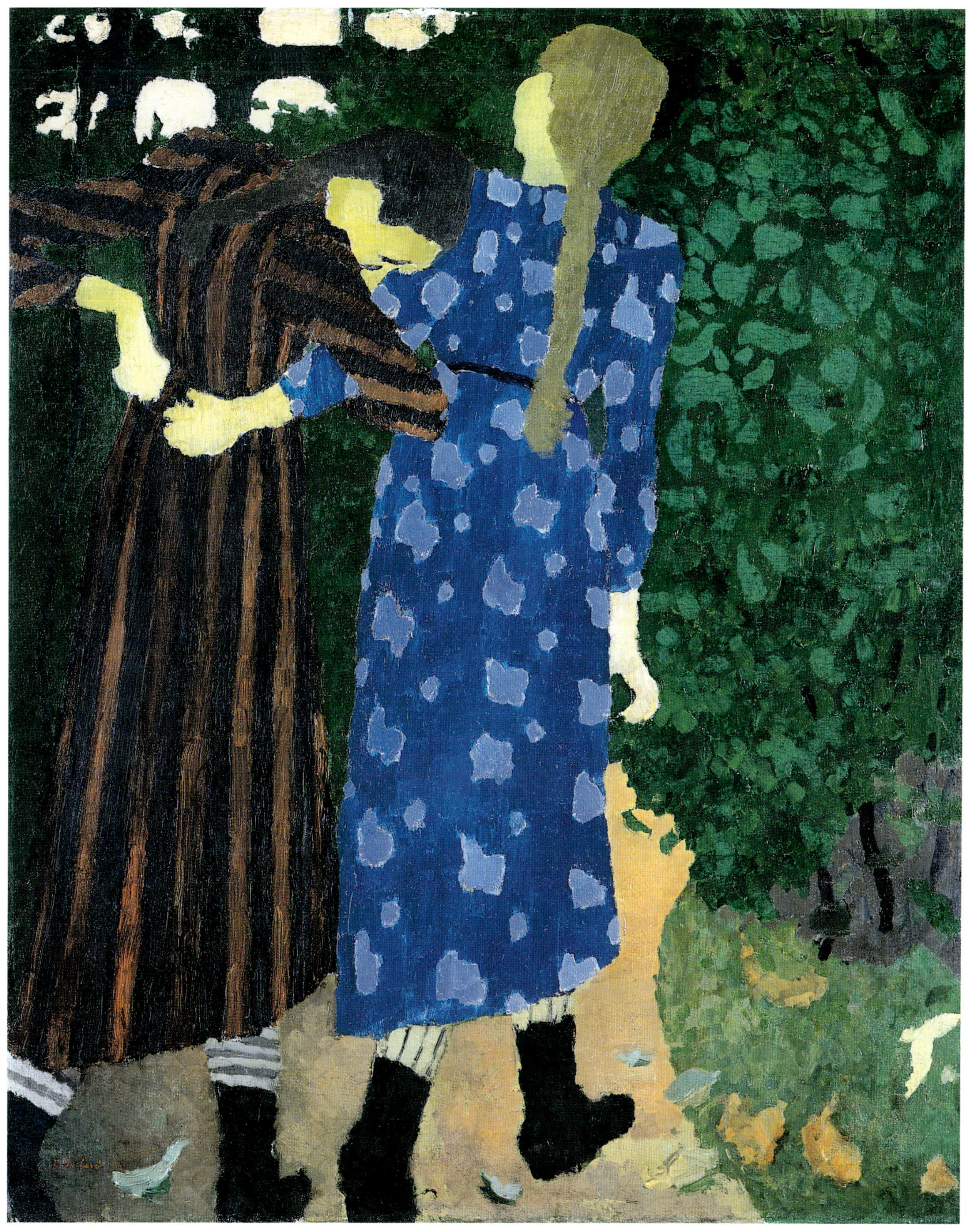

Pablo Picasso's *Child with a Dove* (fig. 133) was painted in 1901, just after the young artist's first visit to Paris in 1900, and it shows the impact on him of works by Lautrec, Van Gogh and especially Gauguin. A sense of primeval gravity invests this image, despite its appealingly sweet components, among which the long white dress, big green sash and laced-up little shoes instantly seize the eye. Other precious details are the small creature cherished in both hands, the toy on the ground, the red lips and long lashes in the dear little face, the artless little ear; but we are not allowed to condescend to any of these. The severely painted figure commands respect, as if Picasso were invoking sacred mysteries, following Gauguin's way with Pacific Islanders and rural Bretons. A touch of Goya appears in the uneven line dividing the indeterminate background, and in the sashed white dress, a mode current in Goya's day; but this dress has an austere formality beyond Goya or Gauguin. Picasso makes its white simplicity give the figure an icon-like flavour, evoked by the sacramental hands around the dove, the rigidly paired feet and the thin dark outline around each shape.

The simplicity and tight fit of this dress are unusual, since little children's clothes in the early twentieth century tended towards the overburdened look, with collars and layers, such as Picasso paints on his own little son Paolo in the early 1920s. Here, however, the artist has given the unearthly look of painted nudity we saw in Blake, following Michelangelo and Pontormo, to this baby's bodice; and the dress itself is not unlike the one he put on another 1901 standing child (*Mother and Child*, private collection), with clasped hands, being caressed by what looks like a fourteenth-century Madonna in her enveloping, blue mantle. The present child has a similar august, religious look, to which the dove adds, and from which the green sash and multi-coloured toy can't entirely detract. We can see suggestions of medieval pictorial design, of Italian images of the Virgin from a time when they still resembled earlier Greek icons, and the arts of antiquity were still alive, still undergoing a formal devolution not yet widely seen to need basic change. An Umbrian *Virgin and Child* of about 1260 (fig. 132) has a certain affinity with this Picasso, and with some other evolving imagery of the early twentieth century.

In the icon there is a visible effort to arrange inventively, for decorative use on a flat surface, what had begun generations earlier as a stylised reduction of illusionistic rendering. By now, however, the conventional image has long been detached from the original aim for three-dimensional illusion. Faces, fingers and especially folds are nevertheless recognisable to us as refined and varied derivations from long-ago realistic art – not as visions directly abstracted from the look of a present reality. Their new aesthetic value as elements in the new pictorial design is ratified by an old artistic heritage, and that has helped engender in this new image its own kind of intensified realism.

Behind Picasso's modernising eyes as he makes this child's image there seems to lie an old iconic model like this *Virgin*, an example of creative distillation from an earlier realistic tradition, not the invention of a wholly new realism. Similarly, the one authentic (if legendary) portrait of the Virgin – which is said by the eighth-century Eastern Christian theologian John of Damascus to have been painted from life by Saint Luke the Evangelist himself, doubtless in the naturalistic Greco-Roman style of the first century, the single picture of her from which all Eastern Christian icons allegedly derive, in hundreds of copies reductively re-copied hundreds of times – lies behind the eyes of the Umbrian master himself. We saw a comparison in Chapter I between a Greek

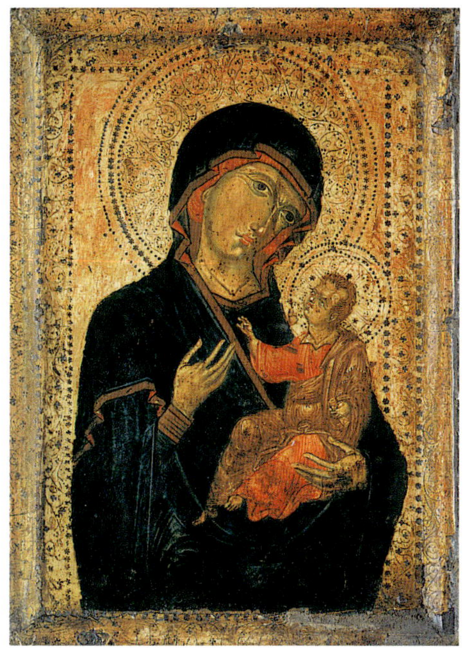

132
Umbrian, about 1260
The Virgin and Child
Tempera on wood,
32.4 × 22.8 cm
National Gallery,
London
NG 6572

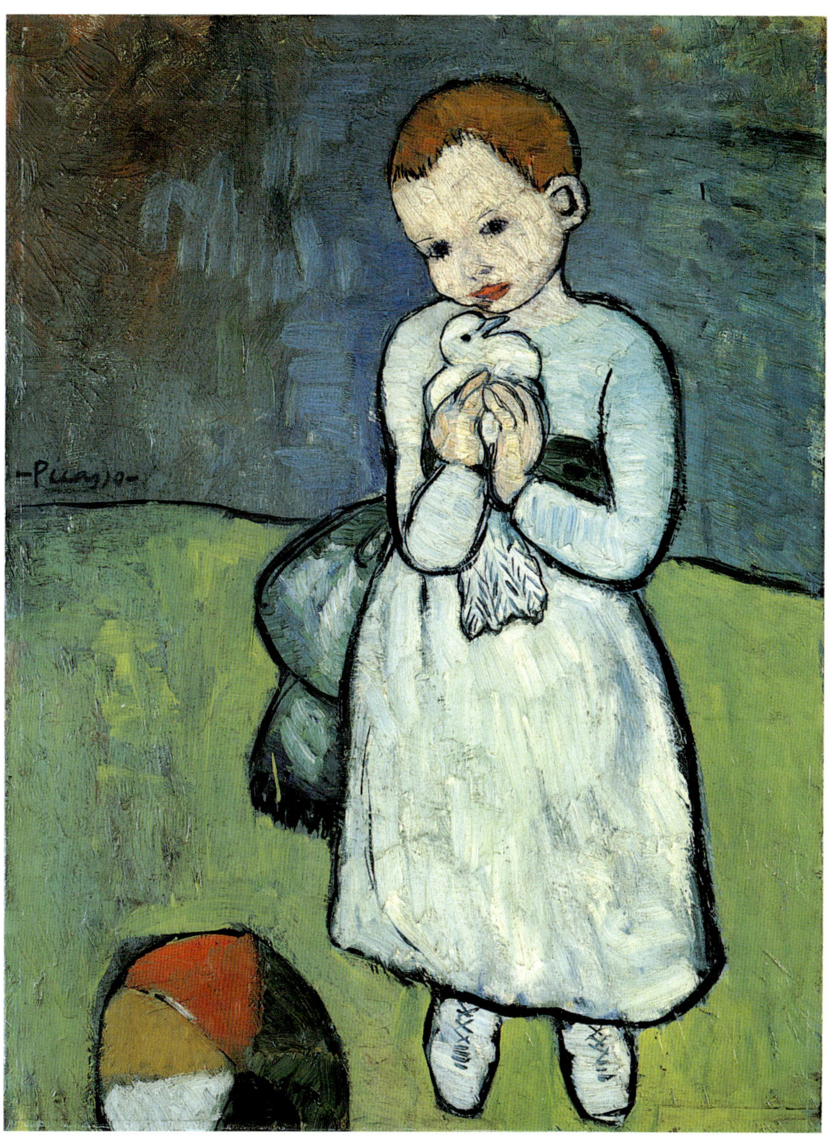

133
Pablo Picasso (1881–1973)
Child with a Dove, 1901
Oil on canvas, 73 × 54 cm
National Gallery, London,
on loan from a private
collection
L9

classical sculpture and a thirteenth-century Tuscan icon (see figs. 3, 4) that suggests the way ancient folds might gradually transform into medieval folds, and so be brought to lead a new life.

The fingers in both these works have the same intensified look, so do the faces, although naturally the clothing differs in them. The once realistic folds of Mary's classical *palla*, which drape her bust and head, and those of the once classical male garments draping the boy Christ's body now form stylised tracery, rivers and eddies of colour, purely pictorial beauties honouring the holiness of the image. In a manner inherited from earlier ways to reduce and sanctify a realistic image, Picasso makes the reduced, clarified shapes and outlines of dress and sash and the decorative strokes of feather and shoelace do the same thing for this modern image that glorifies the child.

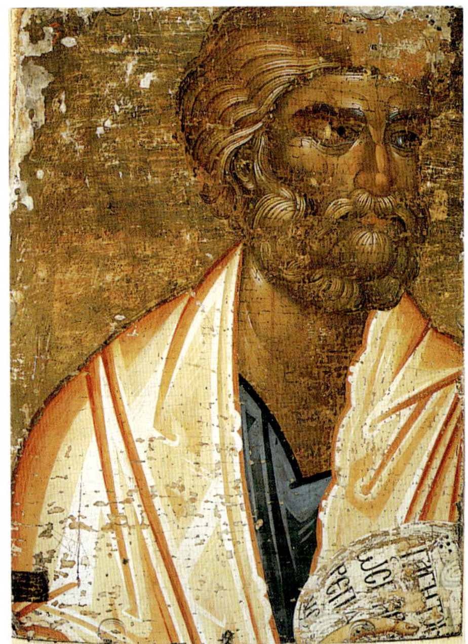

134
Byzantine, about 1320
Saint Peter
Tempera and gold leaf on cedar panel, 68.7 × 50.6 cm
The British Museum, London

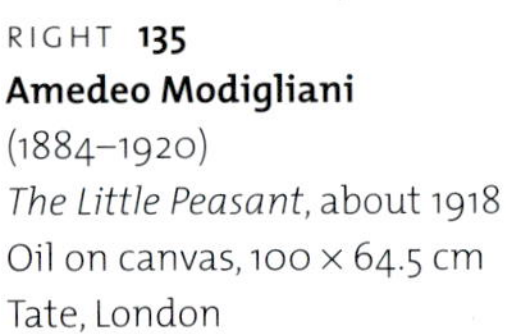

RIGHT **135**
Amedeo Modigliani
(1884–1920)
The Little Peasant, about 1918
Oil on canvas, 100 × 64.5 cm
Tate, London

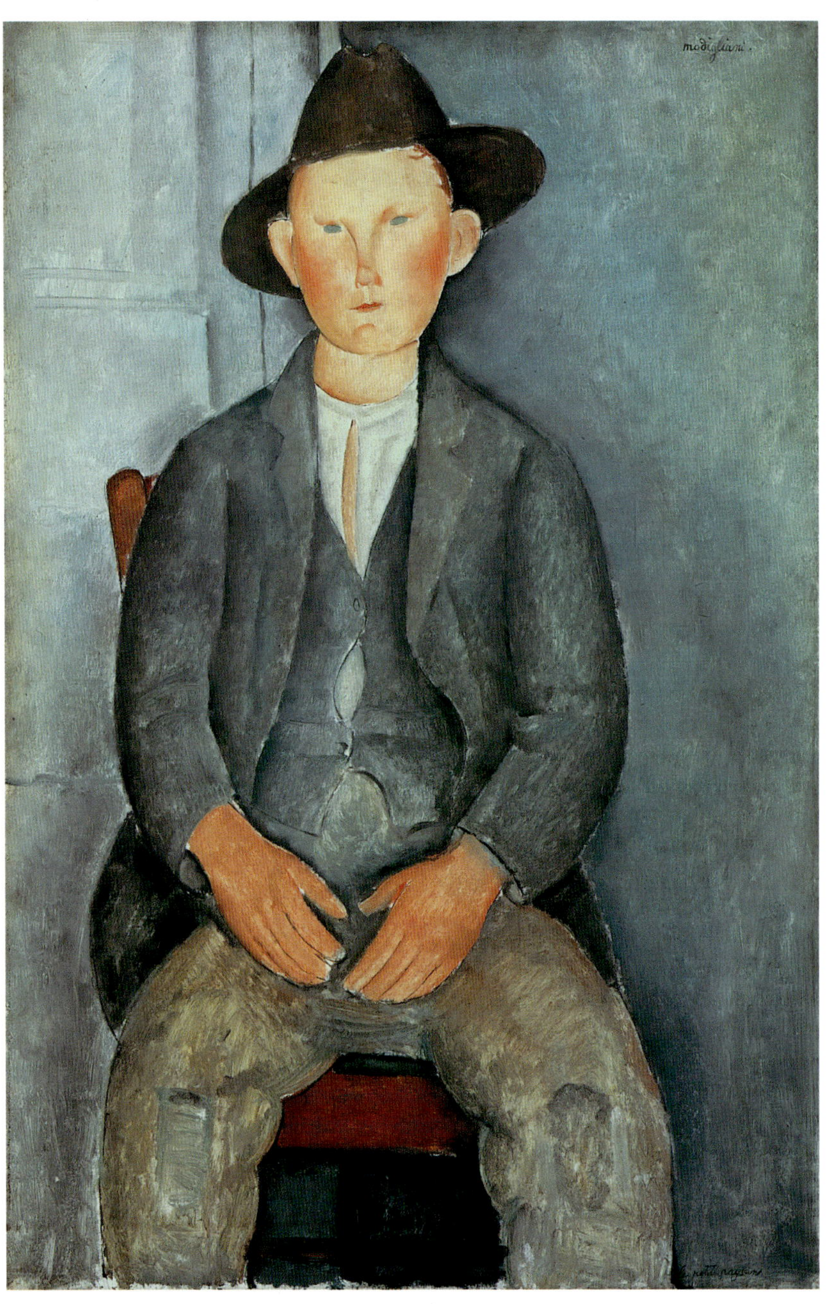

An icon-like style of composition appears in other early twentieth-century works showing a clothed figure, so that they, too, seem to derive their modern realism through the lengthy distillation of an original realistic pictorial model, just as an icon does, and to exemplify the same condensation an icon embodies. A certain honorific, celebratory character invests such images, without adding any explicit sanctity to the subject at all. Amedeo Modigliani's *Little Peasant* of about 1918 (fig. 135) is the conventional portrait of an ordinary man, the subject supported by centuries of art history, out of which the painter has drawn this lyrically concentrated figure composed in icon-like shapes, including the set of lines delineating the face. This modern icon is more refined than Picasso's, following the more delicate clarity of Florentines who created icon-like figures in the fifteenth rather than the thirteenth century.

There is a refined Italian look to this curving coat and waistcoat that gape so gracefully over this collarless shirt, the hat a black shape as well balanced in relation to the head as the simple black hats in Italian Renaissance portraits. His ham-like hands and patched knees announce his peasant condition; and Velázquez or Rembrandt, say, would have dwelt on the lack of refinement in such details, would have given their crudity an intrinsic visual importance in such a subject. But Modigliani gives the peasant's hands a simple, Masaccio-like look, placing them in an iconic central position; and after delicately making the patches blend into the texture of each trousered knee, he makes the inner line of this peasant's spreading legs into a symmetrical scalloped arch that Verrocchio might have invented. Similar scallops even appear along the edge of Saint Peter's robe in an icon from the early fourteenth century (fig. 134). Modigliani has conceived his peasant in an icon format, infusing it with further quasi-religious respect – recalling that of these icon-painters for their originally humble subject – by means of a considerable elegance in the formal composition itself.

Henri Matisse's 1937 *Woman in Blue* (fig. 136) is a much later and more sophisticated version of the same idea, deploying flat shapes with clear outlines in iconic ways, to give a single clothed figure a numinous presence. This painter has made an icon full of joy in honour of a beauty on a smiling sofa, her head silhouetted against a halo of flowers, its yellow explosion even recalling the collar of Lautrec's raffish clown. But this dress has its own Madonna-like blue power, serious, noble and stable. The central fall of bodice frills divides and pours majestically over the skirt in two white rivers that look like medieval painted water; they seem not to be wayward ornaments but vectors of celebration, echoed by the golden arms and red sides of the sofa's hieratic-looking throne. The white lines embellishing the black and red background areas seem not unlike the lines of gold in the icon illustrated in Chapter I (see fig. 3), a web of optical glitter to decorate the revered image. Even the fingers retain simple, icon-like shapes, here enlarged and generous like the spreading dress. Now, however, we see the modern addition, similar to the toy and sash in the Picasso, of the manifest element of pleasure, here the notably pink hand enlaced with a necklace and placed over the crotch, quite opposed to the white hand above that supports and points to the brain. Red lips are here, too, as also in Picasso.

Modern, smoothly curving flat shapes used for rendering a group of clothed figures could be composed with enough spatial sophistication to seem abstracted from pictorial traditions much later than the Middle Ages. In Vanessa Bell's *Conversation* of about 1913–16 (fig. 137), the foreground woman muffles her neck and shoulders in a fashionable wrapped cloak, made to form plump brown and ochre whorls in contrast to the subdued black dress worn by the woman on the left. The third woman, behind, is an auxiliary version of the first, both figures wrapped, hatted and drawn up in opposition to the hatless woman facing them, who leans forward with an eager, bare-necked, bare-handed gesture. For all the folds, flatness is modified and modelled to give them extra prominence, much more than for the dresses in the earlier Picasso or the later Matisse. With its group of half-length clothed figures attended by flowers, draperies and a bit of distance, this modern composition shows a clear debt to seventeenth-century genre and religious painting. The

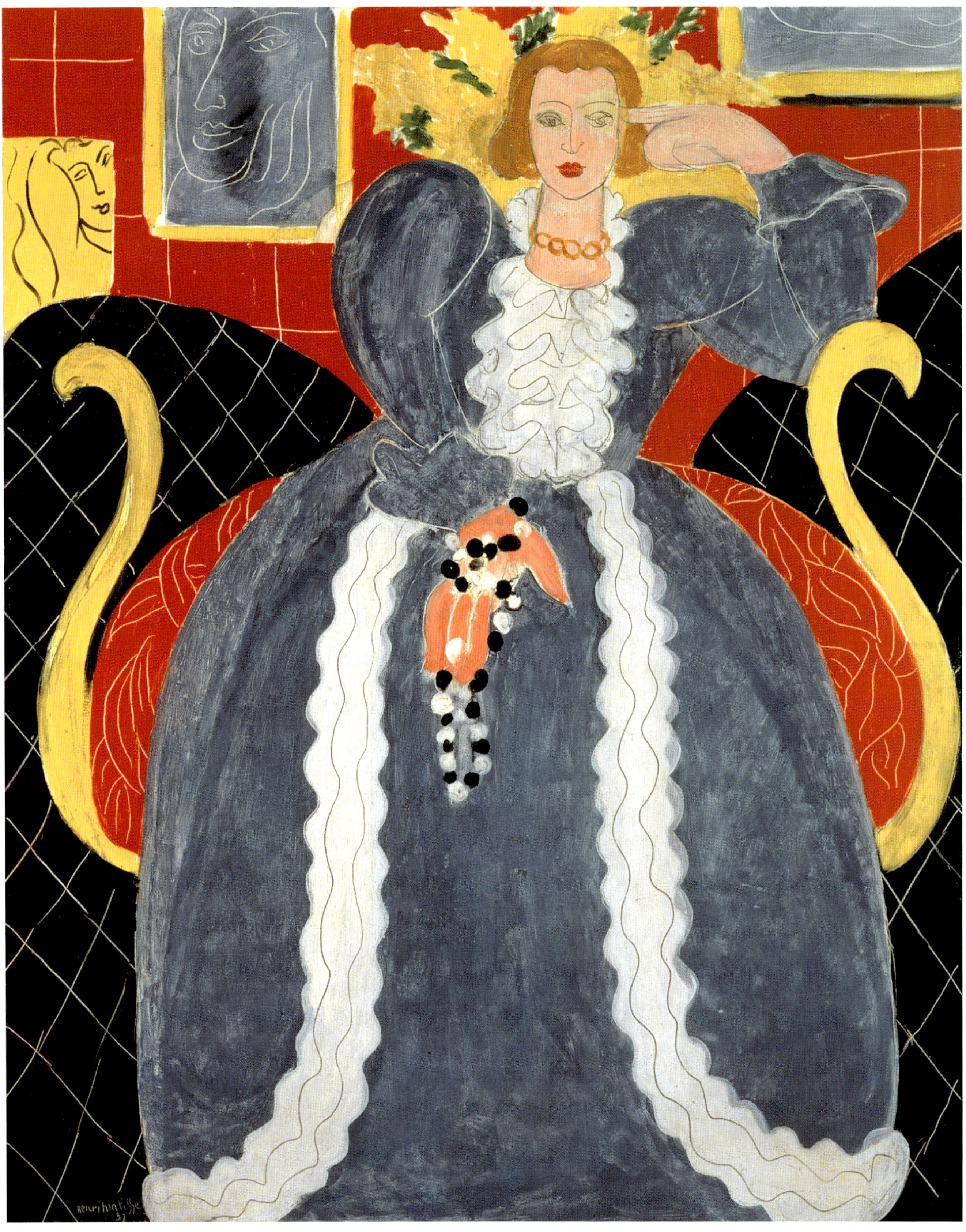

137
Vanessa Bell (1879–1961)
A Conversation, about 1913–16
Oil on canvas, 86.6 × 81 cm
Courtauld Institute Gallery, London, on extended loan from a private collection

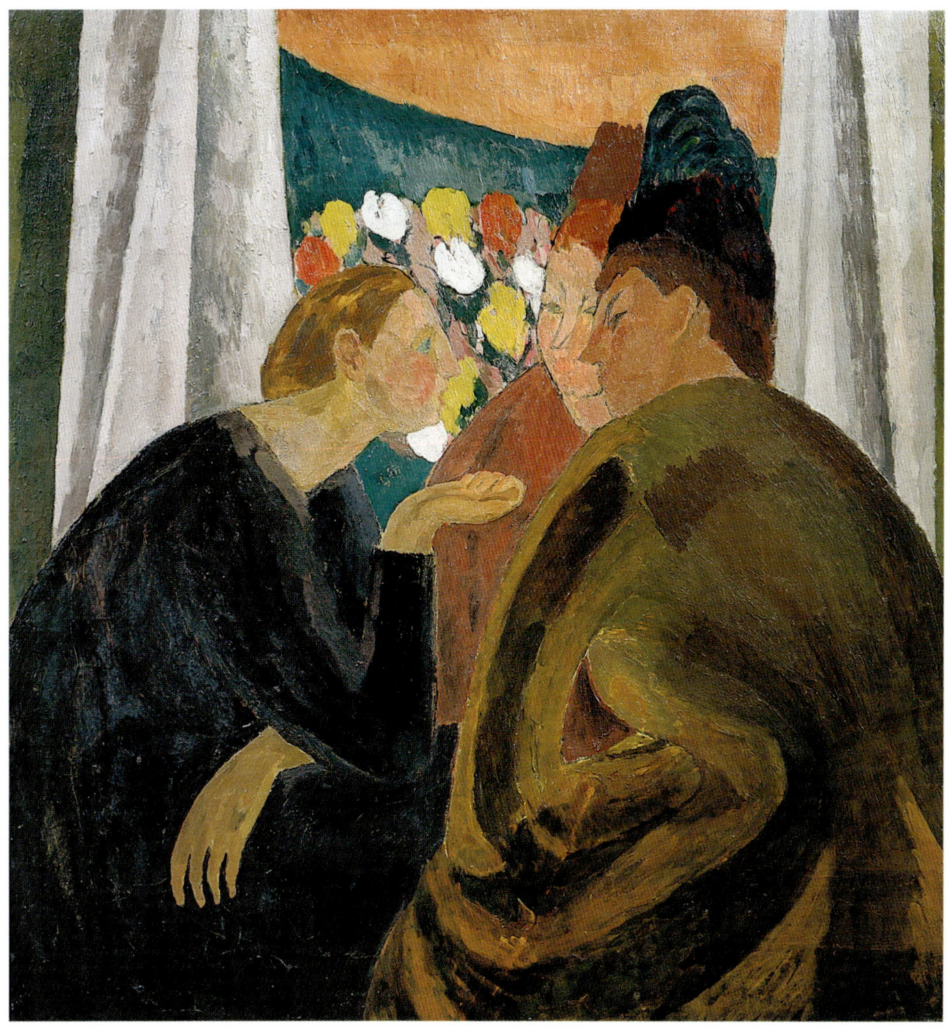

large folds of foreground cloak are fermented memories of the ones on soldiers in Ter Borch and Honthorst, or on biblical characters in Guercino and Guido Reni; and Bell's background draperies have a similar submerged Baroque pròvenance. But the modern painter insists on the detached formal power of the props and draped elements, as Guido and Vermeer did not. She dims the faces, and she vigorously stylises hands, folds and contrasting areas of colour, so that the real conversation is amongst them.

Perhaps the most influential movement in early twentieth-century painting was Cubism, which proposed cutting off painterly relations with any earlier stages of realism dependent on optical impressions from a certain perspective, however reduced, stylised or abstracted they might have been. Cubists aimed instead to construct the image of a more comprehensive form of perception. The viewer was invited to consider the three-dimensional subject's qualities all at once, translated into a painting where its visual characteristics – seen from all sides, even from the inside – were broken down and entirely re-created in an interlocking set of abstractly painted formal components.

In such a scheme, garments and bodies were free of their differences, and distinction vanished between the elements composing figure and ground. For the single clothed

OPPOSITE **136**
Henri Matisse (1869–1954)
Woman in Blue, 1937
Oil on canvas, 92.7 × 73.6 cm
Philadelphia Museum of Art, Gift of Mrs John Wintersteen

figure, the ancient iconic format would not serve: a human object would not be forced into the prison of its outline, nor would a human group be herded inside a fence of non-human surroundings. The break-up of the painted universe made all its abstract units free to substitute for each other – and it eventually made them free of all subjects, so that later developments inevitably led to absolute abstraction, form painted for its own sake.

Cubism was begun by Picasso and Georges Braque in 1907, but European painters were affected differently by the idea in the succeeding decade. The Russian artist Kazimir Malevich was among those who wished to go beyond subject and object into the pure play of painted form; but he made some concessions to subject-matter, of which *Morning in the Village after Snowstorm* is one from 1912 (fig. 138). We can see his effort to geometrise the smoke from village chimneys, and to carve into sharp-edged monuments the fluffy snowdrifts piled up during the night. Women's heavy skirts, boots and kerchiefs were easier to show as pure geometry, certainly when a back view reduced a thickly clad woman to the shapes of her clothes. The milk-pails match the skirts in conical form, the sky matches them in rosy colour, the smoke matches the tree-tops, the hills match the roof-tops. The painter makes the point that rising smoke and fallen snow, women, trees, huts and hills are all of one substance under his hand – that is, paint in its full array of tints, moulded into an impersonal system of volumes. The universe he makes of it stops at the frame, and this village has no other life.

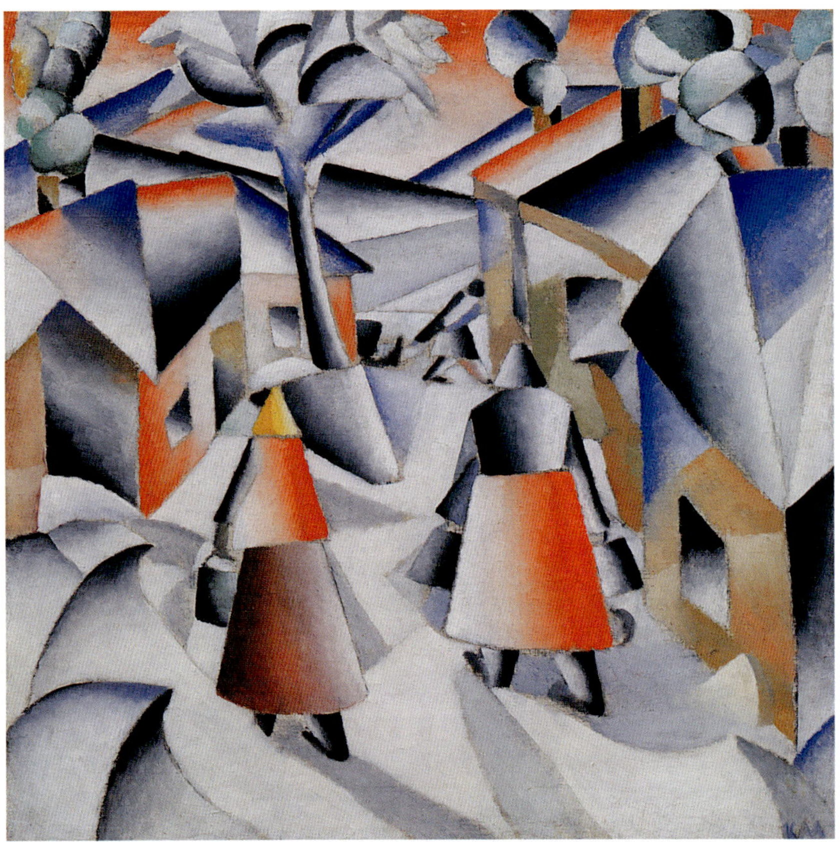

138
Kazimir Malevich (1878–1935)
Morning in the Village after Snowstorm, 1912
Oil on canvas, 80.7 × 80.8 cm
Solomon R. Guggenheim Museum, New York

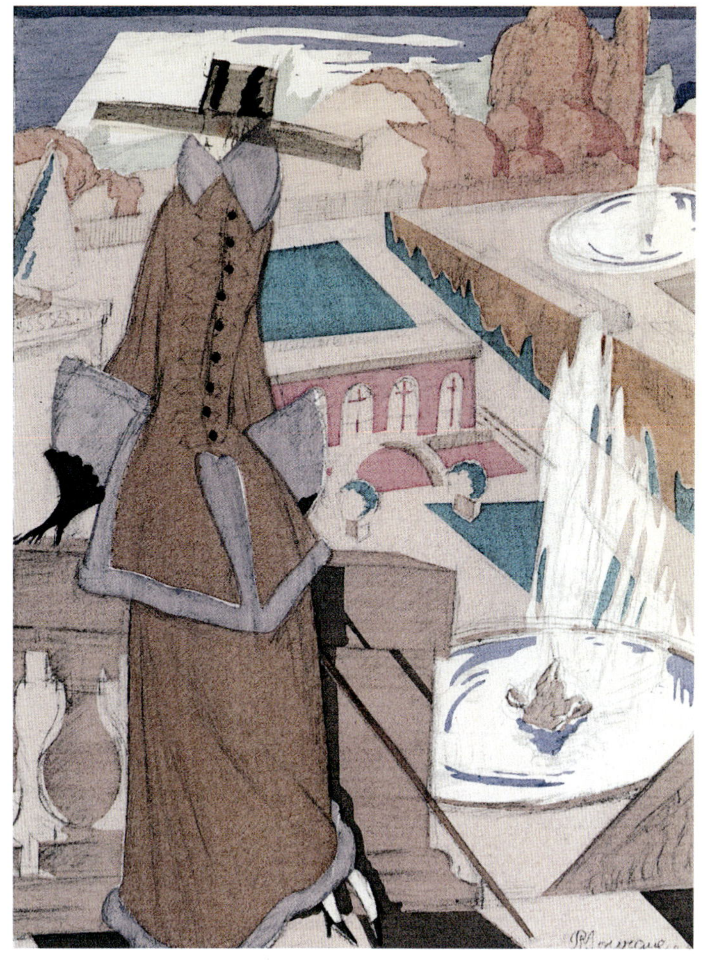

139
La Petite Mademoiselle, 1922, from *Gazette du Bon Ton*, no. 1, 1922, pl. 1
Thomas J. Watson Library, Rogers Fund, The Metropolitan Museum of Art, New York (inv. 233.4/G25)

A French fashion plate from ten years later (fig. 139) shows how Cubist influence came to affect the art that conveyed the desired perception of fashion – focusing especially on the impulse to turn the dressed female figure into a faceless set of abstract shapes. Most of this plate is the setting – a Cubist-like view of the gardens at Versailles, which makes the costume into a Cubist-like version of a seventeenth-century lady's riding habit, as the subtitle says it is. The style of the picture suggests the right blend of high-level modern chic with high-level Modern art; and if it were not a fashion illustration, this plate might well be a set-and-costume design for a Cocteau play or a Diaghilev ballet.

To be elegant in France in 1922, a woman's looks had to lend themselves to the ambient French Cubism, here casting its refractory eye on the august Grand Siècle, which this illustrator suggests has no life outside this plate. The image exemplifies the depersonalising character of fashion plates, here nicely emphasised by the Cubist trimmings. The illustrator has given no consideration to the humanity of any possible wearer of the pictured costume: we see only an extreme version of a particular abstract visual effect, and no wearer, only some apparently detachable body parts. He has departed from Cubism enough to record the specific details of cut, trim and accessory, to instruct a possible human customer for the ensemble.

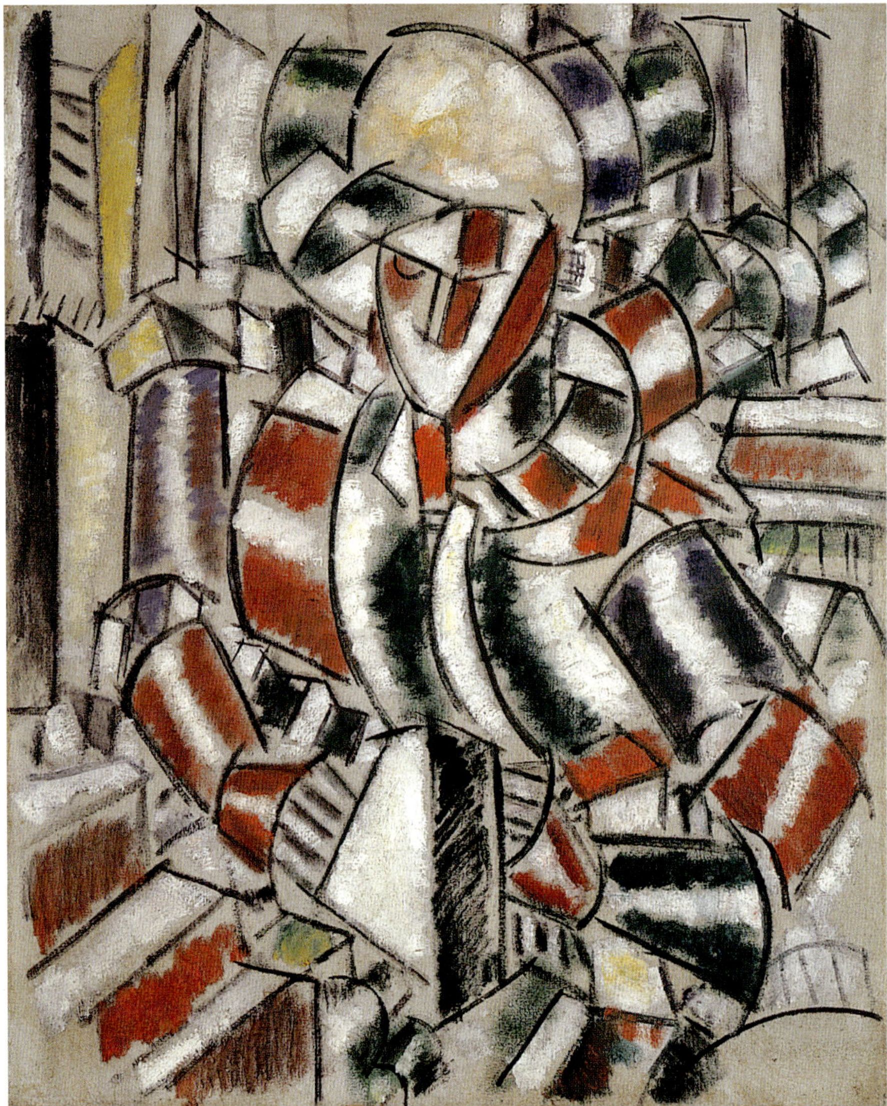

140
Fernand Léger (1881–1955)
Woman in Red and Green, 1914
Oil on canvas, 100 × 81 cm
Centre Georges Pompidou, Musée national d'art moderne, Paris

OPPOSITE **141**
Robert Delaunay (1885–1941)
A Woman with a Parasol (La Parisienne), 1913
Oil on canvas, 122 × 85.5 cm
Museo Thyssen-Bornemisza, Madrid

The opposite effect was achieved in the vigorous painting of a single female figure wrought in Fernand Léger's brand of Cubism in 1914, *Woman in Red and Green* (fig. 140). Here the details of the garments are unintelligible, but the humanity of the woman is strongly suggested by the energy of the concerted cubic and tubular forms that make up her clad and hatted body and her sharp-angled hands and face – with its eloquent single eyelid – as she moves along her urban street. The street has no details, either; but we get a sense of busy buildings and a busy costume, a particular woman moving in some haste, a life in progress in a lively place. The white sheen on everything suggests bright sunlight; and the clothes act on our eye as they often do in cities, as parts of a passer-by's vivid flash, parts of the whole flickering street we're in. This work shows how well Modern artists could make garments strike the mind through the eye with entirely new forms of painted reality.

Robert Delaunay was another who wished to move completely beyond subject-matter into the rhythms of pure colour, but he sometimes allowed those to allude to actualities,

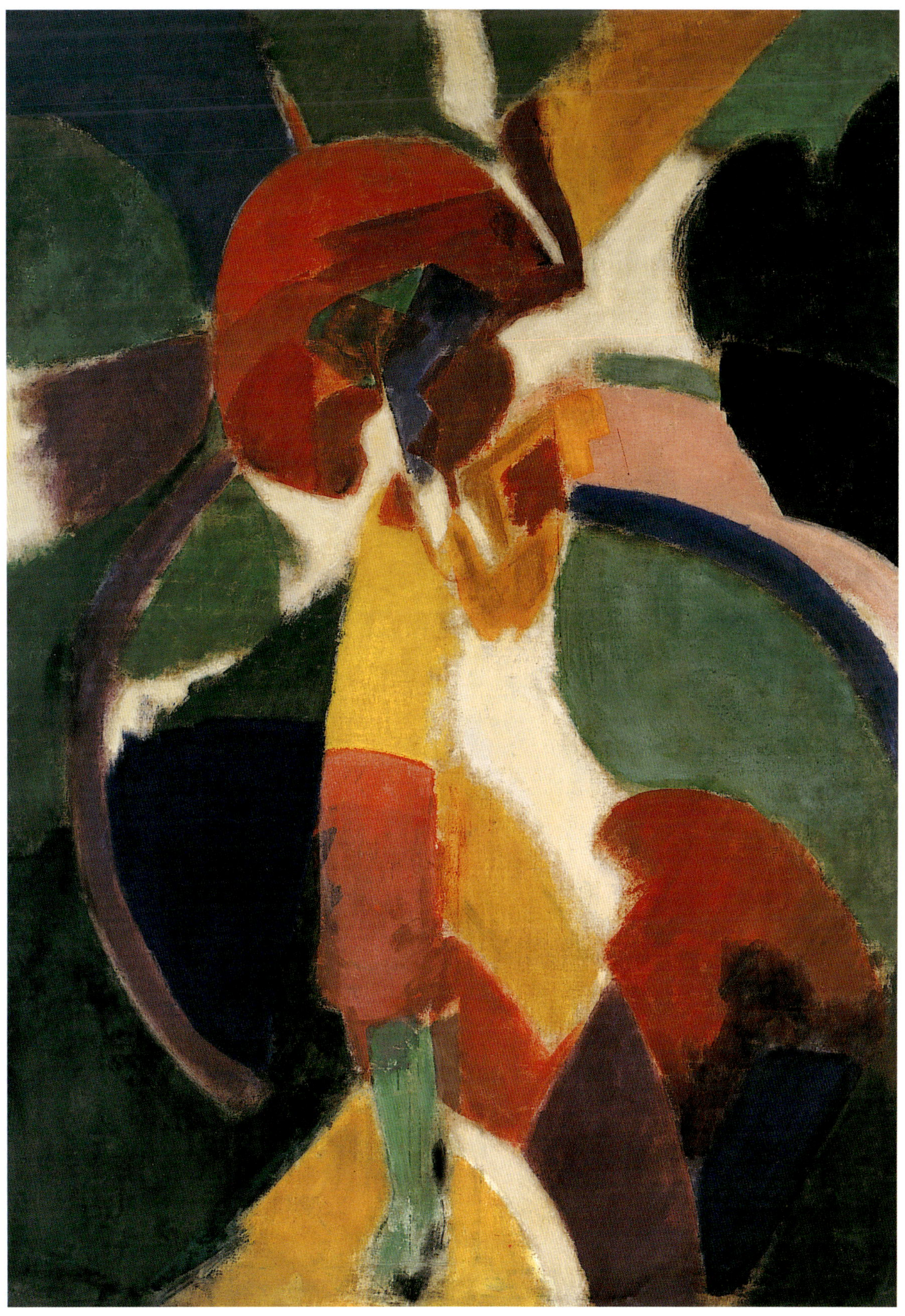

as in *A Woman with a Parasol* from 1913 (fig. 141). This work was also called *La Parisienne*, a title usually suggesting a woman deliberately on view and in no hurry. The shapes creating the woman's clothes are quite different from those in the Léger, here floating in arcs and screens of colour that never sharpen into edgy glitter; and the woman remains at a distance, keeping still. We can't really see her at all except for the neat little patches of black shoe the painter gives her to stand in, so it's upwards of them that we follow the indolent, richly coloured curve of her pose without taking note of what she wears or what she's like – we only perceive that her costume is simple, in few but luminous colours. The painter lets the palest and brightest streaks in this chromatic symphony arrive to cluster around her as if she drew in the light, which the parasol's russet dome seems to capture and fracture. Beyond that the whole warm sweep of surroundings seems another parasol itself, enclosing light and woman together in this magnetic stretch of park. Clothes are again painted as integral to a momentary whole, inseparable from all that's seen and felt at once inside this frame.

For dress in portraits, Modern painters have had infinite choices of register, able to make clothes a part both of the person and of the setting, to use them for the display of vibrant colour contrast or of concordant shapes, of surface texture or of psychological tension. At mid-century, the Modern portrait could, moreover, be doubly traditional, adhering to modern and ancient traditions at once. In his 1949 portrait of T. S. Eliot (fig. 142), Patrick Heron presents the sitter's bare face and clothed body as a set of painted fragments reunited to suggest a man with two selves – a divided face, rising from a divided suit, standing out against a divided background. The candid, tweedy green-and-white left half of the coat and the pallor of the left half-face are threatened from the right by the heavy purple profile, its blade-like nose the focus of the picture, its big ear swallowing the small one. The half-coat below it is an undisciplined and harsh mélange of russet, lavender, deep purple and sand encroaching on the white shirt's no man's land, the lapels distorted in thickness of stroke. High above, a silvery cloud over the poet's head divides the background in reverse, the peaceable on the right, the turbulent on the left.

At the same time, this is a straightforward bust portrait with the light coming from the window on the left, the lighted and shaded areas broken up as differently wrought and distributed areas of painted colour. The serpentine white strokes at upper left suggest light caught by hanging draperies as it enters to bathe the face and drape the coat-shoulder on that side. The dim strokes at upper right figure a shadowed interior, the less crisp rendering of the suit's details on the right and its rougher colours suggest the dimmer illumination there. The unmatching halves of face and suit produce a disunity of response, perhaps intended by the painter in the context of the original Cubist proposal, which allowed many disparately effective visual elements to be combined in one image. The suit-coat itself is made into an agent of visual disharmony, displaying its naturally matching sides as if they were at war.

As a foil to the conceptual character of Cubism, with its constant pictorial analysis of form itself, the Surrealist movement was founded in 1924 to plumb the stuff of dreams, unconscious fantasies, free association and uncontrolled thought as a source for pictorial imagery. In real life, visualisations in this domain tend to be specifically detailed and naturalistic, asleep or awake; and bodies and garments, so deeply connected with sex

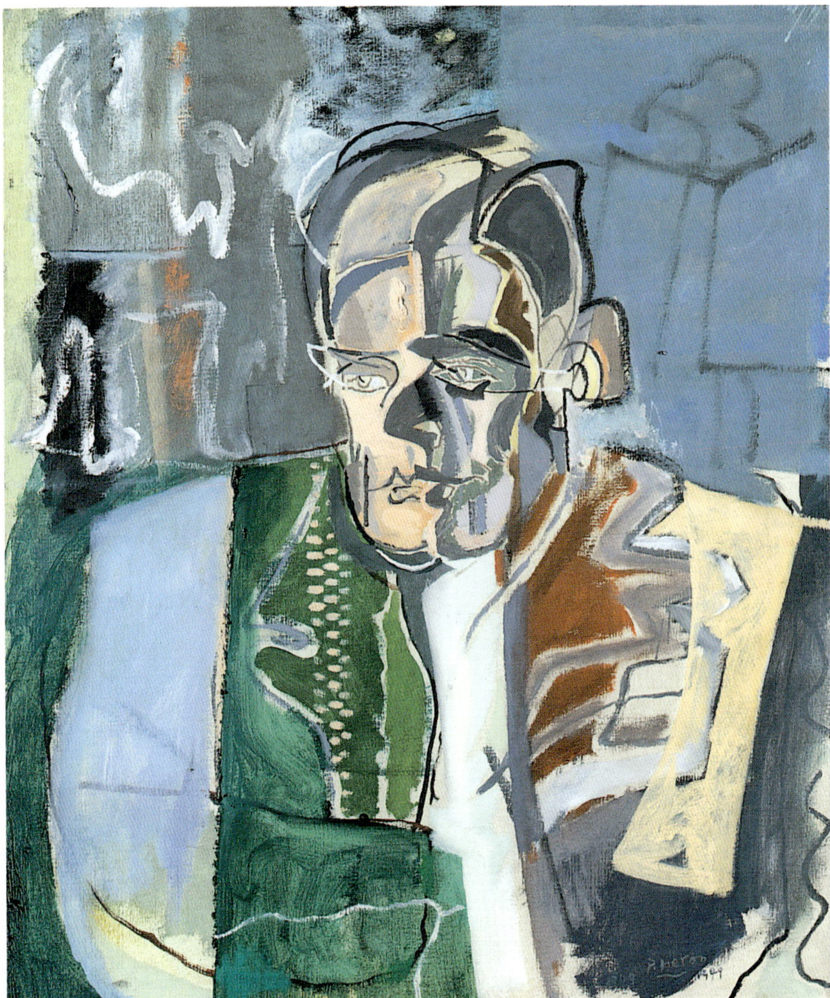

142
Patrick Heron (1920–1999)
Thomas Stearns Eliot, 1949
Oil on canvas, 76.2 × 62.9 cm
National Portrait Gallery, London

and self, often appear in them. Surrealist painters made use of both, not always at the same time, and often in strange ways. Max Ernst's picture called *Saint Cecilia* (fig. 143) was painted a year before Surrealism was officially founded, but this work already shows Ernst as one of its best exponents, always ready to provide concreteness for any stretch of visual fantasy.

This dressed feminine figure opposes the sort of imagery we saw in the Cubist works, where all form was re-arranged to construct a new visual programme for the subject, as if to make a perpetual assertion of the painter's authority over the vision. Ernst keeps the formal representation traditional, subverting the idea of subject in a different way. He leaves it open to the infinite play of the inner eye, suggesting that he has only tapped into an endless well of extant visual material, of which examples would be accessible to anyone who would draw them up from within.

This Saint Cecilia plays in the air on a half built, half ruined, half absent piano. She is half imprisoned, half enthroned but essentially clad in a hooded opera cloak, made entirely of ancient masonry adorned with incised, eye-like carvings. The cloak, the piano and their platforms are all held together with round-headed bolts connected by thin

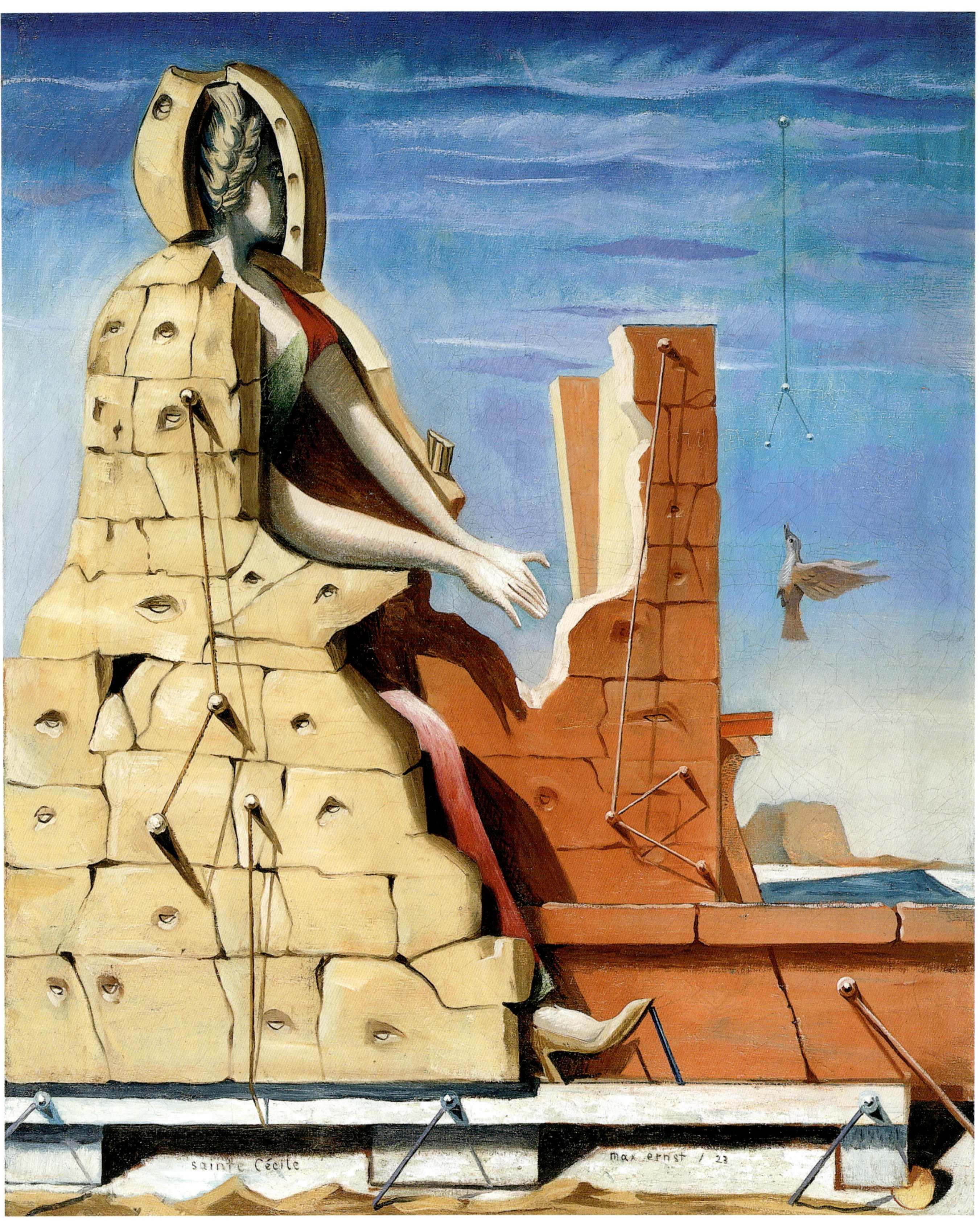
sainte Cécile
max ernst / 23

144
René Magritte (1898–1967)
Philosophy in the Boudoir, 1948
Oil on canvas, 46 × 37 cm
Private collection

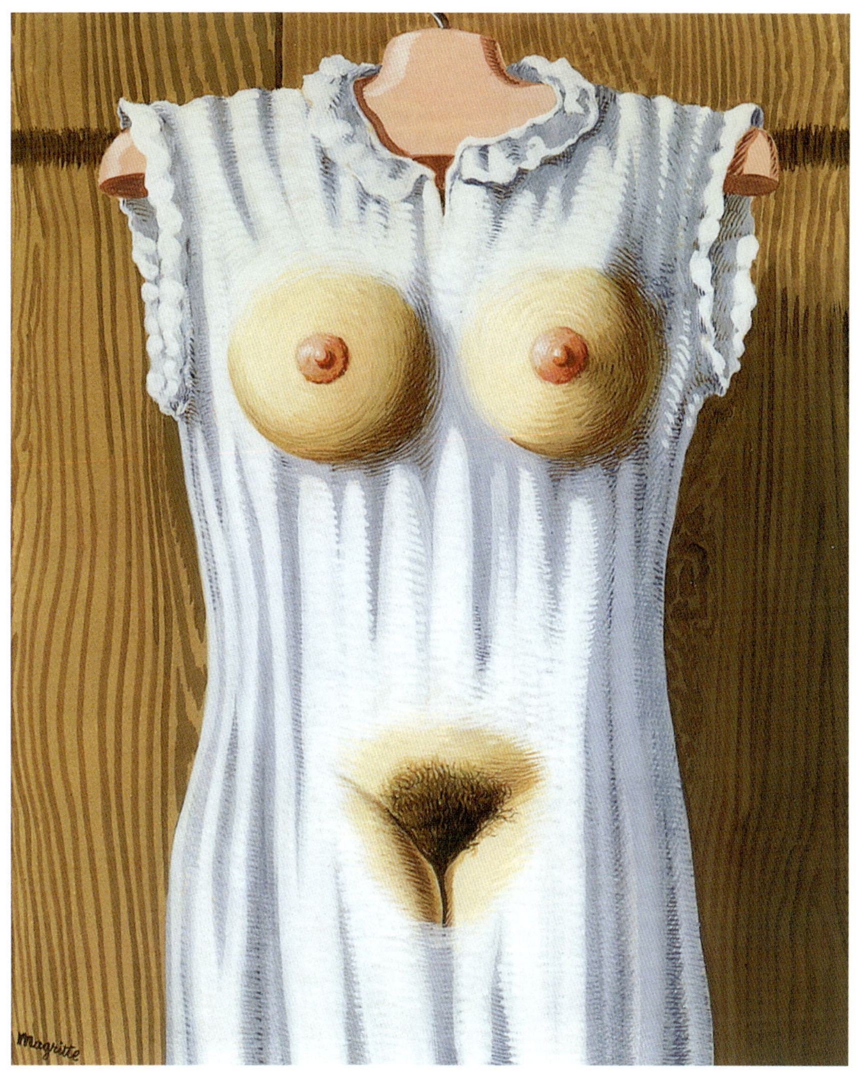

rods; and so is the sky. The saint's attractive high-heeled shoe, dressed knee and bosom, coiffure and nude arms emerge delicately from her stony cloak; and again her face is obscured, just as in both the fashion plates we saw before, and in Delaunay's painting of the Parisienne. We get the sense that the face, the fantasy's identity, may be supplied by each viewer.

Surrealism had become an old tradition by the time René Magritte painted *Philosophy in the Boudoir* in 1948 (fig. 144). The title is taken from the Marquis de Sade's book of 1795 listing and describing every kind of erotic pleasure. Magritte has added a gallery to the boudoir, where what can't go on the list may hang on the wall. Magritte's subject is the visual erotic fantasies you need pictures to discover – they can't quite take shape until his matter-of-fact style has conjured them up. Then they are hard to forget. This wooden closet holds only one hanger with one empty dress on the rack. Only one is necessary to evoke the whole elaborate range of women's gear that does nothing to hide from the mind's eye – hers and ours – what is glowing underneath in plain inward sight, even if she never undresses.

OPPOSITE **143**
Max Ernst (1891–1976)
Saint Cecilia – The Invisible Piano, 1923
Oil on canvas, 101 × 82 cm
Staatsgalerie Stuttgart

List of Exhibited Works

COMPILED BY SALLY KORMAN

Figure numbers in brackets refer to illustration numbers in this book.
Preceding numbers are the catalogue numbers of the exhibited works.

NUDE AND MODE

1. (fig. 115)
Paolo Veronese (Verona 1528–1588 Venice)
Portrait of a Woman, about 1565
Oil on canvas, 106 × 87 cm
Musée de la Chartreuse, Douai, inv. 751

The sitter is unknown and the portrait has been dated on the evidence of the costume. Paolo Caliari, called Veronese, painted a number of portraits of patricians and their families, although he is best known for his altarpieces and for the canvases and frescoes he painted for palaces in Venice and its hinterland.

2. (fig. 116)
Attr. to **Jacopo Tintoretto** (Venice 1518–1594 Venice)
Proserpine and Ascalaphus, about 1578–80
Oil on canvas, 101.5 × 128.5 cm
Courtesy of the Marquess of Bath, Longleat House, Warminster

When Proserpine was carried off by Pluto, ruler of the dead, her mother Ceres obtained a promise from Jupiter that her daughter could return if she had eaten nothing in the underworld. Ascalaphus had seen her eat seven pomegranate seeds and betrayed her: she turned him into an owl (Ovid, *Metamorphoses*, V, 535–50). This is one of the many mythological paintings that Jacopo Robusti, known as Tintoretto, painted for Venetian private palaces. He also painted public works for churches and '*scuole*' or confraternities. He may have executed this work together with his son, Domenico (1560–1635). (See also cat. 19.)

3. (fig. 117)
Jacob Ochtervelt (Rotterdam 1634–1682 Amsterdam)
A Woman playing a Virginal, Another singing and a Man playing a Violin, probably 1675–80
Oil on canvas, 84.5 × 75 cm
National Gallery, London, inv. NG 3864

Inscribed on the underside of the virginal's lid: S[?]D[?]E[?].
Signed over the door: *Jac: Ocht*[..]*velt: f.*

Ochtervelt, who worked in Rotterdam and Amsterdam, specialised in domestic interior scenes, usually set in prosperous households. The map on the wall, showing North and South America, is based on an example published in Amsterdam in 1661.

4. (fig. 118)
Jacob Jordaens (Antwerp 1593–1678 Antwerp)
King Candaules of Lydia showing his Wife to Gyges, 1646
Oil on canvas, 193 × 157 cm
Nationalmuseum, Stockholm, inv. NM 1159

King Candaules of Lydia, boasting of his wife's beauty, arranged for his favourite Gyges to spy on her as she undressed. In revenge, the queen forced Gyges to choose between suicide and murdering her husband. Gyges killed Candaules, married the queen and took over the kingdom (Herodotus, *History*, Book 1). Unlike his great Flemish contemporaries Rubens and Van Dyck, Jordaens never became a court painter, but worked almost exclusively for the prosperous bourgeoisie of Antwerp.

5. (fig. 119)
Henry Raeburn (Edinburgh 1756–1823 Edinburgh)
Mrs Scott Moncrieff, about 1814
Oil on canvas, 76.5 × 64 cm
The National Gallery of Scotland, Edinburgh, inv. NG 302

Margaret (or Margaritta) Macdonald (died 1824) was the wife of an Edinburgh wine merchant, Robert Scott Moncrieff. The couple were members of Edinburgh's social and cultural élite, to whom Raeburn was the leading portrait painter, during the period of the Scottish Enlightenment.

6. (fig. 120)
William Etty (York 1787–1849 York)
Venus and Cupid, probably 1820s
Oil on millboard on panel, 80.8 × 39 cm
Russell-Cotes Art Gallery and Museum, Bournemouth inv. RC00769

Etty scandalised many of his Victorian contemporaries by introducing voluptuous female nudes, whom he painted from the life, into classical and mythological scenes. His style shows the influence of two years spent in Italy, where he admired the techniques of Venetian Renaissance painters. Small oil studies such as this were made in preparation for larger works.

7. (fig. 121)
Kees van Dongen (Delftshaven 1877–1968 Monte Carlo)
The Comtesse de Noailles, 1931
Oil on canvas, 196 × 131 cm
Stedelijk Museum, Amsterdam, inv. A642

The poet Anna de Noailles (1876–1933) was born into an aristocratic family in Paris, where she was prominent in fashionable literary and artistic circles. Her friends included the writers Marcel Proust and Jean Cocteau. The Dutch-born Van Dongen lived mostly in Paris, where from 1918 he concentrated on portraits of the *beau monde*, particularly of society women, earning a reputation as a chronicler of the period.

8. (fig. 122)
Pierre Bonnard (Fontenay-aux-Roses, near Paris 1867–1947 Le Cannet)
Standing Nude, 1920
Oil on canvas, 122 × 56 cm
Private collection

The nude woman is glimpsed in her bathroom, reaching out as if to grasp an unseen object. Bonnard was a founder member of the Nabis ('Wise Men'), a group of French artists who greatly admired Gauguin. He painted intimate domestic interiors, many of which show women bathing. The artist often used as a model his lifelong companion Maria ('Marthe') Boursin, whom he married in 1926, although it is not always possible to identify her, as her features are frequently idealised.

CLOTH OF HONOUR

9. (fig. 16)
Greco-Roman, probably 2nd century
Tyche with Cornucopia
Marble, height 98 cm
The British Museum, London, inv. SC1702

Tyche was the Greek goddess of Fortune. The cornucopia, or horn of plenty, refers to the wealth and abundance she could choose to bestow on mortals. The figure was formerly holding a rudder, of which only the lower part of the blade remains. The head is ancient but probably originates from another statue.

10. (fig. 5)
Cretan, about 1425–50
The Deesis (Christ with the Virgin and Saint John the Baptist)
Tempera and gold on wood, 68 × 48 cm
Private collection

The Greek word *deesis* ('calling to witness') refers to the image of Christ enthroned between the Virgin and Saint John the Baptist. Christ's right hand is raised in blessing, while his left holds open a Gospel book inscribed, in Greek, 'Come unto me, all ye that labour and are heavy laden, and I will give you rest. Take my yoke upon you, and learn of me' (Matthew 11: 28–9). The small dimensions of the icon probably indicate that it was made for private devotion.

11. (fig. 10)
Attr. to **Allegretto Nuzi** (Fabriano 1316/20–1373/4 Fabriano)
Saint Catherine and Saint Bartholomew, about 1350
Tempera on wood, 83 × 51 cm
National Gallery, London, inv. NG 5930

Saint Catherine stands by the wheel on which she was tortured and Saint Bartholomew holds the knife used to flay him. The painting was probably the right-hand panel of a triptych or polyptych. Allegretto was from Fabriano in the Italian Marches but his work shows the influence of Florentine painters, particularly Bernardo Daddi.

12. (fig. 15)
Andrea Mantegna (Padua 1430/1–1506 Mantua)
The Virgin and Child with the Magdalen and Saint John the Baptist, about 1490–1500
Tempera on canvas, 139.1 × 116.8 cm
National Gallery, London, inv. NG 274

Inscribed on the scroll: [EC]CE AGNV[S DEI EC]CE Q[UI TOLLIT PEC]CATA M[UN]DI *Andreas Mantinia C.P. F.*[ecit] (Behold the Lamb of God, behold the one who takes away the sins of the world; Andrea Mantegna Count Palatine [or Citizen of Padua] made this)

The Virgin sits on a throne underneath a canopy. The Baptist wears the camel-skin he wore in the desert and a belt made of reeds, while Mary Magdalen carries a small jar of ointment. It is not known who commissioned this altarpiece; it was probably painted in Mantua, where Mantegna worked as a painter to the Gonzaga court, but as it is on canvas it may have been intended for transport elsewhere.

13. (fig. 19)
Bartolomeo Montagna (Vicenza? about 1450–1523 Vicenza)
The Virgin and Child, about 1504–6
Oil on canvas, transferred from wood, 59 × 51 cm
National Gallery, London, inv. NG 1098

Montagna seems to have worked principally in Vicenza, where he was first documented, as a minor, in 1459. He may have trained in Venice in the late 1460s, possibly with Giovanni Bellini, whose influence is reflected in small-scale devotional works such as this. The sleep of the Christ Child prefigures his death.

14. (fig. 17)
Attr. to **Andrea Previtali** (Bergamo, active 1502–1528 Bergamo)
The Virgin and Child with Two Angels, about 1510–20
Oil on canvas, transferred from wood, 63.7 × 92.7 cm
National Gallery, London, inv. NG 3111

The Virgin and Child, adored by two angels, are seated in front of a parapet with a landscape to the rear. The Christ Child holds two cherries, symbols of Paradise. Previtali, who worked in Venice and Bergamo, signs himself in some of his early works as a pupil of Giovanni Bellini. However, this painting is closer in style to the Ferrarese artist Boccaccio Boccaccini, to whom it has also been attributed.

15. (fig. 20)
Rogier van der Weyden (Tournai, about 1399–1464 Brussels)
The Magdalen reading, probably about 1435
Oil on mahogany, transferred from another panel, 61.6 × 54.6 cm
National Gallery, London inv. NG 654

Mary Magdalen is seated reading a devotional book: the jar of ointment she used to anoint Christ's feet is at her side. The standing figure holding a rosary has been identified as Saint Joseph. This is one of several existing fragments of a large altarpiece of the kind for which Van der Weyden, who worked in Brussels, was famous in northern and southern Europe.

16. (fig. 18)
Workshop of Dirk Bouts (Haarlem, about 1400?–1475 Louvain)
The Virgin and Child with Saints Peter and Paul, probably 1460s
Oil on wood, 68.8 × 51.6
National Gallery, London, inv. NG 774

The Virgin is enthroned with the Christ Child. She places her hand on a book held by Saint Peter on the left, while the Child accepts a carnation – a symbol of the Passion – from Saint Paul, who kneels at the right. Bouts had settled in Louvain by September 1457, establishing a sizeable workshop of which his two sons were members.

LIBERATED DRAPERIES

17. (fig. 37)
El Greco (Candia, now Iraklion, Crete, about 1541–1614 Toledo)
Christ driving the Traders from the Temple, about 1600
Oil on canvas, 106.3 × 129.7 cm
National Gallery, London, inv. NG 1457

Christ's expulsion of the traders from the Temple is told in Matthew 21:12–13. The architecture is decorated with two scenes from the Old Testament: the Sacrifice of Isaac, which was understood to prefigure the Crucifixion, and the Expulsion from Eden. The artist, who was born Domenikos Theotokopoulos, painted several versions of this subject. He trained as an icon-painter in his native Crete before travelling to Venice and Rome, settling finally in Toledo.

18. (fig. 29)
Gaudenzio Ferrari (Valduggia, near Vercelli 1475/80–1546 Milan)
Christ rising from the Tomb, about 1540
Oil on poplar, 152.4 × 84.5 cm
National Gallery, London, inv. NG 1465

Christ steps from the tomb carrying the banner of the Resurrection, his right hand raised in blessing. The painting may be the central panel of an altarpiece from the church of San Pietro at Maggianico, near Lecco in northern Italy. Gaudenzio, who trained in the Piedmontese town of Varallo, was active throughout Piedmont and Lombardy.

19. (fig. 36)
Jacopo Tintoretto (Venice 1518–1594 Venice)
Saint George and the Dragon, about 1560
Oil on canvas, 158.3 × 100.5 cm
National Gallery, London, inv. NG 16

The episode of Saint George rescuing a princess from a dragon appears in *The Golden Legend*, the popular thirteenth-century compilation of saints' lives. Unusually, the kneeling princess occupies the foreground, while to the rear Saint George, on horseback, plunges his lance into the monster's eye. The painting was probably made for domestic devotion rather than for a church. (See also cat. 2)

20. (fig. 38)
Honoré-Victorin Daumier (Marseille 1808–1879 Valmondois)
Nymphs pursued by Satyrs, 1850 (with later additions)
Oil on canvas, 131.8 × 97.8 cm
The Montreal Museum of Fine Arts, inv. 1945.880

Daumier, who was a caricaturist, lithographer and sculptor as well as a painter, was known in his lifetime chiefly as a political and social satirist. This painting, which does not appear to depict a particular episode from classical mythology, is one of only four paintings he exhibited at the Paris Salon.

21. (fig. 35)
Damiano Mazza (active in Padua about 1570–90)
The Rape of Ganymede, probably about 1570–90
Oil on canvas, 177.2 × 188.6 cm
National Gallery, London, inv. NG 32

The beautiful shepherd-boy Ganymede was seized by Jupiter in the form of an eagle and taken up to Mount Olympus, where he served as cupbearer to the gods. This painting may have originally decorated a ceiling in the Paduan palace of Francesco Assonica, who also owned works by Titian. Mazza was in style a follower of Titian.

SENSUALITY

22. (fig. 43)
After Titian (Pieve di Cadore, about 1485/90–1576 Venice)
The Toilet of Venus, after about 1555
Oil on canvas, 94.3 × 73.8 cm
Courtauld Institute Gallery, London

Venus, goddess of Love, adjusts her veil whilst gazing at her reflection in a mirror held by Cupid. This picture is based on Titian's Barbarigo *Venus* of about 1555, now in the National Gallery of Art, Washington, D.C. It is generally identified as the work of one of Titian's numerous followers, but has also been attributed to Veronese or his school.

23. (fig. 55)
Guido Reni (Bologna 1575–1642 Bologna)
Lucretia, after about 1620
Oil on canvas, 99 × 76 cm
Dulwich Picture Gallery, London, inv. DPG 204

Lucretia was raped by the son of Tarquinius Superbus, ruler of Rome, and committed suicide to avoid disgrace. The incident led to the establishment of the Roman republic. Reni was widely admired long after his death for this type of history painting, in which he sought to combine ideal beauty with emotional intensity. Several versions of this composition exist, but none can be securely identified as the original.

24. (fig. 53)
Johann Liss (Oldenburg, about 1595–1631 Verona)
Judith in the Tent of Holofernes, mid 1620s
Oil on canvas, 128.5 × 99 cm
National Gallery, London, inv. NG 4597

In the Old Testament Apocrypha, the Jewish heroine Judith entered the enemy camp of the Assyrians. Their commander, Holofernes, invited her into his tent, and she cut off his head with his sword as he slept. Here Judith places the head in a basket held by her maidservant. This was painted early in the German painter Liss's long sojourn in Italy, which lasted from around 1620–1 until his death from plague in 1631.

25. (fig. 45)
Michelangelo Merisi da Caravaggio (Milan or Caravaggio 1571–1610 Porto Ercole)
Boy bitten by a Lizard, about 1595–1600
Oil on canvas, 66 × 49.5 cm
National Gallery, London, inv. NG 6504

The youth starts back in pain as a lizard bites the middle finger of his right hand. A window is reflected in the glass vase, which contains jasmine and a rose; cherries lie on the table nearby. This picture was painted for the art market in Rome, where Caravaggio had specialised as a still-life painter before receiving the important church commissions that made his name.

26. (fig. 44)
Bartolomé Esteban Murillo (Seville 1617–1682 Seville)
A Peasant Boy leaning on a Sill, about 1670–80
Oil on canvas, 52 × 38.5 cm
National Gallery, London, inv. NG 74

This study of a smiling boy has been considered to be the pendant to a picture in a private collection showing *A Young Girl lifting her Shawl*. In addition to his well-known religious works, Murillo painted many scenes of street children in his native Seville.

27. (fig. 57)
Cindy Sherman (born Glenn Ridge, New Jersey, 1954)
Untitled, 1982
Photograph on paper, 115.2 × 76 cm
Tate, London, inv. P77729

The American photographer Cindy Sherman studied at the University College of Buffalo in New York and began exhibiting in 1976. She uses herself as a model to create scenes with a wide range of cultural references, from Old Master paintings to the 'B' movies of the 1950s.

28. (fig. 56)
Friedrich von Amerling (Vienna 1803–1887 Vienna)
Portrait of a Girl, about 1830–40
Oil on canvas, 64 × 50.5 cm
Residenzgalerie Salzburg, inv. 192

Amerling's first important commission was to paint a life-size portrait of the emperor Francis I of Austria, after which he became highly sought after as a portrait painter in his native Vienna. One of his specialities was the 'one-figure genre painting', where the evocation of a particular mood or type implies the presence of a storyline. An almost identical composition with the title *Susanna looking Bashful* dates from 1837.

29. (fig. 61)
Jean-Honoré Fragonard (Grasse 1732–1806 Paris)
A Young Girl on her Bed, making her Dog dance, about 1770
Oil on canvas, 89 × 70 cm
Alte Pinakothek, Bayerische Staatsgemäldesammlungen, Munich, inv. HuW 35

This playful erotic image is one of several paintings by the artist showing semi-clad girls playing with dogs. It is sometimes known as *The Ring Biscuit*; this is incorrect, as – by contrast to other versions – the girl does not offer her dog a biscuit. Fragonard was a pupil of François Boucher, whose own teacher, Jean-Antoine Watteau, originated this type of erotic genre picture. (See also cat. 36.)

HIGH ARTIFICE

30. (fig. 62)
Anthony van Dyck (Antwerp 1599–1641 London)
The Countess of Castlehaven, about 1635–8
Oil on canvas, 133.4 × 101.6 cm
Collection of the Earl of Pembroke, Wilton House, Salisbury

Elizabeth, Countess of Castlehaven (dates unknown) was a daughter of the 5th Lord Chandos. Her husband was James, 13th Baron Audley and 1st Earl of Castlehaven, who had been granted the titles under a new patent in 1634, following the execution of his father. The couple probably married soon afterwards, which may have been the occasion for this portrait, painted during the artist's second period in England.

31. (fig. 73)
Joshua Reynolds (Plympton 1723–1792 London)
Charles Coote, 1st Earl of Bellamont, 1773
Oil on canvas, 241 × 161 cm
National Gallery of Ireland, Dublin, NGI 216

Charles Coote (1738–1800) was created Earl of Bellamont (also spelt 'Bellomont') in 1767. He received the Order of the Bath in 1764 after defeating an insurrection in the North of Ireland. Reynolds became the first president of the Royal Academy in 1768.

32. (fig. 75)
Johann Zoffany (Frankfurt-am-Main 1733–1810 London)
Mrs Michael Woodhull, about 1770
Oil on canvas, 243.8 × 165.1 cm
Tate, London, inv. TO 2217

Catherine Ingram (1744–1808), fourth daughter of the Revd John Ingram of Wolford, Warwickshire, married the poet and translator Michael Woodhull (1740–1816) in 1761. It appears that the portrait was originally commissioned as a half-length, but was enlarged by Zoffany at the Woodhulls' request.

33. (fig. 66)
Hyacinthe Rigaud (Perpignan 1659–1743 Paris)
Antoine Pâris, 1724
Oil on canvas, 144.7 × 110.5 cm
National Gallery, London, inv. NG 6428

Antoine Pâris (1668–1733) was the eldest of four brothers, all of whom were prominent financiers. He sat to the artist for two portraits in the same year. Rigaud enjoyed immense success as a portraitist at the court of Louis XIV. He was extremely prolific and remained fashionable throughout his long career.

34. (fig. 72)
Donato Creti (Cremona 1671–1749 Bologna)
Artemisia drinking the Ashes of Mausolus, about 1713–14
Oil on canvas, 62.7 × 49.9 cm
National Gallery, London, inv. L884

Artemisia was the wife of Mausolus, ruler of the province of Caria in Asia Minor. After his death in around 353–352 BC she drank his ashes. She built the Mausoleum at Halicarnassus, one of the wonders of the ancient world, in his memory. Creti, who remained in Bologna for most of his career, worked mostly on a small scale for private patrons.

35. (fig. 69)
Giovanni Domenico Tiepolo (Venice 1727–1804 Venice)
The Marriage of Frederick Barbarossa and Beatrice of Burgundy, about 1752–3
Oil on canvas, 72.4 × 52.7 cm
National Gallery, London, inv. NG 2100

The marriage of the Emperor Frederick I Barbarossa (ruled 1150–90) to Beatrice, daughter of the Count of Burgundy, was celebrated in the German town of Würzburg in 1156. This painting has also been attributed to the artist's father, Giovanni Battista Tiepolo (see cat. 37, below), who painted a fresco of the same subject in about 1750 for the palace of Karl Philipp von Greiffenklau, Prince-Bishop of Würzburg.

36. (fig. 71)
Jean-Honoré Fragonard (Grasse 1732–1806 Paris)
Psyche showing her Sisters her Gifts from Cupid, 1753
Oil on canvas, 168.3 × 192.4 cm
National Gallery, London, inv. NG 6445

The story is told by Apuleius in *The Golden Ass*. Cupid, god of love, became enamoured of the mortal Psyche, whom he visited at night. Her sisters, jealous of the gifts Psyche had received from her lover, tried to convince her that he was a monster and persuade her to murder him. She brought a lamp to bed in order to look at him, but he awoke and abandoned her, and she was forced to undergo a series of trials to win him back. (See also cat. 29.)

37. (fig. 68)
Giovanni Battista Tiepolo (Venice 1696–1770 Madrid)
The Meeting of Antony and Cleopatra, about 1743
Oil on canvas, 66.8 × 38.4 cm
The National Gallery of Scotland, Edinburgh, inv. NG 91

The meeting between the Roman general Mark Antony and the Egyptian queen Cleopatra took place in 41 BC. The painting is probably a preparatory sketch for a section of Tiepolo's fresco of the same subject in Palazzo Labia, Venice. Tiepolo decorated numerous churches and palaces in Venice and its hinterland; he also worked in Spain and Germany, notably at Würzburg (see cat. 35 above).

ROMANTIC SIMPLICITY

38 (fig. 93)
Louis-Léopold Boilly (La Bassée, near Lille 1761–1845 Paris)
M. d'Aucourt de Saint-Just, about 1800
Oil on canvas, 56 × 46 cm
Musée des Beaux-Arts, Lille, inv. 1949

39 (fig. 84)
Mme d'Aucourt de Saint-Just, about 1800
Oil on canvas, 56 × 46 cm
Musée des Beaux-Arts, Lille, inv. 1950

The sitters in these small full-length companion portraits may be M. and Mme d'Ancourt de Saint-Just. Boilly, who painted genre subjects as well as portraits, also produced engravings and lithographs, and was an accomplished watercolourist.

40. (fig. 78)
Agustín Esteve y Marques (Valencia 1753–1820 Madrid)
Doña Joaquina Tellez-Giron, 1798
Oil on canvas, 190 × 116 cm
Museo Nacional del Prado, Madrid, inv. 2581

Inscribed at the lower left: *Su edad 13 años y 4 meses – Esteve* (Her age 13 years and 4 months – Esteve)

The sitter (1784–1851) was the daughter of the 9th Duke of Osuna. This picture was painted in January 1798, along with a companion portrait of her sister. From 1780, Esteve worked as an assistant to Francisco de Goya, who also painted Doña Joaquina on two occasions.

41. (fig. 80)
Gottlieb Schick (Stuttgart 1776–1812 Stuttgart)
Frau Wilhelmine von Cotta, 1802
Oil on canvas, 133 × 140.5 cm
Staatsgalerie Stuttgart, inv. GVL 87

Signed on the balustrade to the right: *Schick faciebat 1802*

Ernestine Philippine Wilhelmine Haas (1771–1821), the daughter of a clergyman, was married to the publisher and bookseller Johann Friedrich von Cotta. Schick, who studied with the French Neoclassical painter David, painted this portrait at the couple's home in Tübingen.

42. (fig. 90)
Meredith Frampton (London 1894–1984 Mere, Wiltshire)
Portrait of a Young Woman, 1935
Oil on canvas, 205.7 × 107.9 cm
Tate, London, inv. NO 4820

Inscribed with the date and monogram *19 MF 35*

The artist was the only son of the sculptor and decorative artist Sir George Frampton (1860–1928). The sitter was a young woman named Margaret Austin-Jones, then aged twenty-three, although Frampton did not disclose her name, writing in 1960 that he preferred her to remain anonymous. The vase, made of mahogany, was designed by Frampton himself.

43. (fig. 95)
Ferdinand-Victor-Eugène Delacroix
(Charenton-St-Maurice, near Paris 1798–1863 Paris)
Louis-Auguste Schwiter, 1826–30
Oil on canvas, 217.8 × 143.5 cm
National Gallery, London, inv. NG 3286

Delacroix was the principal artist of the Romantic movement and is best known for his grand history paintings. The background of this portrait is said to have been painted by his friend the landscape artist Paul Huet. Louis-Auguste, later Baron, Schwiter was also a painter and exhibited a portrait of Delacroix at the Paris salon of 1833.

44. (fig. 96)
Henri Lehmann (Kiel, Holstein 1814–1846 Paris)
Franz Liszt, 1839
Oil on canvas, 113 × 86 cm
Musée Carnavalet, Histoire de Paris, Paris, inv. P.1683

Inscribed at the lower left: *AMICVS AMICO/ HL Romae/ MDCCCXXXIX*

The Hungarian composer and virtuoso pianist Franz Liszt (1811–1886) was one of the leading exponents of the Romantic movement in music. Lehmann, who was of German origin, was a pupil of his father Leo (1782–1859) and later of Ingres.

45. (fig. 100)
Edvard Munch (Løten, Hedmark 1863–1944 Oslo)
Harry Graf Kessler, 1906
Oil on canvas, 200 × 84 cm
Staatliche Museen zu Berlin, Neue Nationalgalerie, inv. B50 kat 172

Count Harry Kessler (1868–1937) was born in Paris, the son of a German-Swiss father and an Irish mother, and educated in England. A diplomat, publisher, critic and connoisseur, at the time this portrait was painted he was director of the art academy in Weimar. Kessler was one of several influential patrons acquired by the Norwegian painter Edvard Munch during the visits he made to Germany from 1892 onwards, which led to his becoming a major influence on German Expressionism.

46. (fig. 99)
Philip Wilson Steer (Birkenhead 1860–1942 London)
Walter Sickert, 1894
Oil on canvas, 59.7 × 29.8
National Portrait Gallery, London, inv. NPG 3142

The painter Walter Richard Sickert (1860–1942) is best known for his scenes of modern urban life and the London music hall. Steer was the leading exponent of English Impressionism. He founded the New English Art Club, of which Sickert was also a member.

RESTRAINT AND DISPLAY

47. (fig. 103)
Arthur Hughes (London 1832–1915 London)
The Long Engagement, about 1854–9
Oil on canvas, 105.4 × 52.1 cm
Birmingham Museums and Art Gallery, inv. 1902 P13

This celebrated Pre-Raphaelite image illustrates the plight of Victorian lovers condemned by their parents to lengthy engagements. It was exhibited in 1859 with a quotation from Chaucer: 'For how might ever sweetnesse hav be known / To hym that never tastyd bitternesse.' Hughes himself had had to wait five years before marrying Tryphena Foorde in 1855.

48. (fig. 104)
Alfred Elmore (Clonakilty 1815–1881 London)
On the Brink, 1865
Oil on canvas attached to panel, 114.3 × 83.2 cm
Fitzwilliam Museum, Cambridge, inv. PD.108-1975

Signed and dated lower left, *A. Elmore. 1865*

The painting depicts a woman seemingly about to succumb to a life of adultery or prostitution. An inscription on the reverse, *Homburg*, probably refers to the then fashionable German gambling resort of Homburg-vor-der-Höhe. Elmore may have visited the town during the Continental tour from which he returned in 1844.

49. (fig. 105)
James Tissot
(Nantes 1836–1902 Chateau de Buillon, Doubs)
The Ball, about 1878
Oil on canvas, 90.2 × 50.2 cm
Musée d'Orsay, Paris, inv. RF 2253

The model was the artist's mistress Kathleen Newton. The French-born Tissot lived in London from 1871 to 1882. He painted scenes of society balls and entertainments, and was fascinated by travel. In later life he underwent a religious conversion and produced a series of Biblical illustrations.

50. (fig. 109)
Henri de Toulouse-Lautrec
(Albi 1864–1901 Château de Malromé)
The Englishman at the Moulin Rouge, before 1894
Oil and gouache on cardboard, 85.7 × 66 cm
The Metropolitan Museum of Art, New York, inv. 187.108

The Moulin Rouge was the most famous of the Montmartre dance halls. This painting depicts the artist's friend, the English painter William Tom Warrener (1861–1934), and two dancers, Rayon d'Or and La Sauterelle. It served as a preparatory study for a colour lithograph entitled *Flirt*. (See also cat. 57.)

51. (fig. 111)
Frits van den Berghe (Ghent 1883–1939 Ghent)
Paul-Gustave van Hecke and his Wife, 1923–4
Oil on canvas, 160.6 × 120.4 cm
Koninklijk Museum voor Schone Kunsten, Antwerp, inv. 3268

The Belgian painter and printmaker Frits van den Berghe embraced a range of styles from Symbolism to Surrealism. The Brussels gallery owner Paul-Gustav van Hecke (1887–1965?) represented Van den Berghe from 1921, following the artist's return from Holland, where he had lived during the First World War.

WOMAN AS DRESS

52. (fig. 124)
Jean-Baptiste-Camille Corot (Paris 1796–1875 Paris)
The Lady in Blue, 1874
Oil on canvas, 80 × 50.5 cm
Musée du Louvre, Paris, inv. RF 2056

Corot was primarily known as a landscape painter, but he also produced many figure studies, few of which he exhibited. This is one of his last works and is part of a series of paintings showing anonymous models alone in the studio.

53. (fig. 126)
Giacomo Balla (Turin 1871–1958 Rome)
Portrait in the Open Air, 1902
Oil on canvas, 155 × 113.5 cm
Galleria Nazionale d'Arte Moderna e Contemporanea, Rome

The painting depicts Leonilde Imperatori on the balcony of her house overlooking the Piazza di Spagna in Rome, and was commissioned by her father. Balla gradually renounced his successful career as a portrait painter as, after 1897, he became influenced by the artistic and social theories of the Italian Divisionist movement. He later became a leading exponent of Futurism.

54. (fig. 123)
Alfred Stevens (Brussels 1823–1906 Paris)
The Lady in Pink, 1866
Oil on canvas, 87 × 57 cm
Musées royaux des Beaux-Arts de Belgique, Brussels, inv. 1793

A young woman examines a Japanese figurine; behind her are displayed other oriental *objets d'art*. Such exotic accessories feature prominently in the work of the Belgian artist Alfred Stevens, who began by painting social and historical subjects, but turned to depictions of fashionable Parisian women.

55. (fig. 125)
Thomas Wilmer Dewing (Boston 1851–1938 New York)
Lady in Gold, about 1912
Oil on canvas, 61.3 × 46 cm
Brooklyn Museum of Art, New York, inv. 15.322

Dewing was from Boston and studied in Paris. His scenes of elegant young women in poses of reverie, which he referred to as 'decorations', are reminiscent of the American painter James McNeill Whistler, whom he greatly admired.

FORM AND FEELING

56. (fig. 134)
Byzantine, about 1320
Saint Peter
Tempera and gold leaf on cedar panel, 68.7 × 50.6 mm.
The British Museum, London, inv. MME 1983-0401.1

Saint Peter is depicted looking to the left, holding a scroll with the inscription in Greek: 'Beloved, I beseech you as aliens and exiles to abstain from the passions of the flesh that wage war against your soul' (1 Peter 2:11). The panel has been cut down but the saint was probably always shown half-length. The icon may have been made for a monastery, as part of a sanctuary screen.

57. (fig. 128)
Henri de Toulouse-Lautrec
(Albi 1864–1901 Château de Malromé)
Seated Clowness from the Album *Elles*, 1896
Crayon, brush and spatter lithograph in four colours, 52.5 × 40.4 cm
The British Museum, London, inv. 1949-4-11-3635

This print depicts the clowness Cha-U-Kao. The same subject appears in a number of Lautrec's paintings and prints of this period, including a colour lithograph of the following year, *The Clowness at the Moulin Rouge*, in which she wears an identical costume. (See also cat. 50.)

58. (fig. 131)
Edouard Vuillard (Cuiseaux 1868–1940 La Baule)
Young Girls walking, 1891–2
Oil on canvas, 81.2 × 65 cm
National Gallery, London, inv. L652

Vuillard was, with Pierre Bonnard (see cat. 8), a leading member of the Nabis group. This study of two young girls seen from behind, their arms linked, is typical of the artist's early works in its deliberately flat and silhouette-like character.

59. (fig. 129)
Félix Vallotton (Lausanne 1865–1925 Paris)
The Lie, 1897
Oil on artist's board, 24 × 33.3 cm
Baltimore Museum of Art, inv. BMA 1950.298

This image of a couple embracing is related to the first in a series of ten woodcuts entitled *Intimités*, in which the artist satirises the hypocrisies of bourgeois marital life. Vallotton was born in Lausanne, Switzerland, and was active in Paris as a painter, printmaker, sculptor and writer.

60. (fig. 137)
Vanessa Bell (London 1879–1961 Charleston)
A Conversation, about 1913–16
Oil on canvas, 86.6 × 81 cm
Courtauld Institute Gallery, on extended loan from a private collection, inv. P.1935.RF.24

Three women are silhouetted against a curtained window, through which a flower garden is visible. Bell was a central figure in the Bloomsbury Group, along with her sister the novelist Virginia Woolf, her husband the painter Clive Bell, and the artist and critic Roger Fry, with whom she had a daughter.

61. (fig. 135)
Amedeo Modigliani (Livorno 1884–1920 Paris)
The Little Peasant, about 1918
Oil on canvas, 100 × 64.5 cm
Tate, London, inv. N05269

This is one of a small group of paintings of youths by the Italian painter and sculptor Modigliani. Although the title identifies the sitter as a 'peasant boy', the same model appears in a painting in the Louvre entitled *The Young Apprentice*. Modigliani was greatly influenced by Cézanne, and it seems likely that this painting was a homage to Cézanne's series of country workers.

62. (fig. 136)
Henri Matisse (Le Cateau Cambrésis, now Le Cateau 1869–1954 Nice)
Woman in Blue, 1937
Oil on canvas, 92.7 × 73.6 cm
Philadelphia Museum of Art, inv. 1956-23-1

The sitter was Lydia Delectorskaya, who posed for Matisse during the 1930s, and had worked as his studio assistant earlier in the decade. The painting demonstrates Matisse's mastery of colour, pattern and symmetry, and illustrates his preoccupation at this time with portraying single women in interiors.

63. (fig. 133)
Pablo Picasso (Malaga 1881–1973 Mougins)
Child with a Dove, 1901
Oil on canvas, 73 × 54 cm
National Gallery, London, inv. L9

The child clasps the dove and stands beside a multi-coloured ball. The whole canvas is heavily worked in thick impasto, and may have been painted over an earlier picture. The simplified forms of this picture, which was painted in Paris, are typical of the style Picasso adopted before the development of Cubism.

64.
Fernand Leger (Argentan 1881–1955 Gif-sur-Yvette)
Drawing for *Femme en rouge et vert*, 1913
Gouache and ink on ochre paper, 65 × 50 cm
Centre Georges Pompidou, Musée national d'art moderne, Paris, inv. AM 1984–580

This is one of a number of gouache studies that Léger made in preparation for his 1914 painting *Femme en rouge et vert* (fig. 140, Centre Georges Pompidou, Paris). Both show him working in a semi-abstract style, strongly influenced by Cubism, which he developed in the 1910s. Léger was also active as a printmaker and illustrator and in later years made designs for the ballet and for ceramics, mosaics and stained glass.

65. (fig. 141)
Robert Delaunay (Paris 1885–1941 Montpellier)
A Woman with a Parasol (*La Parisienne*), 1913
Oil on canvas, 122 × 85.5 cm
Museo Thyssen-Bornemisza, Madrid, inv. 517

The figure of a woman holding a red parasol emerges from geometric blocks of yellow, green, red and purple. The painting belongs to what the artist termed his 'constructive' phase of 1912–14, in which teasing references to real objects are combined with a concentration on abstract form and colour. One of the main points of departure for this work was Delaunay's interest in Cubism, which grew in the years following his marriage in 1910 to the painter Sonia Terk.

66. (fig. 142)
Patrick Heron (Leeds 1920–1999 St Ives)
Thomas Stearns Eliot, 1949
Oil on canvas, 76.2 × 62.9 cm
National Portrait Gallery, London, inv. NPG 4467

T.S. Eliot (1888–1965) was one of the most important twentieth-century poets writing in English. American by birth but resident in Britain, he was the author of *The Wasteland* (1922) and *Four Quartets* (1943). Heron was associated with the St Ives group of painters and also wrote influentially on the visual arts. His later work became much more abstract.

67. (fig. 143)
Max Ernst (Brühl 1891–1976 Paris)
Saint Cecilia – The Invisible Piano, 1923
Oil on canvas, 101 × 82 cm
Staatsgalerie Stuttgart, inv. 3194

Saint Cecilia is the patron saint of music. The German-born Ernst worked in Paris from 1922 until 1941, when he moved to the USA. He became an American citizen in 1948, but later returned to France, where he was naturalised in 1958. He was one of the leading Surrealists, and his paintings and collages, with their irrational combinations of imagery, reflect his interest in dreams and the unconscious.

List of Lenders

AUSTRIA

Salzburg, Residenzgalerie cat. no. 28

BELGIUM

Antwerp, Koninklijk Museum voor Schone Kunsten cat. no. 51

Brussels, Musées royaux des Beaux-Arts de Belgique cat. no. 54

CANADA

Montreal, Quebec, Montreal Museum of Fine Arts cat. no. 20

ENGLAND

Birmingham Museums and Art Gallery cat. no. 47

Bournemouth, Russell-Cotes Art Gallery and Museum cat. no. 6

Cambridge, Lent by the Syndics of The Fitzwilliam Museum cat. no. 48

London

- British Museum cat. nos. 9, 56, 57
- Collection of Sir Denis Mahon on loan to the National Gallery cat.no. 34
- Courtauld Institute Gallery cat. no. 22
- Dulwich Picture Gallery cat. no. 23
- National Gallery cat. nos. 3, 11, 12, 13, 14, 15, 16, 17, 18, 19, 21, 24, 25, 26, 33, 35, 36, 43
- National Portrait Gallery cat. nos. 46, 66
- Tate cat. nos. 27, 32, 42, 61
- Warminster, Wiltshire, Longleat House, Courtesy of the Marquess of Bath cat. no. 2
- Wilton, Salisbury, Collection of the Earl of Pembroke cat. no. 30

FRANCE

Douai, Musée de la Chartreuse cat. no. 1

Lille, Musée des Beaux-Arts cat. nos. 38, 39

Paris

- Musée Carnavalet, Histoire de Paris cat. no. 44
- Musée du Louvre cat. no. 52
- Musée national d'art moderne, Centre Georges Pompidou cat. no. 64
- Musée d'Orsay cat. no. 49

GERMANY

Berlin, Neue Nationalgalerie, Staatliche Museen zu Berlin cat. no. 45

Munich, Alte Pinakothek, Bayerische Staatsgemäldesammlungen cat. no. 29

Stuttgart Staatsgalerie cat. nos. 41, 67

IRELAND

Dublin, The National Gallery of Ireland cat. no. 31

ITALY

Rome, Galleria Nazionale d'Arte Moderna e Contemporanea cat. no. 53

THE NETHERLANDS

Amsterdam, Stedelijk Museum cat. no. 7

SCOTLAND

Edinburgh, The National Gallery of Scotland cat. nos. 5, 37

SPAIN

Madrid

- Museo Nacional del Prado cat. no. 40
- Museo Thyssen-Bornemisza cat. no. 65

SWEDEN

Stockholm, Nationalmuseum cat. no. 4

UNITED STATES OF AMERICA

Baltimore Museum of Art cat. no. 59

New York

- Brooklyn Museum of Art cat. no. 55
- The Metropolitan Museum of Art cat. no. 50

Philadelphia Museum of Art cat. no. 62

Private collections cat. nos. 8, 10

Private collection, on extended loan to the Courtauld Institute Gallery cat. no. 60

Private collections, on loan to the National Gallery cat. nos. 58, 63

Photographic Credits

AMSTERDAM
© Rijksmuseum, Amsterdam: fig. 64
Stedelijk Museum © ADAGP, Paris and DACS, London 2002. Photo Stedelijk Museum: fig. 121

ANTWERP
Antwerp Cathedral © Provinciebestuur van Antwerpen: fig. 49
Koninklijk Museum voor Schone Kunsten © DACS 2002, London. Photo Koninklijk Museum voor Schone Kunsten: fig. 111

ATHENS
Acropolis Museum © Hellenic Ministery of Culture/TAP: fig. 1

BALTIMORE
© Baltimore Museum of Art: fig. 129

BERLIN
Antikensammlung © Staatliche Museen zu Berlin. Bildarchiv Preussischer Kulturbesitz. Photo Erich Lessing: fig. 2
Gemäldegalerie © Staatliche Museen zu Berlin. Bildarchiv Preussischer Kulturbesitz. Photo Jörg P. Anders: fig. 21
Neue Nationalgalerie © Munch Museum/Munch–Ellingsen Group, BONO, Oslo, DACS, London 2002. Photo Staatliche Museen zu Berlin. Bildarchiv Preussischer Kulturbesitz. Jörg P. Anders: fig. 100

BIRMINGHAM
© Birmingham Museums and Art Gallery: fig. 103

BOURNEMOUTH
Russell-Cotes Art Gallery and Museum © The Bridgeman Art Library, London: fig. 120

BRUSSELS
© Musées royaux des Beaux-Arts de Belgique, Brussels. Photo d' Art Kunstfoto Speltdoorn, Brussels: figs. 22, 123 (detail on page 164)

CAMBRIDGE
Lent by the Syndics of The Fitzwilliam Museum © Fitzwilliam Museum, University of Cambridge: fig. 104

CAMBRIDGE, USA
Courtesy of the Busch-Reisiger Museum, Harvard University Art Museums © DACS 2002, London. Photo President and Fellows of Harvard College, Harvard University/Katya Kallsen: fig. 101
Courtesy of The Fogg Art Museum, Harvard University Art Museums © President and Fellows of Harvard College, Harvard University: fig. 94

DOUAI
© Musée de la Chartreuse. Photo Hugo Maertens: fig. 115

DRESDEN
© Gemäldegalerie Alte Meister, Staatliche Kunstsammlungen Dresden. Photo Estel Klut, Dresden: fig. 52

DUBLIN
© The National Gallery of Ireland, Dublin: fig. 73 (detail on page 8)

EDINBURGH
National Gallery of Scotland © National Galleries of Scotland. Photo Antonia Reeve: figs. 50, 68, 74, 119
Scottish National Portrait Gallery © National Galleries of Scotland. Photo Antonia Reeve: figs. 79, 91

FLORENCE
Brancacci Chapel, Santa Maria del Carmine © Photo SCALA, Florence: fig. 11
Galleria degli Uffizi © Photo SCALA, Florence: figs. 12, 41 (detail on page 2)
Galleria Palatina, Palazzo Pitti © Photo SCALA, Florence: fig. 25
Museo Mediceo, Palazzo Medici Riccardi © Photo SCALA, Florence: fig. 31
Santa Felicita © Photo SCALA, Florence: fig. 27

FORT WORTH, USA
© Kimbell Art Museum, Fort Worth, Texas: figs. 76, 98

HAMPTON COURT
The Royal Collection © 2002, Her Majesty Queen Elizabeth II. Photo The Royal Collection, Windsor: fig. 24

HARTFORD, USA
© Wadsworth Atheneum, Hartford, Connecticut: fig. 51

ISTANBUL
Archaeological Museum © Photo SCALA, Florence: fig. 7

LILLE
Musée des Beaux-Arts © RMN, Paris. Photo Bernard: figs. 84, 93 (detail on page 118)

LIVERPOOL
Walker Art Gallery © Board of Trustees of the National Museums and Galleries on Merseyside. Photo John Mills, Liverpool: fig. 87

LONDON
British Museum © Copyright The British Museum: fig. 16, 128, 134
Courtauld Institute Gallery © Courtauld Institute Gallery, London: figs. 32, 43
Courtauld Institute Gallery, on extended loan from a private collection © 1961 Estate of Vanessa Bell, courtesy of Henrietta Garnett. Photo Courtauld Institute Gallery: fig. 137
Dulwich Picture Gallery © By Permission of the Trustees of the Dulwich Picture Gallery, London: fig. 55
Kobal Collection © Photo The Kobal Collection, London: fig. 58
Magnum Photo, London. Courtesy CMG Worldwide Inc. Los Angeles. TM/© 2002 Marilyn Monroe LLC by CMG Worldwide Inc., www.MarilynMonroe.com. Photo Magnum: fig. 59
National Gallery
© National Gallery: figs. 3, 10 (detail on page 12), 14, 15, 17, 18, 19, 20, 23, 26, 29, 35 (detail on page 36), 36, 37, 44, 45, 53 (detail on page 56), 54, 66 (detail on page 78), 69, 71, 77, 95, 106, 117, 132
National Gallery, on loan from a private collection © ADAGP, Paris and DACS, London 2002. Photo National Gallery. Courtesy of the owner: fig. 131 (detail on page 176);
© Succession Picasso/DACS 2002. Photo National Gallery. Courtesy of the owner: fig. 133
National Gallery, on loan from the collection of Sir Denis Mahon © Courtesy of the owner. Photo National Gallery: fig. 72
National Portrait Gallery © By Courtesy of the National Portrait Gallery: figs. 63, 85; © Courtesy of the artist's estate/Tate 2002. Photo National Portrait Gallery: fig. 99; © Estate of Patrick Heron 2002. All Rights Reserved. DACS, London 2002. Photo National Portrait Gallery: fig. 142
Queen's Gallery, Buckingham Palace, The Royal Collection © 2002, Her Majesty Queen Elizabeth II. Photo The Royal Collection, Windsor: fig. 9
Royal Academy of Arts © The Royal Academy of Arts, London: fig. 86
Tate © Tate 2002 figs. 75, 89, 90, 135; © Courtesy of the artist and Metro Pictures, New York: fig. 57
Victoria and Albert Museum © The Board of Trustees of the Victoria and Albert Museum, London: fig. 30

LUGANO (CASTAGNOLA)
Thyssen-Bornemisza Collection © Lucian Freud. Courtesy of Acquavella Galleries, New York. Photo Thyssen-Bornemisza Collection, Lugano: fig. 102

MADRID
© Museo Nacional del Prado: figs. 42, 78
Museo Thyssen-Bornemisza © Copyright Museo Thyssen-Bornemisza: fig. 65; © L&M Services B.V. Amsterdam 20020306. Photo Museo Thyssen-Bornemisza: fig. 141

MILAN
Pinacoteca di Brera © Photo SCALA, Florence: fig. 33

MONTERCHI
Santa Maria a Nomentana © Photo SCALA, Florence: fig. 13

MONTREAL, CANADA
© The Montreal Museum of Fine Arts, Montreal, Quebec. Photo Brian Merrett: fig. 38

MUNICH
Alte Pinakothek © Bayerische Staatsgemäldesammlungen, Munich. Photo Artothek, Joachim Blauel: fig. 61

NEW HAVEN, CONNECTICUT
Yale Center for British Art © Photo Bridgeman Art Library, London: fig. 92

NEW YORK
Brooklyn Museum of Art © Brooklyn Museum of Art, New York: fig. 125
Condé Nast © Norman Parkinson LTD/Fiona Cowan, London. Photo Condé Nast Permissions, New York: fig. 127
Frick Collection © The Frick Collection, New York: fig. 34
Solomon R. Guggenheim Museum © The Solomon R. Guggenheim Foundation, New York. Photo David Heald: fig. 138
Metropolitan Museum of Art © The Metropolitan Museum of Art, New York. Photograph 1979: fig. 109, photograph 1987: fig. 108, photograph 1988: fig. 67, photograph 1990: fig. 107, photograph 1997: fig. 4, photograph 2002: figs. 130, 139

OXFORD
Ashmolean Museum © Copyright in this photograph is reserved to the Ashmolean Museum, Oxford: fig. 70

PADUA
Capella degli Scrovegni © Photo SCALA, Florence: fig. 6

PARIS
Centre Georges Pompidou, Musée national d'art moderne / Centre de création industrielle © ADAGP, Paris and DACS, London 2002. Photo RMN, Paris: fig. 140
Musée Carnavalet, Histoire de Paris © Mairie de Paris, Photothèque des Musées de la Ville de Paris. Photo P. Pierrain: fig. 96
Musée d'Orsay © RMN, Paris. Photo H. Lewandowski: fig. 105 (detail on page 138)
Musée du Louvre © RMN, Paris. Photo H. Lewandowski: fig. 124, Photo Arnaudet: fig. 60, Photo Gérard Blot: fig. 83, Photo Gérard Blot/C. Jean: fig. 81, Photo R.G. Ojeda: figs. 28, 47

PHILADELPHIA
Philadelphia Museum of Art © Succession H. Matisse/DACS 2002, London. Photo Philadelphia Museum of Art. Graydon Wood: fig. 136

PRIVATE COLLECTIONS
© The appearance of Fred Astaire has been arranged through a special licence with Mrs Fred Astaire. All rights reserved. *Top Hat* © 1935, courtesy of RKO Pictures, inc. Photo Courtesy of the author: fig. 112
© ADAGP, Paris and DACS, London 2002. Photo Courtesy of the owner: fig. 122
© Courtesy of the owner. Photo British Museum, London: fig. 5
© Courtesy of the owner. Photo. John T. Spike: fig. 46
© Petworth House, The Egremont Collection (The National Trust). Photo The National Trust Picture Library/A. C. Cooper: fig. 40
© Photothèque R. Magritte–ADAGP, Paris and DACS, London 2002: fig. 144

ROME
Galleria Nazionale d'Arte Moderna e Contemporanea © DACS 2002, London. Photo Soprintendenza Speciale alla galleria D'Arte Moderna e Contemporanea di Roma. Araldo de Luca, Rome: fig. 126
Santa Maria del Popolo © Photo SCALA, Florence: fig. 48

SALZBURG
© Residenzgalerie Salzburg. Photo Ulrich Ghezzi, Oberalm: fig. 56

STOCKHOLM
Nationalmuseum © The National Art Museums of Sweden: fig. 118 (detail on page 152)

STUTTGART
Staatsgalerie © ADAGP, Paris and DACS, London 2002. Photo Staatsgalerie Stuttgart: fig. 143; © E.L. Kirchner / Ingeborg & Dr. Wolfgang Henze-Ketterer, Wichtrach/Bern. Photo Staatsgalerie Stuttgart: fig. 110 (detail on page 5);
© Staatsgalerie Stuttgart: fig. 80 (cover & detail on page 100)

VIENNA
© Kunsthistorisches Museum, Vienna: fig. 114
© Österreichische Nationalbibliothek, Vienna: fig. 113

VATICAN CITY, ROME
Vatican Museums © Musei Vaticani, Archivio Fotografico Musei Vaticani. Photo M. Sarri: fig. 8

WARMINSTER, WILTSHIRE
Longleat House. Courtesy of the Marquess of Bath © Reproduced by permission of the Marquess of Bath, Longleat House, Warminster, Wiltshire: fig. 116

WASHINGTON, DC
© National Gallery of Art, Washington. Board of Trustees, Photograph 2002. Photo Bob Grove: figs. 39, 82

WILTON, SALISBURY
Collection of the Earl of Pembroke, Wilton House © Wilton House, Wilton, Salisbury. Photo Ian Jackson Photography Oakgate Southampton: fig. 62

ZURICH
Kunsthaus, Zurich © 2002 Kunsthaus Zürich. All rights reserved: fig. 88; © ADAGP, Paris and DACS, London 2002. Photo 2002 Kunsthaus Zürich. All rights reserved: fig. 97

Index

Numbers in *italics* refer to figure numbers for illustrations.

ANNE HOLLANDER is an independent art historian, critic and historian of dress who is renowned for her bold studies of the evolution of dress. A Fellow of the New York Institute for the Humanities and former President of PEN American Center, she is the author of the influential books *Seeing through Clothes* (1978), a study of costume, nudity and fabric in art, and *Sex and Suits* (1994, UK edition 2002) about the aesthetics of the modern suit. She has also published *Moving Pictures* (1989), a book about the influence of painting and the graphic arts on the cinema, and *Feeding the Eye* (1999) a selection of essays.